1650 INTELLIGENT WORDS

To ace any standardized verbal test and to read great books

The Best Example Sentences from Great English and American Books

Appendix: 120 Key Science Terms

Stephen Choi

Manufactured by CreateSpace, an Amazon company

in the United States of America

Acknowledgments

I gladly thank Arleen Tarantino, an English instructor at Monterey Peninsula College, for her tips and advice on publishing this book. My special thanks go to Charles E. Shaw, PhD, a geologist, for editing the appendix: **120 ESSENTIAL SCIENCE TERMS**. I also thank the editorial and design service teams of CreateSpace, an Amazon company, for helping me publish this book.

ISBN-13: 9781502497840

ISBN-10: 1502497840

Library of Congress Control Number: 2014917748
CreateSpace Independent Publishing Platform
North Charleston, South Carolina

This book is available on **amazon.com, wordsandnarratives.com, amazon.cn, amazon.in, amazon.co.jp, amazon.com.br, Amazon Europe,** other retail outlets, and in Kindle Edition.

* Online wholesaler for resellers: createspace.com/pub/1/createspacedirect.do

* Any question about placing order: info@createspace.com

CONTENTS

Introduction

There are many vocabulary preparation resources for standardized verbal tests that include example sentences, but most of them are so humdrum that students often become bored with reading through them. No one has ever written a word-study guide that contains symbolic, philosophical, and exciting example sentences exclusively from great English and American books. That's why I wrote this book especially for **you, intelligent students who seek college or graduate school readiness.**

Great books are discourses full of great ideas. Reading the example sentences from great books is one of the best ways to become a creative intellectual who can change the world for the better. This book includes **1,650 intelligent words** most often tested on the verbal section of any standardized test, **the example sentences and 195 aphorisms** totally from great books, and **120 essential science terms.** Also, the book contains **review exercises**. In order to both maximize your test score and read great books, you must know these intelligent words and science terms. The book would be a milestone in your test and career.

If you read the book thoroughly, following the tips in both sections, **How to Optimize Your Reading of This Book** and **Reminder** on the next page, you can dramatically boost your score on any standardized verbal test. Better still, you can saturate your mind with the great spirits of the great writers who have reformed the world.

This book could be not just a vocabulary preparation resource but a new beacon of intelligence for **you, intelligent students, who will make history.**

Stephen Choi

How to Optimize Your Reading of This Book

1. Please read each example sentence to understand the bold-faced word without referring to its synonyms below the group of example sentences.
2. You may skip any familiar word and its example sentence.
3. If you can't understand a word's meaning, please mark it with a check, and then read the sentence at least three more times, **trying to gather its contextual clues**.
4. If you still can't decipher it even after some effort to grasp the word, please look up its meaning in the synonym / definition section.
5. Please return to the example sentence and read it three more times, **creating your own impressive idea of the word** to lodge it deep in your mind.
6. Please review every eight pages in the **review exercise**. ※ Please don't write down your entry from the choices in the blank, but just read it. Then you can go over the exercise again and again without looking at the entry.
7. Once you have finished reading through the book, please repeat the above steps at least two more times.

♣ If you are a verbal test taker without enough time, you can concentrate your efforts only on the **review exercise.**

Reminder

Whenever you encounter a tough word in an example sentence, **please build up your own short, funny sentence** using the word, based on the example sentence or its more simplified one in the **review exercise**, with a pun, joke, or witticism. You can construct your own sentence; for instance, "***Abjure** this crazy love so as not to be abjured by your family*" from p. 1, no. 6 example sentence. **Please make a list of your own sentences**, reciting them repeatedly, which will remarkably help you upgrade your vocabulary, reading comprehension, and writing skills.

☆☆☆☆☆☆☆☆☆☆☆☆☆☆

This book is neither a no-brainer that you can breeze through, nor a set of flash cards filled with synonyms that you must memorize by rote. The text is elaborately designed for you, intelligent students, to enhance your mind and vocabulary by reading through great example sentences, which are so gripping yet somewhat weighty. **Are you ready to give your gritty concentration to them?**

Let's start reading the example sentences of 1,650 intelligent words and 120 essential science terms. Good luck to you!

1. Nothing **abashed** him, nor was he appalled by the display and culture and power around him. —Jack London, *Burning Daylight*

2. Though a king may **abdicate** for his own person, he cannot abdicate for the monarchy. —Edmund Burke, *Reflections on the Revolution in France*

3. The more **aberrant** any form is, the greater must be the number of connecting forms which have been exterminated* and utterly lost. —Charles Darwin, *The Origin of Species*

4. . . . the sea has never been friendly to man. At most it has been the accomplice* of human restlessness, and playing the part of dangerous **abettor** of world-wide ambitions. —Joseph Conrad, *The Mirror of the Sea*

5. They [the Yahoos] are strong and hardy, but of a cowardly* spirit, and, by consequence, insolent,* **abject**, and cruel. —Jonathan Swift, *Gulliver's Travels*

6. O, something soundeth in mine ears
"**Abjure** this magic, turn to God again!"
—Christopher Marlowe, *Doctor Faustus*

****

1. **abash**; confuse, confound, embarrass, bewilder, nonplus. —abashment.
2. **abdicate**; abandon (a throne or power), renounce, relinquish. —abdication.
3. **aberrant**; abnormal, deviant, digressive, divergent, erratic, queer, anomalous. —aberration, —aberrance. * exterminate; eradicate.
4. **abettor**; provoker, inciter, prodder, instigator. —abet: *aid and abet an attempt on the queen's life*. * accomplice; confederate, a partner in a wrong doing.
5. **abject**; base, mean, ignoble, despicable, detestable. —abjection, —abjectly. * cowardly; timid, recreant. * insolent; impudent, brazen, *see p. 165, no. 3.*
6. **abjure**; renounce, recant, forswear, retract, waive. —abjuration.

♣ Hitch your wagon to a star. —R. W. Emerson, *Society and Solitude*

1. She soared so far above him that there seemed nothing else for him to do than die for her. . . . It was the sublime **abnegation** of true love that comes to all lovers. —Jack London, *Martin Eden*

2. People were only civil to her at all from fear of the malice of her tongue; for to their faces and behind their backs she said **abominable** things. —W. Somerset Maugham, Of *Human Bondage*

3. Who is the Trustee? What is the **aboriginal** Self, on which a universal reliance may be grounded? —R. W. Emerson, *Self-Reliance*

4. As long as the criminal remains upon two legs so long must there be some indentation,* some **abrasion**, some trifling displacement which can be detected by the scientific searcher. —Arthur Conan Doyle, *The Return of Sherlock Holmes*

5. It shall please you to **abrogate** scurrility.* —Shakespeare, *Love's Labour's Lost*

6. You **absconded** with money, leaving your debts unpaid; you forsook my mother; . . . you have become a gambler. —George Eliot, *Daniel Deronda*

****

1. **abnegation**; denial, renunciation, relinquishment. —abnegator.
2. **abominable**; loathsome, disgusting, detestable. —abominate *v.*
3. **aboriginal**; original, native, indigenous. —aborigine; original inhabitant.
4. **abrasion**; wearing away, rubbing, friction. —abrade, —abrasive. * indentation; cut, notch, *see p. 157, no. 4.*
5. **abrogate**; abolish, repeal, annul, nullify, rescind. —abrogation, —abrogable. * scurrility; vulgarism, gross abuse, *see p. 283, no. 3.* —scurrile *or* scurrilous.
6. **abscond**; escape, flee, bolt, run away, make off.

♣ The very greatest men have been among the least believers in the power of genius. —Samuel Smiles, *Self Help*

1. . . . he was an **abstemious** epicure.* —G. K. Chesterton, *The Wisdom of Father Brown*

2. Very few have abilities requisite for the discovery of **abstruse** truth; and of those few some want leisure and some resolution. —Samuel Johnson, *The Rambler*

3. Razumov, in his chair, leaning his head on his hand, spoke as if from the bottom of an **abyss**.
   "You believe in God, Haldin?" —Joseph Conrad, *Under Western Eyes*

4. To the species of medical treatment, however, I would by no means **accede**, much as he insisted upon it. —Herman Melville, *Typee*

5. Quite elated* at being so near the Happars,* I pushed up the **acclivity**, and soon gained its summit. —Herman Melville, *Typee*

6. Aylward, you are a trusty soldier, for all that your shoulder has never felt **accolade**, nor your heels worn the gold spurs. —Arthur Conan Doyle, *The White Company*

****

1. **abstemious**; moderate, temperate, abstinent, continent. ※ abstain; refrain: —abstention. * epicure; 1. hedonist. ***ant.*** ascetic, *see p. 308, no. 5*. 2. gourmet.
2. **abstruse**; profound, recondite, arcane, cryptic, enigmatic. —abstrusity.
3. **abyss**; 1. bottomless pit or depth. 2. hell. —abysmal. ※ zenith. ***ant.*** nadir.
4. **accede**; agree, assent, consent. —accedence.
5. **acclivity**; upward slope. ***ant.*** declivity. —acclivitous. * elated; exhilarated. * the Happars; the friendly tribe, not the cannibalistic one in the novel, *Typee*.
6. **accolade**; award, bestowal, honor.

♣ The better part of valor is discretion.

—Shakespeare, King Henry IV, Part I

1. She did show favour to the youth in your sight only to exasperate you, to awake your dormouse* valour, to put fire in your heart, . . . You should then have **accosted** her. —Shakespeare, *Twelfth Night*

2. . . . her sole idea seemed to be to shun* mankind—or rather that cold **accretion** called the world . . . —Thomas Hardy, *Tess*

3. Just at the very instant when his heart was exulting in meditations on the happiness which would **accrue** to him by Mr Allworthy's death, he himself—died of an apoplexy.* —Henry Fielding, *Tom Jones*

4. It is well known that great scholars who have shown the most pitiless **acerbity** in their criticism of other men's scholarship have yet been of a relenting and indulgent temper in private life. —George Eliot, *Adam Bede*

5. The **acme** of bliss, which would have been a marriage with the tragedian, was not for her in this world. —Kate Chopin, *The Awakening*

6. She promised **acquiescence**, and tried to obey. —W. M. Thackeray, *Vanity Fair*

****

1. **accost**; approach and address. * dormouse; 1. sleeping, slumbering, dozing, drowsing. 2. small squirrellike rodent.
2. **accretion**; addition, increment. —accrete *v.* * shun; escape, evade, eschew.
3. **accrue**; add up, pile up. —accrual. * apoplexy; stroke. ※ *accrued interest* .
4. **acerbity**; 1. sharpness, bitterness, acridity, acrimoniousness. 2. sourness, acidity. ***ant.*** mildness, sweetness. —acerbate *v.*, —acerbic.
5. **acme**; apex, culmination, consummation, zenith, apogee. ***ant.*** nadir; the lowest point: *My life reached its nadir when I lost my wife and son in the traffic accident.*
6. **acquiescence**; tacit acceptance or consent, compliance. —acquiesce.

♣ Expect poison from the standing water.

—William Blake, *The Marriage of Heaven and Hell*

1. They locked horns* with him, tete-a-tete*
   In **acrimonious** debate.

   —Ambrose Bierce, *Devil's Dictionary*

2. Mr. Rochester had sometimes read my unspoken thoughts with an **acumen** to me incomprehensible. —Charlotte Brontë, *Jane Eyre*

3. All things are flowing, even those that seem immovable. The **adamant** is always passing into smoke. —R. W. Emerson, *Farming*

4. No invalidating proof being **adduced**, the plaintiffs were cast* in the suit and the cannibal reputation of the defendant fully established. —Herman Melville, *Typee*

5. The president can only **adjourn** the national legislature in the single case of disagreement about the time of adjournment. —Alexander Hamilton, *The Federalist Papers*

6. He was the man with power to buy, to build, to choose, to endow, to sit on committees and **adjudicate** upon designs . . . —George Bernard Shaw, *An Unsocial Socialist*

****

1. **acrimonious**; sarcastic, caustic, trenchant, vitriolic, astringent. —acrimony. * lock horns; contend, fight. * tete-a-tete; 1. face-to-face. 2. privately.
2. **acumen**; keenness, acuteness, discernment, astuteness, perspicacity.
3. **adamant**; 1. hard as rock, stiff. 2. *n.* very rigid substance. 3. determined, uncompromising, inflexible. —adamancy *or* adamance.
4. **adduce**; illustrate, cite as evidence. —adduction, —adducible. * cast; defeat.
5. **adjourn**; put off, delay, defer, postpone. —adjournment.
6. **adjudicate**; judge, adjudge, umpire, referee, settle judicially. —adjudication, —adjudicative, —adjudicator; judge, umpire.

♣ There is no good in arguing with the inevitable. —James Russell Lowell, *Democracy*

1. Learning is but an **adjunct** to ourself,
   And where we are our learning likewise is.
   —Shakespeare, *Love's Labour's Lost*

2. I have been offered mock **adulation**, treated with mock reserve or with mock devotion . . . —Joseph Conrad, *The Arrow of Gold*

3. He was as splendid a brute—an **adumbration** of the splendid human conquerors and rulers, higher on the ladder of evolution, who have appeared in other times and places. —Jack London, *Jerry of the Islands*

4. With the **advent** of Burning Daylight the whole place became suddenly brighter and cheerier. —Jack London, *Burning Daylight*

5. His **adversary** had fallen senseless with excessive pain and the flow of blood, that gushed from an artery or a large vein. —Emily Brontë, *Wuthering Heights*

6. While prosperity is apt to harden the heart to pride, **adversity** in a man of resolution will serve to ripen it into fortitude.* —Samuel Smiles, *Self Help*

****

1. **adjunct**; attachment, supplement, appurtenance, appendage. —adjunctive; auxiliary, subsidiary. ※ ancillary; adjunctive: *ancillary effects of the war.*
2. **adulation**; flattery, fawning, sycophancy. —adulator, —adulate.
3. **adumbration**; prefiguration, outlining, foreshadowing. —adumbrative.
4. **advent**; arrival, onset. ※ Adventist; believer in Christ's return. —Adventism. ※ adventitious; 1. accidental. 2. extrinsic.
5. **adversary**; enemy, opponent, foe, antagonist. —adverse; opposing, contrary.
6. **adversity**; misfortune, calamity, mishap. * fortitude; valor, grit, intrepidity, *see p. 127, no. 2.* —fortitudinous. ※ fortuitous; accidental, *see p. 127, no. 3.*

♣ To err is human; to forgive, divine.
—Alexander Pope, *An Essay on Criticism*

1. The regions ruled by the north-east and south-east Trade Winds are serene. . . . Those citizens of the ocean feel sheltered under the **aegis** of an uncontested law, of an undisputed dynasty. —Joseph Conrad, *The Mirror of the Sea*

2. She is all **affability** and condescension.* —Jane Austen, *Pride and Prejudice*

3. He was even ready to make an **affidavit** that he had been slaughtered. —James Fenimore Cooper, *Autobiography of a Pocket-Handkerchief*

4. It ought also to be added that Buffon wrote and published all his great works while **afflicted** by one of the most painful diseases to which the human frame is subject. —Samuel Smiles, *Self Help*

5. Pierre was the only son of an **affluent**, and haughty widow. —Herman Melville, *Pierre*

6. It is almost an **affront** to look a man in the face without being introduced. —R. W. Emerson, *English Traits*

****

1. **aegis;** protection, patronage, auspices. ※ nepotism; unjust patronage or favoritism to relatives: *nepotism in the oligarchy.** * oligarchy; *see p. 206, no. 5.*
2. **affability**; amiability, geniality, sociability, amicability, bonhomie. *condescension; 1. civility, humility. 2. patronage, superciliousness. —condescend.
3. **affidavit**; written pledge, testimony. ※ subpoena; court order, writ of summons, *see p. 302, no.3.*
4. **afflict**; distress, torment, inflict, ail, harass. —affliction, —afflictive.
5. **affluent**; rich, wealthy, opulent, prosperous, well-off. —affluence.
6. **affront**; insult, offense, slight. —affrontive.

♣ Excellence in art, as in everything else, can only be achieved by dint of pains-taking labour. —Samuel Smiles, *Self Help*

1. He only wanted to **aggrandize** and enrich himself. —Jane Austen, *Emma*

2. It is the duty of every man to endeavour that something may be added by his industry to the hereditary **aggregate** of knowledge and happiness. —Samuel Johnson, *The Rambler*

3. They would often spring, and bound, and leap, with prodigious **agility**. —Jonathan Swift, *Gulliver's Travels*

4. He proclaimed himself an **agnostic**. —Sherwood Anderson, *Winesburg, Ohio*

5. I saw they'd got to the **agrarian** laws of Caius Gracchus,* and I wondered if they knew anything about agrarian troubles in Ireland. —W. Somerset Maugham, *Of Human Bondage*

6. The good purpose once formed must be carried out with **alacrity** and without swerving.* —Samuel Smiles, *Self Help*

****

1. **aggrandize**; enlarge, extend, expand, magnify. —aggrandizement.
2. **aggregate**; sum, total, assemblage, accumulation, compound. —aggregative. ※ aggravate; 1. worsen: *aggravating the disease*. 2. vex.
3. **agility**; quickness, swiftness, nimbleness, alacrity, alertness, briskness. —agile.
4. **agnostic**; one who believes that the existence of God is beyond human understanding. ※ atheist ***ant.*** theist. ※ deist; one who believes that God started the Universe but has not controlled it. ※ pagan; heretic; heathen.
5. **agrarian**; farming, agricultural. —agrarianism. * Caius Gracchus; Roman politician (154 BC–121 BC) who made land reforms for the lower classes.
6. **alacrity**; alertness, agility, nimbleness. —alacritous. * swerve; alter course, turn, deflect. ※ veer; swerve*: The plane veered off course to the Antarctic.*

♣ It appears probable that disuse has been the main agent in rendering organs rudimentary. —Charles Darwin, *The Origin of Species*

1. A king may _______ just for his own person, not for the monarchy.
2. The more _______ any form is, the more must be the connecting forms.
3. Nothing _______ him, nor was he appalled by the power around him.
4. The sea has played the part of the dangerous _______ of world-wide ambitions.
5. The Yahoos were insolent, _______, and cruel.
6. _______ this magic, turn to God again!

[**abjure, abashed, abdicate, abject, aberrant, abettor**]

****

1. His death was the sublime _______ of true love.
2. What is the _______ Self, on which a universal reliance may be grounded?
3. To their faces and behind their backs she said _______ things.
4. It shall please you to _______ scurrility.
5. You _______ with money, leaving your debts unpaid.
6. There must be some indentation or _______ in the venue.

[**abrasion, abnegation, aboriginal, absconded, abominable, abrogate**]

****

1. He was an _______ epicure.
2. I pushed up the _______, and soon gained its summit.
3. Your shoulder has never felt _______, nor your heels worn the gold spur.
4. Very few have abilities requisite for the discovery of _______ truth.
5. Razumov, in his chair, spoke as if from the bottom of an _______.
6. I would by no means _______ to this species of medical treatment.

[**abyss, accede, abstemious, accolade, abstruse, acclivity**]

****

1. Her sole idea shunned mankind—or rather that cold _______ called the world.
2. Happiness would _______ to him by Mr Allworthy's death.
3. She showed him favor to exasperate you. You should then have _______ her.
4. They have shown the most pitiless _______ in their criticism of others.
5. She promised _______, and tried to obey.
6. The _______ of bliss was not for her in this world.

[**accosted, acerbity, acme, acquiescence, accretion, accrue**]

Review Exercise: Sentence Completions (pp. 5–8)

1. He read my unspoken thoughts with an _______ to me incomprehensible.
2. The _______ is always passing into smoke.
3. They locked horns with him, tete-a-tete in _______ debate.
4. The president can _______ the national legislature in some case.
5. He was the man with power to sit on committees and _______ upon designs.
6. No invalidating proof being _______, the plaintiffs were cast in the suit.

[**acumen, adjudicate, adduced, adjourn, acrimonious, adamant**]

****

1. His _______ had fallen senseless with excessive pain and the flow of blood.
2. Learning is but an _______ to ourself.
3. I have been offered mock _______, treated with mock reserve.
4. He was an _______ of the splendid human conquerors and rulers.
5. With the _______ of Burning Daylight the whole place became brighter.
6. _______ in a man of resolution will serve to ripen the heart into fortitude.

[**adversity, adversary, adjunct, advent, adulation, adumbration**]

****

1. It is almost an _______ to look a man in the face without being introduced.
2. The citizens feel sheltered under the _______ of an uncontested law.
3. He was even ready to make an _______ that he had been slaughtered.
4. She is all _______ and condescension.
5. Buffon wrote and published all his great works while _______ by the disease.
6. He was the only son of an _______, and haughty widow.

[**affability, aegis, affidavit, affront, affluent, afflicted**]

****

1. I saw they'd got to the _______ laws of Caius Gracchus.
2. He only wanted to _______ and enrich himself.
3. He can add something to the hereditary _______ of knowledge and happiness.
4. They would often spring, and bound, and leap, with prodigious _______.
5. He proclaimed himself an _______.
6. The good purpose once formed must be carried out with _______.

[**agnostic, aggrandize, alacrity, aggregate, agility, agrarian**]

1. We spend more on almost any article of bodily **aliment** or ailment than on our mental aliment. —Henry David Thoreau, *Walden*

2. Resignation is the willing endurance of a pain that is not **allayed**—that you don't expect to be allayed. —George Eliot, *The Mill on the Floss*

3. From all our observations we may collect with certainty, that misery is the lot of man, but cannot discover in what particular condition it will find most **alleviations**. —Samuel Johnson, *The Rambler*

4. The two chambermaids being again left alone, began a second bout at **altercation**, which soon produced a combat of a more active kind. —Henry Fielding, *Tom Jones*

5. Nature designed Mirah to fall in love with me. The **amalgamation** of races demands it—the mitigation of human ugliness demands it—the affinity of contrasts assures it. —George Eliot, *Daniel Deronda*

6. The smallest marshes are the most dangerous, being surrounded, as at Vera Cruz and Carthagena, with an arid and sandy soil, which raises the temperature of the **ambient** air." —Charles Darwin, *The Voyage of the Beagle*

****

1. **aliment**; nourishment, sustenance, nutrition, victuals. —alimentary; nutritious.
2. **allay**; calm, soothe, appease, pacify, assuage, mollify, relieve, alleviate.
3. **alleviations**; relief, mitigation, assuagement, mollification, palliation.
4. **altercation**; dispute, argument, quarrel, wrangle. —altercate.
5. **amalgamation**; mixture, fusion, conflation. —amalgamate, —amalgamable.
6. **ambient**; surrounding, atmospheric, encircling. —ambience. ※ ambivalence; coexistence of conflicting feelings. —ambivalent. ※ ambiversion; character showing both introversion and extroversion. ※ extrovert. ***ant.*** introvert.

♣ Servility creates despotism. —Charlotte Brontë, *The Professor*

1. Adam Smith sowed the seeds of a great social **amelioration** in that dingy old University of Glasgow where he so long laboured, and laid the foundations of his "Wealth of Nations." —Samuel Smiles, *Self Help*

2. The humanities and **amenities** of life had no attraction for him—its peaceful enjoyments no charm. —Charlotte Brontë, *Jane Eyre*

3. Ossipon, my feeling for you is **amicable** contempt. You couldn't kill a fly. —Joseph Conrad, *The Secret Agent*

4. The most menacing* political condition is a period of international **amity**. —Ambrose Bierce, *The Devil's Dictionary*

5. 'Ataxic*' and '**amnesic**' aphasia,* 'word-deafness,' and 'associative aphasia' are all practical losses of word-memory. —William James, *The Principles of Psychology*

6. He was supremely happy, perched like an **amorphous** bundle on the high stool, with his head thrown back, his eyes fixed on the opposite cornice,* and his lips wide open . . . —George Eliot, *The Mill on the Floss*

****

1. **amelioration**; improvement, advancement. —ameliorate, —ameliorable.
2. **amenity**; geniality, amiability, affability. ※ amenable; docile, acquiescent.
3. **amicable**; friendly, amiable, sociable. —amicability.
4. **amity**; friendship, fellowship, fraternity. * menacing; threatening, intimidating.
5. **amnesic**; forgetful, oblivious. —amnesia. * ataxic; of incoordination (inability to control physical movement). —ataxia *n.* * aphasia; inability to articulate or understand ideas.
6. **amorphous**; shapeless, formless. —amorphism. ※ amorous; romantic: *the beast's amorous advance.* * cornice; ornamental projection crowning a wall.

♣ Poetry is connate with the origin of man. —P. B. Shelley, *A Defence of Poetry*

1. Shakespeare's introducing it [handkerchief] into the play of "Othello" is an **anachronism**. —Ambrose Bierce, *The Devil's Dictionary*

2. Each new invention would violate a great number of known **analogies**. —Charles Lyell, *The Progress of Geology*

3. He shrank from the venerable saint, as if to avoid an **anathema**. —Nathaniel Hawthorne, *Young Goodman Brown*

4. Hence some extremely remote progenitor* of the whole vertebrate kingdom appears to have been hermaphrodite* or **androgynous**. —Charles Darwin, *The Descent of Man*

5. The old servant was worn and wasted; her gown hung loose on her **angular** body. —Wilkie Collins, *I Say No*

6. Life appears to me too short to be spent in nursing **animosity**, or registering wrongs. —Charlotte Brontë, *Jane Eyre*

****

1. **anachronism**; 1. something outdated. 2. superannuated person.
2. **analogy**; similarity, parallel, homology. —analogous, —analogize.
3. **anathema**; curse, damn, malediction, execration. —anathematize.
4. **androgynous**; having both sexes, monoecious. ***ant.*** dioecious; unisexual. —androgyne *n.* * progenitor; ancestor. * hermaphrodite; bisexual.
5. **angular**; 1. skinny, bony, gaunt. 2. forming an angle, angulate. —angularity.
6. **animosity**; hatred, malice, enmity, rancor, animus.

♣ The whole man seems to be an enigma, a grotesque assemblage of incongruous qualities, selfishness and generosity, cruelty and benevolence, craft and simplicity, abject villainy and romantic heroism. —Thomas Babington Macaulay, *Machiavelli*

1. I have shown that no society of slaves can endure, because, in its very nature, such society must **annul** the law of development. —Jack London, *Martin Eden*
2. Nothing can heal her! no **anodyne** can give her sleep! no poppies forgetfulness! —Oscar Wilde, *A Woman of No Importance*
3. In the expression of the countenance, which was beaming all over with smiles, there still lurked (incomprehensible **anomaly**!) that fitful stain of melancholy . . . —Edgar Allan Poe, *The Assignation*
4. I like to know the manners of my time—contemporary gossip, not **antediluvian**. —George Eliot, *Daniel Deronda*
5. London is religion's opportunity—not the decorous* religion of theologians, but **anthropomorphic**, crude. —E. M. Forster, *Howards End*
6. Thou art as opposite to every good
   As the **Antipodes** are unto us,
   Or as the south to the septentrion.*

   —Shakespeare, *Henry VI, Part III*

****

1. **annul**; cancel, void, nullify, invalidate. —annulment.
2. **anodyne**; 1. painkiller, analgesic *or* analgetic. 2. palliative. 3. *adj.* analgesic. ※ narcotic; 1. opiate: *narcotic addicts.* 2. anesthetic.
3. **anomaly**; irregularity, abnormality, deviation, aberration. —anomalous.
4. **antediluvian**; 1. ancient, of the time before the Flood. 2. antiquated, archaic, passé. ※ antiquarian; 1. antique. 2. antiquary. ※ anterior; previous, antecedent. ***ant.*** posterior. ※ the status quo ante; the previous state.
5. **anthropomorphic**; humanlike, ascribing human attributes to things or animals. —anthropomorphism, —anthropomorphize. * decorous; dignified.
6. **antipodes**; two places exactly opposite to each other on the globe. —antipodal. * septentrion; the north, Northern regions. —septentrional.

1. He shares Mary's **apathetic** and listless look; he seems to have more length of limb than vivacity of blood or vigour of brain. —Charlotte Brontë, *Jane Eyre*

2. The **apex** of the triangle of dark-blue sky was growing brighter and bluer. —G. K. Chesterton, *The Wisdom of Father Brown*

3. He has that ***aplomb*** which results from a good adjustment of the moral and physical nature and the obedience of all the powers to the will. —R. W. Emerson, *English Traits*

4. They say it [apocrypha] is **apocryphal**. The word itself, I've heard from the pulpit, implies something of uncertain credit. —Herman Melville, *The Confidence-Man*

5. Anarchists don't marry. It's well known. They can't. It would be **apostasy**. —Joseph Conrad, *The Secret Agent*

6. The ecstasy of faith almost **apotheosized** her; it set upon her face a glowing irradiation,* and brought a red spot into the middle of each cheek. —Thomas Hardy, *Tess*

****

1. **apathetic**; indifferent, uninterested, impassive, listless. —apathy.
2. **apex**; top, tip, pinnacle, vertex, acme, zenith. ※ apogee; apex: *The movement reached its apogee at the end of 1960s.*
3. **aplomb**; calmness, composure, poise, equanimity, sangfroid.
4. **apocryphal**; doubtful, dubious, unauthentic, equivocal. —apocrypha; Christian writings considered uncanonical. ※ uncanonical; unorthodox, heterodox.
5. **apostasy**; backsliding, recantation, renegade. —apostate, —apostatize.
6. **apotheosize**; 1. exalt. 2. deify. —apotheosis. * irradiation; illumination.

♣ To the rarest genius it is the most expensive to succumb and conform to the ways of the world. —Henry David Thoreau, *A Week on the Concord and Merrimack Rivers*

1. It is not the quantity of study that one gets through, or the amount of reading, that makes a wise man, but the **appositeness** of the study to the purpose for which it is pursued. —Samuel Smiles, *Self Help*
2. He stands among partial men for the complete man, and **apprises** us not of his wealth, but of the common wealth. —R. W. Emerson, *The Poet*
3. The desire for **approbation** is perhaps the most deeply seated instinct of civilized man. —W. Somerset Maugham, *The Moon and Sixpence*
4. . . . the sheriff was legal custodian of the Manton farm and **appurtenances** thereunto belonging. —Ambrose Bierce, *Can Such Things Be?*
5. **Arable** lands are few and limited; with but slight exceptions the prospect is a broad rich mass of grass and trees, mantling minor hills and dales within the major. —Thomas Hardy, *Tess*
6. Safety from external danger is the most powerful director of national conduct. Even the **ardent** love of liberty will, after a time, give way to its dictates.* —Alexander Hamilton, *The Federalist Papers*

****

1. **appositeness**; aptness, opportuneness, relevance. —apposite; appropriate, apropos. ***ant.*** malapropos. ※ malapropism; misuse of a word, malaprop (e.g., "hear" for "here"). ※ oxymoron; a figure using contradictions (e.g., *cruel love*).
2. **apprise**; inform, notify, apprize. ※ appraise; estimate: *appraise her property.*
3. **approbation**; approval, sanction, ratification, praise. ***ant.*** disapprobation.
4. **appurtenances**; accessories, belongings, appendages. —appurtenant.
5. **arable**; farmable, cultivable, tillable. —arability. ※ edible; eatable. ※ eligible; qualified. ※ legible; readable. ※ portable; handy. ※ potable; drinkable.
6. **ardent**; passionate, fervid, fiery, zealous, impassioned, fervent, vascular. —ardour; fervor, zeal, zest, verve. ※ cardiovascular; of the heart and blood vessels: *cardiovascular disease.* * dictates; ordinance.

1. It [The good old office] was not a very **arduous** office, but very pleasantly remunerative.* —Herman Melville, *Bartleby*

2. He was tired out by the violence of his passion. His soul was filled on a sudden with a singular **aridity**. —W. Somerset Maugham, *Of Human Bondage*

3. Shakespeare himself is to be adored, not **arraigned**; but, so we do it with humility, we may a little canvass* his characters. —Herman Melville, *The Confidence-Man*

4. My mother glances submissively at them [Mr. Murdstone and Miss Murdstone], shuts the book, and lays it by as an **arrear** to be worked out when my other tasks are done. —Charles Dickens, *David Copperfield*

5. The human and fallible should not **arrogate** a power with which the divine and perfect alone can be safely entrusted. —Charlotte Brontë, *Jane Eyre*

6. There is in my nature a strain of **asceticism**, and I have subjected my flesh each week to a more severe mortification.* —W. Somerset Maugham, *The Moon and Sixpence*

****

1. **arduous**; hard, tough, formidable. * remunerative; profitable, lucrative.
2. **aridity**; dullness, lifelessness, dryness, barrenness. —arid, —aridly.
3. **arraign**; accuse, indict, inculpate. —arraignment. * canvass; explore, analyze.
4. **arrear**; overdue debt, unpaid liabilities or indebtedness. —arrearage.
5. **arrogate**; seizure, usurp, appropriate. —arrogation.
6. **asceticism**; stoicism, monasticism. ***ant.*** hedonism; epicurism, epicureanism. —ascetic. * mortification; 1. discipline. 2. humiliation.

♣ *Recreation* is as necessary as labour or food. —John Locke, *Some Thoughts Concerning Education*

1. Still I love the Old Travelers. I love them for their witless platitudes*; for their supernatural ability to bore; for their delightful **asinine** vanity. —Mark Twain, *The Innocents Abroad*

2. "Call me Tess," she would say, **askance**; and he did. —Thomas Hardy, *Tess*

3. "Do you see any prospect of solving this mystery, Mr. Holmes?" she asked, with a touch of **asperity** in her voice. —Arthur Conan Doyle, *The Memoirs of Sherlock Holmes*

4. Elsewhere in this volume the slanderous* **aspersion** has been disproved,* that the vocation of whaling is throughout a slatternly,* untidy business. —Herman Melville, *Moby Dick*

5. . . . disputing, excusing, caviling* upon mandates and directions, is a kind of shaking off the yoke,* and **assay** of disobedience. —Francis Bacon, *Essays*

6. Instantly Fritz, with a scream of anger, flew at the bulky Rogers and began **assiduously** to pommel* that surprised free-booter* with his fists. —O. Henry, *A Chaparral Prince*

****

1. **asinine**; like an ass, stupid. —asininity. ※ bovine; like a cow, equine; like a horse. ※ canine; like a dog. ※ simian; apelike. * platitude; cliché, triteness.
2. **askance**; 1. sideways, with squinting eyes. 2. suspiciously. 3. obliquely.
3. **asperity**; bitterness, crossness, acerbity. —asperous.
4. **aspersion**; slander, libel, calumny, disparagement, vilification. —asperse *v.* *slanderous; defamatory. * disprove; refute. * slatternly; slovenly.
5. **assay**; 1. evaluation, assessment, appraisal. 2. *v.* evaluate, appraise. —assay able. ※ essay; try, test, experiment: *The slave essayed escapes, but all of them were failures.* * cavil; find fault, quibble. * yoke; bondage.
6. **assiduously**; busily, diligently, industriously. —assiduity. * pommel; pummel. ※ barrage; salvo, volley. * free-booter; sea robber, pirate, buccaneer.

1. We spend more on any article of bodily _______ than on our mental aliment.
2. We cannot discover in what particular condition misery will find most _______.
3. The two maids being again left alone, began a second bout at _______.
4. Nature designed her to fall in love with me. The _______ of races demands it.
5. Resignation is the willing endurance of a pain that is not _______.
6. The arid and sandy soil raises the temperature of the _______ air.

[**ambient, aliment, allayed, altercation, alleviations, amalgamation**]

****

1. The humanities and _______ of life had no attraction for him.
2. Ossipon, my feeling for you is _______ contempt. You couldn't kill a fly.
3. Adam Smith sowed the seeds of a great social _______ in the university.
4. The most menacing political condition is a period of international _______.
5. He was very happy, perched like an _______ bundle on the high stool.
6. 'Ataxic' and '_______' aphasia is a practical loss of word-memory.

[**amorphous, amnesic, amity, amicable, amenities, amelioration**]

****

1. He shrank from the venerable saint, as if to avoid an _______.
2. Shakespeare's introducing handkerchief into the play is an _______.
3. Each new invention would violate a great number of known _______.
4. The progenitor of the vertebrate kingdom appears to have been _______.
5. She was worn and wasted; her gown hung loose on her _______ body.
6. Life appears to me too short to be spent in nursing _______.

[**analogies, anathema, anachronism, angular, androgynous, animosity**]

****

1. Nothing can heal her! No _______ can give her sleep!
2. There still lurked (incomprehensible _______ !) that fitful stain of melancholy.
3. I like to know the manners of my time—contemporary gossip, not _______.
4. Thou art as opposite to every good as the _______ are unto us.
5. It is not the decorous religion of theologians, but _______, crude.
6. The society of slaves must _______ the law of development.

[**annul, anthropomorphic, antipodes, anodyne, anomaly, antediluvian**]

Review Exercise: Sentence Completions (pp. 15–18)

1. Anarchists don't marry. It's well known. They can't. It would be _______.
2. The ecstasy of faith almost _______ her.
3. He shares Mary's _______ and listless look.
4. The _______ of the triangle of dark-blue sky was growing brighter and bluer.
5. He has the _______ resulting from the obedience of all the powers to the will.
6. They say it [apocrypha] is _______.

[**apathetic, apocryphal, aplomb, apex, apotheosized, apostasy**]

****

1. He was legal custodian of the farm and _______ thereunto belonging.
2. It is the _______ of the study to the purpose that makes a wise man.
3. He _______ us not of his wealth, but of the common wealth.
4. The desire for _______ is perhaps the most deeply seated instinct of man.
5. _______ lands are few and limited.
6. Even the _______ love of liberty will, after a time, give way to its dictates.

[**ardent, appurtenances, arable, appositeness, apprises, approbation**]

****

1. Shakespeare himself is to be adored, not _______.
2. My mother shuts the book, and lays it by as an _______ to be worked out.
3. Man should not _______ a power with which the divine can be entrusted.
4. It was not a very _______ office, but very pleasantly remunerative.
5. His soul was filled on a sudden with a singular _______.
6. There is in my nature a strain of _______.

[**arraigned, arduous, asceticism, aridity, arrear, arrogate**]

****

1. "Call me Tess," she would say, _______; and he did.
2. "Can you solve this mystery?" She asked, with a touch of _______ in her voice.
3. Disputing is a kind of shaking off the yoke, and _______ of disobedience.
4. The _______ has been disproved that whaling is an untidy business.
5. Still I love the Old Travelers for their delightful _______ vanity.
6. Fritz began _______ to pommel that surprised free-booter with his fists.

[**assiduously, asinine, askance, assay, asperity, aspersion**]

1. Poetry enlarges the circumference of the imagination by replenishing* it with thoughts of ever new delight, which have the power of attracting and **assimilating** to their own nature all other thoughts. —P. B. Shelley, *A Defence of Poetry*

2. They say that 'time **assuages**,'—
Time never did assuage.
—Emily Dickinson, "They say that 'time assuages'"

3. A strong, **astringent**, bilious* nature has more truculent* enemies than the slugs* and moths that fret* my leaves. —R. W. Emerson, *Fate*

4. Some novel movements were evidently working in her mind, and they showed their nature on her **astute** brow. —Charlotte Brontë, *The Professor*

5. There is always the suggestion of dangerous primal instincts within us, something of the past that can recur, **atavistic**, destructive, and uncontrolled. —Arthur Conan Doyle, *The Hound of the Baskervilles*

6. Poor devil! Whatever his crimes, he has suffered something to **atone** for them. —Arthur Conan Doyle, *The Hound of the Baskervilles*

****

1. **assimilate**; digest, ingest, absorb, imbibe. * replenish; refill, reinforce.
2. **assuage**; allay, relieve, mitigate, alleviate. —assuagement, —assuasive.
3. **astringent**; 1. severe, stern, austere, rigid, rigorous, grim, exacting. 2. acerbic, caustic. * bilious; peevish, *see p. 31, no. 6.* * truculent; aggressive. * slug; shell-less snail. * fret; 1. gnaw, corrode. 2. vex. —fretful.
4. **astute**; keen, acute, shrewd. —astuteness.
5. **atavistic**; of recurrence of ancestral idiosyncrasies. —atavist.
6. **atone**; 1. repent, expiate, aby *or* abye. 2. redress, compensate. —atonement.

♣ Nothing great was ever achieved without enthusiasm. —R. W. Emerson, *Circles*

1. The police are confounded* by the seeming absence of motive—not for the murder itself—but for the **atrocity** of the murder. —Edgar Allan Poe, *The Murders in the Rue Morgue*

2. He had to listen to her in a silence that he made no immediate effort to **attenuate**, feeling her doubly woeful amid all her dim diffused* elegance. —Henry James, *The Ambassadors*

3. Here, in a corner my indentures* were duly signed and **attested**, and I was "bound". —Charles Dickens, *Great Expectations*

4. Down the sides of every great rib of ice poured limpid* rills* in gutters carved by their own **attrition**. —Mark Twain, *A Tramp Abroad*

5. When discords, and quarrels, and factions, are carried openly and **audaciously**, it is a sign the reverence of government is lost. —Francis Bacon, *Essays*

6. To fret* over unavoidable evils, or **augment** them by anxiety, was no part of her disposition. —Jane Austen, *Pride and Prejudice*

****

1. **atrocity**; ruthlessness, savagery, ferocity. —atrocious. * confound; mystify.
2. **attenuate**; weaken, dilute, diminish. —attenuation. * diffused; scattered.
3. **attest**; verify, certify, corroborate, notarize. —attestation. ※ notary; notary public, a person licensed to certify documents. * indentures; (usu. in *pl.*) contract.
4. **attrition**; 1. wearing down, friction, abrasion, detrition: *war of attrition*. 2. regret, rue, contrition. —attrite *adj.* * limpid; clear, pellucid. * rill; stream, brook, rivulet.
5. **audaciously**; boldly, dauntlessly, pluckily, intrepidly. —audacity.
6. **augment**; increase, expand, dilate, amplify. —augmentation. * fret; worry, nag.

♣ Hallucinations and histrionic delusions generally go with a certain depth of the trance, and are followed by complete forgetfulness. —William James, *The Principles of Psychology*

1. The best **augury** of a man's success in his profession is that he thinks it the finest in the world. —George Eliot, *Daniel Deronda*

2. . . . his **august** friends, the Duke and Duchess, were everything that was kind and civil. —W. M. Thackeray, *Vanity Fair*

3. There was also a tradition that the soup course should be light and unpretending*—a sort of simple and **austere** vigil* for the feast of fish that was to come. —G. K. Chesterton, *The Innocence of Father Brown*

4. The ocean has the conscienceless temper of a savage **autocrat** spoiled by much adulation. He cannot brook* the slightest appearance of defiance . . . —Joseph Conrad, *The Mirror of the Sea*

5. His [Wellington's] great character stands untarnished* by ambition, **avarice**, or any low passion. —Samuel Smiles, *Self Help*

6. He said I was a capricious* witch, and that he would rather sing another time; but I **averred** that no time was like the present. —Charlotte Brontë, *Jane Eyre*

****

1. **augury**; omen, auspice, divination, presage. —augur *v.* —augural.
2. **august**; majestic, magnificent, splendid, regal.
3. **austere**; stern, solemn, stringent. —austerity. * unpretending; simple, unpretentious. * vigil; 1. rite on the eve of a festival. 2. watch, surveillance.
4. **autocrat**; dictator, tyrant, despot, absolutist, czar. —autocracy. * brook; tolerate.
5. **avarice**; greed, rapacity. —avaricious; covetous, ravenous, voracious, devouring, esurient. * untarnished; untainted, unblemished, unsullied.
6. **aver**; insist, affirm, assert. ※ avert; divert, avoid, forefend: *avert a crisis to avert a calamity*. * capricious; impulsive, unpredictable, freakish, *see p. 42, no. 3.*

♣ He who desires but acts not, breeds pestilence.

—William Blake, *The Marriage of Heaven and Hell*

1. He thought, or rather felt, that Tom had an **aversion** to looking at him; every one, almost, disliked looking at him; and his deformity was more conspicuous when he walked. —George Eliot, *The Mill on the Floss*

2. Philip, his restless mind **avid** for new things, became devout.* —W. Somerset Maugham, *Of Human Bondage*

3. Wilfred Bohun stood rooted to the spot long enough to see the idiot go out into the sunshine, and even to see his dissolute* brother hail him with a sort of **avuncular** jocularity. —G. K. Chesterton, *The Innocence of Father Brown*

4. Thou aimest all **awry**.

   —Shakespeare, *King Henry VI, Part II*

5. "Mademoiselle is a fairy," he said, whispering mysteriously. Whereupon I told her not to mind his **badinage**. —Charlotte Brontë, *Jane Eyre*

6. "Overdue" was the title he had decided for it, and its length he believed would not be more than sixty thousand words—a **bagatelle** for him with his splendid vigor of production. —Jack London, *Martin Eden*

****

1. **aversion**; antipathy, abhorrence, loathing, repugnance, disgust. —averse *adj.*; opposed, disinclined: *averse to the "new" project because it is not new.*
2. **avid**; greedy, devouring, avaricious, ravenous, rapacious, esurient. —avidity. * devout; 1. religious, pious. 2. zealous, ardent, impassioned.
3. **avuncular**; like an uncle, benevolent. * dissolute; libertine, wanton, profligate, licentious. ※ dissolution; decomposition, disintegration: *dissolution of the club.*
4. **awry**; askew, obliquely, crookedly, lopsidedly.
5. **badinage**; ridicule, banter, raillery.
6. **bagatelle**; 1. easy and short piece. 2. trifle, triviality, frivolity.

♣ Every sweet hath its sour; every evil its good. —R. W. Emerson, *Compensation*

1. Sliding down the ropes like **baleful** comets, the two Canallers rushed into the uproar, and sought to drag their man out of it towards the forecastle. —Herman Melville, *Moby Dick*

2. A thin carpet of moss, scarcely covering the ragged beds of pudding-stone, tantalized* and **balked** his [a miserable horse's] hunger. —Washington Irving, *The Devil and Tom Walker*

3. Then there must be some middle counsellors, to keep things steady; for without that **ballast** the ship will roll too much. —Francis Bacon, *Essays*

4. They had no longer any surprises for me, . . . even their love-affairs had a tedious **banality**. —W. Somerset Maugham, *The Moon and Sixpence*

5. You intimated that to have a sullied* memory was a perpetual **bane**. —Charlotte Brontë, *Jane Eyre*

6. The sky too was monotonously gray; the atmosphere was stagnant and humid; yet amidst all these deadening influences, my fancy budded fresh and my heart **basked** in sunshine. —Charlotte Brontë, *Villette*

****

1. **baleful**; harmful, malignant, malevolent, sinister. —bale; evil, harm.
2. **balk**; 1. baffle, thwart, stymie. 2. shrink, quail. ※ stymie; 1. frustrate: *The beauty stymied the other beauty contestants.* 2. obstacle, block, obstruction. * tantalize; tease.
3. **ballast**; 1. heavy substance for a vessel's stability. 2. stabilizer.
4. **banality**; triteness, humdrumness. —banal; pedestrian, run-of-the-mill.
5. **bane**; 1. death, calamity, disaster. 2. poison, canker. —baneful; noxious, noisome, pernicious. * sullied; disgraced, defiled.
6. **bask**; 1. sunbathe, toast oneself. 2. rejoice, indulge.

♣ Language is the archives of history. —R. W. Emerson, *The Poet*

bastion

1. Two of the sweeping **bastions** appeared to rest on the water which washed their bases. —James Fenimore Cooper, *The Last of the Mohicans*

2. The child amidst his **baubles** is learning the action of light, motion, gravity, muscular force. —R. W. Emerson, *Divinity School Address*

3. . . . bloody, **bawdy** villain!
   Remorseless, treacherous,* lecherous, kindless villain!
   O, vengeance!*

   —Shakespeare, *Hamlet*

4. Modest doubt is call'd
   The **beacon** of the wise.

   —Shakespeare, *Troilus and Cressida*

5. He seemed, at times, so lost in the **beatific** vision, that he forgot my stumblings in the philological darkness, till I appealed to him for help. Then he would read aloud with that magnificent rhythm . . . —W. Dean Howells, *My Literary Passions*

6. As usual, she was extraordinarily festooned* and **bedizened**, with a limp* Leghorn hat* anchored to her head by many windings of faded gauze.* —Edith Wharton, *The Age of Innocence*

****

1. **bastion**; stronghold, fortress, citadel, bulwark.
2. **bauble**; cheap and showy toy, trinket, gewgaw, knickknack.
3. **bawdy**; lecherous, ribald. * treacherous; traitorous. * vengeance; revenge.
4. **beacon**; guiding light, signal fire, buoy, signal, bonfire.
5. **beatific**; 1. blissful, rapturous, exalted. 2. *adj.* blessing. —beatify, —beatitude.
6. **bedizen**; 1. attire garishly. 2. adorn gaudily. —bedizenment. * festoon; 1. decorate with garlands. 2. n. wreath. * limp; 1. flexible. 2. lame walk. * Leghorn hat; hat made from Italian straw. * gauze; thin, transparent fabric.

1. They [the dogs] quarreled and bickered* more than ever among themselves, till at times the camp was a howling **bedlam**. —Jack London, *The Call of the Wild*

2. He was dressed in a **bedraggled** suit of khaki, and his hands would have been all the better for a wash. —W. Somerset Maugham, *The Moon and Sixpence*

3. Please do not misunderstand. There was no drunkenness, as drunkenness is ordinarily understood—no staggering and rolling around, no **befuddlement** of the senses. —Jack London, *John Barleycorn*

4. I am not merry; but I do **beguile**
   The thing I am, by seeming otherwise.
   —Shakespeare, *Othello*

5. **Belabored** by their officers, they began to move forward. —Stephen Crane, *The Red Badge of Courage*

6. I cannot think that any Scottish or French rovers* could land in such force as to **beleaguer** the fortalice.* —Arthur Conan Doyle, *The White Company*

****

1. **bedlam**; tumult, turmoil, uproar, commotion, pandemonium. * bicker; argue.
2. **bedraggled**; 1. untidy, muddy, soiled, disheveled. 2. wet, drenched.
3. **befuddlement**; perplexity, bewilderment, bemusement, bafflement, obfuscation.
4. **beguile**; delude, deceive, cheat. —beguilement. ※ guile; cunning, slyness. —guileful. ※ gullible; naive, credulous: *a gullible husband and his guileful wife.*
5. **belabor**; 1. beat, thrash, whip. 2. explain unduly, harp on.
6. **beleaguer**; 1. beset, besiege, surround and assail. 2. annoy, beset. * rover; 1. pirate. 2. tramp. * fortalice; fortress, fort, citadel, stronghold.

♣ The history of persecution is a history of endeavors to cheat nature, to make water run up hill, to twist a rope of sand. —R. W. Emerson, *Compensation*

1. The business of eating interposed a brief truce between the **belligerents**. —Charlotte Brontë, *The Professor*
2. Humanity and good policy conspire to dictate, that the **benign** prerogative* of pardoning should be as little as possible fettered* or embarrassed. —Alexander Hamilton, *The Federalist Papers*
3. Now I read over the works of Aristotle and Plato, with the rest of those inestimable treasures which ancient Greece had **bequeathed** to the world. —Henry Fielding, *Tom Jones*
4. Regardless of the vindictive* threats of the bullets, he went about coaxing, **berating**, and bedamning. —Stephen Crane, *The Red Badge of Courage*
5. A mob is a society of bodies voluntarily **bereaving** themselves of reason and traversing* its work. —R. W. Emerson, *Compensation*
6. I threw myself on my knees before him and **besought** him to acknowledge me as his Grand Child. —Jane Austen, *Love and Friendship*

****

1. **belligerent**; 1. nation at war, or fighter. 2. *adj.* aggressive, pugnacious, bellicose. —belligerence. ※ jingoism; 1. chauvinism. 2. belligerence, hawkishness.
2. **benign**; temperate, benevolent, complaisant, clement. ***ant.*** malignant. —benignancy. * prerogative; privilege, *see p. 235, no. 3.* * fetter; chain, tether.
3. **bequeath**; hand down, will, inherit. —bequest *n. or* bequeathal.
4. **berate**; reproach, reprove, upbraid, lambaste, objurgate. * vindictive; spiteful.
5. **bereave**; deprive, strip. —bereft *p., pp.* ※ the bereaved; the survivors. * traverse; 1. thwart. 2. cross, go through.
6. **beseech**; plead, implore, entreat, conjure, adjure, petition, supplicate.

♣ Love is never quite devoid of sentimentality. —W. Somerset Maugham, *The Moon and Sixpence*

1. They have the power of _______ to their own nature all other thoughts.
2. Some novel movements showed their nature on her _______ brow.
3. Something of the past can recur, _______, destructive, and uncontrolled.
4. Whatever his crimes, he has suffered something to _______ for them.
5. They say that 'time _______,'—time never did assuage.
6. An _______ nature has more enemies than the moths that fret my leaves.

[**assuages, assimilating, astute, astringent, atone, atavistic**]

****

1. He listened to her in a silence that he made no immediate effort to _______.
2. Here, in a corner my indentures were duly signed and _______.
3. Down the sides of every great rib of ice poured limpid rills in gutters carved by their own _______.
4. To _______ unavoidable evils by anxiety was no part of her disposition.
5. Quarrels and factions were carried openly and _______.
6. He was confounded by the absence of motive for the _______ of the murder.

[**atrocity, augment, audaciously, attenuate, attested, attrition**]

****

1. Much adulation spoiled the savage _______.
2. Wellington's great character stands untarnished by ambition or _______.
3. So favorable was the _______ for his success in the profession.
4. His _______ friends were everything that was kind and civil.
5. It was a sort of simple and _______ vigil for the feast of fish.
6. He would sing another time; but I _______ that no time was like the present.

[**august, avarice, averred, augury, austere, autocrat**]

****

1. Philip, his restless mind _______ for new things, became devout.
2. His dissolute brother hailed him with a sort of _______ jocularity.
3. I told her not to mind his _______.
4. Thou aimest all _______.
5. The work was a _______ for him with his splendid vigor for production.
6. He thought, or rather felt, that Tom had an _______ to looking at him.

[**awry, badinage, aversion, bagatelle, avid, avuncular**]

Review Exercise: Sentence Completions (pp. 25–28)

1. Sliding down the ropes like _______ comets, they rushed into the uproar.
2. To have a sullied memory was a perpetual _______.
3. My fancy budded fresh and my heart _______ in sunshine.
4. A thin carpet of moss tantalized and _______ the horse's hunger.
5. Without that _______ the ship will roll too much.
6. Even their love-affairs had a tedious _______.

[**balked, ballast, banality, baleful, basked, bane**]

****

1. He seemed, at times, lost in the _______ vision.
2. She was extraordinarily festooned and _______, with a limp Leghorn hat.
3. The child amidst his _______ is learning the action of light, motion, gravity.
4. Two of the sweeping _______ appeared to rest on the water.
5. Bloody, _______ villain! Remorseless, lecherous villain! O, vengeance!
6. Modest doubt is call'd the _______ of the wise.

[**bedizened, bastions, beatific, beacon, bawdy, baubles**]

****

1. _______ by their officers, they began to move forward.
2. He was dressed in a _______ suit of khaki.
3. The dogs quarreled and bickered till the camp was a howling _______.
4. There was no drunkenness, and no _______ of the senses.
5. I am not merry; I do _______ the thing I am, by seeming otherwise.
6. Any Scottish rovers could land in such force as to _______ the fortalice.

[**beleaguer, befuddlement, belabored, beguile, bedlam, bedraggled**]

****

1. The _____ prerogative of pardoning should be as little as possible fettered.
2. He went about coaxing, _______, and bedamning.
3. A mob is a society of bodies voluntarily _______ themselves of reason.
4. I _______ him to acknowledge me as his Grand Child.
5. The business of eating interposed a brief truce between the _______.
6. Ancient Greece had _______ those inestimable treasures to the world.

[**berating, belligerents, besought, bereaving, bequeathed, benign**]

1. Love was too fine and noble, and he was too loyal a lover for him to **besmirch** love with criticism. —Jack London, *Martin Eden*

2. When he looked at her he knew that he no longer loved her . . . Watching her gravely, he asked himself why he had been so **besotted** with passion for her. —W. Somerset Maugham, *Of Human Bondage*

3. **Betrothed**, or not betrothed, she was equally far from me. —Wilkie Collins, *The Woman in White*

4. Walter Scott was all but a dunce when a boy, always much readier for a "**bicker**," than apt at his lessons. —Samuel Smiles, *Self Help*

5. I am not **bigoted** to my plans, and I can overturn them myself. I can substitute some other plans. —Charles Dickens, *David Copperfield*

6. He gorged* himself habitually at table, which made him **bilious**, and gave him a dim and bleared eye and flabby* cheeks. —Charlotte Brontë, *Jane Eyre*

****

1. **besmirch**; smear, tarnish, taint, sully, denigrate. —besmirchment.
2. **besot**; charm, intoxicate, captivate, infatuate. —besottedness, —besottedly.
3. **betrothed**; engaged, affianced, plighted. —betrothal *or* betrothment, —betroth.
4. **bicker**; argument, dispute, contention, quarrel, squabble, wrangle. —bickerer.
5. **bigoted**; biased, prejudiced, narrow-minded, opinioned. —bigot *n.*, —bigotry; bias. ※ tendentious; 1. biased, partial. 2. partisan, sectarian.
6. **bilious**; nasty, irascible, peevish, petulant, choleric, splenetic, liverish. —biliously, —biliousness. * gorge; overeat, gluttonize. * flabby; loose, sagging.

♣ Never was ruler so absolute as he [Abraham Lincoln], nor so little conscious of it; for he was the incarnate common-sense of the people. —James Russell Lowell, *Abraham Lincoln*

1. I don't intend to **bilk** my lodgings; but I have a private reason for not taking a formal leave. —Henry Fielding, *Tom Jones*

2. In the world's broad field of battle,
   In the **bivouac** of Life,
   Be not like dumb, driven cattle!
   Be a hero in the strife!

   —H. W. Longfellow, "A Psalm of Life"

3. He was quite calm. He denied everything. He denied with **bland** effrontery.* —W. Somerset Maugham, *Of Human Bondage*

4. Those sensitive creatures [ships] have no ears for our **blandishments**. It takes something more than words to cajole* them to do our will, to cover us with glory. —Joseph Conrad, *The Mirror of the Sea*

5. It was great **blasphemy** when the devil said, *I will ascend and be like the Highest.* —Francis Bacon, *Essays*

6. O, I know he's a good fellow—you needn't frown—an excellent fellow, . . . but a hide-bound* pedant* for all that; an ignorant, **blatant** pedant. —R. L. Stevenson, *Dr. Jekyll and Mr. Hyde*

****

1. **bilk**; 1. elude, evade paying and flee. 2. cheat, defraud, swindle. —bilker.
2. **bivouac**; 1. camping site or ground. 2. camp, encampment.
3. **bland**; 1. mild, smooth, suave. 2. dull, insipid, vapid. —blandness, —blandly. * effrontery; boldness, presumption, impudence, *see p. 95, no. 6.*
4. **blandishment**; coaxing, enticement, inveiglement. * cajole; seduce, wheedle.
5. **blasphemy**; profanity, sacrilege, desecration. —blasphemous.
6. **blatant**; 1. unashamed, brazen, impudent. 2. plain, overt. —blatancy. * hide-bound; narrow-minded, bigoted, tendentious. * pedant; pedagogue.

1. I'll give no **blemish** to her honour, none.

—Shakespeare, *The Winter's Tale*

2. His form was of the same strong and stalwart* contour* as ever: . . . not in one year's space, by any sorrow, could his athletic strength be quelled,* or his vigorous prime **blighted**. —Charlotte Brontë, *Jane Eyre*

3. And hark! how **blithe** the throstle sings!
   He, too, is no mean preacher.

—William Wordsworth, "The Tables Turned"

4. Strickland employed not the rapier* of sarcasm but the **bludgeon** of invective.* —W. Somerset Maugham, *The Moon and Sixpence*

5. As I walked over the long causeway* made for the railroad through the meadows, I encountered many a **blustering** and nipping* wind, for nowhere has it freer play. —Henry David Thoreau, *Walden*

6. A sceptre* snatch'd with an unruly hand
   Must be as **boisterously** maintain'd as gain'd.

—Shakespeare, *King John*

****

1. **blemish**; 1. stain, flaw, defect, disgrace, taint. 2. *v.* mar, spoil, deface, blur.
2. **blight**; 1. wither, shrivel, blast. 2. misery. * stalwart; stout, robust, hefty, sinewy, *see p. 296, no. 4.* * contour; 1. outline. 2. limn. * quell; subdue, suppress.
3. **blithe**; merry, cheerful, lighthearted, gleeful, jaunty. —blithely.
4. **bludgeon**; short but heavy club. * rapier: slender sword. * invective; venom.
5. **blustering**; violent, gusty, stormy. * causeway; raised road. * nipping; bitter.
6. **boisterously**; clamorously, obstreperously, rambunctiously, vociferously. * sceptre *also* scepter; regal power, sovereignty.

♣ Nature is no sentimentalist,—does not cosset or pamper us. —R. W. Emerson, *Fate*

1. An idle brain is the devil's workshop, and a lazy man the devil's **bolster**. —Samuel Smiles, *Self Help*

2. Then, because he did not reply for several days, Miss Wilkinson **bombarded** him with letters. —W. Somerset Maugham, *Of Human Bondage*

3. He [Shakespeare] is many times flat and insipid*; his comic wit degenerating into clenches, his serious swelling into **bombast**. —Samuel Johnson, *Preface to Shakespeare*

4. My **boon** I make it that you know me not.

   —Shakespeare, *King Lear*

5. **Boor** as he was, Sir Pitt was a stickler* for his dignity while at home, and seldom drove out but with four horses. —W. M. Thackeray, *Vanity Fair*

6. In April, high in air, the beautiful and **bountiful** horse-chestnuts, candelabra-wise, proffer* the passer-by their tapering* upright cones of congregated* blossoms. —Herman Melville, *Moby Dick*

****

1. **bolster**; pad, cushion, support, prop, brace.
2. **bombard**; assault, blast, barrage, batter, pepper, blitz. —bombardment. ※ incursion; raid, foray: *making incursions into the king's territory.* —incursive.
3. **bombast**; grandiloquence, magniloquence, bravado. —bombastic. ※ magniloquent; bombastic, pompous, rhetorical: *magniloquent voice.* * insipid; dull.
4. **boon**; blessing, mercy, favor, benefit.
5. **boor**; rustic, churl. * stickler; one who maintains something obstinately.
6. **bountiful**; lavish, unstinted, munificent. —bounty *n.* * proffer; offer. * taper; 1. diminish, attenuate. 2. thin candle. * congregated; assembled.

♣ Great minds are to make others great. —W. Ellery Channing, *On the Elevation of the Laboring Classes*

1. Gaining the more open water, the **bracing** breeze waxed* fresh. —Herman Melville, *Moby Dick*

2. She is **bragged** of, but not brags. —Herman Melville, *Pierre*

3. Comets, importing change of times and states,
Brandish your crystal tresses* in the sky.
—Shakespeare, *King Henry VI, Part I*

4. When I got to camp I warn't feeling very **brash**, there warn't much sand in my craw.* —Mark Twain, *The Adventures of Huckleberry Finn*

5. I do not believe the people who tell me they do not care a row of pins for the opinion of their fellows. It is the **bravado** of ignorance. —W. Somerset Maugham, *The Moon and Sixpence*

6. . . . he was brown and **brawny**, like most old seamen, and heavily rolled up in blue pilot-cloth, cut in the Quaker style. —Herman Melville, *Moby Dick*

****

1. **bracing**; refreshing, invigorating, tonic, fortifying, rejuvenating. —brace; 1. support, buttress. 2. reinforce, stimulate. * wax; 1. become, grow. 2. increase.
2. **brag**; boast, flaunt, vaunt, bravado. —braggart.
3. **brandish**; wave threateningly, flourish, flaunt. * tress; a long braid of hair.
4. **brash**; 1. energetic, spirited. 2. impudent, forward. * craw; stomach, tummy.
5. **bravado**; swagger, boast, vainglory, brag, fanfaronade, bombast, vaunt.
6. **brawny**; muscular, robust, sturdy, hefty, sinewy, stalwart. —brawn; sinew.

♣ All impediments in fancy's course
Are motives of more fancy.
—Shakespeare, *All's Well That Ends Well*

1. It is an established doctrine on the subject of treaties, that all the articles are mutually conditions of each other; that a **breach** of any one article is a breach of the whole treaty. —James Madison, *The Federalist Papers*

2. A frowsy,* bearded **brigand** sprang into the road with a shout, and flourished a musket in the light of the moon! —Mark Twain, *The Innocents Abroad*

3. I better brook the loss of **brittle** life
Than those proud titles thou hast won of me.
—Shakespeare, *Henry IV, Part I*

4. It was in mid-winter, when Billy, with quite a deal of obvious reluctance,* **broached** a money matter to Saxton. —Jack London, *The Valley of the Moon*

5. Why, he is no more than a ponderous* **bromide** . . . —Jack London, *Martin Eden*

6. His keen grey eye, impersonal and **brusque**, flashed upon her half impatiently. —O. Henry, *The Romance of a Busy Broker*

****

1. **breach**; violation, infraction, offense, transgression, infringement.
2. **brigand**; outlaw, bandit, highwayman. —brigandage. * frowsy; untidy, slovenly.
3. **brittle**; frail, fragile, friable, frangible. —brittleness, —brittly.
4. **broach**; introduce, bring up, open up, approach. —broacher. * reluctance; dislike, aversion, loathing, *see p. 264, no. 3.*
5. **bromide**; 1. dull person, bore. 2. commonplace, platitude, cliché, truism, banality, triteness. —bromidic. * ponderous; 1. dull, tedious. 2. awkward.
6. **brusque**; blunt, curt, gruff. —brusquely, —brusqueness.

♣ The good of the whole is the same with the good of all its parts. —Samuel Johnson, *Rasselas*

1. He had a handsome face, thin, ascetic,* with dark eyes; he wore his fantastic garb with the dashing air of a **buccaneer**. —W. Somerset Maugham, *Of Human Bondage*

2. The Pollio* of Virgil, with all its elevation, is a composition truly **bucolic**, though rejected by the critics. —Samuel Johnson, *The Rambler*

3. Here I expect we shall be told that the militia of the country is its natural **bulwark**, and would be at all times equal to the national defence. —Alexander Hamilton, *The Federalist Papers*

4. I was still annoyed at his **bumptious** style of conversation. —Arthur Conan Doyle, *A Study in Scarlet*

5. Ignorance and **bungling** with love are better than wisdom and skill without. —Henry David Thoreau, *A Week on the Concord and Merrimack Rivers*

6. His vivacity betrays itself at all points, in his manners, in his respiration, and the inarticulate noises he makes in clearing the throat;—all significant of **burly** strength. —R. W. Emerson, *English Traits*

****

1. **buccaneer**; pirate. ※ pirate; 1. sea robber, rover. 2. plagiarist, infringer: *copyright pirate*. * ascetic; severe, Spartan. —asceticism; *see p. 17, no. 6.*
2. **bucolic**; pastoral, rustic, rural, idyllic, Arcadian. * The Pollio; Virgil's fourth eclogue.
3. **bulwark**; fortress, bastion, buttress, citadel, rampart.
4. **bumptious**; arrogant, insolent, overbearing, conceited, brash, forward.
5. **bungling**; mismanaging, blundering, bumbling, botching. —bunglesome.
6. **burly**; stout, muscular, sturdy, brawny, hefty. —burliness, —burlily.

♣ The mind must not be tied down by rigid rules. —W. Ellery Channing, *On the Elevation of the Laboring Classes*

1. Mislike me not for my complexion,
   The shadow'd livery* of the **burnish'd** sun,
   To whom I am a neighbour and near bred.
   —Shakespeare, *The Merchant of Venice*

2. While an unbounded field for **cabal** and intrigue lies open, all idea of responsibility is lost. —Alexander Hamilton, *The Federalist Papers*

3. From a **cache** behind a hollow rotting log my companion brought out a variety of things,—a fifty-pound sack of flour, tinned foods of all sorts . . . and, last and most important, a large coil of stout rope. —Jack London, *The Iron Heel*

4. There were deep hollows at his temples. His body was **cadaverous**. —W. Somerset Maugham, *The Moon and Sixpence*

5. He coaxed, wheedled, **cajoled**, and complimented Jos Sedley with a perseverance* and cordiality of which he was not aware himself, very likely. —W. M. Thackeray, *Vanity Fair*

6. Drudgery,* **calamity**, exasperation, want, are instructors in eloquence and wisdom. —R. W. Emerson, *The American Scholar*

****

1. **burnished**; polished, glossed, sheened. —burnisher. * livery; attire.
2. **cabal**; plot, intrigue, scheme, conspiracy.
3. **cache**; secret repository, hidden store.
4. **cadaverous**; pallid, gaunt. —cadaverousness.
5. **cajole**; coax, entice, wheedle, inveigle. —cajolery. * perseverance; persistence.
6. **calamity**; 1. misfortune, adversity, misery. 2. disaster. * drudgery; toil, hard work.

♣ Singularity is almost invariably a clue. —Arthur Conan Doyle, *The Adventures of Sherlock Holmes*

1. Walter Scott was always much readier for a _______ than apt at his lessons.
2. I am not _______ to my plans, and I can overturn them myself.
3. He was too loyal a lover for him to _______ love with criticism.
4. _______, or not betrothed, she was equally far from me.
5. He asked himself why he had been so _______ with passion for her.
6. He gorged himself habitually at table, which made him ______.

[**bigoted, bicker, besmirch, besotted, betrothed, bilious**]

****

1. He is a good fellow, but an ignorant, _______ pedant.
2. I don't intend to _______ my lodgings.
3. In the _______ of life, be not like dumb, driven cattle, be a hero in the strife.
4. He was quite calm. He denied everything. He denied with _______ effrontery.
5. Those sensitive creatures [ships] have no ears for our _______.
6. It was great _______ when the devil said, *I will ascend and be like the Highest.*

[**bilk, bland, bivouac, blatant, blasphemy, blandishments**]

****

1. And hark! How _______ the throstle sings! He, too, is no mean preacher.
2. I'll give no _______ to her honour, none.
3. Not in one year's space, by any sorrow, could his vigorous prime be _______.
4. I encountered many a _______ and nipping wind.
5. A sceptre snatch'd with an unruly hand must be _______ maintain'd.
6. Strickland employed not the rapier of sarcasm but the _______ of invective.

[**boisterously, blemish, blustering, bludgeon, blithe, blighted**]

****

1. He did not reply for several days. She _______ him with letters.
2. My _______ I make it that you know me not.
3. An idle brain is the devil's workshop, and a lazy man the devil's _______.
4. _______ as he was, Sir Pitt was a stickler for his dignity while at home.
5. His comic wit degenerates into clenches, his serious swelling into _______.
6. In April, high in air, the horse-chestnuts were beautiful and _______.

[**bolster, bombarded, boon, bombast, bountiful, boor**]

Review Exercise: Sentence Completions (pp. 35–38)

1. Comets _______ your crystal tresses in the sky.
2. When I got to camp I warn't feeling very _______.
3. He said he doesn't care for the others' opinion. It is the ______ of ignorance.
4. She is _______ of, but not brags.
5. Gaining the more open water, the _______ breeze waxed fresh.
6. He was brown and _______, like most old seamen.

[**brash, bravado, bragged, bracing, brawny, brandish**]

****

1. Why, he is no more than a ponderous _______.
2. A _______ of any one article is a breach of the whole treaty.
3. A frowsy, bearded _______ sprang into the road with a shout.
4. I better brook the loss of _______ life than those proud titles.
5. He, with quite a deal of reluctance, _______ a money matter to Saxton.
6. His keen grey eye, impersonal and _______, flashed upon her half impatiently.

[**brittle, brigand, broached, bromide, brusque, breach**]

****

1. I was still annoyed at his _______ style of conversation.
2. He wore his fantastic garb with the dashing air of a _______.
3. The Pollio of Virgil, with all its elevation, is a composition truly _______.
4. Ignorance and _______ with love are better than wisdom and skill without.
5. His manners and respiration . . . , all are significant of _______ strength.
6. The militia of the country is its natural _______.

[**burly, bungling, bumptious, buccaneer, bucolic, bulwark**]

****

1. An unbounded field for _______ and intrigue lies open.
2. From a _______ behind a hollow rotting log he brought out a variety of things.
3. He coaxed, wheedled, and _______ her with a perseverance and cordiality.
4. There were deep hollows at his temples. His body was _______.
5. Drudgery, _______, want, are instructors in eloquence and wisdom.
6. Mislike me not for my complexion, the shadow'd livery of the _______ sun.

[**cabal, cache, cadaverous, cajoled, calamity, burnish'd**]

1. . . . she was merely bored with her husband and went to Strickland out of a **callous** curiosity. —W. Somerset Maugham, *The Moon and Sixpence*

2. Such a downy* tip was on his **callow** chin, that he seemed half fledged like a young bird. —Charles Dickens, *Little Dorrit*

3. To spread suspicion, to invent **calumnies**, to propagate* scandal, requires neither labour nor courage. —Samuel Johnson, *The Rambler*

4. He had lived all his life in the working-class world, and the ***camaraderie*** of labor was second nature with him. —Jack London, *Martin Eden*

5. In London that night poor Henderson's telegram describing the gradual unscrewing of the shot was judged to be a **canard**. —H. G. Wells, *The War of the Worlds*

6. Of all the **cants** which are canted in this canting world—though the cant of hypocrites may be the worst—the cant of criticism is the most tormenting! —Laurence Sterne, *Tristram Shandy*

****

1. **callous**; unsympathetic, indifferent, apathetic. ***ant.*** pathetic; sympathetic, empathic. —callosity. ※ empathetic; pathetic: *the empathetic doctors.*
2. **callow**; immature, green, unfledged, puerile, jejune. * downy; soft, fluffy.
3. **calumny**; slander, libel, vilification, aspersion, denigration. —calumniate, —calumnious. * propagate; 1. distribute, publicize. 2. breed. —propagation.
4. **camaraderie**; fellowship, comradeship, companionship.
5. **canard**; false story, groundless rumor, fabrication.
6. **cant**; 1. hypocrisy, duplicity, affectation, pretense. 2. *v.* speak hypocritically.

♣ Natural abilities are like natural plants, that need pruning by study. —Francis Bacon, *Essays*

1. I turned away to pay off my taxi, the driver of which was very **cantankerous** and abusive* over his fare. —Arthur Conan Doyle, *The Poison Belt*

2. I am ashamed to think how easily we **capitulate** to badges and names, to large societies and dead institutions. —R. W. Emerson, *Self-Reliance*

3. The aunt was a **capricious** woman, and governed her husband entirely. —Jane Austen, *Emma*

4. Far be from us the **captious** and fault-finding spirit, my dear sir. —Herman Melville, *The Confidence-Man*

5. Plato apprehended* the **cardinal** facts. —R. W. Emerson, *Plato; or, the Philosopher*

6. The door slammed to because it was on the **careened** side. —Mark Twain, *The Adventures of Huckleberry Finn*

****

1. **cantankerous**; ill-natured, bad-tempered, grumpy, crusty. —cantankerousness, —cantankerously. * abusive; offensive, maligning.
2. **capitulate**; yield, surrender, submit, succumb. —capitulation.
3. **capricious**; fickle, fitful, whimsical, freakish, arbitrary. —caprice.
4. **captious**; faultfinding, caviling, carping. —captiously, —captiousness.
5. **cardinal**; main, fundamental, primary, foremost, principal, paramount. * apprehend; 1. comprehend, grasp. 2. dread, fear. —apprehension, —apprehensive.
6. **careen**; 1. lean over, tilt, lurch. 2. pitch, sway.

♣ We may, and must, assume our opinion to be true for the guidance of our own conduct: and it is assuming no more when we forbid bad men to pervert society by the propagation of opinions which we regard as false and pernicious. —John Stuart Mill, *On Liberty*

1. Rome was never sated* of **carnage** and conquest. —Alexander Hamilton, *The Federalist Papers*.

2. We have reason to cool our raging motions, our **carnal** stings, our unbitted* lusts. —Shakespeare, *Othello*

3. It was fight or look on, all day and every day; and sing, gamble, dance, **carouse** half the night every night. —Mark Twain, *A Connecticut Yankee*

4. Shame not these woods
   By putting on the cunning of a **carper**.
   —Shakespeare, *Timon of Athens*

5. My unfortunate limb was now left much in the same condition as a rump-steak after undergoing the **castigating** process which precedes cooking. —Herman Melville, *Type*

6. She goes about her business indifferent to wars, revolutions, and **cataclysms**. —W. Somerset Maugham, *Of Human BondageMy*

****

1. **carnage**; mass murder, slaughter, massacre, holocaust. * sate; surfeit, cloy.
2. **carnal**; sexual, fleshly, sensual, libidinous. * unbitted; unrestrained.
3. **carouse**; revel, spree, roister. —carousal, —carousing; orgiastic, bacchic, bacchanal, bacchanalian, inebriated.
4. **carper**; faultfinder, censurer, caviler, quibbler. —carp
5. **castigate**; reprove, chastise, chide, lambaste *also* lambast, objurgate.
6. **cataclysm**; 1. upheaval, disaster, catastrophe. 2. great flood, deluge.

♣ A state without the means of some change is without the means of its conservation. —Edmund Burke, *Reflections on the Revolution in France*

1. He was **catholic**. He had not only a true appreciation of the old masters, but sympathy with the moderns. —W. Somerset Maugham, *The Moon and Sixpence*

2. She was indolent,* passive, the **caustic** even called her dull. —Edith Wharton, *The Age of Innocence*

3. The **cavalcade** had not long passed, before the branches of the bushes that formed the thicket were cautiously moved asunder*. . . —James Fenimore Cooper, *The Last of the Mohicans*

4. "Well, where is Guinea?" said the man in gray; "where is he? Let us at once find him, and refute beyond **cavil** this injurious hypothesis." —Herman Melville, *The Confidence-Man*

5. Either **cede** your daughter to my disposal, or take her wholly to your own surprising discretion. —Henry Fielding, *Tom Jones*

6. **Celerity** is never more admired
   Than by the negligent.*

   —Shakespeare, *Anthony and Cleopatra*

****

1. **catholic**; all-embracing, universal, comprehensive. —catholicity, —catholicize. ※ eclectic; 1. catholic: *The villain has an eclectic taste in reading.* 2. selective.
2. **caustic**; acrid, pungent, edgy, vitriolic. —causticity. * indolent; sluggish.
3. **cavalcade**; parade, procession, promenade. * asunder: apart.
4. **cavil**; find fault, censure, carp, niggle, quibble. —caviler. ※ bowdlerize; erase, censor, sanitize, expurgate: *The expurgator bowdlerized the romantic movie.*
5. **cede**; yield, surrender, concede, relinquish. —cession.
6. **celerity**; nimbleness, alacrity. * negligent; slack. ※ celebrity; dignitary.

♣ Many valuable preparations of chemistry, are supposed to have risen from unsuccessful enquiries after the grand elixir. —Samuel Johnson, *The Adventurer*

1. Marriage has many pains, but **celibacy** has no pleasures. —Samuel Johnson, *Rasselas*

2. The *Idler* is naturally **censorious**; those who attempt nothing themselves think everything easily performed. —Samuel Johnson, *The Idler*

3. . . . as the poise of my body depends on the equilibrium* of **centrifugal** and centripetal forces, so the hours should be instructed by the ages and the ages explained by the hours. —R. W. Emerson, *History*

4. He was down on the rank* wet grass, filing at his iron like a mad man, and not minding me or minding his own leg, which had an old **chafe** upon it and was bloody. —Charles Dickens, *Great Expectations*

5. Silence is the universal refuge, the sequel to all dull discourses and all foolish acts, a balm to our every **chagrin**. —Henry David Thoreau, *A Week on the Concord and Merrimack Rivers*

6. **Charlatanism** is for confusing or obliterating* the distinctions between excellent and inferior, sound and unsound or only half-sound, true and untrue or only half-true. —Matthew Arnold, *The Study of Poetry*

****

1. **celibacy**; 1. singleness, bachelorhood or spinsterhood. 2. abstinence, continence. —celibate, —celibatarian.
2. **censorious**; faultfinding, carping, caviling. —censor *v.* ※ censure; criticize.
3. **centrifugal**; moving from a center. ***ant.*** centripetal; moving toward a center. —centrifugation. * equilibrium; symmetry, equipoise.
4. **chafe**; 1. *n.* sore, gall. 2. *v.* warm by rubbing. 3. abrade. * rank; 1. flourishing, lush. 2. foul.
5. **chagrin**; dissatisfaction, mortification, vexation, displeasure.
6. **charlatanism**; fraud, imposture, quackery. —charlatan; quack, impostor, fraudster, mountebank. —charlatanic. * obliterate; erase, delete.

1. The **chariest** maid is prodigal* enough
   If she unmask her beauty to the moon.

   —Shakespeare, *Hamlet*

2. **Chaste** women are often proud and forward,* as presuming* upon the merit of their chastity. —Francis Bacon, *Essays*

3. It is always distressing when outraged morality does not possess the strength of arm to administer direct **chastisement** on the sinner. —W. Somerset Maugham, *The Moon and Sixpence*

4. After the word **chicanery** there was a growing noise, half of murmurs and half of hisses . . . —George Eliot, *Middlemarch*

5. I will **chide** no breather in the world but myself, against whom I know most faults. —Shakespeare, *As You Like It*

6. The Rev. B. B. Gordon was a man by nature ill-suited to be a schoolmaster: he was impatient and **choleric**. —W. Somerset Maugham, *Of Human Bondage*

****

1. **chary**; wary, prudent, circumspect. * prodigal; 1. lavish, bountiful, profuse. 2. spendthrift, *see p. 238, no. 1.*
2. **chaste**; pure, virginal. —chastity. * forward; bold, brash, impudent. * presuming; haughty, overbearing, arrogant, presumptuous.
3. **chastisement**; chiding, castigation, objurgation. ※ chasten; discipline.
4. **chicanery**; cheating, duplicity, deception, trickery, fraud. —chicane *v.*
5. **chide**; scold, upbraid, reproach, reprove, reprimand, lambaste.
6. **choleric**; irritable, touchy, peevish, waspish, irascible, splenetic. —choler *n.*

♣ He [the true gentleman] will not boast of his wealth, or his strength, or his gifts. He will not be puffed up by success, or unduly depressed by failure. —Samuel Smiles, *Self Help*

1. You deserve perpetual isolation from your species for your **churlish** inhospitality. —Emily Brontë, *Wuthering Heights*

2. I have now told you everything without an attempt at **circumlocution** or concealment. —Arthur Conan Doyle, *The Return of Sherlock Holmes*

3. On the banks of the St. Cruz, in certain **circumscribed** spaces, which were generally bushy and all near the river, the ground was actually white with bones. —Charles Darwin, *The Voyage of the Beagle*

4. We must not expect a lively young man to be always so guarded and **circumspect**. —Jane Austen, *Pride and Prejudice*

5. Offer your prayers to Him who can give us wisdom to **circumvent** the cunning of the devils who fill these woods. —James Fenimore Cooper, *The Last of the Mohicans*

6. Sometimes we see a cloud that's dragonish;
   A vapour sometime like a bear or lion,
   A tower'd **citadel**, a pendant* rock,
   A forked mountain, or blue promontory.*
   —Shakespeare, *Anthony and Cleopatra*

****

1. **churlish**; uncivil, rustic, rude, harsh, vulgar, boorish, uncouth. —churl; boor.
2. **circumlocution**; roundabout or evasive expression, beating about the bush, periphrasis. —circumlocutory; periphrastic, ambagious. ***ant.*** plain; express, outright. ※ peripheral; circumferential, marginal, tangential, perimetric.
3. **circumscribe**; limit, encircle, encompass, demarcate. —circumscription.
4. **circumspect**; cautious, discreet, prudent, guarded, judicious. —circumspection.
5. **circumvent**; bypass, elude, outwit, foil. —circumvention, —circumventive.
6. **citadel**; fortress, rampart. * pendant; hanging. * promontory; headland.

1. . . . when Mr. Tulliver speaks **civil** to me, I'll speak civil to him. —George Eliot, *The Mill on the Floss*

2. I used to think you were a **clairvoyant** and that was the reason why you were so bitter against other clairvoyants, wanting to keep your monopoly. —George Eliot, *The Lifted Veil*

3. When a law is considered as immutable,* and the immutable law happens at the same time to be too foolish and mischievous to be endured, instead of being repealed,* it is **clandestinely** evaded, or openly violated. —Sydney Smith, *Fallacies of Anti-Reformers*

4. In matters of human feeling the **clement** judge is the most successful pleader. —Robert L. Stevenson, *Truth of Intercourse*

5. Hie* thee to France,
   And **cloister** thee in some religious house.

   —Shakespeare, *King Richard II*

6. O, who can hold a fire in his hand
   By thinking on the frosty Caucasus?
   Or **cloy** the hungry edge of appetite
   By bare imagination of a feast?

   —Shakespeare, *King Richard II*

****

1. **civil**; polite, courteous, decorous. —civility; courtesy, decorum.
2. **clairvoyant**; 1. seer, diviner. 2. *adj.* perspicacious, prescient. —clairvoyance.
3. **clandestinely;** underhand, covertly, stealthily, surreptitiously, furtively. *immutable; invariable. * repeal; abolish, abrogate, annul, see p. 265, no. 6.
4. **clement**; merciful, benevolent, magnanimous. ***ant.*** inclement. —clemency.
5. **cloister**; 1. isolate, seclude. 2. monastery. ※ convent; nunnery. * hie; hasten.
6. **cloy**; satiate, surfeit, pamper. ※ blasé; 1. bored, cloyed, jaded. 2. apathetic.

1. The _______ of labor was second nature with him.
2. Such a downy tip was on his _______ chin, that he seemed half fledged.
3. To invent _______ requires neither labour nor courage.
4. Poor Henderson's telegram was judged to be a _______.
5. Of all the _______, the cant of criticism is the most tormenting!
6. She went to Strickland out of a _______ curiosity.

[**callow, cants, callous, camaraderie, calumnies, canard**]

****

1. How easily we _______ to badges and names!
2. The aunt was a _______ woman and governed her husband entirely.
3. Far be from us the _______ and fault-finding spirit, my dear sir.
4. The driver was very _______ and abusive over his fare.
5. Plato apprehended the _______ facts.
6. The door slammed to because it was on the _______ side.

[**captious, cantankerous, capitulate, cardinal, careened, capricious**]

****

1. Shame not these woods by putting on the cunning of a _______.
2. We have reason to cool our raging motions and our _______ stings.
3. Rome was never sated of _______ and conquest.
4. It was sing, gamble, dance, _______ half the night every night.
5. She goes about her business indifferent to wars, revolutions, and _______.
6. The rump-steak underwent the _______ process which preceded cooking.

[**carnal, carnage, carper, carouse, cataclysms, castigating**]

****

1. She was indolent, passive, the _______ even called her dull.
2. He was _______, enjoying the old masters and understanding the moderns.
3. The _______ had passed through the bushes.
4. _______ is never more admired than by the negligent.
5. Let us at once find him, and refute beyond _______ this injurious hypothesis.
6. Either _______ your daughter to my disposal, or take her to your discretion.

[**celerity, cede, cavil, cavalcade, caustic, catholic**]

Review Exercise: Sentence Completions (pp. 45–48)

1. The idler is naturally _______.
2. The poise of my body depends on that of _______ and centripetal forces.
3. He did not mind his own leg, which had an old _______ upon it.
4. Marriage has many pains, but _______ has no pleasures.
5. _______ is for confusing the distinctions between true and untrue.
6. Silence is the universal refuge . . . , and a balm to our every _______.

[**censorious, centrifugal, chafe, charlatanism, chagrin, celibacy**]

****

1. I will _______ no breather in the world but myself.
2. The Rev. B. B. Gordon was impatient and _______.
3. The _______ maid is prodigal enough if she unmask her beauty to the moon.
4. The morality doesn't have the strength to administer _______ on the sinner.
5. After the word _______ there was a growing noise.
6. _______ women are often proud and forward.

[**chastisement, chaste, chariest, chicanery, choleric, chide**]

****

1. We must not expect a lively young man to be always so _______.
2. He can give us wisdom to _______ the cunning of the devils.
3. He deserves isolation from his species for his _______ inhospitality.
4. I have now told you everything without an attempt at _______.
5. In certain _______ spaces, the ground was actually white with bones.
6. We see a vapour sometime like a bear, a tower'd _______, or a pendant rock.

[**circumlocution, churlish, circumscribed, circumspect, citadel, circumvent**]

****

1. A law considered as immutable and foolish is _______ evaded.
2. In matters of human feeling the _______ judge is the most successful pleader.
3. Hie thee to France, and _______ thee in some religious house.
4. Who can _______ the hungry edge of appetite by bare imagination of a feast?
5. When Mr. Tulliver speaks _______ to me, I'll speak civil to him.
6. You must be a _______ because you are so bitter against other clairvoyants.

[**cloy, cloister, clement, clandestinely, clairvoyant, civil**]

1. The huge pool of blood in front of her was already assuming the iridescence* of **coagulation**; and when the sun rose a million prismatic* hues were reflected from it. —Thomas Hardy, *Tess*

2. Men of affectionate temper and bright fancy will **coalesce** a great deal sooner than those who are cold and dull. —James Boswell, *The Life of Samuel Johnson*

3. . . . my sister, in her capricious and violent **coercion**, was unjust to me. —Charles Dickens, *Great Expectations*

4. My bed shall be abused, my **coffers** ransacked,* my reputation gnawn* at; . . . —Shakespeare, *The Merry Wives of Windsor*

5. Were the ends of nature so great and **cogent**, as to exact this immense sacrifice of men? —Ralph Waldo Emerson, *Nature*

6. Generally, youth is like the first **cogitations**, not so wise as the second. —Francis Bacon, *Essays*

****

1. **coagulation**; solidification, congealment, clotting, curdling. —coagulant *n.*, —coagulate. * iridescence; rainbow color. * prismatic; multicolored.
2. **coalesce**; mix, fuse, unify, blend, merge, consolidate, incorporate, integrate, commingle, amalgamate, conflate. —coalescence, —coalescent.
3. **coercion**; enforcement, compulsion, constraint. —coerce.
4. **coffer**; chest, casket, vault, strongbox. * ransack; rummage. * gnaw; nibble.
5. **cogent**; persuasive, convincing, potent. —cogency, —cogently.
6. **cogitation**; meditation, contemplation, rumination. —cogitate, —cogitative.

♣ Upon the accuracy with which similitude in dissimilitude, and dissimilitude in similitude are perceived, depend our taste and our moral feelings. —William Wordsworth, *Preface to Lyrical Ballads*

1. The regiment left a **coherent** trail of bodies. —Stephen Crane, *The Red Badge of Courage*

2. There was no **cohesion** among the particles, and it could not be moulded into snow-balls. —Jack London, *Burning Daylight*

3. The parts of a judge in hearing are four: to direct the evidence; to moderate length, repetition, or impertinency of speech; to recapitulate,* select, and **collate** the material points of that which hath been said; and to give the rule or sentence. —Francis Bacon, *Essays*

4. There was **collusion**, sir, or that villain never would have escaped. —W. M. Thackeray, *Vanity Fair*

5. According to Liebig, man's body is a stove, and food the fuel which keeps up the internal **combustion** in the lungs. —Henry David Thoreau, *Walden*

6. The stakes were high and the risk was great; the prize therefore must have been **commensurate**. —Henry James, *The American*

****

1. **coherent**; 1. consistent, corresponding. 2. harmonious. —coherence.
2. **cohesion**; consolidation, adhesion, coalescence. —cohesive, —cohere.
3. **collate**; collect and verify. —collation, —collative, —collator. ※ collateral; 1. parallel. 2. auxiliary: *collateral duty*. * recapitulate; epitomize.
4. **collusion**; plot, scheme, intrigue, conspiracy. —collude, —collusive.
5. **combustion**; burning, ignition, inflammation. —combustible.
6. **commensurate**; corresponding, equivalent, proportionate, compatible, analogous. —commensuration, —commensurately.

♣ Brevity is the soul of wit.

—Shakespeare, *Hamlet*

1. I have often observed with concern that distress is more apt to excite contempt than **commiseration** . . . —Henry Fielding, *Tom Jones*

2. The mansion was stately without, **commodious** and elegant within. —Anne Brontë, *Agnes Grey.*

3. The damsels wear nothing but flowers and their **compendious** gala* tunics. —Herman Melville, *Typee*

4. With infinite **complacency** men went to and fro over this globe about their little affairs, serene in their assurance of their empire over matter. —H. G. Wells, *The War of the Worlds*

5. One thinks that everything is to be carried by spirit and vigor; that art is meanness, and that versatility* and **complaisance** are the refuge of pusillanimity* and weakness. —4th Earl of Chesterfield, *Letters to His Son*

6. ACCOMPLICE, *n.* One associated with another in a crime, having guilty knowledge and **complicity**, as an attorney who defends a criminal, knowing him guilty. —Ambrose Bierce, *The Devil's Dictionary*

****

1. **commiseration**; pity, sympathy, compassion, pathos. —commiserate.
2. **commodious**; spacious, roomy, capacious. —commodiousness.
3. **compendious**; brief, concise. —compendium. * gala; 1. festival, feast. 2. festive.
4. **complacency**; satisfaction, gratification, contentment. —complacent.
5. **complaisance**; civility, courtesy, deference. —complaisant. * versatility; 1. inconstancy. 2. skillfulness, having various skills. —versatile; 1. all-around, protean. 2. multifarious. * pusillanimity; cowardice. —pusillanimous.
6. **complicity**; conspiracy, collusion, connivance. —complicitous *also* complicit.

♣ Man is a force; so is the sun. —Henry Adams, *The Education of Henry Adams*

1. The good lieutenant immediately **complied** with his desires . . . —Henry Fielding, *Tom Jones*

2. Mr. Linton stood looking at her in sudden **compunction** and fear. He told me to fetch some water. She had no breath for speaking. —Emily Brontë, *Wuthering Heights*

3. The natural world may be conceived of as a system of **concentric** circles. —R. W. Emerson, *Circles*

4. He was an expert at **concocting** strong drinks. —Kate Chopin, *The Awakening*

5. Suspicion is, indeed, a temper so uneasy and restless, that it is very justly appointed the **concomitant** of guilt. —Samuel Johnson, *The Rambler*

6. He fosters the spirit of **concord** and justice, in whose work there is as much glory to be reaped as in the deeds of arms. —Joseph Conrad, *The Mirror of the Sea*

****

1. **comply**; conform, yield, acquiesce, submit. —compliance.
2. **compunction**; remorse, penitence, qualm, contrition. —compunctious.
3. **concentric**; having a common center. ***ant.*** eccentric; 1. having a different center. 2. anomalous. —concentricity, —concentrically.
4. **concoct;** mix, brew, compound. —concoction. ※ pastiche; mixture, medley, hodgepodge *or* hotchpotch, motley: *The movie is a pastiche of spy films.*
5. **concomitant**; attendant, concurrent, accompaniment. —concomitance.
6. **concord**; harmony, agreement, accord, unison, consonance, concert. ***ant.*** discord. —concordance, —concordant.

♣ Battle for freedom wherever you can,
And, if not shot or hang'd, you'll get knighted.
—Lord Byron, "When a man hath no freedom to fight for at home"

1. There is no great **concurrence** between learning and wisdom. —Francis Bacon, *The Advancement of Learning*

2. When a lady **condescends** to apologize, there is no keeping one's anger, of course. —Anne Brontë, *The Tenant of Wildfell Hall*

3. You will the more easily **condone** any mental aberration* upon your own part when you realize that even I have had moments when my balance has been disturbed. —Arthur Conan Doyle, *The Poison Belt*

4. The life I led, Miss Manette, is not **conducive** to health. —Charles Dickens, *A Tale of Two Cities*

5. They [The North and South Winds] depend upon local causes—the **configuration** of coasts, the shapes of straits, the accidents of bold promontories round which they play their little part. —Joseph Conrad, *The Mirror of the Sea*

6. To bereave a man of life, [says he] or by violence to **confiscate** his estate, without accusation or trial, would be so gross and notorious an act of despotism, as must at once convey the alarm of tyranny throughout the whole nation. —Alexander Hamilton, *The Federalist Papers*

****

1. **concurrence**; agreement, concord, accord, harmony. —concur, —concurrent; 1. concerted, harmonious. 2. simultaneous, concomitant, synchronic, coeval.
2. **condescend**; stoop, deign, descend, humble oneself. —condescension.
3. **condone**; forgive, pardon. —condonation. * aberration; abnormality, deviation.
4. **conducive**; helpful, contributive, instrumental.
5. **configuration**; 1. figure, outline, contour, conformation. 2. arrangement. —configure, —configurable.
6. **confiscate**; seize, usurp, impound, expropriate, commandeer. —confiscator, —confiscable. ※ conscript; draft, recruit, conscribe, commandeer.

1. . . . an immense **confluence** of persons of all ranks hastened upon the appointed morning to the place of combat. —Walter Scott, *Ivanhoe*
2. Long discourse, and philosophical reasonings, at best, amaze and **confound**, but do not instruct children. —John Locke, *Some Thoughts Concerning Education*
3. My blood **congeals**, and I can write no more.—Christopher Marlowe, *Doctor Faustus*
4. Holmes returned to his seat with that quiet look of inward satisfaction which meant that he had a **congenial** task before him. —Arthur Conan Doyle, *The Hound of the Baskervilles*
5. An anatomist—even a mere physiognomist*—would have seen that the deformity of Philip's spine was not a **congenital** hump, but the result of an accident in infancy. —George Eliot, *The Mill on the Floss*
6. The strata are of sandstone, and one layer was remarkable from being composed of a firmly-cemented **conglomerate** of pumice* pebbles . . . —Charles Darwin, *The Voyage of the Beagle*

****

1. **confluence**; convergence, concourse, juncture, conflux. —confluent.
2. **confound**; perplex, bewilder, baffle, nonplus, befuddle. ※ disorient; confound
3. **congeal**; freeze, solidify, coagulate, clot, curdle. —congealment.
4. **congenial**; 1. agreeable, pleasant, genial, affable, convivial, complaisant. 2. sympathetic, compatible. —congeniality.
5. **congenital**; inborn, inbred, inherent, innate, hereditary. —congenitally. * physiognomist; one who judges nature from appearance. —physiognomy.
6. **conglomerate**; 1. mass, cluster. 2. large corporation. —conglomeratic. * pumice; volcanic rock. —pumiceous.

♣ Money is like muck, not good except it be spread. —Francis Bacon, *Essays*

1. Rumor is a pipe
   Blown by surmises, jealousies, **conjectures**.
   —Shakespeare, *King Henry IV, Part II*

2. Mr. and Mrs. Norris began their career of **conjugal** felicity* with very little less than a thousand a year. —Jane Austen, *Mansfield Park*

3. "Mr Todhunter," explained Father Brown placidly,* "is learning to be a professional **conjurer**, as well as juggler, ventriloquist,* and expert in the rope trick." —G. K. Chesterton, *The Wisdom of Father Brown*

4. Thou must **connive** at her escape, Malvoisin, and I will transport her to some place of greater security and secrecy. —Walter Scott, *Ivanhoe*

5. He wore expensive clothes; and was a **connoisseur** in starvation. —O. Henry, *An Unfinished Story*

6. Though these two were in **consanguinity** so nearly related, they were in their dispositions almost the opposites to each other. —Henry Fielding, *Tom Jones*

****

1. **conjecture**; 1. supposition, surmise, presumption. 2. *v.* assume. —conjectural.
2. **conjugal**; of the relations between spouses, connubial. —conjugality. ※ marital; of marriage, matrimonial, nuptial: *marital status*. ※ nubile; marriageable. * felicity; eudaemonia, *see p. 118, no. 6.*
3. **conjurer**; bewitcher, charmer, enchanter. —conjury. * placidly; calmly. * ventriloquist; an entertainer who can make his voice sound like coming from another source.
4. **connive**; plot, conspire, intrigue, collude, scheme. —connivance.
5. **connoisseur**; gourmet, aesthete, esthete, expert in food or the fine arts. ※ gourmand; 1. gourmet, epicure. 2. glutton.
6. **consanguinity**; kinship, affinity, cognation. —consanguineous *also* consanguine. ※ cognate; consanguine. —cognation, —cognately.

1. Silence is the general **consecration** of the universe. —Herman Melville, *Pierre*

2. Ah! how cheerfully we **consign** ourselves to perdition!* —Herman Melville, *Moby Dick*

3. In the very aspect of those primitive and rugged trees there was, methinks, a tanning* principle which hardened and **consolidated** the fibers of men's thoughts. —Henry David Thoreau, *Walking*

4. A government founded on principles more **consonant** to the wishes of the larger States, is not likely to be obtained from the smaller States. —Alexander Hamilton, *The Federalist Papers*

5. The ladies Lynn and Ingram continued to **consort** in solemn conferences; where they nodded their two turbans at each other, and held up their four hands in confronting gestures of surprise, or mystery, or horror, according to the theme. —Charlotte Brontë, *Jane Eyre*

6. He never ran if he could help it, because he knew it made his limp* more **conspicuous** . . . —W. Somerset Maugham, *Of Human Bondage*

****

1. **consecration**; hallowing, sanctification, deification. ***ant.*** desecration. —consecrate. ***ant.*** deconsecrate; desecrate, unhallow.
2. **consign**; hand over, entrust, deliver. —consignation *also* consignment, —consigner, —consignee. * perdition; ruin, destruction, *see p. 218, no. 4.*
3. **consolidate**; 1. conjoin, combine, amalgamate. 2. fortify, strengthen, solidify. —consolidation, —consolidator, —consolidatory. * tanning; whipping.
4. **consonant**; harmonious, correspondent, congruous. —consonance.
5. **consort**; associate, keep company, pal around, fraternize. —consortium.
6. **conspicuous**; outstanding, noticeable, arresting, striking. —conspicuity. * limp; lame walk or gait.

1. My sister, in her capricious and violent _______, was unjust to me.
2. The huge pool of blood was already assuming the iridescence of _______.
3. Men of affection and fancy will ______ sooner than those who are cold and dull.
4. My bed shall be abused, my _______ ransacked, my reputation gnawn at.
5. Were the ends of nature so great and _______, as to exact this sacrifice of men?
6. Generally, youth is like the first _______, not so wise as the second.

[**coffers, coercion, coalesce, coagulation, cogitations, cogent**]

****

1. There was no _______ among the particles.
2. One part of a judge is to recapitulate, select, and _______ the material points.
3. There was _______, sir, or that villain never would have escaped.
4. Food keeps up the internal _______ in the lungs.
5. The regiment left a _______ trail of bodies.
6. The risk was great; the prize therefore must have been _______.

[**cohesion, coherent, collate, collusion, commensurate, combustion**]

****

1. Distress is more apt to excite contempt than _______.
2. Versatility and _______ are the refuge of pusillanimity and weakness.
3. The mansion was stately without, _______ and elegant within.
4. The damsels wear nothing but flowers and their _______ gala tunics.
5. With infinite _______ men went to and fro over this globe.
6. Accomplice is one associated with another in a crime, having guilty _______.

[**commodious, commiseration, compendious, complicity, complaisance, complacency**]

****

1. Mr. Linton stood looking at her in sudden _______ and fear.
2. The natural world may be conceived of as a system of _______ circles.
3. He fosters the spirit of _______ and justice.
4. He was an expert at _______ strong drinks.
5. Suspicion is a temper so uneasy that it is justly appointed the _______ of guilt.
6. The good lieutenant immediately _______ with his desires.

[**compunction, complied, concocting, concentric, concord, concomitant**]

Review Exercise: Sentence Completions (pp. 55–58)

1. The life I led, Miss Manette, is not _______ to health.
2. There is no great _______ between learning and wisdom.
3. When a lady _______ to apologize, there is no keeping one's anger.
4. You would not easily _______ any mental aberration upon your part.
5. They tried to _______ his estate.
6. The North and South winds depend upon the _______ of coasts.

[**configuration, condescends, condone, concurrence, conducive, confiscate**]

****

1. Philosophical reasonings, at best, _______, but do not instruct children.
2. My blood _______, and I can write no more.
3. He had a _______ task before him.
4. The deformity of Philip's spine was not a _______ hump.
5. An immense _______ of persons hastened upon the morning to the place.
6. One layer was composed of a firmly-cemented _______ of pumice pebbles.

[**congeals, confound, confluence, conglomerate, congenital, congenial**]

****

1. Mr. and Mrs. Norris began their career of _______ felicity.
2. Mr Todhunter is learning to be a professional _______, as well as juggler.
3. He wore expensive clothes; and was a _______ in starvation.
4. Thou must _______ at her escape, Malvoisin.
5. Rumor is a pipe blown by surmises, jealousies, _______.
6. These two were in _______ so nearly related.

[**connive, consanguinity, connoisseur, conjurer, conjugal, conjectures**]

****

1. The ladies Lynn and Ingram continued to _______ in solemn conferences.
2. He never ran if he could help it, because it made his limp more _______.
3. Silence is the general _______ of the universe.
4. Ah! How cheerfully we _______ ourselves to perdition!
5. The fibers of men's thoughts have been _______ by a tanning principle.
6. The principles are more _______ to the wishes of the larger States.

[**consort, conspicuous, consecration, consign, consonant, consolidated**]

1. And then a spasm* **constricted** her mouth for an instant. —Charlotte Brontë, *Jane Eyre*

2. He was a **consummate** eavesdropper* and spy. —Joseph Conrad, *The Mirror of the Sea*

3. By looking through the two **contiguous** object-glasses, I found that the interjacent* air exhibited rings of colours, as well by transmitting light as by reflecting it. —Isaac Newton, *Optics*

4. He [Lord Wellington] left nothing whatever to chance, but provided for every **contingency**. —Samuel Smiles, *Self Help*

5. Right in the midst there lay the body of a man sorely* **contorted** and still twitching. —Robert L. Stevenson, *Dr. Jekyll and Mr. Hyde*

6. . . . musketeers went into St. Giles's, to search for **contraband** goods, and the mob fired on the musketeers, and the musketeers fired on the mob . . . —Charles Dickens, *A Tale of Two Cities*

****

1. **constrict**; compress, contract. —constriction, —constrictive. * spasm; convulsion, paroxysm, *see p. 294, no. 2.* —spasmodic.
2. **consummate**; 1. perfect, accomplished. 2. finish, fulfill. —consummation; culmination. ※ coda; finale, denouement. * eavesdropper; informant, snooper.
3. **contiguous**; neighboring, bordering, touching, adjoining, adjacent, abutting. —contiguity. * interjacent; intervening.
4. **contingency**; accident, eventuality. —contingent; haphazard, fortuitous.
5. **contort**; twist, distort, wrench, warp. —contortion. * sorely; badly.
6. **contraband**; smuggling, black-marketing, bootlegging. —contrabandist.

♣ If you would convince others, seem open to conviction yourself. —4th Earl of Chesterfield, *Letters to His Son*

1. In action he easily incurs the charge of antinomianism* by his avowal* that he, who has the Law-giver, may with safety not only neglect, but even **contravene** every written commandment. —R. W. Emerson, *The Transcendentalist*

2. . . . she was all **contrition** on the instant.
   "Forgive me for laughing," she said across the gate. —Jack London, *Burning Daylight*

3. We feel defrauded* of the retribution* due to evil acts, because the criminal adheres to his vice and **contumacy** and does not come to a crisis or judgment anywhere in visible nature. —R. W. Emerson, *Compensation*

4. I was once, I remember, called to a patient who had received a violent **contusion** in his tibia* . . . —Henry Fielding, *Tom Jones*

5. He is fond of enigmas, of **conundrums**, of hieroglyphics*; exhibiting in his solutions of each a degree of *acumen* which appears to the ordinary apprehension preternatural.* —Edgar Allan Poe, *The Murders in the Rue Morgue*

6. She is tolerably **convalescent**. —Charles Dickens, *David Copperfield*

****

1. **contravene**; violate, breach, infract. —contravention. * antinomianism; belief that Christians are freed from any secular morality. * avowal; profession.
2. **contrition**; remorse, penance. —contrite *adj.*
3. **contumacy**; 1. rebelliousness, noncompliance. 2. obstinacy. —contumacious; insubordinate, refractory. * defrauded; swindled. * retribution; retaliation.
4. **contusion**; bruise, swelling, trauma. —contuse, —contusive. * tibia; shinbone.
5. **conundrum**; riddle, enigma. * hieroglyphics; 1. illegible writing. 2. pictograph. * preternatural; superhuman.
6. **convalescent**; restoring, recuperating, in remission. —convalescence.

1. The callous palms of the laborer are **conversant** with finer tissues of self-respect and heroism, whose touch thrills the heart, than the languid* fingers of idleness. —Henry David Thoreau, *Walking*

2. Mr. Micawber was uncommonly **convivial**. I never saw him such good company. —Charles Dickens, *David Copperfield*

3. The senses were oppressed by mingled and conflicting perfumes, reeking up from strange **convolute** censers* . . . —Edgar Allan Poe, *The Assignation*

4. She was withal* a little of a **coquette**, as might be perceived even in her dress. —Washington Irving, *The Legend of Sleepy Hollow*

5. . . . and if people are to quarrel often, it follows as a **corollary** that their quarrels cannot be protracted* beyond certain limits. —George Eliot, *The Mill on the Floss*

6. As natural selection works solely by and for the good of each being, all **corporeal** and mental endowments will tend to progress towards perfection. —Charles Darwin, *The Origin of Species*

****

1. **conversant**; well-informed, versed in, au fait, au courant. * languid; feeble.
2. **convivial**; merry, jovial, sociable, genial, jolly. —conviviality.
3. **convolute**; winding, coiling, curved. —convolution. * censer; incense vessel.
4. **coquette**; flirter, vamp. * withal; 1. in addition, moreover. 2. at the same time.
5. **corollary**; deduction, inference, consequence, upshot. * protract; extend.
6. **corporeal**; bodily, physical, material, corporal, somatic. —corporeality.

♣ As the best law is founded upon reason, so are the best manners. —Jonathan Swift, *A Treatise on Good Manners and Good Breeding*

1. He was middle-aged, short and **corpulent**, with a black beard and dark, greasy hair. —W. Somerset Maugham, *Of Human Bondage*

2. Dr. Unanùe states that hydrophobia* was first known in South America in 1803: this statement is **corroborated** by Azara and Ulloa having never heard of it in their time. —Charles Darwin, *The Voyage of the Beagle*

3. Care is no cure, but rather **corrosive**. —Shakespeare, *King Henry VI, Part I*

4. Mast-heads and funnel-tops of ships peep above the ranges of **corrugated** iron roofs. —Joseph Conrad, *The Mirror of the Sea*

5. Every member of the respectable **coterie** appeared plunged in his own reflections; not excepting the dog . . . —Charles Dickens, *Oliver Twist*

6. George neither spoke to nor looked at Legree, who did not **countermand** his orders, but stood, whistling, with an air of forced unconcern. —Harriet Beecher Stowe, *Uncle Tom's Cabin*

****

1. **corpulent**; fat, obese, portly, rotund, plump. —corpulence.
2. **corroborate**; verify, vindicate, validate. —corroboration. * hydrophobia; rabies.
3. **corrosive**; progressively destructive, erosive. —corrode, —corrosion.
4. **corrugated**; wrinkled, crinkled, creased, puckered. —corrugation.
5. **coterie**; club, circle, group, bevy, assemblage.
6. **countermand**; cancel, repeal, annul, retract, revoke, rescind.

♣ Our healing is not in the storm or in the whirlwind, it is not in monarchies, or aristocracies, or democracies, but will be revealed by the still small voice that speaks to the conscience and the heart, prompting us to a wider and wiser humanity. —James Russell Lowell, *Democracy*

1. Gowns* and pecuniary* foundations, though of towns of gold, can never **countervail** the least sentence or syllable of wit. —R. W. Emerson, *The American Scholar*

2. My heart this **covenant** makes, my hand thus seals it.—Shakespeare, *King Richard II*

3. Like knavish* cards, the leaves of all great books were **covertly** packed. —Herman Melville, *Pierre*

4. Here, crouching and **cowering** behind some trees, the men clung with desperation, as if threatened by a wave. —Stephen Crane, *The Red Badge of Courage*

5. There were many **crass** minds in Middlemarch whose reflective scales could only weigh things in the lump. —George Eliot, *Middlemarch*

6. Accursed fate! that the unconquerable captain in the soul should have such a **craven** mate! —Herman Melville, *Moby Dick*

****

1. **countervail**; counteract, offset, compensate, counterbalance. * gown; the faculty and student body in a college town. * pecuniary; monetary.
2. **covenant**; agreement, contract, treaty. ※ convent; nunnery.
3. **covertly**; secretly, clandestinely, surreptitiously. * knavish; roguish.
4. **cower**; shrink, wince, cringe, quail.
5. **crass**; 1. unrefined, boorish. 2. doltish, witless. —crassly, —crassness.
6. **craven**; cowardly, recreant, pusillanimous.

♣ He who resorts to the easy novel, because he is languid, does no better than if he took a nap. —Henry David Thoreau, *A Week on the Concord and Merrimack Rivers*

1. The sea was as a **crucible** of molten gold, that bubblingly leaps with light and heat. —Herman Melville, *Moby Dick*

2. I'm glad to see you spot the **crux** so quickly, Bunny. —E. W. Hornung, *A Thief in the Night*

3. "You are **cryptic**," said Philip. —W. Somerset Maugham, *Of Human Bondage*

4. When he speaks, although his words are **culled** with the choicest art, yet they flow with rapidity and unparalleled eloquence. —Mary Shelley, *Frankenstein*

5. Now the thing stands thus. You have done nothing which you could have avoided—nothing, certainly, which renders you **culpable**. —Edgar Allan Poe, *The Murders in the Rue Morgue*

6. Whilst the privileges of nobility are passing to the middle class, the badge is discredited, and the titles of lordship are getting musty and **cumbersome**. —R. W. Emerson, *English Traits*

****

1. **crucible**; 1. container used to melt substances, melting pot. 2. harsh trial.
2. **crux**; essence, core, kernel, nucleus, pith, marrow. —cruxes *or* cruces *pl.*
3. **cryptic**; enigmatic, occult, esoteric, rarefied. ※ cryptography; encoding.
4. **cull**; 1. select, choose, pick out, winnow. 2. gather, collect.
5. **culpable**; guilty, sinful, blameworthy. ***ant.*** inculpable. —culpa; sin, guilt. —culprit; sinner, offender, criminal. ※ inculpate; accuse, incriminate. ※ mea culpa; through my error: *The team lost the match, and the coach cried, "Mea culpa."*
6. **cumbersome**: burdensome, unwieldy, cumbrous, onerous. —cumbersomeness.

♣ The pedigree of honey
Does not concern the bee.

—Emily Dickinson, "The pedigree of honey"

1. I could not imagine a human being so blinded by **cupidity** as to sell poison to such an atrocious* creature. —Joseph Conrad, *The Mirror of the Sea*

2. No churlish old **curmudgeon** could have been the owner of that grove of bread-fruit trees, or of these gloriously yellow bunches of bananas. —Herman Melville, *Typee*

3. Prudence is of more frequent use than any other intellectual quality; it is exerted* on slight occasions, and called into act by the **cursory** business of common life. —Samuel Johnson, *The Idler*

4. Well, sir, let us do what we can to **curtail** this visit, which can hardly be agreeable to you, and is inexpressibly irksome* to me. —Arthur Conan Doyle, *The Lost World*

5. "Of course. Everyone is of consequence in this dreary* country," said Gwendolen, **curtly**. —George Eliot, *Daniel Deronda*

6. His august Majesty, the Emperor Aurelius, occupied the imperial box, and was the **cynosure** of all eyes. —Mark Twain, *The Innocents Abroad*

****

1. **cupidity**; greed, avarice, rapacity, avidity. * atrocious; cruel, heinous.
2. **curmudgeon**; miser, skinflint, niggard.
3. **cursory**; careless, superficial, slapdash, perfunctory. —cursoriness, —cursorily. * exert; 1. exercise, employ. 2. belabor.
4. **curtail**; shorten, abridge, abbreviate. —curtailment. ※ syncopate; 1. shorten a word (e.g., ne'er). 2. modify rhythm. —syncopation. * irksome; boring.
5. **curtly**; abruptly, bluntly, tersely. —curtness. * dreary; gloomy, dismal.
6. **cynosure**; 1. object of admiration. 2. guiding star.

♣ Nobody knows how many rebellions besides political rebellions ferment in the masses of life which people earth. —Charlotte Brontë, *Jane Eyre*

1. Marriage, uncle! alas! my years are young;
   And fitter is my study and my books,
   Than wanton* **dalliance** with a paramour.*
   —Shakespeare, *King Henry VI, Part I*

2. Philip smiled, for it leaped to one's eyes that the artist in life had produced no more than a wretched **daub**. —W. Somerset Maugham, *Of Human Bondage*

3. To that **dauntless** temper of his mind,
   He hath a wisdom that doth guide his valour
   To act in safety.
   —Shakespeare, *Macbeth*

4. He [Napoleon] declared that he beat the Austrians because they never knew the value of time; while they **dawdled**, he overthrew them. —Samuel Smiles, *Self Help*

5. Two canine animals, in a time of **dearth**, may be truly said to struggle with each other which shall get food and live. —Charles Darwin, *The Origin of Species*

6. The Brunswickers were routed* and had fled—their Duke was killed. It was a general **debacle**. —W. M. Thackeray, *Vanity Fair*

****

1. **dalliance**; dawdling, flirtation. —dally. * wanton; lewd. * paramour; lover.
2. **daub**; 1. smudge, blemish, crude painting. 2. *v.* smear. —daubery, —daubingly.
3. **dauntless**; courageous, gallant, valiant. —dauntlessness, —dauntlessly.
4. **dawdle**; 1. loaf, loiter, dally. 2. flirt. —dawdler.
5. **dearth**; 1. famine. 2. lack, shortage, deficiency.
6. **debacle**; 1. defeat. 2. downfall, collapse. * rout; defeat utterly, stampede.

♣ Too swift arrives as tardy as too slow
—Shakespeare, *Romeo and Juliet*

1. He was a _______ eavesdropper and spy.
2. He left nothing whatever to chance, but provided for every _______.
3. Looking through the two _______ object-glasses, I found the fact.
4. Right in the midst there lay the body of a man sorely _______.
5. Musketeers went into St. Giles's, to search for _______ goods.
6. And then a spasm _______ her mouth for an instant.

[**consummate, constricted, contingency, contiguous, contorted, contraband**]

****

1. The patient had received a violent _______ in his tibia.
2. He avows that he may _______ every written commandment.
3. She was all _______ on the instant.
4. The criminal adheres to his vice and _______.
5. She is tolerably _______.
6. He is fond of enigmas, of _______, of hieroglyphics.

[**contravene, contrition, contusion, contumacy, convalescent, conundrums**]

****

1. She was withal a little of a _______, as might be perceived even in her dress.
2. The palms of the laborer are _______ with finer tissues of self-respect.
3. He was uncommonly _______. I never saw him such good company.
4. All _______ and mental endowments tend to progress towards perfection.
5. Conflicting perfumes reeked up from the _______ censers.
6. If people are to quarrel often, it follows as a _______ that they are all wrong.

[**convivial, convolute, conversant, corporeal, corollary, coquette**]

****

1. The statement was _______ by Azara and Ulloa having never heard of it.
2. He was middle-aged, short and _______.
3. George did not look at Legree, who did not _______ his orders.
4. Care is no cure, but rather _______.
5. Mast-heads of ships peep above the ranges of _______ iron roofs.
6. Every member of the respectable _______seemed plunged in his own musing.

[**coteries, countermand, corpulent, corroborated, corrosive, corrugated**]

Review Exercise: Sentence Completions (pp. 65–68)

1. The foundations can never _______ the least sentence or syllable of wit.
2. Like knavish cards, the leaves of all great books were _______ packed.
3. Crouching and _______ behind some trees, the men clung with desperation.
4. There were many _______ minds in Middlemarch.
5. The unconquerable captain in the soul should have such a _______ mate!
6. My heart this _______ makes, my hand thus seals it.

[**covenant, countervail, cowering, covertly, craven, crass**]

****

1. You have done nothing—nothing, certainly, which renders you _______.
2. The sea was a _______ of molten gold.
3. I'm glad to see you spot the _______ so quickly, Bunny.
4. His words were _______ with the choicest art.
5. "You are _______," said Philip.
6. The titles of lordship are getting musty and _______.

[**crux, crucible, culled, cryptic, cumbersome, culpable**]

****

1. "Everyone is of consequence in this dreary country," said he _______.
2. The Emperor occupied the imperial box, and was the _______ of all eyes.
3. He was so blinded by _______ as to sell poison to such an atrocious creature.
4. No churlish old _______ can be the owner of that grove of bread-fruit trees.
5. Prudence is called into act by the _______ business of common life.
6. Let's do what we can to _______ this visit, which can't be agreeable to you.

[**cursory, curmudgeon, cupidity, cynosure, curtly, curtail**]

****

1. The artist in life had produced no more than a wretched _______.
2. To that _______ temper of his mind, he has a wisdom that controls his valour.
3. While they _______, he overthrew them.
4. Two dogs, in a time of _______, may be truly said to struggle with each other.
5. Fitter is my study and my books, than wanton _______ with a paramour.
6. The Brunswickers were routed and had fled. It was a general _______.

[**daub, dalliance, dawdled, dauntless, debacle, dearth**]

1. To **debauch** a young woman, however low her condition was, appeared to him a very heinous* crime. —Henry Fielding, *Tom Jones*
2. The crowd that throngs the wharf as the steamer draws alongside is gay and **debonair**; it is a noisy, cheerful, gesticulating crowd. —W. Somerset Maugham, *The Moon and Sixpence*
3. Here and there lay the **debris** of belated fugitives, carts, and dead bodies of horses and men. —H. G. Wells, *The War in the Air*
4. Dionysius I,* who had threatened to **decapitate** the broad-browed philosopher [Plato], was a usurper* and a despot. —Ambrose Bierce, *The Devil's Dictionary*
5. Annual and perennial* plants, **deciduous** and evergreen trees, plants inhabiting different stations and fitted for extremely different climates, can often be crossed with ease. —Charles Darwin, *The Origin of Species*
6. You must remember that the Revolution **decimated** my family. —E. Phillips Oppenheim, *The Yellow Crayon*

****

1. **debauch**; corrupt, deprave, pollute. —debauchery. * heinous; abominable.
2. **debonair**; sprightly, jaunty, buoyant. —debonairness; buoyancy, —debonairly.
3. **debris**; 1. fragments, remains, remnants. 2. wreckage. ※ shard; fragment, a piece of broken pottery.
4. **decapitate**; behead, guillotine, decollate. ※ gibbet; gallows. ※ pillory; 1. wooden framework to punish offenders. 2. *v.* ridicule, stigmatize. * Dionysius I; Greek tyrant of Syracuse. * usurper; seizer.
5. **deciduous**; annual. ***ant.*** evergreen. * perennial; lasting many years. ※ biennial; lasting two years. ※ centennial; of one hundred years. ※ annuity; 1. yearly allowance. 2. the right to be a recipient of an annuity.
6. **decimate**; massacre, slaughter. —decimation.

1. Among the favorite topics of moral **declamation**, may be numbered the miscarriages* of imprudent boldness, and the folly of attempts beyond our power. —Samuel Johnson, *The Rambler*

2. Their rage is **decorous** and prudent, for they [the cultivated classes] are timid, as being very vulnerable* themselves. —R. W. Emerson, *Self-Reliance*

3. His slow, limping step and bowed shoulders gave the appearance of **decrepitude**. —Arthur Conan Doyle, *The Adventures of Sherlock Holmes*

4. What we are accustomed to **decry** as great social evils, will, for the most part, be found to be but the outgrowth of man's own perverted* life. —Samuel Smiles, *Self Help*

5. Of course her **defection** had cut me to the quick*? —Charlotte Brontë, *The Professor*

6. Born up by this high idea ["reverence himself"], he will not **defile** his body by sensuality, nor his mind by servile* thoughts. —Samuel Smiles, *Self Help*

****

1. **declamation**; speech, oration. —declaim. * miscarriage; error, failure.
2. **decorous**; polite, decent. —decorum. * vulnerable; susceptible.
3. **decrepitude**; weakness by old age, senility, senescence, caducity. —decrepit *adj.*; senile, senescent. ※ dementia; dotage. ※ Alzheimer's disease; brain degeneration, a common type of senile dementia. ※ amentia; idiocy.
4. **decry**; denounce, condemn, censure, disparage, depreciate. —decrial, —decrier. * perverted; distorted, warped. —perversion, —pervert, —perversive.
5. **defection**; abandonment of allegiance, backsliding, renegading. —defect. ※ quick; 1. very sensitive flesh. 2. core. * cut me to the quick; upset me.
6. **defile**; 1. soil, tarnish, besmirch. 2. debase. 3. profane. 4. march in files. —defilement. * servile; mean, slavish, abject.

1. Never crave him; we are **definitive**.

   —Shakespeare, *Measure for Measure*

2. As by the cultivation of various sciences a language is amplified, it will be more furnished with words **deflected** from their original sense. —Samuel Johnson, *Preface to the English Dictionary*

3. Plato, called "the divine" by reason of the excellence of his wisdom, **defrayed** his travelling expenses in Egypt by the profits derived from the oil which he sold during his journey. —Samuel Smiles, *Self Help*

4. Mr. Wickham, after a few moments, touched his hat—a salutation* which Mr. Darcy just **deigned** to return. —Jane Austen, *Pride and Prejudice*

5. She was subject to no disorder but hypochondriac* **dejection**. —Samuel Johnson, *The Rambler*

6. Sweet are the oases in Sahara; charming the isle-groves of August prairies; **delectable** pure faith amidst a thousand perfidies.* —Herman Melville, *The Paradise of Bachelors*

****

1. **definitive**; 1. complete, consummate, absolute. 2. conclusive, decisive, ultimate. —definitiveness, —definitively.
2. **deflect**; divert, deviate, swerve, veer. —deflection, —deflective.
3. **defray**; pay, meet, cover. —defrayable, —defrayment.
4. **deign**; stoop, condescend, descend. * salutation; greeting, salute, obeisance.
5. **dejection**; gloom, depression, despondency, despair. —deject; discourage, baffle, dishearten, demoralize. —dejected. * hypochondriac; 1. of hypochondria (neurotic anxiety about one's ailments). 2. patient of hypochondria.
6. **delectable**; 1. pleasant, agreeable. 2. tasty, palatable, luscious. —delectation; happiness, felicity, beatitude, eudemonia. ※ palatable; 1. savoury: *palatable appetizer*. 2. acceptable: *palatable changes*. * perfidy; treason.

1. . . . he became ambitious to **delineate** the varieties of human character. —Samuel Smiles, *Self Help*

2. . . . as the swift monster drags you deeper and deeper into the frantic* shoal, you bid adieu to circumspect* life and only exist in a **delirious** throb. —Herman Melville, *Moby Dick*

3. The great winding-sheets,* that bury all things in oblivion,* are two; **deluges** and earthquakes. —Francis Bacon, *Essays*

4. We are acquainted with a mere pellicle* of the globe on which we live. Most have not **delved** six feet beneath the surface, nor leaped as many above it. —Henry David Thoreau, *Walden*

5. The expectation of the vital and great can only be satisfied by the **demeanor** of the vital and great. —Walt Whitman, *Preface to Leaves of Grass*

6. They [animals] do not lie awake in the dark and weep for their sins,
They do not make me sick discussing their duty to God,
Not one is dissatisfied, not one is **demented** with the mania of owning things.
—Walt Whitman, "Song of Myself"

****

1. **delineate**; portray, depict, represent, limn, contour. —delineative.
2. **delirious**; 1. hysterical, frantic, raving, demented. 2. ecstatic. —delirium. * frantic; frenetic. * circumspect; careful, judicious, sagacious, *see p. 47, no. 4.*
3. **deluge**; great flood, inundation. * winding-sheet; shroud. * oblivion; blankness.
4. **delve**; search, explore, probe, investigate. * pellicle; membrane, film.
5. **demeanor**; bearing, deportment. —demean *v.* ※ misdemeanor. ***ant.*** felony.
6. **dement**; derange, madden, craze. —demented; hysterical, delirious.

♣ The only sin is limitation. —R. W. Emerson, *Circles*

1. At his lamented **demise**, he was found himself to be possessor of many of his heir's bonds, purchased for their benefit. —W. M. Thackeray, *Vanity Fair*

2. After some delay and **demur**, the door grudgingly turned on its hinges a very little way, and allowed Mr. Jerry Cruncher to squeeze himself into court. —Charles Dickens, *A Tale of Two Cities*

3. Farther down, before one of the cottages, a lady in black was walking **demurely** up and down, telling her beads.* —Kate Chopin, *The Awakening*

4. I will **denounce** a curse upon his head.

   —Shakespeare, *King John*

5. An uncommon prudence is habitual with the subtler **depravity**, for it has everything to hide. —Herman Melville, *Billy Budd*

6. They had betaken* themselves to their work; I, less to divert my mind than to **deprecate** conversation, had provided myself with a book. —Anne Brontë, *The Tenant of Wildfell Hall*

****

1. **demise**; death, passing, decease.
2. **demur**; objection, disagreement, dissent. —demurral, —demurrable.
3. **demurely**; prudishly, primly. —demureness. * telling her beads; pray.
4. **denounce**; blame, criticize, censure, condemn, impugn, accuse, reprobate. —denunciation; denouncement. —denunciative.
5. **depravity**; degradation, corruption, immorality, degeneracy, vitiation, iniquity. —deprave, —depravation.
6. **deprecate**; condemn, denounce, accuse. —deprecation. * betake; devote.

♣ Nature herself occasionally quarters an inconvenient parasite on an animal towards whom she has otherwise no ill-will. —George Eliot, *The Mill on the Floss*

1. In reality, to **depreciate** a book maliciously, or even wantonly,* is at least a very ill-natured office; and a morose* snarling critic may, I believe, be suspected to be a bad man. —Henry Fielding, *Tom Jones*

2. I am determined to see the law executed to the letter, on all such **depredators**. —James Fenimore Cooper, *The Pioneers*

3. The farther I penetrated into London, the profounder grew the stillness. . . . It was a city condemned and **derelict**. —H. G. Wells, *The War of the Worlds*

4. Besides, in **derogatory** comments upon anyone against whom they have a grudge, or for any reason or no reason mislike, sailors are much like landsmen; they are apt to exaggerate or romance it. —Herman Melville, *Billy Budd*

5. Nay, now you are too flat*;
   And mar the concord,* with too harsh a **descant**.
   —Shakespeare, *The Two Gentlemen of Verona*

6. Little Dorrit thought she **descried** a slight thaw of triumph in a corner of her frosty eye. —Charles Dickens, *Little Dorrit*

****

1. **depreciate**; underrate, devaluate. ***ant.*** appreciate. —depreciation, —depreciatory. * wantonly; arbitrarily. * morose; sour, pessimistic.
2. **depredator**; plunderer, pillager, ransacker. —depredation, —depredate.
3. **derelict**; 1. discarded, deserted, forsaken. 2. abandoned property at sea. 3. vagrant, tramp. —dereliction.
4. **derogatory**; defamatory, disparaging, debasing, detracting, depreciatory. —derogation, —derogate. ※ pejorative; derogatory: *pejorative words*.
5. **descant**; 1. discourse, detailed comment. 2. *v.* discuss at length. * flat; dull, monotonous. * concord; harmony, accord, unison, *see p. 54, no. 6*.
6. **descry**; catch sight of, discover, detect, espy.

1. Why should we **desecrate** noble and beautiful souls by intruding on them? —R. W. Emerson, *Friendship*

2. But as they entered the town a change more ominous and startling than the **desiccation** of the landscape forced itself upon them. The town was still there, but where were the inhabitants? —Bret Harte, *Devil's Ford*

3. A lynx's* lair* is not **despoiled** with impunity.* —Jack London, *White Fang*

4. I sat about in the darkness of the scullery,* in a state of **despondent** wretchedness. —H. G. Wells, *The War of the Worlds*

5. I had lived a dreadful life, perfectly **destitute** of the knowledge and fear of God. —Daniel Defoe, *Robinson Crusoe*

6. This old house had wasted more from **desuetude** than it would have wasted from use, twenty years for one. —Charles Dickens, *Our Mutual Friend*

****

1. **desecrate**; profane, blaspheme, deconsecrate. ***ant.*** consecrate; sanctify.
2. **desiccation**; 1. lifelessness, inanimation. 2. drying out, dehydration. —desiccator.
3. **despoil**; rob, plunder, pillage, rifle. —despoliation; despoilment. * lynx; bobcat, one of wildcats. * lair; den. * impunity; exemption, absolution, *see p. 153, no. 2.*
4. **despondent**; depressed, disheartened, dejected. —despondence, —despond. * scullery; small room (near to the kitchen) for washing and storing dishes.
5. **destitute**; totally lacking, devoid, indigent. —destituteness, —destitutely.
6. **desuetude**; disuse, inactivity.

♣ Mind without heart, intelligence without conduct, cleverness without goodness, are powers in their way, but they may be powers only for mischief. —Samuel Smiles, *Self Help*

1. Conquests would be as easy to be made as difficult to be retained. War, therefore, would be **desultory** and predatory.* —Alexander Hamilton, *The Federalist Papers*

2. She was growing a little stout, but it did not seem to **detract** an iota* from the grace of every step, pose, gesture. —Kate Chopin, *The Awakening*

3. Indeed, toward the last of his life his whole mind seemed to have fixed itself upon religious matters, perhaps to the **detriment** of his worldly affairs. —O. Henry, *Cherchez la Femme*

4. Those who have attempted much, have seldom failed to perform more than those who never **deviated** from the common roads of action. —Samuel Johnson, *The Adventurer*

5. . . . he balanced the tea-spoon **dexterously** on the milk jug. —W. M. Thackeray, *Vanity Fair*

6. . . . no man, that ever I heard of, ever committed a **diabolical** murder for sweet charity's sake. —Herman Melville, *Bartleby*

****

1. **desultory**; random, haphazard. —desultoriness. * predatory; 1. rapacious, ravening. 2. carnivorous. ***ant.*** herbivorous. ※ insectivorous; feeding on insects.
2. **detract**; lessen, diminish, reduce. —detraction, —detractive. * iota; bit, jot.
3. **detriment**; harm, damage, impairment. —detrimental, —detrimentally.
4. **deviate**; diverge, digress, stray, swerve. —deviation, —deviant.
5. **dexterously**; skillfully, adroitly, deftly. —dexterity.
6. **diabolical**; devilish, satanic, demonic, fiendish. —diabolism, —diabolize.

♣ Cheerfulness gives elasticity to the spirit. Spectres fly before it; difficulties cause no despair. —Samuel Smiles, *Self Help*

1. You must remember that the Revolution _______ my family.
2. To _______ a young woman appeared to him a very heinous crime.
3. The crowd that throngs the wharf is gay and _______.
4. Here and there lay the _______ of belated fugitives.
5. Dionysius I had threatened to _______ Plato.
6. _______ and evergreen trees can often be crossed with ease.

[**debauch, decimated, debonair, deciduous, debris, decapitate**]

****

1. His limping step and bowed shoulders gave the appearance of _______.
2. Their rage is _______ and prudent, for they are timid.
3. Among the favorite topics of moral _______, may be numbered imprudence.
4. We _______ but the outgrowth of man's own perverted life as social evils.
5. He will not _______ his body by sensuality, nor his mind by servile thoughts.
6. Of course her _______ had cut me to the quick.

[**decry, declamation, defile, decorous, defection, decrepitude**]

****

1. The words have been _______ from their original sense.
2. Never crave him; we are _______.
3. Plato _______ his expenses in Egypt by the profits from the sale of oil.
4. He touched his hat—a salutation which Mr. Darcy just _______ to return.
5. She was subject to no disorder but hypochondriac _______.
6. Sweet are the oases; _______ pure faith amidst a thousand perfidies.

[**delectable, dejection, deigned, defrayed, deflected, definitive**]

****

1. They are _______ with the mania of owning things.
2. You bid adieu to circumspect life and only exist in a _______ throb.
3. He became ambitious to _______ the varieties of human character.
4. The shrouds that bury all things in oblivion are two; _______ and earthquakes.
5. They have not _______ six feet beneath the surface.
6. The expectation of the vital can only be satisfied by the _______ of the vital.

[**delved, delineate, deluges, delirious, demented, demeanor**]

Review Exercise: Sentence Completions (pp. 75–78)

1. I will _______ a curse upon his head.
2. An uncommon prudence is habitual with the subtler _______.
3. After some delay and _______, the door grudgingly turned on its hinges.
4. A lady in black was walking _______ up and down, telling her beads.
5. At his _______, he was found to be possessor of many of his heir's bonds.
6. I, less to divert my mind than to _______ conversation, walked out of the bar.

[**deprecate, demise, depravity, demur, denounce, demurely**]

****

1. I am determined to see the law executed to the letter, on all such _______.
2. It was a city condemned and _______.
3. In reality, to _______ a book maliciously is at least a very ill-natured office.
4. In _______ comments upon anyone, they are apt to exaggerate it.
5. Little Dorrit _______ a slight thaw of triumph in a corner of her frosty eye.
6. Nay, now you are too flat; and mar the concord, with too harsh a _______.

[**derelict, derogatory, descant, descried, depreciate, depredators**]

****

1. I had lived a dreadful life, perfectly _______ of the knowledge and fear of God.
2. A change more ominous than the _______ of the house forced itself upon him.
3. A lynx's lair is not _______ with impunity.
4. I sat about in the darkness of the room, in a state of _______ wretchedness.
5. This old house had wasted more from _______ than from use.
6. Why should we _______ noble and beautiful souls by intruding on them?

[**desiccation, desecrate, destitute, despoiled, desuetude, despondent**]

****

1. She was stout, but it did not _______ an iota from the grace of every step.
2. His mind has fixed itself upon religion, to the _______ of his worldly affairs.
3. They never _______ from the common roads of action.
4. He balanced the tea-spoon _______ on the milk jug.
5. No man ever committed a _______ murder for sweet charity's sake.
6. War would be _______ and predatory.

[**detract, desultory, deviated, detriment, diabolical, dexterously**]

1. Life is not **dialectics**. —R. W. Emerson, *Experience*

2. He is so **diametrically** opposite to what I imagined my husband should be. — Anne Brontë, *The Tenant of Wildfell Hall*

3. To behold the day-break!
   The little light fades the immense and **diaphanous** shadows,
   The air tastes good to my palate.*
   —Walt Whitman, "Song of Myself"

4. Lost! lost! My dear Miss Lucy, during our political **diatribes** we have taken a wrong turning. —E. M. Forster, *A Room with a View*

5. . . . there is no justice in your **dictums**. —Charlotte Brontë, *The Professor*

6. He was too **diffident** to do justice to himself. —Jane Austen, *Sense and Sensibility*

****

1. **dialectics**; method of discovering truth by the interchange of arguments (e.g., Hegelian dialectic: combining thesis and antithesis into a synthesis or truth). —dialectical: *dialectical materialism*.
2. **diametrically**; completely, totally, absolutely. —diametrical; opposite, contrary.
3. **diaphanous**; see-through, transparent, pellucid. —diaphaneity. ※ translucent; lucid, *see p. 318, no. 3.* * palate; taste. —palatable; savoury, delectable.
4. **diatribe**; violent criticism, vituperation, bitter denunciation. —diatribist.
5. **dictum**; 1. statement, assertion. 2. maxim, epigram, aphorism, adage.
6. **diffident**; shy, coward, timid, timorous. ***ant.*** confident. —diffidence.

♣ The standing is slippery, and the regress is either a downfall, or at least an eclipse, which is a melancholy thing. —Francis Bacon, *Essays*

1. The moon shone into empty halls and galleries stripped of their transient* splendor, stained and **dilapidated** by time, and hung with cobwebs. —Washington Irving, *Legend of the Two Discreet Statues*

2. The nostrils **dilated** and collapsed violently as he breathed. —Joseph Conrad, *Lord Jim*

3. Ah, mortal! then, be heedful; for so, in all this **din** of the great world's loom,* thy subtlest thinkings may be overheard afar. —Herman Melville, *Moby Dick*

4. 'Tis some mischance; the cry is very **direful**.

   —Shakespeare, *Othello*

5. The mourner sat with bowed head, rocking her body heavily to and fro, and crying out in a high, strained voice that sounded like a **dirge** on some forlorn* pipe. —Stephen Crane, *Maggie: A Girl of the Streets*

6. The first step of worthiness will be to **disabuse** us of our superstitious associations with places and times, with number and size. —R. W. Emerson, *Heroism*

****

1. **dilapidate**; decay, crumble, wear out, break down. —dilapidation. * transient; fleeting, ephemeral, evanescent, *see p. 318, no. 1.*
2. **dilate**; swell, widen, expand, enlarge, distend. —dilation *or* dilatation, —dilative. ※ dilatory; belated, tardy: *The professor got angry about the dilatory papers.*
3. **din**; noise, clamor, uproar. * loom; apparatus for weaving.
4. **direful**; ominous, portentous, inauspicious. —dire; dreadful, dismal.
5. **dirge**; funeral song, requiem, threnody. * forlorn; forsaken.
6. **disabuse**; undeceive, disillusion, free from delusion.

♣ People will, in a great degree, and not without reason, form their opinion of you, upon that which they have of your friends. —4th Earl of Chesterfield, *Letters to His Son*

1. . . . if any State should be **disaffected** to the authority of the Union, it could at any time obstruct the execution of its laws . . . —Alexander Hamilton, *The Federalist Papers*

2. The arbor* was vacant, and its floor, table, and circular bench were still damp, and bestrewn* with twigs and the **disarray** of the past storm. —Nathaniel Hawthorne, *The House of the Seven Gables*

3. He **disavowed** nothing; he seemed as if he would defy all things. —Charlotte Brontë, *Jane Eyre*

4. I felt shame that I had ever joyed in his **discomfiture** or pain. —Jack London, *The Sea Wolf*

5. I have **disconcerted** him already by my calm reserve . . . —Jane Austen, *Lady Susan*

6. He was a little **disconsolate** that no one had come to meet him. —W. Somerset Maugham, *Of Human Bondage*

****

1. **disaffected**; 1. discontented, disgruntled. 2. rebellious. —disaffection.
2. **disarray**; 1. confusion, chaos. 2. *v.* undress. * arbor; bower. * bestrew; scatter.
3. **disavow**; deny, refuse, negate, disclaim, disown. —disavowal.
4. **discomfiture**; frustration, embarrassment, disappointment. —discomfit.
5. **disconcert**; 1. confuse, upset, bewilder. 2. trouble, frustrate.
6. **disconsolate**; gloomy, doleful, desolate, dejected, miserable. —disconsolation.

♣ O, it is excellent
To have a giant's strength, but it is tyrannous
To use it like a giant.

—Shakespeare, *Measure for Measure*

1. . . . a maid-servant's **discordant** voice profaned* the holy calm . . . —Mark Twain, *The Adventures of Tom Sawyer*

2. Whoever is on the stage, it is always Shakespeare who is speaking to me, and perhaps this is the reason why in the past I can trace no **discrepancy** between reading his plays and seeing them. —W. Dean Howells, *My Literary Passions*

3. Albert was the captain's hammock-boy, a sort of sea valet in whose **discretion** and fidelity his master had much confidence. —Herman Melville, *Billy Budd*

4. It is hard to keep a busy eye steadily fixed upon evanescent* atoms, or a **discursive** mind upon evanescent truth. —Samuel Johnson, *Preface to Shakespeare*

5. Hundreds of stampeders,* after staking on other creeks than Bonanza, had gone on **disgruntled** down river to Forty Mile and Circle City. —Jack London, *Burning Daylight*

6. For a true expression of **dishevelled** wildness there is nothing like a gale* in the bright moonlight of a high latitude.* —Joseph Conrad, *The Mirror of the Sea*

****

1. **discordant**; disharmonious, dissonant, cacophonous, incongruous. —discord. ※ cacophony; discord: *cacophony of yells*. * profane; blaspheme. —profanity.
2. **discrepancy**; difference, disparity, divergence. —discrepant.
3. **discretion**; carefulness, prudence, circumspection. —discreet. ※ discrete; different, separate, distinct: *The building has its discrete security system*.
4. **discursive**; diffuse, desultory. —discursion. * evanescent; fleeting.
5. **disgruntle**; displease, dissatisfy, vex, make discontent. —disgruntlement. * stampeders; a crowd of people who flee hurriedly in panic.
6. **dishevelled**; untidy, ruffled, tousled, rumpled, unkempt. * gale; windstorm. * a high latitude; an area near the north or south pole. ※ latitudes (usu. in *pl.*); region, clime.

1. . . . the practitioners resolved to **disinter** the body and dissect* it at leisure, in private. —Edgar Allan Poe, *The Premature Burial*

2. Two great yellow caravans had halted one morning before the door and men had come tramping into the house to **dismantle** it. —James Joyce, *A Portrait of the Artist as a Young Man*

3. Miss Frances married, in the common phrase, to **disoblige** her family. —Jane Austin, *Mansfield Park*

4. **Disparage** not the faith thou dost not know.
—Shakespeare, *A Midsummer Night's Dream*

5. I might have seen that there was too great a **disparity** between the ages of the parties to make it likely that they were man and wife. —Emily Brontë, *Wuthering Heights*

6. Nothing was found to be so efficacious in **dispelling** the royal megrims* as the power of music. —Washington Irving, *Legend of the Rose of the Alhambra*

****

1. **disinter**; disentomb, unearth, exhume. —disinterment. * dissect; anatomize. ⋇ autopsy; examination of a corpse, postmortem examination, necropsy. —autopsist. ⋇ parse; analyze syntactically: *to parse a long sentence shortly.*
2. **dismantle**; take apart, disassemble, strip down. —dismantlement.
3. **disoblige**; annoy, offend, upset. —disobliging; unkind. ***ant***. obliging.
4. **disparage**; belittle, slight, depreciate, decry. —disparagement, —disparagingly. ⋇ debunk; 1. disparage, belittle. 2. expose: *The doctor debunked the cure-all.*
5. **disparity**; inequality, imparity, discrepancy. —disparate, —disparately.
6. **dispel**; drive away, scatter, disperse. —dispellable. * megrim; migraine.

♣ What is now proved was once, only imagin'd.
—William Blake, *The Marriage of Heaven and Hell*

1. Life is, in few instances, and at rare intervals, the diapason* of a heavenly melody; oftenest the fierce jar of **disruptions** and convulsions,* which, do what we will, there is no disregarding.* —Thomas Carlyle, *Characteristics*

2. If a man **dissemble**, deceive, he deceives himself, and goes out of acquaintance with his own being. —R. W. Emerson, *Divinity School Address*

3. Flowers and fruit have been rendered conspicuous by brilliant colours in contrast with the green foliage, in order that the flowers may be readily seen, visited and fertilized by insects, and the seeds **disseminated** by birds. —Charles Darwin, *The Origin of Species*

4. However, as the chief expressed the liveliest satisfaction at the result, I was too wise to **dissent** from his opinion. —Herman Melville, *Typee*

5. **DISSIMULATION** is but a faint kind of policy or wisdom. —Francis Bacon, *Essays*

6. Time **dissipates** to shining ether* the solid angularity* of facts. —R. W. Emerson, *History*

****

1. **disruption**; 1. disturbance, perturbation, disarray. 2. rupture. —disruptive. * diapason; consonance. * convulsion; spasm. * disregard; ignore.
2. **dissemble**; 1. conceal, disguise, dissimulate. 2. feign, affect. —dissemblance.
3. **disseminate**; diffuse, scatter, disperse. —dissemination.
4. **dissent**; oppose, object, demur. —dissentient; 1. dissenter, nonconformist. 2. *adj.* dissenting. ※ maverick; dissentient: *The old politician was regarded as a maverick in the political world.* ※ dissentious; argumentative.
5. **dissimulation**; concealment, disguise, dissemblance. ※ dissimilar; different, disparate. —dissimilitude, —dissimilation.
6. **dissipate**; drive away, scatter, disperse. * ether; 1. air, atmosphere. 2. the upper parts of the sky. * angularity; 1. rigidity. 2. angular contour.

1. Beauty is as summer fruits, which are easy to corrupt, and cannot last; and for the most part it makes a **dissolute** youth, and an age a little out of countenance.* —Francis Bacon, *Essays*

2. As day advances the **dissonant** din augments. With ear-splitting cries the wild birds celebrate their matins.* —Herman Melville, *The Encantadas*

3. The skin about the abdomen* is much looser than that on the back; hence, during the inflation, the lower surface becomes far more **distended** than the upper; and the fish, in consequence, floats with its back downwards. —Charles Darwin, *The Voyage of the Beagle*

4. "Good heavens, my nerves are all **distraught**," he said. "you nearly frightened me out of my wits." —W. Somerset Maugham, *Moon and Sixpence*

5. Even the abridger, compiler and translator, though their labours cannot be ranked with those of the **diurnal** historiographer,* yet must not be rashly doomed to annihilation. —Samuel Johnson, *The Rambler*

6. It is an interesting question how far men would retain* their relative rank if they were **divested** of their clothes. —Henry David Thoreau, *Walden*

****

1. **dissolute**; corrupt, degenerate, debauched, depraved. —dissolutely. ※ dissolve; 1. melt. 2. vanish. —dissolution. * out of countenance; disconcerted.
2. **dissonant**; discordant, inharmonious, unmelodious, cacophonic. ***ant.*** consonant. —dissonance. * matin; morning song.
3. **distend**; expand, extend, swell, bulge, dilate. —distension *or* distention, —distensible. * abdomen; belly.
4. **distraught**; distracted, distressed, deranged, agitated. —distraughtly.
5. **diurnal**; 1. daytime. ***ant.*** nocturnal. 2. daily. * historiographer; historian.
6. **divest**; strip, denude, disarray. —divestment *or* divestiture. * retain; keep.

1. Unwittingly* here a secret has been **divulged**, which perhaps might more properly, in set way, have been disclosed before. —Herman Melville, *Moby Dick*

2. "A noble boy, and **docile**"—she murmured—"he has all the frolicsomeness* of youth, with little of its giddiness.* And he does not grow vain-glorious in sophomorean wisdom . . ." —Herman Melville, *Pierre*

3. The word ***doctrinaire***—word full of terror to the British mind—reappeared from time to time between his explosions. —Oscar Wilde, *The Picture of Dorian Grey*

4. The interment* over, some good-natured forecastle poet and artist seizes his paintbrush, and inscribes a **doggerel** epitaph.* —Herman Melville, *The Encantadas*

5. . . . his 'Biology' took the wind out of my sails, and his 'Psychology' left me butting around in the **doldrums** for many a day. —Jack London, *The Sea Wolf*

6. . . . whether in the house or abroad I could not at first tell, but it recurred, doubtful yet **doleful** at every lull*; at last I made out it must be some dog howling at a distance. —Charlotte Brontë, *Jane Eyre*

****

1. **divulge**; reveal, disclose, uncover. —divulgence. * unwittingly; unawares.
2. **docile**; compliant, tractable, amenable, pliable. —docility, —docilely. * frolicsomeness; friskiness. * giddiness; 1. flippancy. 2. dizziness.
3. **doctrinaire**; 1. dogmatist, drumbeater. 2. dogmatic, dictatorial. —doctrinarism.
4. **doggerel**; 1. poor, crude. 2. bad poetry, trivial verse. * interment; burial. * epitaph; tomb inscription. ※ obituary; notice of one's death.
5. **doldrums**; 1. slump, stagnation, inertia. 2. gloom, blues, melancholy.
6. **doleful**; sad, gloomy, woeful, dolorous. * lull; pause, interval, respite.

♣ No pleasure is comparable to the standing upon the vantage ground of truth. —Francis Bacon, *Essays*

1. The little light fades the immense and _______ shadows.
2. During our political _______ we have taken a wrong turning.
3. He was too _______ to do justice to himself.
4. There is no justice in your _______.
5. He is so _______ opposite to what I imagined my husband should be.
6. Life is not _______.

[diaphanous, diametrically, dialectics, diffident, dictums, diatribes]

****

1. The moon shone into empty galleries stained and _______ by time.
2. The first step of worthiness will be to _______ us of our superstition.
3. In all this _______ of the world's loom, thy thinkings may be overheard afar.
4. The nostrils _______ and collapsed violently as he breathed.
5. He cried out in a high voice that sounded like a _______ on some forlorn pipe.
6. 'Tis some mischance; the cry is very _______.

[direful, dilapidated, dilated, disabuse, dirge, din]

****

1. I have _______ him already by my calm reserve.
2. He was a little _______ that no one had come to meet him.
3. The State was _______ to the authority of the Union.
4. The arbor was bestrewn with twigs and the _______ of the past storm.
5. I felt shame that I had ever joyed in his _______ or pain.
6. He _______ nothing; he seemed as if he would defy all things.

[disconsolate, disconcerted, discomfiture, disavowed, disaffected, disarray]

****

1. For an expression of _____ wildness there is nothing like a gale in the moonlight.
2. I can trace no _______ between reading Shakespeare's plays and seeing them.
3. The captain had much confidence in his _______ and fidelity.
4. A maid-servant's _______ voice profaned the holy calm.
5. It is hard to keep a _______ mind upon evanescent truth.
6. They had gone on _______ down river to Forty Mile and Circle City.

[discrepancy, dishevelled, discordant, disgruntled, discretion, discursive]

Review Exercise: Sentence Completions (pp. 85–88)

1. Men had come tramping into the house to _______ it.
2. The practitioner resolved to _______ the body and dissect it at leisure.
3. Miss Frances married, in the common phrase, to _______ her family.
4. _______ not the faith thou dost not know.
5. Nothing was so efficacious in _______ the royal megrims as music.
6. There was a great _______ between the ages of the parties.

[disinter, disoblige, disparity, dispelling, disparage, dismantle]

****

1. _______ is but a faint kind of policy or wisdom.
2. Time _______ to shining ether the solid angularity of facts.
3. Life is oftenest the fierce jar of _______ and convulsions.
4. If a man _______, deceive, he deceives himself.
5. The seeds are _______ by birds.
6. I was too wise to _______ from his opinion.

[disseminated, dissent, dissemble, disruptions, dissipates, dissimulation]

****

1. As day advances the _______ din augments.
2. The lower surface becomes far more _______ than the upper.
3. For the most part beauty makes a _______ youth.
4. My nerves are all _______. You nearly frightened me out of my wits.
5. Their labours cannot be ranked with those of the _______ historiographer.
6. The men were _______ of their clothes.

[dissonant, dissolute, distraught, divested, diurnal, distended]

****

1. The word _______ reappeared from time to time between his explosions.
2. The poet seized his paintbrush and inscribed a _______ epitaph.
3. His 'Psychology' left me butting around in the _______ for many a day.
4. Unwittingly here a secret has been _______.
5. A noble boy, and _______, he has all the frolicsomeness of youth.
6. The mournful under-sound recurred, doubtful yet _______ at every lull.

[docile, *doctrinaire*, doggerel, doldrums, doleful, divulged]

1. Take off thine eye! more intolerable than fiends' glarings is a **doltish** stare! —Herman Melville, *Moby Dick*

2. She has left the paternal **domicile**. She is launched. —Henry James, *The American*

3. She, sweet lady, **dotes**,
   Devoutly* dotes, dotes in idolatry,*
   Upon this spotted* and inconstant man.
   —Shakespeare, *A Midsummer Night's Dream*

4. . . . and he looked up with no very pleased expression upon his **dour** features. —Arthur Conan Doyle, *The Return of Sherlock Holmes*

5. Her gown was **dowdy** and expensive. —W. Somerset Maugham, *The Moon and Sixpence*

6. His broad-brim* was placed beside him; his legs were stiffly crossed; his **drab** vesture* was buttoned up to his chin; . . . —Herman Melville, *Moby Dick*

****

1. **doltish**; stupid, idiotic, imbecile. —dolt; blockhead, dunce, jerk, simpleton.
2. **domicile**; residence, dwelling, abode. —domiciliary, —domiciliate *v.*
3. **dote**; 1. adore, like excessively. 2. age, be senile, dodder. —dotage; senility. ※ superannuated; 1. be too old and retired. 2. outmoded. * devoutly; devotedly. * idolatry; blind worship of idols. * spotted; stained, specked.
4. **dour**; gloomy, sullen, morose. —dourness.
5. **dowdy**; outmoded, antiquated, desuete. —dowdiness, —dowdily.
6. **drab**; 1. shabby, lackluster, dingy. 2. cheerless, dreary, gloomy. —drabness, —drably. * broad-brim; hat with a broad brim. * vesture; clothing, apparel.

♣ Facility will come with practice, and strength and fortitude with repeated effort. —Samuel Smiles, *Self Help*

1. In the name of God, peace, peace! You drive me mad with your **drivel**! —Jack London, *Michael, Brother of Jerry*

2. . . . fat female singers, who had bawled* obscurely for twenty years, were discovered to possess inimitable* **drollery**. —W. Somerset Maugham, *Of Human Bondage*

3. His own verses are often rude and defective. The gold does not yet run pure, is **drossy** and crude. —R. W. Emerson, *Thoreau*

4. In most conditions of life, **drudgery** and toil are to be cheerfully endured as the best and most wholesome discipline. —Samuel Smiles, *Self Help*

5. Bingley was endeared* to Darcy by the easiness, openness, **ductility** of his temper, though no disposition could offer a greater contrast to his own. —Jane Austen, *Pride and Prejudice*

6. I cannot think, that in this most mild and **dulcet** air, the invisible agencies are plotting treasons* against our loves. —Herman Melville, *Pierre*

****

1. **drivel**; 1. stupid or meaningless talk, twaddle, prate. 2. *v.* talk stupidly. 3. *v.* drool, slobber. 4. saliva.
2. **drollery**; humor, joke, clowning, waggery. —droll *v.*, —drolly *ad.* * bawl; cry out, shout. * inimitable; matchless, nonpareil.
3. **drossy**; rubbish, trivial. —dross *n.* ※ nugatory; drossy: *a nugatory ordinance.*
4. **drudgery**; hard work, grind, toil, donkey work. —drudge *v.*, —drudgingly.
5. **ductility**; flexibility, elasticity, plasticity, malleability, tractability. —ductile; tensible, tractile. —ductilely. ※ tensile; ductile: *the tensile force of the metal.* ※ duct; pipe, tube, channel, conduit: *tear duct.* * endear; charm, attract.
6. **dulcet**; 1. sweet, mellifluent, luscious. 2. harmonious, euphonious. 3. soothing, agreeable. —dulcify. * treason; treachery, mutiny. ***ant.*** fealty; fidelity, allegiance.

1. . . . they have not yet had time to become accomplished in **duplicity**; they will tell lies, but they do it inartificially, and you know they are lying. —Charlotte Brontë, *The Professor*

2. The crowd without gave way, and several warriors entered the place, bringing with them the hapless* conjurer,* who had been left so long by the scout* in **duress**. —James Fenimore Cooper, *The Last of Mohicans*

3. He was now an intelligent man of sixteen, but **dyspeptic** and difficile.* —E. M. Forster, *Howards End*

4. His **ebullient** spirits were always on tap to spill over on the slightest provocation . . . —Jack London, *Michael, Brother of Jerry*

5. He [Vaucanson] made for a miniature chapel the figures of some angels which waved their wings, and some priests that made several **ecclesiastical** movements. —Samuel Smiles, *Self Help*

6. The logs drifted on out of the **eddy** and swept away down the stream. —Jack London, *Before Adam*

****

1. **duplicity**; double-dealing, hypocrisy, fraud, deception.
2. **duress**; restraint, compulsion, coercion. * hapless; unfortunate. * conjurer; magician, sorcerer, *see p. 57, no. 3.* * scout; 1. reconnoiterer. 2. *v.* reconnoiter.
3. **dyspeptic**; 1. irritable, liverish, irascible, bilious. 2. of indigestion. —dyspeptia. ***ant.*** eupepsia. * difficile; stubborn.
4. **ebullient**; 1. enthusiastic, exuberant. 2. boiling, effervescent. —ebullience.
5. **ecclesiastical**; clerical, priestly, churchly, religious, holy.
6. **eddy**; 1. whirlpool, swirl, maelstrom, vortex. 2. whirl, swirl *v.*

♣ Beings inferior, as your worships all know, syllogize by their noses. —Lawrence Sterne, *Tristram Shandy*

1. Try thy cunning, Thyreus;
   Make thine own **edict** for thy pains.
   —Shakespeare, *Antony and Cleopatra*

2. My love with words and errors still she feeds,
   But **edifies** another with her deeds.
   —Shakespeare, *Troilus and Cressida*

3. From these paintings (vivid as their images now are before me) I would in vain endeavour to **educe** more than a small portion which should lie within the compass* of merely written words. —Edgar Allan Poe, *The Fall of the House of Usher*

4. As it grew dark, the wind rose: it blew yesterday evening, not as it blows now—wild and high—but 'with a sullen,* moaning sound' far more **eerie**. —Charlotte Brontë, *Jane Eyre*

5. The intellectual part of his nature was already **effaced**; he had power only to feel, and feeling was torment. —Ambrose Bierce, *An Occurrence at Owl Creek Bridge*

6. We are not always to conclude that a wise man is not hurt because he doth not cry out and lament himself, like those of a childish or **effeminate** temper. —Henry Fielding, *Tom Jones*

****

1. **edict**; order, decree, mandate, ordinance. —edictal, —edictally.
2. **edify**; educate, instruct, enlighten. —edification. ※ edifice; building.
3. **educe**; derive, elicit. —eduction, —educible. * compass; 1. extent. 2. instrument for navigation. ※ purview; compass: *It's beyond the purview of moral law.*
4. **eerie** *also* **eery**; frightening, weird, uncanny. —eeriness. * sullen; sulky.
5. **efface**; erase, delete, obliterate, expunge. —effacement, —effaceable.
6. **effeminate**; feminine, effete, sissy. ***ant.*** macho; manly, virile. —effeminacy.

1. Shortly, however, the **effervescence** began to abate. —Anne Brontë, *The Tenant of Wildfell Hall*
2. There are nations not blinded to Science, not given over hand and foot to **effete** snobocracies* and Degenerate Decadents. —H. G. Wells, *The War in the Air*
3. . . . the marble **effigies** of thirty generations of kings and queens lay stretched at length upon the tombs. —Mark Twain, *The Innocents Abroad*
4. In enforcing a truth, we need severity rather than **efflorescence** of language. —Edgar Allan Poe, *The Poetic Principle*
5. In the cow-pox no pustules* appear, nor does it seem possible for the contagious matter to produce the disease from **effluvia**, or by any other means than contact. —Edward Jenner, *Vaccination against Smallpox*
6. He was generous, and the needy, laughing at him because he believed so naively their stories of distress, borrowed from him with **effrontery**. —W. Somerset Maugham, *The Moon and Sixpence*

****

1. **effervescence**; bubbling, simmering, seething, ebullition. —effervescent.
2. **effete**; 1. declining, feeble. 2. sissy. —effeteness. * snobocracy; snobs.
3. **effigy**; 1. image, statue. 2. idol. —effigial.
4. **efflorescence**; blossom, flower, bloom. —efflorescent, —effloresce *v.* ※ effluence; outflow. ※ fluorescence; visible light, radiation.
5. **effluvium,** *pl.* **effluvia**; 1. offensive odor or vapor. 2. emission, exhalation. —effluvial. * pustule; swelling, pimple, blister with pus.
6. **effrontery**; impudence, brazenness, brashness, cheekiness, presumption.

♣ A great mind is formed by a few great ideas, not by an infinity of loose details. —W. Ellery Channing, *On the Elevation of the Laboring Classes*

1. Ligeia grew ill. The wild eyes blazed with a too—too glorious **effulgence**. —Edgar Allan Poe, *Ligeia*

2. The Frau* Professor came in, a short, very stout* woman with tightly dressed hair and a red face; she had little eyes, sparkling like beads, and an **effusive** manner. —W. Somerset Maugham, *Of Human Bondage*

3. Several eminent characters have, in numberless instances of their lives, played the fool **egregiously** in earnest; so far as to render it a matter of some doubt whether their wisdom or folly was predominant. —Henry Fielding, *Tom Jones*.

4. The waters of the great deep have ingress and **egress** to the soul. —R. W. Emerson, *Intellect*

5. The autumn air, blithe* and vivacious,* **elated** Philip. —W. Somerset Maugham, *Of Human Bondage*

6. There are men "in society" now, as rich as Croesus, who have no consideration extended towards them, and **elicit** no respect. —Samuel Smiles, *Self Help*

****

1. **effulgence**; brilliance, radiance, refulgence, luster. —effulgent.
2. **effusive**; demonstrative, gushing. —effusion. * Frau; Madam. * stout; 1. muscular, sturdy, stalwart. 2. fat, plump.
3. **egregiously**; shockingly, flagrantly, outrageously. —egregiousness.
4. **egress**; exit, way out, outlet. ***ant.*** ingress. ※ regress. ***ant.*** progress.
5. **elate**; uplift, exhilarate, exalt. —elation, —elated; joyous, jubilant, animated. * blithe; cheery, *see p. 33, no. 3.* * vivacious; lively.
6. **elicit**; draw out, derive, educe. —elicitation.

♣ By labour, the earth has been subdued, and man redeemed from barbarism; nor has a single step in civilization been made without it. —Samuel Smiles, *Self Help*

1. Among other derivatives* I have been careful to insert and **elucidate** the anomalous plurals of nouns and preterites* of verbs, which in the Teutonic dialects are very frequent. —Samuel Johnson, *Preface to the English Dictionary*

2. Her figure was slim and sufficiently tall, her face rather **emaciated**, so that its sculpturesque beauty was the more pronounced,* her crisp hair perfectly black. —George Eliot, *Daniel Deronda*

3. Good humour is a state between gayety and unconcern; the act or **emanation** of a mind at leisure to regard the gratification of another. —Samuel Johnson, *The Rambler*

4. Nature is made to conspire with spirit to **emancipate** us. —R. W. Emerson, *Nature*

5. If he resigned himself to their tender mercies he would soon be completely **emasculated**. —Henry David Thoreau, *Walden*

6. A large portion of the cylinder had been uncovered, though its lower end was still **embedded**. —H. G. Wells, *The War of the Worlds*

****

1. **elucidate**; explain, expound, explicate. —elucidation. * derivative; word derived from a primitive. * preterite *also* preterit; past tense.
2. **emaciated**; gaunt, haggard, skinny, wizened. * pronounced; distinct.
3. **emanation**; emission, effusion, ejection, discharge. —emanate.
4. **emancipate**; free, liberate, unfetter, unbridle. —emancipation.
5. **emasculate**; 1. weaken, enervate, debilitate. 2. castrate. —emasculation.
6. **embed**; implant, infix, lodge, insert.

♣ The shape of a crystal is determined solely by the molecular forces, and it is not surprising that dissimilar substances should sometimes assume the same form. —Charles Darwin, *The Origin of Species*

1. The geologist has discovered that the figures of serpents, griffins, flying dragons, and other fanciful **embellishments** of heraldry, have their prototypes in the forms of fossil species which were extinct before man was created. —Henry David Thoreau, *Walking*

2. And how long have you been so thick* with Dunsey that you must *collogue** with him to **embezzle** my money? —George Eliot, *Silas Marner*

3. It is a very justifiable cause of a war, to invade a country after the people have been wasted by famine, destroyed by pestilence, or **embroiled** by factions among themselves. —Jonathan Swift, *Gulliver's Travels*

4. Important changes in the **embryo** or larva will probably entail changes in the mature animal. —Charles Darwin, *The Origin of Species*

5. I dispatched **emissaries** down this path, and that path, and at last went wandering in search of her myself. —Emily Brontë, *Wuthering Heights*

6. Fortunately, on one occasion, running short of boiling oil, he [Paré] substituted a mild and **emollient** application.* . . . Such was the casual origin of one of Paré's greatest improvements in the treatment of gunshot wounds. —Samuel Smiles, *Self Help*

****

1. **embellishment**; decoration, ornament, adornment.
2. **embezzle**; misappropriate, peculate, defalcate. —embezzlement. * thick; intimate. * collogue; conspire.
3. **embroil**; involve, entangle, implicate. —embroilment.
4. **embryo**; fertilized egg, fetus, germ, seed, nucleus, crux. —embryonic.
5. **emissary**; 1. messenger, courier. 2. envoy, delegate, deputy.
6. **emollient**; softening, soothing, relieving. * application; drug applied, such as an ointment.

1. He looked up with no very pleased expression upon his _______ features.
2. She has left the paternal _______. She is launched.
3. Take off thine eye! More intolerable than fiends' glarings is a _______ stare!
4. She devoutly _______ , dotes in idolatry, upon this spotted and inconstant man.
5. Her gown was _______ and expensive.
6. His _______ vesture was buttoned up to his chin.

[**domicile, drab, dowdy, doltish, dotes, dour**]

****

1. Fat female singers were discovered to possess inimitable _______.
2. The gold does not yet run pure, is _______ and crude.
3. In this most mild and _______ air, they are plotting treasons against our loves.
4. In the name of God, peace, peace! You drive me mad with your _______!
5. In most conditions of life, _______ and toil are to be cheerfully endured.
6. Bingley was endeared to Darcy by the openness and _______ of his temper.

[**drossy, drivel, drollery, drudgery, dulcet, ductility**]

****

1. The hapless conjurer had been left so long by the scout in _______.
2. He was now an intelligent man of sixteen, but _______ and difficile.
3. His _______ spirits were on tap to spill over on the slightest provocation.
4. He made the figures of some priests that made several _______ movements.
5. They have not yet had time to become accomplished in _______.
6. The logs drifted on out of the _______ and swept away down the stream.

[**duress, duplicity, ebullient, dyspeptic, eddy, ecclesiastical**]

****

1. From these paintings I would in vain endeavor to _______ something great.
2. It blew yesterday evening with a sullen, moaning sound far more _______.
3. My love with words and errors she feeds, but _______ another with her deeds.
4. The intellectual part of his nature was already _______.
5. He lamented himself, like those of a childish or _______ temper.
6. Try thy cunning, Thyreus; make thine own _______ for thy pains.

[**eerie, effeminate, effaced, edict, edifies, educe**]

Review Exercise: Sentence Completions (pp. 95–98)

1. There are nations not given over hand and foot to _______ snobocracies.
2. Shortly, however, the _______ began to abate.
3. The needy borrowed from him with _______.
4. The marble _______ of the kings and queens lay stretched upon the tombs.
5. In enforcing a truth, we need severity rather than _______ of language.
6. It is impossible for the contagious matter to produce the disease from _______.

[**effete, effrontery, effervescence, effigy, efflorescence, effluvia**]

****

1. Several eminent characters have played the fool _______ in earnest.
2. Ligeia grew ill. The wild eyes blazed with a too—too glorious _______.
3. She had little eyes, sparkling like beads, and an _______ manner.
4. There are men in society now, as rich as Croesus, who _______ no respect.
5. The waters of the great deep have ingress and _______ to the soul.
6. The autumn air, blithe and vivacious, _______ Philip.

[**effulgence, elated, elicit, effusive, egregiously, egress**]

****

1. I have _______ the anomalous plurals of nouns and preterites of verbs.
2. Good humor is the _______ of a mind at leisure to see another's gratification.
3. Nature is made to conspire with spirit to _______ us.
4. If he resigned himself to her tender mercies he would be soon _______.
5. The lower end of the cylinder was still _______ in the deep pit.
6. Her figure was slim and sufficiently tall, her face rather _______.

[**embedded, elucidated, emaciated, emanation, emancipate, emasculated**]

****

1. I dispatched _______ down this path, and that path.
2. _______ of heraldry have their prototypes in the forms of fossil species.
3. The people have been _______ by factions among themselves.
4. Changes in the _______ will probably entail changes in the mature animal.
5. Running short of boiling oil, Pare substituted a mild and _______ application.
6. You collogued with him to _______ my money.

[**embezzle, embryo, emissaries, emollient, embroiled, embellishments**]

1. With an **emphatic** gesture he held his nose and whistled through his teeth. —W. Somerset Maugham, *Of Human Bondage*

2. He was not so much interested in surgery as in medicine, which, a more **empirical** science, offered greater scope to the imagination. —W. Somerset Maugham, *Of Human Bondage*

3. Of the Ancients, enough remains to excite our **emulation**, and direct our endeavours. —Samuel Johnson, *The Idler*

4. She remembered that she had been passionately **enamored** of a dignified and sad-eyed cavalry officer who visited her father in Kentucky. —Kate Chopin, *The Awakening*

5. I can pronounce no **encomiums** on her beauty, for she was not beautiful; nor offer condolence on her plainness, for neither was she plain. —Charlotte Brontë, *The Professor*

6. The orators, the poets, the commanders **encroach** on us only as fair women do, by our allowance and homage.* —R. W. Emerson, *Divinity School Address*

****

1. **emphatic**; 1. marked, striking. 2. emphasized.—emphatically. ※ empathetic; empathic, sympathetic, *see p. 41, no. 1.* —empathy, —empathize.
2. **empirical**; experimental, experiential. —empiricism. ※ heuristics; learning method especially through trial- and-error, *see p. 352, no. 6.*
3. **emulation**; competition, contest. —emulator, —emulate; vie, contend.
4. **enamor**; charm, fascinate, enchant, captivate, enthrall, entrance, trance.
5. **encomium**; eulogy, panegyric, paean, extolment. —encomiast, —encomiastic.
6. **encroach**; intrude, trespass, infringe, impinge. * homage; admiration.

♣ There is nothing makes a man suspect much, more than to know little. —Francis Bacon, *Essays*

1. With dismal monotony and startling variety the uncanny* and multiform shapes of the cacti lift their twisted trunks and fat, bristly* hands to **encumber** the way. —O. Henry, *The Caballero's Way*

2. New Zealand in its **endemic** planes is much more closely related to Australia, the nearest mainland, than to any other region. —Charles Darwin, *The Origin of Species*

3. What is the nature of the luxury which **enervates** and destroys nations? —Henry David Thoreau, *Walden*

4. . . . if a man have the fortitude and resolution to **enfranchise** himself at once, that is the best. —Francis Bacon, *Essays*

5. An unguided ramble into its [a vale's*] recesses* in bad weather is apt to **engender** dissatisfaction with its narrow, tortuous,* and miry ways. —Thomas Hardy, *Tess*

6. Miss Bingley was **engrossed** by Mr. Darcy, her sister scarcely less so. —Jane Austen, *Pride and Prejudice*

****

1. **encumber**; 1. obstruct, hinder, impede, hamper. 2. restrict, restrain, inhibit. —encumbrance. * uncanny; weird, eerie. * bristly; thick with stiff hairs.
2. **endemic**; local, native, indigenous. —endemism *or* endemicity.
3. **enervate**; weaken, enfeeble, debilitate. —enervation.
4. **enfranchise**; 1. set free, liberate, deliver. 2. grant the vote. ***ant.*** disfranchise *or* disenfranchise. —enfranchisement; 1. franchise, suffrage. 2. deliverance.
5. **engender**; cause, generate, beget. —engenderment. * vale; valley, ravine. * recess; 1. corner, nook. 2. alcove. * tortuous; winding, sinuous.
6. **engross**; preoccupy, arrest, absorb, intrigue, enthrall. —engrossment.

♣ A great mind must be androgynous. —S. T. Coleridge, *The Table Talk*

1. The oratory* closed, the dormitory became the scene of ablutions,* arrayings and bedizenings curiously elaborate. To me it was, and ever must be an **enigma**, how they contrived to spend so much time in doing so little. —Charlotte Brontë, *Villette*

2. One of Pythagoras's wisest maxims, in his 'Golden Verses,' is that with which he **enjoins** the pupil to "reverence himself." —Samuel Smiles, *Self Help*

3. So will I turn her virtue into pitch,*
   And out of her own goodness make the net
   That shall **enmesh** them all.

   —Shakespeare, *Othello*

4. And life was not so ample I
   Could finish **enmity**.

   —Emily Dickinson, "I had no time to hate"

5. Undoubtedly the very tedium and **ennui** which presume to have exhausted the variety and the joys of life are as old as Adam. —Henry David Thoreau, *Walden*

6. Back in the yard was a room for servants, in which old Celestine had been **ensconced**. —Kate Chopin, *The Awakening*

****

1. **enigma**; riddle, puzzle, conundrum. —enigmatic. * oratory; 1. small church. 2. speech. * ablution; bathing as a ritual.
2. **enjoin**; 1. order, demand, direct, command. 2. prohibit, forbid.
3. **enmesh**; entangle, ensnare, embroil, ensnarl. —enmeshment. * pitch; filth.
4. **enmity**; hostility, rancor, animosity, animus.
5. **ennui**; boredom, weariness, tedium, lassitude. —ennuye; weary.
6. **ensconce**; 1. settle comfortably. 2. enshrine, cherish as holy.

♣ A man's fortunes are the fruit of his character. —R. W. Emerson, *Fate*

1. Mine ear is much enamor'd of thy note;
   So is mine eye **enthralled** to thy shape;
   And thy fair virtue's force perforce* doth move me.
   —Shakespeare, *A Midsummer Night's Dream*

2. There is nothing more **enticing**, disenchanting,* and enslaving than the life at sea. —Joseph Conrad, *Lord Jim*

3. . . . and she liked and required the **entourage** which wealth could give her. —Kate Chopin, *The Kiss*

4. Thus the doctor and the disease meet in fair and equal conflict; whereas, by giving time to the latter, we often suffer him to fortify and **entrench** himself, like a French army. —Henry Fielding, *Tom Jones*

5. The importance of an aggregate of characters, even when none are important, alone explains the aphorism **enunciated** by Linnæus, namely, that the characters do not give the genus,* but the genus gives the characters. —Charles Darwin, *The Origin of Species*

6. Honor is venerable to us because it is no **ephemera**. —R. W. Emerson, *Self-Reliance*

****

1. **enthral**; charm, captivate, intrigue, fascinate, entrance. * perforce; necessarily.
2. **enticing**; seducing, alluring. —enticement. * disenchanting; disillusioning.
3. **entourage**; attendant, retinue, suite.
4. **entrench** *or* **intrench**; 1. establish solidly, settle. 2. secure. —entrenchment.
5. **enunciate**; state, proclaim, pronounce, enounce. —enunciation. ※ enumerate; count, list. * genus; category, species. ※ homogeneous. ***ant.*** heterogeneous.
6. **ephemera** (*pl.* –eras *or* -erae); 1. something transitory, ephemeron. 2. dayfly, ephemerid. —ephemeral; fleeting, transient, evanescent, fugacious.

1. . . . Stubb heeded not the mumblings of the banquet that was going on so nigh him, no more than the sharks heeded the smacking of his own **epicurean** lips. —Herman Melville, *Moby Dick*

2. In my humble opinion, the true characteristic of the present beau monde* is rather folly than vice, and the only **epithet** which it deserves is that of frivolous.* —Henry Fielding, *Tom Jones*

3. . . . he preserved his usual **equable** smile notwithstanding that his body was dangling in a most uncomfortable position . . . —Charles Dickens, *The Old Curiosity Shop*

4. The little party recovered its **equanimity** at sight of the fragrant feast. —Emily Brontë, *Wuthering Heights*

5. With a view to establishing the **equilibrium** of power and the peace of that part of the world, all the resources of negotiation were exhausted, and triple and quadruple alliances were formed. —Alexander Hamilton, *The Federalist Papers*

6. **Equivocating**, evading, shuffling, in order to remove a present danger or inconveniency, is something so mean, and betrays so much fear, that whoever practices them always deserves to be, and often will be kicked. —4th Earl of Chesterfield, *Letters to His Son*

****

1. **epicurean**; 1. overindulgent toward pleasures. 2. hedonistic. —epicure; gourmet.
2. **epithet**; term to distinguish a person or thing: *Samuel Johnson the Great.* * beau monde; high society. * frivolous; trivial, trifling, *see p. 128, no. 5.*
3. **equable**; 1. calm, placid, serene. 2. constant, consistent. —equability.
4. **equanimity**; calmness, tranquility, composure, sangfroid. —equanimous.
5. **equilibrium**; symmetry, equipoise, counterpoise, counterbalance. —equilibrate.
6. **equivocate**; dodge, hedge, fudge, evade, shuffle, prevaricate. —equivocal.

1. . . . and I was pleased with my role of the trusted friend bringing back the **errant** husband to his forgiving wife. —W. Somerset Maugham, *The Moon and Sixpence*
2. Throughout a large part of the United States, **erratic** boulders and scored* rocks plainly reveal a former cold period. —Charles Darwin, *The Origin of Species*
3. You see as plain as can be, that I write as a man of **erudition**; that even my similes, my allusions, my illustrations, my metaphors, are erudite. —Laurence Sterne, *Tristram Shandy*
4. No one then observing me, I took the first step towards my **escapade**, and filled both pockets of my coat with biscuit. —Robert L. Stevenson, *Treasure Island*
5. I **eschewed** upbraiding, I curtailed remonstrance*; I tried to devour my repentance and disgust in secret. —Charlotte Brontë, *Jane Eyre*
6. The ancient philosophies were of two kinds,—*exoteric*, those that the philosophers themselves could partly understand, and ***esoteric***, those that nobody could understand. —Ambrose Bierce, *The Devil's Dictionary*

****

1. **errant**; 1. wandering, roving. 2. erring, deviant, straying.
2. **erratic**; 1. shifting, wandering. 2. abnormal. ※ erroneous; incorrect: *making erroneous inferences from the erroneous premise.* * scored; scratched.
3. **erudition**; learning, knowledge, scholarliness. —erudite *adj.*, —eruditely.
4. **escapade**; adventure, daring or unsafe task.
5. **eschew**; avoid, evade, shun. —eschewal. * remonstrance; 1. reproof. 2. protest.
6. **esoteric**; mystical, occult, cryptic, rarefied. ***ant.*** exoteric; 1. popular. 2. external. —esotericism.

♣ Come forth into the light of things,
Let Nature be your Teacher.

—William Wordsworth, "The Table Turned"

1. How dare you lock me in? This is not your house. Let me pass! I am tired of all this stupid **espionage**. —E. Phillips Oppenheim, *The Yellow Crayon*

2. When I left college, I was sent out to Jamaica, to **espouse** a bride already courted for me. —Charlotte Brontë, *Jane Eyre*

3. . . . she was fain* to betake herself into some corner, lest Clifford should **espy** her agitation. —Nathaniel Hawthorne, *The House of the Seven Gables*

4. He lived in the finest house in town, kept a carriage and was a most **estimable** man variously. —Ambrose Bierce, *Can Such Things Be?*

5. The same **ethereal** figure which stood before me the preceding night upon the steps of the Ducal Palace, stood before me once again. —Edgar Allan Poe, *The Assignation*

6. . . . and with persistency* and practice, he [Richard Cobden] became at length one of the most persuasive and effective of public speakers, extorting* the disinterested **eulogy** of even Sir Robert Peel himself. —Samuel Smiles, *Self Help*

****

1. **espionage**; watching, spying, surveillance, vigilance.
2. **espouse**; 1. marry. 2. support. —espousal; betrothal, wedding ceremony.
3. **espy**; discover, detect, descry. —espial. * fain; willing, eager.
4. **estimable**; 1. respectable, esteemed. 2. computable, valuable. —estimation.
5. **ethereal**; 1. celestial. 2. aerial. —ether *or* aether, —ethereal, —etherealize.
6. **eulogy**; high praise, encomium, panegyric, extolment. —eulogize, —eulogistic.
   * persistency; grit, tenacity. * extort; force, *see p. 115, no. 5.*

♣ His [man's] life is a battle, in so far as it is an entity at all. —Thomas Carlyle, *Sir Walter Scott*

1. . . . she had all sorts of **euphemisms** for common objects, she always chose an elaborate word as more becoming than a simple one. —W. Somerset Maugham, *Of Human Bondage*

2. The real name of the little man was Harris, but it had gradually merged into the less **euphonious** one of Trotters . . . —Charles Dickens, *The Old Curiosity Shop*

3. Friendship is **evanescent** in every man's experience, and remembered like heat lightning in past summers. —Henry David Thoreau, *A Week on the Concord and Merrimack Rivers*

4. The answer was **evasive**—I should have liked something clearer. —Charlotte Brontë, *Jane Eyre*

5. The Basts had just been **evicted** for not paying their rent, and had wandered no one knew whither. —E. M. Forster, *Howards End*

6. Some of them are unmannered, rough, intractable,* as well as ignorant; but others are docile, have a wish to learn, and **evince** a disposition* that pleases me. —Charlotte Brontë, *Jane Eyre*

****

1. **euphemism**; mild or vague expression. —euphemistic, —euphemize.
2. **euphonious**; harmonious, melodious. ***ant.*** cacophonous. —euphony.
3. **evanescent**; transient, fugacious, ephemeral. —evanescence, —evanesce *v.*
4. **evasive**; vague, circumventing, ambiguous. —evasion, —evade.
5. **evict**; expel, eject, oust, dislodge. —eviction, —evictor, —evictee.
6. **evince**; demonstrate, exhibit, attest. —evincible. * intractable; headstrong, uncompromising, *see p. 168, no. 1.* ※ intransigent; intractable, tenacious: *to maintain her intransigent stance.* * disposition; nature, temperament, tendency.

♣ Do not suffer life to stagnate. —Samuel Johnson, *Rasselas*

Review Exercise: Sentence Completions (pp. 101–4)

1. Medicine, a more _______ science, offered greater scope to the imagination.
2. Of the Ancients, enough remains to excite our _______.
3. With an _______ gesture he held his nose and whistled through his teeth.
4. She had been passionately _______ of a dignified cavalry officer.
5. The poets _______ on us only as fair women do.
6. I can pronounce no _______ on her beauty, for she was not beautiful.

[**emphatic, empirical, encroach, encomiums, emulation, enamored**]

****

1. What is the nature of the luxury which _______ and destroys nations?
2. An unguided ramble in bad weather is apt to _______ dissatisfaction.
3. The cacti lift their twisted trunks and fat, bristly hands to _______ the way.
4. New Zealand in its _______ planes is closely related to Australia.
5. Miss Bingley was _______ by Mr. Darcy, her sister scarcely less so.
6. He has the fortitude and resolution to _______ himself at once.

[**enervates, endemic, engender, enfranchise, engrossed, encumber**]

****

1. Out of her own goodness I will make the net that shall _______ them all.
2. And life was not so ample I could finish _______.
3. The very tedium and _______ have exhausted the variety and the joys of life.
4. Old Celestine had been _______ in a room for servants.
5. To me it was an _______, how they spent so much time in doing so little.
6. He _______ the pupil to reverence himself.

[**enmesh, ennui, enigma, enjoined, enmity, ensconced**]

****

1. There is nothing more _______ and disenchanting than the life at sea.
2. She liked and required the _______ which wealth could give her.
3. We often suffer him to fortify and _______ himself, like a French army.
4. Honor is venerable to us because it is no _______.
5. Linnaeus _______ the aphorism that the genus gives the characters.
6. Mine ear is much enamor'd of thy note; So is mine eye _______ to thy shape.

[**ephemera, enthralled, enunciated, enticing, entourage, entrench**]

Review Exercise: Sentence Completions (pp. 105–8)

1. The sharks did not heed the smacking of his own _______ lips.
2. To establish the _______ of power, all the resources were exhausted.
3. _______ or shuffling is something mean, and betrays much fear.
4. The only _______ which the present beau monde deserves is that of frivolous.
5. He preserved his usual _______ smile although his body was uneasy.
6. The little party recovered its _______ at sight of the fragrant feast.

[**epithet, epicurean, equanimity, equable, equivocating, equilibrium**]

****

1. _______ boulders and scored rocks plainly reveal a former cold period.
2. You see as plain as can be, that I write as a man of _______.
3. No one then observing me, I took the first step towards my _______.
4. The ancient philosophies were of two kinds—exoteric and _______.
5. The trusted friend brought back the _______ husband to his forgiving wife.
6. I _______ upbraiding, I curtailed remonstrance.

[**eschewed, esoteric, errant, erratic, erudition, escapade**]

****

1. I was sent out to Jamaica to _______ a bride already courted for me.
2. He lived in the finest house in town, and was a most _______ man variously.
3. The same _______ figure which stood before me stood before me once again.
4. She betook herself into some corner lest Clifford should _______ her agitation.
5. He extorted the disinterested _______ of even Sir Robert Peel himself.
6. I am tired of all this stupid _______.

[**espy, espouse, espionage, eulogy, ethereal, estimable**]

****

1. They have a wish to learn, and _______ a disposition that pleases me.
2. His real name, Harris, had gradually merged into the less _______ one of Trotters.
3. Friendship is _______ in every man's experience.
4. She had all sorts of _______ for common objects.
5. The answer was _______—I should have liked something clearer.
6. The Basts had just been _______ for not paying their rent.

[**evince, euphemisms, euphonious, evanescent, evicted, evasive**]

1. . . . I thought it prudent not to **exacerbate** the growing moodiness of his temper by any comment. —Edgar Allan Poe, *The Gold Bug*

2. The violence of the northern savages **exasperated** Christianity into power. —R. W. Emerson, *English Traits*

3. The genius* of the people will ill brook the inquisitive* and peremptory* spirit of **excise** laws. —Alexander Hamilton, *The Federalist Papers*

4. The corpse of the young lady was much bruised and **excoriated**. —Edgar Allan Poe, *The Murders in the Rue Morgue*

5. The unblushing Macdonald, without even endeavouring to **exculpate** himself from the crime he was charged with, meanly endeavoured to reproach Sophia with ignobly* defrauding* him of his money. —Jane Austen, *Love and Friendship*

6. His clothes were apt to look oily, and smell of eating-houses. He wore his pantaloons very loose and baggy in summer. His coats were **execrable**; his hat not to be handled. —Herman Melville, *Bartleby*

****

1. **exacerbate**; worsen, aggravate. —exacerbation.
2. **exasperate**; irritate, enrage, infuriate, incense, inflame. —exasperation.
3. **excise**; 1. tax on the production and sale of goods. 2. tax for a license. * genius; character, inclination, knack, propensity. * inquisitive; curious, inquiring, prying. * peremptory; compelling, *see p. 218, no. 5.*
4. **excoriate**; 1. strip off, skin, flay. 2. denunciate, objurgate. —excoriation.
5. **exculpate**; acquit, absolve, purge, remit, exonerate. —exculpation, —exculpatory. * ignobly; despicably, meanly. * defraud; cheat, swindle.
6. **execrable**; detestable, abhorrent, loathsome, abominable. —execrate.

♣ A single word even may be a spark of inextinguishable thought. —P. B. Shelley, *A Defence of Poetry*

1. The very dogs that sullenly bay the moon from farmyards in these nights, excite more heroism in our breasts than all the civil **exhortations** or war sermons of the age. —Henry David Thoreau, *A Week on the Concord and Merrimack Rivers*

2. The coffin was **exhumed** and broken open. —R. L. Stevenson, *The Body Snatcher*

3. Great powers cannot be exerted, but when great **exigencies** make them necessary. —Samuel Johnson, *The Idler*

4. Her mother was a small, spare, light person, with a wandering eye, a very **exiguous** nose, and a large forehead, decorated with a certain amount of thin, much frizzled* hair. —Henry James, *Daisy Miller*

5. Surely, the poor child's story, faithfully repeated to these men, will be sufficient to **exonerate** him. —Charles Dickens, *Oliver Twist*

6. Why should we not meet, not always as dyspeptics,* to tell our bad dreams, but sometimes as eupeptics, to congratulate each other on the ever-glorious morning? I do not make an **exorbitant** demand, surely. —Henry David Thoreau, *Life without Principle*

****

1. **exhortation**; urge, incitement. —exhort, —exhortative.
2. **exhume**; unbury, unearth, disinter. —exhumation.
3. **exigency**; crisis, urgency. —exigent; 1. critical. 2. exacting, demanding.
4. **exiguous**; scanty, meager. —exiguity, —exiguously. * frizzled; curly.
5. **exonerate**; pardon, excuse, absolve, acquit, remit, purge, exculpate. —exoneration. ※ parole; 1. conditionally early release of a prisoner. 2. promise, word.
6. **exorbitant**; excessive, inordinate. * dyspeptic; 1. pessimist. 2. one suffering from indigestion. 3. of dyspepsia. ***ant.*** eupeptic, *see p. 93, no. 3.*

1. Sir John Herschel, in completion of the work of his father, who had made the catalogue of the stars of the northern hemisphere, **expatriated** himself for years at the Cape of Good Hope, finished his inventory* of the southern heaven, came home, and redacted* it in eight years more. —R. W. Emerson, *English Traits*

2. Nature suggests every economical **expedient** somewhere on a great scale. —R. W. Emerson, *Farming*

3. He silently and **expeditiously** encased himself in the covering of the beast. —James Fenimore Cooper, *The Last of the Mohicans*

4. Pain is no **expiation**. —Jane Austen, *Emma*

5. Man is **explicable** by nothing less than all his history. —R. W. Emerson, *History*

6. I found how the world had been misled by prostitute writers, to ascribe the greatest **exploits** in war, to cowards. —Jonathan Swift, *Gulliver's Travels*

****

1. **expatriate**; 1. exile, deport, expel, banish, ostracize. ***ant.*** repatriate. 2. *n.* exile, expat. —expatriation. ※ ostracize; expel, expatriate: *The beauty was ostracized because she was a beauty.* ※ extradite; surrender a suspect to another country's jurisdiction: *The criminal was extradited from the USA to our country.* * inventory; catalogue, directory. * redact; edit, revise, correct. —redaction.
2. **expedient**; 1. means, device, resource, recourse. 2. advantageous, beneficial, useful, suitable, appropriate. —expedience, —expediently.
3. **expeditiously**; fast, quickly, rapidly. —expeditiousness.
4. **expiation**; penance, repentance, atonement. —expiate.
5. **explicable**; explainable, accountable, justifiable. —explication; interpretation, explanation, exposition, exegesis. —explicate.
6. **exploit**; 1. feat, accomplishment, achievement. 2. *v.* utilize, manipulate.

♣ A man's friends are his magnetisms. —R. W. Emerson, *Fate*

1. He had a considerable reputation in England as a critic and was the accredited* **exponent** in this country of modern French literature. —W. Somerset Maugham, *Of Human Bondage*

2. Laws are a dead letter without courts to **expound** and define their true meaning and operation. —Alexander Hamilton, *The Federalist Papers*

3. The **expropriated** farmers took forcible possession of the state governments. —Jack London, *The Iron Heel*

4. They [oysters] open their shells to their fullest extent, and then suddenly contracting them, the **expulsion** of the water forwards gives a motion backwards. —Henry David Thoreau, *Cape Cod*

5. Every lash* inflicted is a tongue of fame; . . . every burned book or house enlightens the world; every suppressed or **expunged** word reverberates through the earth from side to side. —R. W. Emerson, *Compensation*

6. The World's Charity is to be a society whose members shall comprise deputies from every charity and mission **extant**. —Herman Melville, *The Confidence-Man*

****

1. **exponent**; 1. interpreter, expounder. 2. *adj.* expository. —exponential. * accredited; official, authorized, credential.
2. **expound**; elucidate, explicate, expatiate. ※ exposition; 1. explication, interpretation: *the technician's exposition of the apparatus.* 2. expo, exhibition.
3. **expropriate**; confiscate, commandeer, appropriate. —expropriation; seizure.
4. **expulsion**; ejection, eviction, expelling, banishment. —expulsive.
5. **expunge**; erase, delete, obliterate, excise. * lash; whip, scourge.
6. **extant**; present, existing, existent, subsisting. ***ant.*** extinct.

♣ Every human being is a volume worthy to be studied. —W. Ellery Channing, *On the Elevation of the Laboring Classes*

1. The style of preaching he had chosen was the **extemporaneous**, which was held little short of* the miraculous in rural parishes like King's Lorton. —George Eliot, *The Mill on the Floss*

2. Speak of me as I am; nothing **extenuate**,
   Nor set down aught in malice.
   —Shakespeare, *Othello*

3. We must simply **extirpate** the scoundrels.* —Joseph Conrad, *Under Western Eyes*

4. The greatness of Charles Strickland was authentic. . . . it is no longer a mark of eccentricity to defend or of perversity* to **extol** him. —W. Somerset Maugham, *The Moon and Sixpence*

5. Are my chests fill'd up with **extorted** gold?
   Is my apparel sumptuous* to behold?
   —Shakespeare, *King Henry VI, Part II*

6. The country is the real thing, the substantial thing, the eternal thing; . . . institutions are **extraneous**, they are its mere clothing, and clothing can wear out . . .
   —Mark Twain, *A Connecticut Yankee*

****

1. **extemporaneous**; offhand, impromptu, improvised, ad-lib, extempore, extemporary. —extemporaneity, —extemporize. ※ contemporary; 1. contemporaneous, synchronic, coeval. 2. current. * little short of; almost.
2. **extenuate**; excuse, justify, palliate, mitigate. —extenuation.
3. **extirpate**; uproot, eliminate, annihilate, exterminate, eradicate, deracinate. —extirpation; extermination, eradication. * scoundrel; rogue, bastard.
4. **extol**; laud, eulogize, panegyrize. —extolment. * perversity; obstinacy.
5. **extort**; 1. rob, blackmail, force. 2. wrest, extract, wring, squeeze. —extortion. * sumptuous; luxurious, splendid, extravagant, *see p. 305, no. 2.*
6. **extraneous**; extra, peripheral, supplementary, nonessential. —extraneousness.

1. The charming furniture of her house, the flowers among which she lived even in winter, suggested an **extravagance** which he deplored. —W. Somerset Maugham, *Of Human Bondage*

2. Several mighty efforts of the wild-cat to **extricate** herself from the jaws of the dog followed, but they were fruitless . . . —James Fenimore Cooper, *The Pioneers*

3. There was no bar to their marriage. Class difference was the only difference, and class was **extrinsic**. It could be shaken off. —Jack London, *Martin Eden*

4. He was heart-broken because he had no whisky, wanted to make coffee for me, racked* his brain for something he could possibly do for me, and beamed and laughed, and in the **exuberance** of his delight sweated at every pore. —W. Somerset Maugham, *The Moon and Sixpence*

5. A man will see his character emitted in the events that seem to meet, but which **exude** from and accompany him. —R. W. Emerson, *Fate*

6. As he spoke his boyish face was wreathed in a gleeful smile, and his voice had an **exultant** ring. —Stephen Crane, *The Red Badge of Courage*

****

1. **extravagance**; wastefulness, squandering, prodigality. —extravagant.
2. **extricate**; free, liberate, deliver, release, disengage. —extrication, —extricable.
3. **extrinsic**; external, unessential, extraneous. ***ant.*** intrinsic; innate, inherent.
4. **exuberance**; abundance, profusion, luxuriance. * rack; torture, agonize.
5. **exude**; emit, emanate. —exudation. ※ secrete; excrete, ooze: *to secrete juice.*
6. **exultant**; rejoicing, jubilant, elated, gleeful. —exultance, —exultation, —exult.

♣ Only an unmitigated despotism demands that the individual citizen shall obey unconditionally every mandate of persons in authority. —John Stuart Mill, *Considerations On Representative Government*

1. Their humor was a low **facetiousness**. —W. Somerset Maugham, *Of Human Bondage*
2. Most men, even in this comparatively free country, through mere ignorance and mistake, are so occupied with the **factitious** cares and superfluously coarse labors of life that its finer fruits cannot be plucked by them. —Henry David Thoreau, *Walden*
3. Our intellectual activity is exercised in winding through the labyrinths* of **fallacy**. —Samuel Johnson, *The Rambler*
4. The two years during which his mind had lain **fallow** had refreshed him, he fancied, and he was able now to work with energy. —W. Somerset Maugham, *Of Human Bondage*
5. An often quoted expression at this day is that "Knowledge is power"; but so also are **fanaticism**, despotism, and ambition. —Samuel Smiles, *Self Help*
6. He was at the same time haughty, reserved, and **fastidious**, and his manners, though well bred, were not inviting. —Jane Austen, *Pride and Prejudice*

****

1. **facetiousness**; fun, jesting, jocularity, jesting. —facetious.
2. **factitious**; unnatural, artificial, contrived. ***ant.*** natural.
3. **fallacy**; 1. error. 2. misconception. —fallacious. ※ infallible; perfect, impeccable, foolproof: *infallible evidence, see p. 161, no. 5.* * labyrinth; maze.
4. **fallow**; 1. uncultivated, uncultured, unaccomplished. 2. untilled.
5. **fanaticism**; zeal, frenzy, franticness. —fanatical; frenzied, phrenetic, maniacal. —fanaticize. ※ frenetic; fanatical: *frenetic effort to escape his doom.*
6. **fastidious**; meticulous, scrupulous, squeamish. —fastidiousness.

♣ Morals and manners, which give colour to life, are of much greater importance than laws. —Samuel Smiles, *Self Help*

1. "I am, of course, a mere student," said I, with **fatuous** smile, "hardly more, I might say, than an earnest inquirer." —Arthur Conan Doyle, *The Lost World*

2. It is evident that the **fauna** during any one great period in the earth's history will be intermediate in general character between that which preceded and that which succeeded it. —Charles Darwin, *The Origin of Species*

3. You show'd your teeth like apes, and **fawn'd** like hounds,
   And bow'd like bondmen,* kissing Cæsar's feet.
   —Shakespeare, *Julius Caesar*

4. We were doing what was needed and **feasible**. —Joseph Conrad, *The Mirror of the Sea*

5. In some Compositæ,* the male florets,* which of course cannot be **fecundated**, have a rudimentary pistil,* for it is not crowned with a stigma,* —Charles Darwin, *The Origin of Species*

6. The pencil of the Holy Ghost hath laboured more in describing the afflictions of Job than the **felicities** of Solomon. —Francis Bacon, *Essays*

****

1. **fatuous**; stupid, silly, idiotic, witless, asinine. —fatuity, — fatuously.
2. **fauna**; animals of a region or time. ※ flora (*pl.* floras *or* florae); plants of a region or time : *the flora of the Nile.*
3. **fawn**; flatter, toady. —fawner; toady, sycophant. * bondman; slave.
4. **feasible**; possible, practicable, workable, applicable, viable. ***ant.*** infeasible. —feasibility. ※ viability; feasibility: *financial viability of the project.*
5. **fecundate**; impregnate, fertilize, inseminate. —fecund *adj.*; fruitful, fertile. —fecundity. * Compositæ; a large family of dicotyledonous (of two cotyledon) plants with flower heads. ※ cotyledon; seed leaf. * floret; small flower. * pistil; female organ of a flower. * stigma; 1. the top of a pistil. 2. stain, disgrace.
6. **felicity**; 1. ecstasy, delectation, eudaemonia. 2. propriety. —felicitous.

Review Exercise: Sentence Completions (pp. 111–14)

1. The genius of the people will ill brook the peremptory spirit of _______ laws.
2. He endeavored to _______ himself from the crime he was charged with.
3. His coats were _______; his hat not to be handled.
4. The corpse of the young lady was much bruised and _______.
5. The violence of the northern savages _______ Christianity into power.
6. It is prudent not to _______ the growing moodiness of his temper.

[**exasperated, execrable, exacerbate, excise, excoriated, exculpate**]

****

1. I do not make an _______ demand, surely.
2. Great _______ make great powers necessary.
3. The coffin was _______ and broken open.
4. Her mother was a small person with a wandering eye and a very _______ nose.
5. The very dogs that bay the moon excite more heroism than all the civil _______.
6. The poor child's story will be sufficient to _______ him.

[**exhumed, exhortations, exigencies, exiguous, exorbitant, exonerate**]

****

1. Nature suggests every economical _______ somewhere on a great scale.
2. He silently and _______ encased himself in the covering of the beast.
3. Sir John Herschel _______ himself for years at the Cape of Good Hope.
4. Pain is no _______.
5. Man is _______ by nothing less than all his history.
6. The world had ascribed the greatest _______ in war to cowards.

[**expeditiously, expiation, explicable, expedient, exploits, expatriated**]

****

1. Laws are a dead letter without courts to _______ their true meaning.
2. The members comprise deputies from every charity and mission _______.
3. He was the accredited _______ in this country of modern French literature.
4. The _______ farmers took forcible possession of the state governments.
5. The _______ of the water forwards gives a motion backwards.
6. Every _______ word reverberates through the earth from side to side.

[**expound, expropriated, expulsion, exponent, extant, expunged**]

Review Exercise: Sentence Completions (pp. 115–18)

1. We must simply _______ the scoundrels.
2. Speak of me as I am; nothing _______, nor set down aught in malice.
3. Are my chests fill'd up with _______ gold?
4. The style of preaching he had chosen was the _______.
5. It is no longer a mark of eccentricity to defend or of perversity to _______ him.
6. The country is the real thing . . . institutions are _______.

[**extenuate, extemporaneous, extol, extirpate, extraneous, extorted**]

****

1. The wild-cat made efforts to _______ herself from the jaws of the dog.
2. Class was _______. It could be shaken off.
3. In the _______ of his delight he sweated at every pore.
4. A man will see his character emitted in the events which _______ from him.
5. As he spoke, his voice had an _______ ring.
6. The charming furniture suggested an _______ which he deplored.

[**exultant, exude, exuberance, extravagance, extricate, extrinsic**]

****

1. Our intellectual activity is exercised in winding through the mazes of _______.
2. Their humor was a low _______.
3. Most men are occupied with the _______ cares and coarse labors of life.
4. The two years during which his mind had lain _______ had refreshed him.
5. He was at the same time haughty, reserved, and _______.
6. Knowledge is power, but so also are _______, despotism, and ambition.

[**fastidious, fanaticism, fallow, fallacy, factitious, facetiousness**]

****

1. Crocodiles belong to tropical or subtropical _______.
2. You show'd your teeth like apes, and _______ like hounds.
3. The male florets of course cannot be _______.
4. We were doing what was needed and _______.
5. The pencil of the Holy Ghost described the _______ of Solomon in detail.
6. "I am, of course, a mere student," said I, with _______ smile.

[**fatuous, fawn'd, fauna, feasible, felicities, fecundated**]

1. . . . here [in Paraguay] neither cattle nor horses nor dogs have ever run wild, though they swarm* southward and northward in a **feral** state. —Charles Darwin, *The Origin of Species*

2. He left Glasgow in a **ferment**. —E. Phillips Oppenheim, *The Yellow Crayon*

3. For many years past the whale-ship has been the pioneer in **ferreting** out the remotest and least known parts of the earth. —Herman Melville, *Moby Dick*

4. The **fervent** red of her face turned almost to purple. —Stephen Crane, *Maggie: A Girl of the Streets*

5. It was now the sweetest hour of the twenty-four:—"Day its **fervid** fires had wasted," and dew fell cool on panting plain and scorched* summit. —Charlotte Brontë, *Jane Eyre*

6. . . . and here and there the tortured flesh was beginning to **fester**. —Jack London, *Martin Eden*

****

1. **feral**; 1. wild, natural, untamed, undomesticated. 2. savage, brutal, bestial, ferocious. * swarm; 1. *v.* flock, throng. 2. *n.* crowd, horde.
2. **ferment**; 1. agitation, excitement, fever. 2. commotion, turmoil. 3. *v.* brew.
3. **ferret**; hunt, search, uncover, scour. —ferreter, —ferrety *adj.*
4. **fervent**; fervid, ardent, zealous, vehement, torrid. —fervency; passion, zeal. ※ verve; fervency: *playing the piano from memory, with amazing verve!*
5. **fervid**; glowing, impassioned, fervent. —fervidity; fervor. * scorch; burn, parch.
6. **fester**; form pus, suppurate, putrefy.

♣ Feeling without judgment is a washy draught indeed; but judgment untempered by feeling is too bitter and husky a morsel for human deglutition.* —Charlotte Brontë, *Jane Eyre*

* deglutition; swallowing.

fetid

1. Does the black **fetid** mud, abounding with organic matter, yield the sulphur and ultimately the sulphuric acid? —Charles Darwin, *The Voyage of the Beagle*

2. As he moved, a chain clanked; to his wrists were attached **fetters**. —Charlotte Brontë, *Jane Eyre*

3. Oh, I'm not a tragical failure! I have not fallen from a height, and my **fiasco** has made no noise. —Henry James, *The American*

4. There is no permanent wise man except in the **figment** of the Stoics. —R. W. Emerson, *Spiritual Laws*

5. With cunning hast thou **filch'd** my daughter's heart.
—Shakespeare, *A Midsummer Night's Dream*

6. Nature seemed to me benign and good; I thought she loved me, outcast as I was; and I, who from man could anticipate only mistrust, rejection, insult, clung to her with **filial** fondness. —Charlotte Brontë, *Jane Eyre*

****

1. **fetid**; stinking, malodorous, foul, rancid, noisome. —fetidness, —fetidly.
2. **fetters** (usu. in *pl.*); 1. chain, shackle, manacle. 2. restraint.
3. **fiasco**; complete failure or miscarriage.
4. **figment**; fiction, invention, fabrication.
5. **filch**; steal, thieve, pilfer. —filcher.
6. **filial**; devoted to one's parents, as a son or daughter. —filially.

♣ One impulse from a vernal wood
May teach you more of man,
Of moral evil and of good,
Than all the sages can.

—William Wordsworth, "The Tables Turned"

1. Once again he touched him on the breast, as though his finger were the fine point of a small sword, with which, in delicate **finesse**, he ran him through the body . . . —Charles Dickens, *A Tale of Two Cities*

2. In order to maintain authority in her school, it became necessary to remove this rebel, this monster, this serpent, this **firebrand**. —W. M. Thackeray, *Vanity Fair*

3. Gusts of sulphurous steam issued silently and invisibly from a thousand little cracks and **fissures** in the crater, and were wafted* to our noses with every breeze. —Mark Twain, *The Innocents Abroad*

4. The wind had abated* its violence; coming now in **fitful**, virulent* puffs. —O. Henry, *The Sphinx Apple*

5. Shower has succeeded shower . . . many coats have lost their gloss,* and many curls been moistened to **flaccidity**. —Samuel Johnson, *The Idler*

6. The injustice of the vulgar tone of preaching is not less **flagrant** to Jesus than to the souls which it profanes.* —R. W. Emerson, *Divinity School Address*

****

1. **finesse**; 1. skill, dexterity, craft, tact, savoir faire. 2. artifice, stratagem. ※ savoir faire; 1. craft, finesse. 2. accomplishment: *a lady of great savoir faire.* ※ artifact; artificial product. ※ artisan; craftsman. ※ artifice; device, maneuver.
2. **firebrand**; 1. agitator, instigator, demagogue. 2. piece of burning wood.
3. **fissure**; opening, crack, crevice, fracture. * waft; drift, whiff.
4. **fitful**; intermittent, sporadic, erratic, desultory, spasmodic. * abate; weaken, quell, alleviate. * virulent; spiteful, malignant, malevolent.
5. **flaccidity**; limpness, flabbiness, droop. —flaccid. * gloss; luster.
6. **flagrant**; notorious, heinous, atrocious. * profane; violate, desecrate.

♣ All an appearance can know is mirage. —Jack London, *John Barleycorn*

1. . . . and the flamboyants,* scarlet against the blue sky, **flaunt** their color like a cry of passion. —W. Somerset Maugham, *The Moon and Sixpence*

2. His **flamboyance** was extinguished; and in neat, commonplace, shabby clothes he hurried, a subdued, unassuming* little man, through the departments as though anxious to escape notice. —W. Somerset Maugham, *Of Human Bondage*

3. See, Uncas, your father is **flaying** the scalps already. —James Fenimore Cooper, *The Last of the Mohicans*

4. Over such feeble **fledglings** the directress spread a wing of kindliest protection. —Charlotte Brontë, *The Professor*

5. Nothing could be in worse taste than misplaced **flippancy**. —Edith Wharton, *The Age of Innocence*

6. In the morning, one might say, his face was of a fine **florid** hue, but after twelve o'clock, meridian*—his dinner hour—it blazed like a grate full of Christmas coals. —Herman Melville, *Bartleby*

****

1. **flaunt**; show off, display, flourish, vaunt. —flaunting, —flaunty. * flamboyant; 1. royal poinciana (a tropical tree with scarlet flowers). 2. florid, ornate.
2. **flamboyance**; colorfulness, brilliance, luxuriance, resplendence, ornateness. —flamboyant. * unassuming; modest, humble, unpretentious.
3. **flay**; 1. strip, scalp, skin. 2. upbraid, excoriate.
4. **fledgling**: 1. beginner, amateur, neophyte, novice, tyro. 2. chick. 3. *adj.* learning, unfledged, immature, callow. ***ant.*** full-fledged. —fledge *v.*; feather.
5. **flippancy**; lightness, levity, frivolity. —flippant.
6. **florid**; 1. reddish, ruddy. 2. ornate. —floridness. * meridian; peak, acme.

♣ Read not to contradict and confute; nor to believe and take for granted; nor to find talk and discourse; but to weigh and consider. —Francis Bacon, *Essays*

1. I had forgotten that I was merely a bit of human **flotsam**. —H. G. Wells, *The Island of Doctor Moreau*

2. Go hang yourself, you naughty* mocking uncle!
   You bring me to do, and then you **flout** me too.
   —Shakespeare, *Troilus and Cressida*

3. The stabler of the iron horse was up early this winter morning by the light of the stars amid the mountains, to **fodder** and harness his steed. —Henry David Thoreau, *Walden*

4. I remember a shrewd* politician, in one of our western cities, told me that "he had known several successful statesmen made by their **foible**." —R. W. Emerson, *English Traits*

5. "You **foment** class hatred," I said. —Jack London, *The Iron Heel*

6. As to his dress, it was careful to the verge of **foppishness**, with high collar, black frock-coat, white waistcoat, yellow gloves, patent-leather shoes, and light-coloured gaiters. —Arthur Conan Doyle, *The Adventures of Sherlock Holmes*

****

1. **flotsam**; debris, wreckage. ※ jetsam; discarded cargo, miscellaneous articles. ※ flotsam and jetsam; 1. odds and ends. 2. floating refuse. 3. vagrants.
2. **flout**; sneer, jeer, gibe, scoff. * naughty; 1. wicked. 2. mischievous.
3. **fodder**; 1. feed livestock. 2. *n.* dried hay, food for cattle, forage.
4. **foible**; weakness, shortcoming, defect. ***ant.*** forte. * shrewd; keen, astute.
5. **foment**; agitate, provoke, incite, instigate, goad. —fomentation.
6. **foppishness** *also* **foppery**; dandyism. —fop; beau, coxcomb.

♣ Difficulty is a severe instructor, set over us by the supreme ordinance of a parental Guardian and Legislator, who knows us better than we know ourselves, as he loves us better too. —Edmund Burke, *Reflections on the Revolution in France*

1. She did not speak to him much, but she was quick to **forestall** his wants. —W. Somerset Maugham, *The Moon and Sixpence*.

2. He [Lucifer], the fallen great one, could not bear to think that man, a being of clay, should possess the inheritance which he by his sin had **forfeited** for ever. —James Joyce, *A Portrait of the Artist as a Young Man*

3. Do not, for one repulse,* **forgo** the purpose
   That you resolv'd to effect.

   —Shakespeare, *The Tempest*

4. The sky was **forlorn** and grey. Philip felt infinitely unhappy. —W. Somerset Maugham, *Of Human Bondage*

5. Givens gently patted one of the **formidable** paws that could have killed a yearling* calf with one blow. —O. Henry, *The Princess and the Puma*

6. They trod noiselessly upon a stair carpet that its own loom would have **forsworn**. It seemed to have become vegetable; to have degenerated in that rank,* sunless air to lush* lichen* . . . —O. Henry, *The Furnished Room*

****

1. **forestall**; anticipate, prevent, circumvent. —forestallment.
2. **forfeit**; renounce, surrender, relinquish. —forfeiture, —forfeitable.
3. **forgo**; 1. abandon, renounce. 2. do without. * repulse; denial, rebuff.
4. **forlorn**; 1. desolate, dreary. 2. forsaken, deserted. 3. hopeless, despondent.
5. **formidable**; 1. dreadful, awesome, redoubtable. 2. invincible, indomitable. * yearling; one year old. ※ toddler, minor, juvenile, adolescent.
6. **forswear**; renounce, abjure. * rank; 1. stinking. 2. flourishing. * lush; dense. * lichen; fungus growing with algae.

♣ Beauty without grace is the hook without the bait. —R. W. Emerson, *Beauty*

1. People will instinctively find out, as I have done, that it is not your **forte** to tell of yourself, but to listen while others talk of themselves. —Charlotte Brontë, *Jane Eyre*

2. The virtue of Prosperity is temperance; the virtue of Adversity is **fortitude**. —Francis Bacon, *Essays*

3. My quest was not aimless and **fortuitous**; it had a definite method. —Ambrose Bierce, *Can Such Things Be?*

4. We had a good ship, but she was deep laden, and wallowed* in the sea, so that the seamen every now and then cried out she would **founder**. —Daniel Defoe, *Robinson Crusoe*

5. From the woods beyond came the dull popping of the skirmishers* and pickets,* firing in the fog. From the right came the noise of terrific **fracas**. —Stephen Crane, *The Red Badge of Courage*

6. I never see Uncle Silas speak up so sharp and **fractious** before. —Mark Twain, *Tom Sawyer Detective*

****

1. **forte**; strength, metier. ***ant.*** defect.
2. **fortitude**; courage, bravery, valor, dauntlessness, pluck. —fortitudinous.
3. **fortuitous**; accidental, unintended, inadvertent, contingent, coincidental. —fortuity, —fortuitism. ***ant.*** teleologism; belief in the purposeful phenomena of nature. ※ serendipitous; accidental: *serendipitous discovery.* —serendipity.
4. **founder**; sink, wreck. * wallow; writhe, wriggle, welter.
5. **fracas**; row, fuss, commotion, brawl. * skirmisher; 1. scout, reconnoiterer. 2. minor battle. * picket; a detachment on a forward line.
6. **fractious**; touchy, irritable, peevish, fretful, irascible. —fractiousness.

♣ The jest which is expected is already destroyed. —Samuel Johnson, *The Idler*

1. Her **frantic** joy at beholding me again moved me much. —Charlotte Brontë, *Jane Eyre*

2. . . . interest is still the ruling motive, and the world is yet full of **fraud** and corruption, malevolence* and rapine.* —Samuel Johnson, *The Adventurer*

3. The caprice* of the winds, like the wilfulness of men, is **fraught** with the disastrous consequences of self-indulgence. —Joseph Conrad, *The Mirror of the Sea*

4. A naked savage will fell an oak with a firebrand, and wear a hatchet* out of the rock by **friction**, but I cannot hew the smallest chip out of the character of my Friend, either to beautify or deform it. —Henry David Thoreau, *A Week on the Concord and Merrimack Rivers*

5. He who allows his application to falter, or shirks* his work on **frivolous** pretexts,* is on the sure road to ultimate failure. —Samuel Smiles, *Self Help*

6. He would never refuse to assist a neighbor even in the roughest toil, and was a foremost man at all country **frolics** for husking* Indian corn, or building stone fences. —Washington Irving, *Rip Van Winkle*

****

1. **frantic**; fanatic, frenzied, maniacal, frenetic. —franticness, —frantically.
2. **fraud**; deception, defrauding, imposture, sham, swindling. —fraudulent. * malevolence; malice, spite, *see p. 184, no. 6.* * rapine; robbery, seizure.
3. **fraught**; filled, laden, replenished. * caprice; whim, fancy, vagary.
4. **friction**; 1. rubbing, attrition, detrition, abrasion. 2. conflict, clash. —frictional. ※ frisson; thrill, shudder, fright: *The zombie film aroused a frisson of fear.* * hatchet; short-handled ax, tomahawk.
5. **frivolous**; 1. foolish, silly. 2. trifling, trivial. 3. flippant, flighty. —frivolity. * shirk; avoid, evade, shun. * pretext; excuse, pretense.
6. **frolic**; merriment, gaiety. —frolicsome. * husk; remove seed coverings.

1. The whale-ship has been the pioneer in _______out the remotest parts.
2. The _______ red of her face turned almost to purple.
3. Day its _______ fires had wasted, and dew fell cool on panting plain.
4. He left Glasgow in a _______.
5. Here and there the tortured flesh was beginning to _______.
6. In Paraguay horses swarm southward and northward in a _______ state.

   [**ferment, feral, fervent, ferreting, fester, fervid**]

****

1. As he moved, a chain clanked; to his wrists were attached _______.
2. I have not fallen from a height, and my _______ has made no noise.
3. The swelled black face was a _______ of imagination.
4. With cunning hast thou _______ my daughter's heart.
5. I thought she loved me, outcast as I was. I clung to her with _______ fondness.
6. Does the black _______ mud, abounding with organic matter, yield the sulphur?

   [**fiasco, fetters, fetid, filial, filch'd, figment**]

****

1. Gusts of sulphurous steam issued from a thousand little _______ in the crater.
2. The wind had abated its violence; coming now in _______, virulent puffs.
3. Many curls have been moistened to _______.
4. It is necessary to remove this rebel, this monster, and this _______.
5. The injustice of the vulgar tone of preaching is _______ to Jesus.
6. With his finger, in delicate _______, he ran him through the body.

   [**flagrant, flaccidity, fitful, fissures, firebrand, finesse**]

****

1. Over such feeble _______ she spread a wing of kindliest protection.
2. The flamboyants _______ their color like a cry of passion.
3. See, Uncas, your father is _______ the scalps already.
4. His _______ was extinguished.
5. In the morning, one might say, his face was of a fine _______ hue.
6. Nothing could be in worse taste than misplaced _______.

   [**flippancy, fledglings, flaying, flamboyance, flaunt, florid**]

Review Exercise: Sentence Completions (pp. 125–28)

1. You bring me to do, and then you _______ me too.
2. He had known several successful statesmen made by their _______.
3. The stabler was up early this morning to _______ and harness his steed.
4. "You _______ class hatred," I said.
5. As to his dress, it was careful to the verge of _______.
6. I had forgotten that I was merely a bit of human _______.

[**flout, flotsam, foppishness, foment, foible, fodder**]

****

1. Do not, for one repulse, _______ the purpose that you resolv'd to effect.
2. The sky was _______ and grey. Philip felt infinitely unhappy.
3. He [Lucifer] by his sin had _______ the inheritance for ever.
4. Givens gently patted one of the _______ paws.
5. He trod noiselessly upon a stair carpet that its own loom would have _______.
6. She did not speak to him much, but she was quick to _______ his wants.

[**forgo, forlorn, forfeited, forestall, forsworn, formidable**]

****

1. The virtue of Prosperity is temperance; the virtue of Adversity is _______.
2. It is not your _______ to tell of yourself, but to listen to others' talking.
3. From the right came the noise of terrific _______.
4. I never see Uncle Silas speak up so sharp and _______ before.
5. My quest was not aimless and _______.
6. The seamen every now and then cried out the ship would _______.

[**fractious, fracas, founder, forte, fortitude, fortuitous**]

****

1. The world is yet full of _______ and corruption, malevolence and rapine.
2. Wilfulness is _______ with the disastrous consequences of self-indulgence.
3. A naked savage will wear a hatchet out of the rock by _______.
4. Her _______ joy at beholding me again moved me much.
5. He who shirks his work on _______ pretexts is on the sure road to failure.
6. He was a foremost man at all country _______ for husking Indian corn.

[**fraught, fraud, frivolous, friction, frolics, frantic**]

1. She husbanded* her money, with the utmost **frugality** . . . —James Fenimore Cooper, *Autobiography of a Pocket-Handkerchief*

2. Restless, shifting, **fugacious** as time is a certain vast bulk of the population of the red brick district of the lower West Side. —O. Henry, *The Furnished Room*

3. The head and neck were moved frequently, and apparently with force; and the extended wings seemed to form the **fulcrum** on which the movements of the neck, body, and tail acted. —Charles Darwin, *The Voyage of the Beagle*

4. When he **fulminated** against fashionable society he always spoke of its "trend"; and to Mrs. Archer it was terrifying and yet fascinating to feel herself part of a community that was trending. —Edith Wharton, *The Age of Innocence*

5. It is not my intention to be **fulsome**, but I confess that I covet your skull. —Arthur Conan Doyle, *The Hound of The Baskervilles*

6. Either his **furlough** was up, or he dreaded to meet any witnesses of his Waterloo flight. —W. M. Thackeray, *Vanity Fair*

****

1. **frugality**; saving, economy, thriftiness, sparing, husbandry. —frugal. * husband; save, economize, retrench. —husbandry.
2. **fugacious**; ephemeral, transitory, evanescent. ***ant.*** persistent. —fugacity.
3. **fulcrum**; 1. prop, support, pivot, hub. 2. support of a lever.
4. **fulminate**; upbraid, berate, excoriate, vituperate, inveigh. —fulminatory.
5. **fulsome**; unduly flattering, inordinately fawning, exceedingly sycophantic. —fulsomeness, fulsomely.
6. **furlough**; 1. leave, vacation. 2. temporary layoff.

♣ The principles of human nature may be studied better in a family than in the history of the world. —W. Ellery Channing, *On the Elevation of the Laboring Classes*

1. He was a young man with **furtive** eyes and a sullen look. —W. Somerset Maugham, *The Moon and Sixpence*

2. He greeted her **gallantly**, but with a certain reserve, of which she was at once aware. —E. Phillips Oppenheim, *The Yellow Crayon*

3. Her rigidity was frightful, like the rigor* of a corpse **galvanized** into harsh speech and glittering stare by the force of murderous hate. —Joseph Conrad, *Under Western Eyes*

4. Desiree ate like a raven, **gambolled** day and night in her bed . . . diverted herself with throwing her shoes at her bonne* and grimacing at her sisters. —Charlotte Brontë, *Villette*

5. He ran the **gamut** of denunciation,* rising to heights of wrath that were sublime and almost Godlike, and from sheer* exhaustion sinking to the vilest* and most indecent abuse. —Jack London, *The Sea Wolf*

6. No doubt the reporters had **garbled** his evidence. —Joseph Conrad, *Chance*

****

1. **furtive**; secret, covert, stealthy, clandestine, surreptitious. —furtively.
2. **gallantly**; 1. politely, gentlemanly, chivalrously. 2. bravely, courageously, valiantly. —gallantry, —gallant.
3. **galvanize**; rouse, energize, electrify. * rigor; severity, grimness. —rigorous.
4. **gambol**; caper, romp, frisk, frolic. * bonne; maid, female servant.
5. **gamut**; 1. complete range. 2. whole series of notes. * denunciation; blame. * sheer; 1. complete, absolute. 2. pure, unalloyed, *see p. 287, no. 2.* * vile; 1. base, mean. 2. disgusting.
6. **garble**; confuse, scramble, jumble. —garbler.

♣ Cheerfulness is an excellent working-quality, imparting elasticity to the character. —Samuel Smiles, *Self Help*

1. After the guests had gone, father threw himself into a chair and gave vent to roars of **Gargantuan** laughter. —Jack London, *The Iron Heel*

2. Pay no worship to the **garish** sun.
—Shakespeare, *Romeo and Juliet*

3. At a certain season of the year, when the fruit of the hundred groves of the valley has reached its maturity, and hangs in golden spheres from every branch, the islanders assemble in harvest groups, and **garner** in the abundance which surrounds them. —Herman Melville, *Typee*

4. The flat, plastered roof is **garnished** by picturesque stacks of fresco* materials. —Mark Twain, *The Innocents Abroad*

5. The event of the day—that is, the return of Diana and Mary—pleased him; but the accompaniments of that event, the glad tumult,* the **garrulous** glee* of reception, irked him. —Charlotte Brontë, *Jane Eyre*

6. If your air and address are vulgar, awkward, and ***gauche***, you may be esteemed indeed, if you have great intrinsic merit. —4th Earl of Chesterfield, *Letters to His Son*

****

1. **gargantuan**; huge, colossal, gigantic, titanic, enormous, stupendous.
2. **garish**; flashy, gaudy, tawdry, meretricious. —garishness, —garishly.
3. **garner**; gather and store, reap, harvest. ※ glean; gather, *see p. 135, no. 2.*
4. **garnish**; decorate, ornament, embellish. —garnishment. * fresco; watercolor painting on moist plaster. ※ graffiti; *pl.* of graffito (inscription on a wall). ※ mural; wall painting.
5. **garrulous**; verbose, wordy, mouthy, loquacious. —garrulously. * tumult; turmoil, pandemonium, *see p. 322, no. 6.* * glee; joy, mirth.
6. **gauche**; awkward, unpolished, tactless, clumsy, uncouth. —gaucherie.

1. Costly thy habit as thy purse can buy,
   But not express'd in fancy; rich, not **gaudy**;
   For the apparel oft proclaims the man.

   —Shakespeare, *Hamlet*

2. Far away I saw a **gaunt** cat slink crouchingly along a wall, but traces of men there were none. —H. G. Wells, *The War of the Worlds*

3. A lanky,* **gawky** fellow tumbles over everybody. —W. M. Thackeray, *Vanity Fair*

4. The estuary* of the Thames is not beautiful; it has no noble features, no romantic grandeur of aspect, no smiling **geniality**; but it is wide open, spacious, inviting . . . —Joseph Conrad, *The Mirror of the Sea*

5. He, too, growled, savagely, terribly, voicing the fear that is to life **germane** and that lies twisted about life's deepest roots. —Jack London, *Love of Life*

6. The sperm whale, as with all other species of the Leviathan,* but unlike most other fish, breeds indifferently at all seasons; after a **gestation** which may probably be set down at nine months, producing but one at a time. —Herman Melville, *Moby Dick*

****

1. **gaudy**; showy, flashy, ostentatious, garish, tawdry. —gaudiness, gaudily.
2. **gaunt**; 1. skinny, bony, haggard, emaciated, angular, cadaverous. 2. dreary, bleak, desolate. —gauntly, —gauntness.
3. **gawky**; awkward, clumsy, ungainly, gauche, loutish. —gawkiness, —gawkily. * lanky; 1. tall and ungainly. 2. tall and thin, gangly.
4. **geniality**; amiability, affability, buoyancy, bonhomie. —genial; 1. temperate. 2. jolly. ※ bonhomous; genial: *bonhomous joke*. * estuary; mouth of a river.
5. **germane**; relevant, pertinent, appropriate, applicable. —germaneness.
6. **gestation**; pregnancy or its period. * Leviathan; 1. sea monster in Bible, a large sea animal. 2. behemoth, colossus. 3. anything large.

1. . . . so he held his breath and stepped **gingerly** back; planted his foot carefully and firmly, after balancing, one-legged, in a precarious* way and almost toppling* over, first on one side and then on the other. —Mark Twain, *The Adventures of Tom Sawyer*

2. He could **glean** nothing from their faces; they might as well have been of stone. —Charles Dickens, *Oliver Twist*

3. I can't conceive how you, in any way, can hold him a fool. How he talked—so **glib**, so pat,* so well. —Herman Melville, *The Confidence-Man*

4. Meanwhile, the infant ruffian continued sucking; and **glowered** up at me defyingly, as he slavered* into the jug. —Emily Brontë, *Wuthering Heights*

5. He who distinguishes the true savor of his food can never be a **glutton**; he who does not cannot be otherwise. —Henry David Thoreau, *Walden*

6. There was an iciness, a sinking, a sickening of the heart—an unredeemed dreariness of thought which no **goading** of the imagination could torture into aught* of the sublime. —Edgar Allan Poe, *The Fall of the House of Usher*

****

1. **gingerly**; carefully, cautiously, warily, charily, prudently, circumspectly. * precarious; uncertain, unstable, *see p. 232, no. 3.* * topple; fall over, overturn.
2. **glean**; 1. collect, gather, pick up. 2. collect grains after reapers. —gleaner.
3. **glib**; fluent, voluble. —glibness, —glibly. * pat; 1. opportunely. 2. to the point.
4. **glower**; stare with discontent, frown, scowl. * slaver; slobber, drivel, dribble, slobber, salivate, drool.
5. **glutton**; gourmand, gorger, gobbler. —gluttony. —glut; 1. *v.* gorge, devour. 2. *n.* excess, surfeit. —gluttonous; greedy, insatiable, voracious.
6. **goad**; stimulate, urge, incite, prod, provoke. * aught; 1. anything, ought. 2. nought *or* naught, zero, nothing.

1. At first, Bartleby did an extraordinary quantity of writing. As if long famishing* for something to copy, he seemed to **gorge** himself on my documents. —Herman Melville, *Bartleby*

2. There is nothing like taking all you do at a moderate estimate: it keeps mind and body tranquil; whereas **grandiloquent** notions are apt to hurry both into fever. —Charlotte Brontë, *Villette*

3. Those friends thou hast, and their adoption tried,
Grapple them to thy soul with hoops of steel.
—Shakespeare, *Hamlet*

4. . . . the lover shall not sigh **gratis**. —Shakespeare, *Hamlet*

5. Among all forms of mistake, prophecy is the most **gratuitous**. —George Eliot, *Middlemarch*

6. As with all **gregarious** animals, 'two souls,' as Faust says, 'dwell within his [man's] breast,' the one of sociability and helpfulness, the other of jealousy and antagonism to his mates. —William James, *The Principles of Psychology*

****

1. **gorge**; glut, devour, gluttonize, gobble, gormandize. * famish; starve.
2. **grandiloquent**; bombastic, magniloquent, pompous, rhetorical. —grandiloquence. ※ orotund; grandiloquent: *orotund encomium.* ※ pontificate; 1. term of pontiff. 2. *v.* talk or behave pompously: *The boss pontificated that he had never pontificated.*
3. **grapple**; 1. grasp, grip, clutch. 2. struggle, tussle, wrestle, strive.
4. **gratis**; free, for nothing, without charge.
5. **gratuitous**; free, gratis. —gratuity; tip, bonus. ※ perquisite; gratuity: *"A gratuitous perquisite" is a good example of tautology.* ※ gratitude; appreciation. ※ gravitate; move toward, be attracted. —gravitation; the force of attraction.
6. **gregarious**; sociable, living in flocks. —gregariously, —gregariousness.

1. He was never absent during business hours, unless upon an errand, and then he was represented by his son, a **grisly** urchin* of twelve, who was his express* image. —Charles Dickens, *A Tale of Two Cities*

2. We passed the night in a **grotto** hollowed* in the snow, which afforded us but poor shelter, and I was ill all night. —Mark Twain, *A Tramp Abroad*

3. He believed that a noble-minded woman insensibly elevated the character of her husband, while one of a **grovelling** nature as certainly tended to degrade it. —Samuel Smiles, *Self Help*

4. Two households, both alike in dignity,
   In fair Verona, where we lay our scene,
   From ancient **grudge** break to new mutiny.*
   —Shakespeare, *Romeo and Juliet*

5. For a time the old man resigned himself to the pleasures of **gustatory** reminiscence.* —H. G. Wells, *The War in the Air*

6. . . . in the stalls* and boxes, people smiled a little at the **hackneyed** sentiments and claptrap* situations, and enjoyed the play as much as the galleries* did. —Edith Wharton, *The Age of Innocence*

****

1. **grisly**; frightful, hideous, gruesome, ghastly, macabre. * urchin; mischievous boy, scamp. * express; 1. exact, precise. 2. outright.
2. **grotto**; cave, cavern. * hollow; 1. *v.* scoop. 2. concave. ***ant.*** convex. 3. sunken.
3. **grovelling**; 1. submissive. 2. fawning, cringing. —groveller, —grovellingly.
4. **grudge**; hatred, malevolence, malice, spite, venom, enmity, rancor, animosity. ⋇ begrudge; 1. be loath to give. 2. covet. * mutiny; revolt, rebellion.
5. **gustatory**; of taste. —gusto; relish, zest, smack. * reminiscence; recollection.
6. **hackneyed**; clichéd, trite, banal. * stall; 1. the front seat in a theater. 2. stable. * claptrap; nonsense. * gallery; the cheapest seats (usu. in a theater).

1. I startled my wife at the doorway, so **haggard** was I. —H. G. Wells, *The War of the Worlds*

2. We do not **haggle** with one who only asks a just and reasonable price. —4th Earl of Chesterfield, *Letters to His Son*

3. The saloons were only left void and still, when the blue sky and **halcyon** sunshine of the genial* spring weather called their occupants out into the grounds. —Charlotte Brontë, *Jane Eyre*

4. Joseph was an elderly, nay, an old man: very old, perhaps, though **hale** and sinewy. —Emily Brontë, *Wuthering Heights*

5. In a larger sense, we cannot dedicate—we cannot consecrate—we cannot **hallow**—this ground. The brave men, living and dead, who struggled here, have consecrated it, far above our poor power to add or detract.* —Abraham Lincoln, *Address at Gettysburg*

6. On one occasion he [Walter Scott] said, "Throughout every part of my career I have felt pinched and **hampered** by my own ignorance." —Samuel Smiles, *Self Help*

****

1. **haggard**; skinny, gaunt, wasted, emaciated, cadaverous. —haggardness.
2. **haggle**; 1. bargain, dicker. 2. quarrel, wrangle, bicker. —haggler.
3. **halcyon**; calm, serene, tranquil, placid. * genial; mild.
4. **hale**; 1. hardy, robust, sturdy. 2. vigorous. —haleness. ※ hale and hearty; strong and healthy: *feeling hale and hearty after one hour workout.*
5. **hallow**; consecrate, sanctify. * detract; subtract. ***ant.*** add.
6. **hamper**; obstruct, impede, hinder, encumber, stymie.

♣ Science is the great antidote to the poison of enthusiasm and superstition. —Adam Smith, *The Wealth of Nations*

1. Either his _______ was up, or he dreaded to meet any witnesses of his flight.
2. She husbanded her money, with the utmost _______.
3. Restless, shifting, _______ as time is a certain vast bulk of the population.
4. The extended wings seemed to form the _______.
5. When he _______ against fashionable society he always spoke of its trend.
6. It is not my intention to be _______, but I confess that I covet your skull.

[**furlough, frugality, fugacious, fulcrum, fulsome, fulminated**]

****

1. No doubt the reporters had _______ his evidence.
2. He was a young man with _______ eyes and a sullen look.
3. Her rigidity was frightful, like the rigor of a corpse _____ into glittering stare.
4. He greeted her _______, but with a certain reserve.
5. Desiree ate like a raven, and _______ day and night in her bed.
6. He ran the _______ of denunciation, rising to heights of wrath.

[**gallantly, furtive, galvanized, gamut, gambolled, garbled**]

****

1. The islanders assemble in harvest groups, and _______ in the abundance.
2. The flat, plastered roof is _______ by picturesque stacks of fresco materials.
3. The glad tumult, the _______ glee of reception, irked him.
4. He threw himself into a chair and gave vent to roars of _______ laughter.
5. Pay no worship to the _______ sun.
6. His air and address are vulgar, awkward, and _______.

[**garrulous, gargantuan, gauche, garner, garish, garnished**]

****

1. The sperm whale, after a _______, produces but one at a time.
2. A lanky, _______ fellow tumbles over everybody.
3. The estuary of the Thames is not beautiful; it has no smiling _______.
4. Costly thy habit as thy purse can buy, but . . . ; rich, not _______.
5. Far away I saw a _______ cat slink crouchingly along a wall.
6. He, too, growled, savagely, terribly, voicing the fear that is to life _______.

[**gaudy, gaunt, geniality, gawky, gestation, germane**]

Review Exercise: Sentence Completions (pp. 135–38)

1. He could _______ nothing from their faces.
2. No ______ of the imagination could torture the dullness into a liveliness.
3. The infant ruffian continued sucking, and _______ up at me defyingly.
4. How he talked—so _______, so pat, so well.
5. So he held his breath and stepped _______ back.
6. He who distinguishes the true savor of his food can never be a _______.

[**goading, glowered, glib, glutton, gingerly, glean**]

****

1. _______ them [those friends] to thy soul with hoops of steel.
2. The lover shall not sigh _______.
3. _______ notions are apt to hurry mind and body into fever.
4. Among all forms of mistake, prophecy is the most _______.
5. As with all _______ animals, two souls dwell within man's breast.
6. At first, he seemed to _______ himself on my documents.

[**grapple, gorge, grandiloquent, gregarious, gratis, gratuitous**]

****

1. We passed the night in a _______ hollowed in the snow.
2. Two households, from ancient _______, break to a new mutiny.
3. The old man resigned himself to the pleasures of _______ reminiscence.
4. People smiled a little at the _______ sentiments and claptrap situations.
5. His son was a _______ urchin of twelve, who was his express image.
6. A woman of a _______ nature tends to degrade the character of her husband.

[**hackneyed, gustatory, grisly, grotto, grovelling, grudge**]

****

1. We do not _______ with one who only asks a just and reasonable price.
2. The blue sky and _______ sunshine called them out into the grounds.
3. Joseph was very old, perhaps, though _______ and sinewy.
4. I have felt pinched and _______ by my own ignorance.
5. In a larger sense, we cannot consecrate—we cannot _______ this ground.
6. I startled my wife at the doorway, so _______ was I.

[**hallow, hale, hampered, haggle, halcyon, haggard**]

1. Mr. Allworthy began to **harangue**. He set forth, in a long speech, the many iniquities* of which Jones had been guilty . . . —Henry Fielding, *Tom Jones*

2. Barefaced* impudence* is the noisy and blustering* **harbinger** of a worthless and senseless usurper.* —4th Earl of Chesterfield, *Letters to His Son*

3. At ten he [Samuel Drew] was apprenticed to a shoemaker; and while in this employment he endured much hardship—living, as he used to say, "like a toad* under a **harrow**." —Samuel Smiles, *Self Help*

4. All places that the eye of heaven visits
   Are to a wise man ports and happy **havens**.

   —Shakespeare, *King Richard II*

5. Out of Plato come all things that are still written and debated among men of thought. Great **havoc** makes he among our originalities. —R. W. Emerson, *Plato; or, the Philosopher*

6. If thou delight to view thy **heinous** deeds,
   Behold this pattern of thy butcheries.

   —Shakespeare, *King Richard III*

****

1. **harangue**; make a long and earnest speech, deliver a tirade. —haranguer. ※ babble; chatter, gabble, prattle, gibber: *babbling about the scandal.* * iniquity; injustice, wickedness, turpitude, *see p. 163, no. 3.* —iniquitous.
2. **harbinger**; forerunner, herald, precursor. * barefaced; presumptuous. * impudence; brazenness. * blustering; stormy. * usurper; seizer, supplanter.
3. **harrow**; torment, affliction, distress. * toad; 1. froglike amphibian. 2. disgusting person, something loathsome. ※ toady; flatterer, *see p. 316, no. 3.*
4. **haven**; 1. shelter, refuge. 2. port, harbor, anchorage.
5. **havoc**; devastation, great destruction, ruin.
6. **heinous**; 1. hideous, odious, abhorrent. 2. flagrant, atrocious. —heinousness.

hermetically

1. . . . their perceptions had been **hermetically** sealed against the possibility of the windows having ever been opened at all. —Edgar Allan Poe, *The Murders in the Rue Morgue*

2. "I am afraid," he said quietly, "that there is a **hiatus** in my life somewhere." — E. Phillips Oppenheim, *The Malefactor*

3. I should be sorry for you to think me **hidebound** in my prejudices. —E. Phillips Oppenheim, *The Yellow Crayon*

4. He was not used to thinking of the world as a whole, but as a limitless **hinterland** of happenings beyond the range of his immediate vision. —H. G. Wells, *The War in the Air*

5. Mr. Burns, reestablished in his bed-place, was concealing his **hirsute** cheek in the palm of his hand. —Joseph Conrad, *The Shadow Line*

6. The talented Vincent Crummles, long favourably known to fame as a country manager and actor of no ordinary pretensions, is about to cross the Atlantic on a **histrionic** expedition. —Charles Dickens, *Nicholas Nickleby*

****

1. **hermetically**; airtightly, impermeably, imperviously. —hermetic; 1. sealed, airtight. 2. of alchemy. 3. solitary. ※ hermit; recluse, eremite, anchorite.
2. **hiatus**; 1. break, interval, interim, respite. 2. gap, chasm, aperture, fissure.
3. **hidebound**; 1. narrow-minded, inflexible, rigid. 2. conventional. ※ hideous; 1. frightful, ghastly, weird, eerie. 2. repulsive, disgusting: *hideous color.* ※ macabre; hideous: *The girls were horrified at the macabre scene of the movie.*
4. **hinterland**; remote land, backcountry, rural area. ***ant.*** foreland.
5. **hirsute**; 1. hairy, shaggy. 2. covered with bristles. —hirsuteness.
6. **histrionic**; dramatic, theatrical. —histrionics; theatrical arts. ※ thespian; 1. dramatic. 2. actor, actress: *James Dean was a thespian actor.*

1. To **hoard** for mere wealth's sake is the characteristic of the narrow-souled and the miserly. —Samuel Smiles, *Self Help*

2. . . . the very bell-rope in the porch was frayed* into a fringe, and **hoary** with old age. —Charles Dickens, *The Old Curiosity Shop*

3. He had seen *Lohengrin** and that passed muster.* It was dull but no worse. But *Siegfried*!* . . . It was the greatest **hoax** of the nineteenth century. —W. Somerset Maugham, *Of Human Bondage*

4. . . . and we **hoisted** the flag and fired a salute. —Mark Twain, *The Innocents Abroad*

5. Bessie supplied the hiatus by a **homily** of an hour's length, in which she proved beyond a doubt that I was the most wicked and abandoned child ever reared under a roof. —Charlotte Brontë, *Jane Eyre*

6. It was the dark and dirty corner of a small winding street. The **hovel** of a cutter of wood into lengths for burning, was the only house at that end; all else was wall. —Charles Dickens, *A Tale of Two Cities*

****

1. **hoard**; 1. reserve, stockpile, hive. 2. *n., v.* cache. ※ hoarse; harsh, raucous.
2. **hoary**; 1. white, gray, silvery, grizzled. 2. old, ancient. —hoariness, —hoarily. * fray; become threadbare, tatter.
3. **hoax**; cheat, trick, deception, fraud. —hoaxer. * pass muster; be acceptable. * *Lohengrin* and * *Siegfried*; operas written by Richard Wagner.
4. **hoist**; take up, raise, lift.
5. **homily**; admonitory discourse, moralizing sermon. —homilist.
6. **hovel**; 1. hut, cabin, cottage, shack, shanty. 2. outbuilding, shed.

♣ The largeness of nature or the nation were monstrous without a corresponding largeness and generosity of the spirit of the citizen. —Walt Whitman, *Preface to Leaves of Grass*

1. As Pride sometimes is hid under **humility**, Idleness is often covered by turbulence* and hurry. —Samuel Johnson, *The Idler*

2. An **iconoclast** in literature,* he [Henry D. Thoreau] seldom thanked colleges for their service to him, holding them in small esteem, whilst yet his debt to them was important. —R. W. Emerson, *Thoreau*

3. I suppose that everyone's conception of the passion [love] is formed on his own **idiosyncrasies**, and it is different with every different person. —W. Somerset Maugham, *The Moon and Sixpence*

4. When they came to a glade* which was suitably sylvan,* Miss Chalice, because it was **idyllic**, insisted on taking off her shoes and stockings. —W. Somerset Maugham, *Of Human Bondage*

5. The guilty Clifford! Once a by-word!* Now, an indistinctly remembered **ignominy**! —Nathaniel Hawthorn, *The House of Seven Gables*

6. He felt the **illicit** pleasure of a schoolboy playing truant.* —Jack London, *Burning Daylight*

****

1. **humility**; humbleness, modesty, unpretentiousness. ※ humiliation; shame, mortification. * turbulence; disturbance, commotion, —turbulent.
2. **iconoclast**; destroyer of an idol. —iconoclasm. ***ant.*** iconolatry; idolatry. —iconoclastic. ※ cult; 1. devotion. 2. craze: *the cult of yoga.* * literature; learning.
3. **idiosyncrasy**; characteristic, peculiarity, trait, distinction. —idiosyncratic.
4. **idyllic**; pastoral, Arcadian, rustic, rural, bucolic. —idyll *also* idyl; eclogue. —idyllist. * glade; open space in woods. * sylvan *also* silvan; of the woods.
5. **ignominy**; dishonor, disgrace, infamy. —ignominious. * by-word; 1. proverbial model. 2. adage. 3. object of scorn. .
6. **illicit**; illegal, unlawful, illegitimate. —illicitly, illicitness. * play truant; stay away from school without approval.

1. History is full, down to this day, of the **imbecility** of kings and governors. —R. W. Emerson, *Napoleon; or, the Man of the World*

2. I had **imbibed** from her something of her nature and much of her habits. —Charlotte Brontë, *Jane Eyre*

3. So the great man, that is, the man most **imbued** with the spirit of the time, is the impressionable man. —R. W. Emerson, *Fate*

4. The whole place was **immaculately** clean, and the big, four-posted bed, snow-white, invited one to repose. —Kate Chopin, *The Awakening*

5. If a man lose his balance and **immerse** himself in any trades or pleasures for their own sake, he may be a good wheel or pin, but he is not a cultivated man. —R. W. Emerson, *Prudence*

6. . . . he had been the prisoner's friend, but, at once in an auspicious* and an evil hour detecting his infamy,* had resolved to **immolate** the traitor he could no longer cherish in his bosom, on the sacred altar of his country. —Charles Dickens, *A Tale of Two Cities*

****

1. **imbecility**; 1. stupidity, idiocy, folly, bêtise. 2. feebleness. —imbecile.
2. **imbibe**; 1. absorb, ingest. 2. drink. —imbibition. ※ quaff; gulf, drink deeply, imbibe heartily: *quaff off a glass of Guinness with gusto*.
3. **imbue** *also* **embue**; 1. instill, infuse, inculcate. 2. pervade, permeate, saturate. —imbuement.
4. **immaculately**; spotlessly, flawlessly, impeccably. —immaculacy.
5. **immerse**; 1. preoccupy, absorb, engross. 2. sink, submerge. —immersion.
6. **immolate**; sacrifice, kill as an offering. —immolator. * auspicious; favorable, propitious. ※ auspices; sponsorship. * infamy; dishonor.

♣ "A difficulty," said Lord Lyndhurst, "is a thing to be overcome"; grapple with it at once. —Samuel Smiles, *Self Help*

1. We were **immured** in ice, and should probably never escape. —Mary W. Shelley, *Frankenstein*

2. To truth, justice, love, the attributes of the soul, the idea of **immutableness** is essentially associated. —R. W. Emerson, *The Over-Soul*

3. We are not to indulge our corporeal appetites with pleasures that **impair** our intellectual vigour, nor gratify our minds with schemes which we know our lives must fail in attempting to execute. —Samuel Johnson, *The Rambler*

4. The press still speaks for truth though **impaled**, in the teeth of lies though intrenched.* —Herman Melville, *The Confidence-Man*

5. "A song and dance!" she said, in a deliberate, sweet voice that seemed to clothe her words in a diaphanous* garment of **impalpable** irony. —O. Henry, *By Courier*

6. A great good will **impart** great good. —John Henry Newman, *The Idea of a University*

****

1. **immure**; jail, imprison, incarcerate. —immurement.
2. **immutableness**; unchangeableness, unalterability. —immutability.
3. **impair**; mar, hurt, damage, vitiate. —impairment.
4. **impale**; pierce, transfix. —impalement. * intrench; fortify, secure.
5. **impalpable**; intangible, imperceptible. * diaphanous; transparent, translucent, *see p. 81, no.3.* —diaphanousness, —diaphanously.
6. **impart**; grant, bestow, confer. —impartation *or* impartment, —impartable.

♣ Sweet is the lore which Nature brings;
Our meddling intellect
Mis-shapes the beauteous forms of things:—
We murder to dissect.

—William Wordsworth, "The Tables Turned"

1. Earth, my likeness,
   Though you look so **impassive**, ample and spheric there,
   I now suspect that is not all.
   —Walt Whitman, "EARTH, MY LIKENESS"

2. I breathed deeply, I revelled* in the vastness of the opened horizon, in the different atmosphere that seemed to vibrate with the toil* of life, with the energy of an **impeccable** world. —Joseph Conrad, *Lord Jim*

3. Riches are oftener an **impediment** than a stimulus to action; and in many cases they are quite as much a misfortune as a blessing. —Samuel Smiles, *Self Help*

4. It became **imperative** to lance the flying whale, or be content to lose him. —Herman Melville, *Moby Dick*

5. Yet the Abbot Berghersh was a man of too firm a grain to allow one bold outbreak* to **imperil** the settled order of his great household. —Arthur Conan Doyle, *The White Company*

6. Here we have the man, sly,* subtle, hard, **imperious**, and, withal, cold as ice. —Nathaniel Hawthorne, *The House of Seven Gables*

****

1. **impassive**; unemotional, insensible, callous, apathetic, aloof, phlegmatic. ※ impassioned; fervent, vehement: *delivering an impassioned speech.*
2. **impeccable**; flawless, sinless, perfect, spotless, unimpeachable, immaculate. * revel; rejoice, indulge, bask. —revelry. * toil; 1. labour, drudgery. 2. strife.
3. **impediment**; hindrance, obstacle, occlusion, barrier, encumbrance, stymie. ※ occlusion; blockage, obstruction: *the occlusion of the coronary arteries.*
4. **imperative**; 1. requisite, pressing, compulsory. 2. crucial, exigent.
5. **imperil**; endanger, jeopardize. —imperilment. * outbreak; 1. mutiny, riot, revolt, insurrection. 2. occurrence, eruption, outburst.
6. **imperious**; 1. arrogant, dictatorial. 2. urgent, pressing. * sly; cunning, wily.

1. History is an **impertinence** and an injury if it be anything more than a cheerful apologue* or parable of my being and becoming. —R. W. Emerson, *Self-Reliance*

2. Before winter I built a chimney, and shingled* the sides of my house, which were already **impervious** to rain . . . —Henry David Thoreau, *Walden*

3. The wide, heavy folding doors of the apartment were all at once thrown open, to their full extent, with a vigorous and rushing **impetuosity** that extinguished, as if by magic, every candle in the room. —Edgar Allan Poe, *William Wilson*

4. Through one of the broken panes I heard the rain **impinge** upon the earth, the fine incessant needles of water playing in the sodden* beds. —James Joyce, *Araby*

5. **Implacable** resentment *is* a shade in a character. —Jane Austen, *Pride and Prejudice*

6. Nothing was found to **implicate** him in any way, and there the matter dropped. —Arthur Conan Doyle, *Memoirs of Sherlock Holmes*

****

1. **impertinence**; 1. impudence, insolence. 2. irrelevance. * apologue; fable.
2. **impervious**; impermeable, impenetrable. * shingle; 1. *v.* cover with shingles. 2. *n.* a small thin piece of wood.
3. **impetuosity**; 1. violence, intensity. 2. impulsiveness. —impetuous; hasty, abrupt. ※ impetus; momentum: *The accident gave an impetus to feminism.*
4. **impinge**; strike, collide. —impingement. * sodden; drenched, soggy.
5. **implacable**; unappeasable, uncompromising, relentless, ruthless, inexorable.
6. **implicate**; involve, entangle, entwine, embroil. ***ant.*** dissociate; exclude.

♣ Words are finite organs of the infinite mind. —R. W. Emerson, *Nature*

Review Exercise: Sentence Completions (pp. 141–44)

1. All places that the eye of heaven visits are to a wise man happy _______.
2. Barefaced impudence is the blustering _______ of a worthless usurper.
3. He endured much hardship "like a toad under a _______."
4. Great _______ makes he [Plato] among our originalities.
5. He began to _______. He set forth, in a long speech, the many iniquities.
6. If thou delight to view thy _______ deeds, behold this pattern of thy butcheries.

[**harbinger, harangue, havens, harrow, heinous, havoc**]

****

1. Vincent Crummles is about to cross the Atlantic on a _______ expedition.
2. There is a _______ in my life somewhere.
3. He was used to think of the world as a limitless _______ of happenings.
4. The perceptions had been _______ sealed against the possibility of murder.
5. I should be sorry for you to think me _______ in my prejudices.
6. Mr. Burns was concealing his _______ cheek in the palm of his hand.

[**hidebound, hermetically, hiatus, histrionic, hinterland, hirsute**]

****

1. The bell-rope in the porch was frayed into a fringe, and _______ with old age.
2. *Siegfried*! It was the greatest _______ of the nineteenth century.
3. We _______ the flag and fired a salute.
4. To _______ for mere wealth's sake is the characteristic of the misery.
5. Bessie supplied the hiatus by a _______ of an hour's length.
6. The _______ was the only house at that end; all else was wall.

[**homily, hoard, hoary, hoax, hoisted, hovel**]

****

1. An _______ in literature, he seldom thanked colleges for their service.
2. Everyone's conception of love is formed on his own _______.
3. Because the glade was _______, she insisted on taking off her shoes.
4. Pride sometimes is hid under _______.
5. He felt the _______ pleasure of a schoolboy playing truant.
6. Clifford! Once a by-word! Now, an indistinctly remembered _______!

[**idiosyncrasies, humility, iconoclast, idyllic, illicit, ignominy**]

Review Exercise: Sentence Completions (pp. 145–48)

1. I had _______ from her something of her nature and much of her habits.
2. The man most _______ with the spirit of the time is the impressionable man.
3. The whole place was _______ clean.
4. He has _______ himself in any trades or pleasures for their own sake.
5. History is full, down to this day, of the _______ of kings and governors.
6. He had resolved to _______ the traitor on the sacred altar of his country.

[**immaculately, imbibed, imbued, immersed, immolate, imbecility**]

****

1. Pleasures _______ our intellectual vigour.
2. The press still speaks for truth though _______.
3. Her sweet voice clothed her words in a garment of _______ irony.
4. To truth, justice, love, the idea of _______ is essentially associated.
5. We were _______ in ice, and should probably never escape.
6. A great good will _______ great good.

[**impaled, impair, immutableness, impalpable, impart, immured**]

****

1. The atmosphere seemed to vibrate with the energy of an _______ world.
2. Riches are oftener an _______ than a stimulus to action.
3. Earth, my likeness, you look so _______, ample and spheric there.
4. Here we have the man, sly, subtle, hard, _______, and, withal, cold as ice.
5. It became _______ to lance the flying whale, or be content to lose him.
6. He did not allow any one outbreak to _______ the settled order.

[**impassive, imperious, impediment, impeccable, imperil, imperative**]

****

1. _______ resentment is a shade in a character.
2. Nothing was found to _______ him in any way, and there the matter dropped.
3. Through one of the broken panes I heard the rain _______ upon the earth.
4. History is an _______ and an injury.
5. I shingled the sides of my house, which were already _______ to rain.
6. The doors were all at once thrown open with a rushing _______.

[**impervious, impetuosity, impinge, impertinence, implicate, implacable**]

1. He had **implored** God to heal him as He had healed the Leper and made the Blind to see. —W. Somerset Maugham, *Of Human Bondage*
2. Oh! how immaterial* are all materials! What things real are there, but **imponderable** thoughts? —Herman Melville, *Moby Dick*
3. A passionate desire to have him understand the **import** of life, to learn to interpret it truly and honestly, swept over her. Leaning forward, her lips brushed his cheek. —Sherwood Anderson, *Winesburg, Ohio*
4. They were never **importunate** and yet never listless.* —Henry James, *The Turn of the Screw*
5. He that suffers by **imposture** has too often his virtue more impaired than his fortune. —Samuel Johnson, *The Rambler*
6. As a selfish man will **impoverish** his family and often bring them to ruin, so a selfish king brings ruin on his people and often plunges them into war. —W. M. Thackeray, *Vanity Fair*

****

1. **implore**; beg, entreat, beseech, plead, conjure, supplicate. —imploration; supplication. —imploratory; supplicatory.
2. **imponderable**; immeasurable, incalculable, inestimable, inconceivable. * immaterial; 1. incorporeal, unsubstantial. 2. insignificant, inconsequential.
3. **import**; 1. meaning, significance. 2. *v.* mean, signify.
4. **importunate**; overly begging, persistent, urgent, insistent, beseeching. —importunacy, —importune *v.* * listless; 1. indifferent. 2. sluggish, lethargic.
5. **imposture**; deception, fraud, sham. —impostor.
6. **impoverish**; 1. make poor, pauperize. 2. exhaust, deplete. —impoverished; needy, indigent. ※ impecunious; impoverished: *the impecunious artist.* ※ deplete; 1. use up: *depleting our natural resources.* 2. exhaust, enervate.

1. Curses always recoil on the head of him who **imprecates** them. —R. W. Emerson, *Compensation*

2. Our thoughts like rivulets issuing from distant springs, are each **impregnated** in its course with various mixtures, and tinged by infusions unknown to the other, yet at last easily unite into one stream. —Samuel Johnson, *The Rambler*

3. Eulalie raised her unmoved eye to mine, and seemed to expect, passively but securely, an **impromptu** tribute to her majestic charms. —Charlotte Brontë, *The Professor*

4. Mr. Micawber has his faults. I do not deny that he is **improvident**. . . . but I never will desert Mr. Micawber! —Charles Dickens, *David Copperfield*

5. His long **improvised** dirges will ring forever in my ears. —Edgar Allan Poe, *The Fall of the House of Usher*

6. I am equally confounded* at HER **impudence** and HIS credulity. How dared he believe what she told him in my disfavour! —Jane Austen, *Lady Susan*

****

1. **imprecate**; curse, swear, execrate. —imprecation. ***ant.*** benediction; grace.
2. **impregnate**; 1. infuse, imbue. 2. fertilize, inseminate. —impregnation.
3. **impromptu**; offhand, improvised, unrehearsed, extemporaneous.
4. **improvident**; shortsighted, imprudent. ***ant.*** provident. —improvidence.
5. **improvise**; ad-lib, speak impromptu, extemporize. —improvisation.
6. **impudence**; boldness, cheekiness, brazenness, insolence, impertinence, presumption. —impudent. * confound; perplex, bewilder, stupefy, *see p. 56, no. 2.*
※ obfuscate: confound, obscure, darken: *The sophists obfuscated the truth.*

♣ He that wrestles with us strengthens our nerves, and sharpens our skill. Our antagonist is our helper. —Edmund Burke, *Reflections on the Revolution in France*

1. It skills not* greatly who **impugns** our doom.
—Shakespeare, *King Henry VI, Part II*

2. It is true that bad example may have a pernicious* effect, especially the example of doing wrong to others with **impunity** to the wrong-doer. —John Stuart Mill, *On Liberty*

3. We **impute** deep-laid, far-sighted plans to Caesar and Napoleon; but the best of their power was in nature, not in them. —R. W. Emerson, *Spiritual Laws*

4. His old dog, Pilot, lay on one side, removed out of the way, and coiled up as if afraid of being **inadvertently** trodden upon. —Charlotte Brontë, *Jane Eyre*

5. Philip asked himself desperately what was the use of living at all. It all seemed **inane**. —W. Somerset Maugham, *Of Human Bondage*

6. Each herd was watched by the patient but **inauspicious** eyes of the turkey-buzzard.* —Charles Darwin, *The Voyage of the Beagle*

****

1. **impugn**; negate, challenge, contradict, gainsay. —impugnment, —impugnable. * it skills not; it matters not.
2. **impunity**; acquittal, absolution. * pernicious; harmful, injurious, noxious.
3. **impute**; attribute, ascribe, refer, assign. —imputation.
4. **inadvertently**; 1. carelessly, negligently. 2. unwittingly. —inadvertence.
5. **inane**; 1. empty, vain, worthless, futile. 2. silly. —inanely, —inaneness.
6. **inauspicious**; ill-omened, ominous, sinister, foreboding, unpropitious. * turkey-buzzard *also* turkey vulture; a vulture common in the New World.

♣ All the world's a stage,
And all the men and women merely players:
They have their exits and their entrances.
—Shakespeare, *As You Like It*

1. As the Heat-Ray went to and fro over Weybridge its impact was marked by flashes of **incandescent** white, that gave place at once to a smoky dance of lurid* flames. —H. G. Well, *The War of the Worlds*

2. . . . on the night of the wedding, he was **incarcerated** in the village cage* . . . —Charles Dickens, *The Pickwick Papers*

3. Obscurantism* is better than the light of **incendiary** torches. —Joseph Conrad, *Under Western Eyes*

4. Certainly virtue is like precious odours, most fragrant when they are **incensed** or crushed. —Francis Bacon, *Essays*

5. There was never any more **inception** than there is now,
   Nor any more youth or age than there is now,
   And will never be any more perfection than there is now,
   Nor any more heaven or hell than there is now.
   —Walt Whitman, "Song of Myself"

6. Then his eyes went muddy, as if he had lost his grip on the **inchoate** thought. —Jack London, *Before Adam*

****

1. **incandescent**; 1. shining, brilliant, radiant, luminous. 2. flaming, glowing, blazing. —incandescence. * lurid; bright, fiery, glaring, *see p. 183, no. 3.*
2. **incarcerate**; imprison, confine, immure. * cage; prison. ※ penitentiary; prison, reformatory (correctional) institution.
3. **incendiary**; 1. inflammatory, agitating. 2. arsonist. ※ pyromania; arsonist: *A pyromania set fire to the theater.* * obscurantism; opposition to enlightenment.
4. **incense**; 1. infuriate, enrage, inflame, exasperate. 2. aroma, balm.
5. **inception**; start, commencement, initiation. —inceptive, —incept *v.*
6. **inchoate**; 1. unformed, undeveloped, immature, rudimentary. 2. initial, inceptive, incipient, nascent. —inchoateness, —inchoately.

1. The forms, which are already dominant, or have some advantage over the other forms in their own country, give birth to the greatest number of new varieties or **incipient** species. —Charles Darwin, *The Origin of Species*

2. And let us make **incision** for your love,
   To prove whose blood is reddest, his or mine.
   —Shakespeare, *The Merchant of Venice*

3. The uncertainty of our duration ought at once to set bounds to our designs, and add **incitements** to our industry. —Samuel Johnson, *The Rambler*

4. He crawled out as outcasts go to face an **inclement** world. —Joseph Conrad, *Typhoon*

5. His **incognito**, which had as many holes as a sieve,* was not meant to hide a personality but a fact. —Joseph Conrad, *Lord Jim*

6. His wandering stare went round the table, with an expression incredibly **incongruous** with the words. —Joseph Conrad, *The Arrow of Gold*

****

1. **incipient**; commencing, inchoate, nascent, inceptive. —incipience.
2. **incision**; 1. cutting. 2. cut, slit, gash. —incisive; keen, sharp, acute, piercing, penetrating, sarcastic, mordant, trenchant. —incise *v.*
3. **incitement**; urge, encouragement, provocation, agitation, instigation.
4. **inclement**; severe, harsh, boisterous, tempestuous. —inclemency.
5. **incognito**; 1. anonymity, disguise. 2. *adj.* anonymous, disguised. ※ incognizance; unawareness, —incognizant. * sieve; utensil for sifting.
6. **incongruous**; discordant, dissonant, inconsonant. —incongruity.

♣ Every man's condition is a solution in hieroglyphic to those inquiries he would put. —R. W. Emerson, *Nature*

1. He heard in one room a tittering* and **incontinent**, slack laughter; in others the monologue of a scold, the rattling of dice, a lullaby, and one crying dully. —O. Henry, *The Furnished Room*

2. He was presented to a tutor by his mother with the complimentary accompaniment that he was an **incorrigible** dunce.* —Samuel Smiles, *Self Help*

3. Every year, every month, came some new **increment** to human achievement, a new country opened up, new mines, new scientific discoveries, a new machine! —H. G. Wells, *The War in the Air*

4. Caesarism* is human idolatry in its worst form—a worship of mere power, . . . A far healthier doctrine to **inculcate** among the nations would be that of self-help. —Samuel Smiles, *Self Help*

5. They formed the design of a great Confederacy, which it is **incumbent** on their successors to improve and perpetuate. —James Madison, *The Federalist Papers*

6. She has a faithful soul, an undaunted* spirit, and an **indefatigable** body. — Joseph Conrad, *Under Western Eyes*

****

1. **incontinent**; uncontrolled, unrestrained, uncurbed. —incontinence. * tittering; giggling. ※ snicker; snigger. ※ sneer; ridicule, disdain, gibe, jeer. ※ sneak; move in a furtive way, slink, skulk, lurk.
2. **incorrigible**; irremediable, uncorrectable, ineradicable. * dunce; fool, simpleton.
3. **increment**; addition, accruement, augmentation. ***ant.*** decrement. ※ increscent; waxing. ***ant.*** decrescent; waning. ※ crescendo. ***ant.*** diminuendo.
4. **inculcate**; edify, instill, indoctrinate. —inculcation. * Caesarism; autocracy.
5. **incumbent**; 1. obligatory, required, compulsory, mandatory, imperative. 2. current, sitting. —incumbency.
6. **indefatigable**; untiring, inexhaustible, unwearied, unremitting. * undaunted; gallant, unflinching, dauntless, intrepid, indomitable, gritty.

1. Alone in the world, cast off by it, and with this sole treasure [Pearl] to keep her heart alive, she felt that she possessed **indefeasible** rights against the world, and was ready to defend them to the death. —Nathaniel Hawthorne, *The Scarlet Letter*

2. It ["The Book of the Grotesque"] was never published, but I saw it once and it made an **indelible** impression on my mind. —Sherwood Anderson, *Winesburg, Ohio*

3. I was **indemnified** for so much suffering by a few delightful minutes of conversation with Mr. Huntingdon. —Anne Brontë, *The Tenant of Wildfell Hall*

4. His [John Williams'] services were accepted by the London Missionary Society; and his master allowed him to leave the ironmonger's shop before the expiry of his **indentures**. —Samuel Smiles, *Self Help*

5. Perker, I'll have this fellow prosecuted—**indicted**—I'll—I'll—I'll ruin him. —Charles Dickens, *The Pickwick Papers*

6. It is a fine thing, reader, to be lifted in a moment from **indigence** to wealth—a very fine thing. —Charlotte Brontë, *Jane Eyre*

****

1. **indefeasible**; irreversible, irrevocable, irretrievable, irreparable, unalterable. —indefeasibility, —indefeasibly.
2. **indelible**; inerasable, ineffaceable, unforgettable, inexpungible. —indelibility.
3. **indemnify**; 1. recompense, compensate, reimburse, requite, remunerate. 2. insure, protect. —indemnification. ※ amortize; pay off gradually, liquidate by installments: *He has amortized his college loan for twenty years.*
4. **indentures**; 1. agreement, contract. 2. indentation; jagged cut, nick, notch.
5. **indict**; accuse, charge, incriminate, prosecute, arraign. —indictment.
6. **indigence**; poverty, impoverishment, destitution, penury. —indigent.

1. Certain South American **indigenous** domestic dogs do not readily unite with European dogs. —Charles Darwin, *The Origin of Species*

2. . . . it seemed to him that the tie between husband and wife, even if breakable in prosperity, should be **indissoluble** in misfortune. —Edith Wharton, *The Age of Innocence*

3. None but the frivolous* or the **indolent** will say, "I am too old to learn." —Samuel Smiles, *Self Help*

4. Arkwright was a man of great force of character, **indomitable** courage, much worldly shrewdness, with a business faculty almost amounting to genius. —Samuel Smiles, *Self Help*

5. No power on earth, he swore, would **induce** him to marry his daughter to the son of such a villain. —W. M. Thackeray, *Vanity Fair*

6. Censure is willingly **indulged**, because it always implies some superiority. —Samuel Johnson, *The Rambler*

****

1. **indigenous**; 1. native, endemic, aboriginal. 2. innate, intrinsic, natural. —indigene *also* indigen; *n.* native. —indigenize.
2. **indissoluble**; lasting, insoluble, binding, permanent. —indissolubility.
3. **indolent**; lazy, slothful, sluggish. —indolence. * frivolous; foolish, silly.
4. **indomitable**; unconquerable, unbeatable, unyielding, invincible.
5. **induce**; 1. persuade, urge, incite, provoke, instigate. 2. bring about, cause, motivate, occasion, effect. 3. infer. ***ant.*** deduce. —inducement. —inducible.
6. **indulge**; 1. wallow, luxuriate. 2. pamper, gratify. 3. coddle, cosset. —indulgence, —indulgent. ※ pander; cater: *the farce that panders to people's low tastes.*

♣ The cruelest lies are often told in silence. —Robert L. Stevenson, *Truth of Intercourse*

1. They were never _______ and yet never listless.
2. What things real are there, but _______ thoughts?
3. He that suffers by _______ has his virtue more impaired than his fortune.
4. A selfish man will _______ his family and often bring them to ruin.
5. He had _______ God to heal him.
6. A desire to have him understand the _______ of life swept over her.

[**importunate, implored, import, imponderable, imposture, impoverish**]

****

1. His long _______ dirges will ring forever in my ears.
2. I am equally confounded at her _______ and his credulity.
3. I do not deny that he is _______, but I never will desert Mr. Micawber!
4. She seemed to expect an _______ tribute to her majestic charms.
5. Curses always recoil on the head of him who _______ them.
6. Our thoughts are each _______ in its course with various mixtures.

[**impudence, improvised, impregnated, imprecates, impromptu, improvident**]

****

1. Each herd was watched by the _______ eyes of the turkey-buzzard.
2. His old dog coiled up as if afraid of being _______ trodden upon.
3. Philip asked himself what was the use of living at all. It all seemed _______.
4. It skills not greatly who _______ our doom.
5. It is the example of doing wrong to others with _______ to the wrong-doer.
6. We _______ deep-laid, far-sighted plans to Caesar and Napoleon.

[**inadvertently, inauspicious, impugns, inane, impute, impunity**]

****

1. There was never any more _______ than there is now.
2. On the night of the wedding, he was _______ in the village cage.
3. Virtue is like precious odours, most fragrant when they are _______ or crushed.
4. The impact of the Heat-Ray was marked by flashes of _______ white.
5. Obscurantism is better than the light of _______ torches.
6. Then his eyes went muddy, as if he had lost his grip on the _______ thought.

[**inchoate, incandescent, incendiary, inception, incarcerated, incensed**]

Review Exercise: Sentence Completions (pp. 155–58)

1. The uncertainty of our duration ought to add _______ to our industry.
2. He crawled out as outcasts go to face an _______ world.
3. The expression was incredibly _______ with the words.
4. His _______ was not meant to hide a personality but a fact.
5. Let's make _______ for your love, to prove whose blood is reddest, his or mine.
6. The forms gave birth to the greatest number of _______ species.

[**inclement, incipient, incision, incognito, incongruous, incitements**]

****

1. He was an _______ dunce.
2. She has a faithful soul, an undaunted spirit, and an _______ body.
3. It is _______ on them to improve and perpetuate the Confederacy.
4. He heard in one room a tittering and _______, slack laughter.
5. A healthier doctrine to _______ among the nations would be that of self-help.
6. Every year, every month, came some new _______ to human achievement.

[**incontinent, incumbent, indefatigable, incorrigible, inculcate, increment**]

****

1. She felt that she possessed _______ rights against the world.
2. It is a fine thing to be lifted in a moment from _______ to wealth.
3. I was _______ for suffering by a few minutes of conversation with him.
4. His master allowed him to leave the shop before the expiry of his _______.
5. I'll have this fellow prosecuted—_______—I'll—I'll—I'll ruin him.
6. The book made an _______ impression on me.

[**indigence, indefeasible, indentures, indemnified, indelible, indicted**]

****

1. Censure is willingly _______, because it always implies some superiority.
2. They are South American _______ domestic dogs, not European dogs.
3. No power on earth would _______ him to marry his daughter to such a villain.
4. Arkwright was a man of _______ courage.
5. The tie between husband and wife should be _______ in misfortune.
6. None but the frivolous or the _______ will say, "I am too old to learn."

[**induce, indulged, indigenous, indissoluble, indolent, indomitable**]

1. Arva is the name bestowed upon a root the properties of which are both **inebriating** and medicinal. —Herman Melville, *Typee*
2. She sighed a sigh of **ineffable** satisfaction, as if her cup of happiness were now full. —Charlotte Brontë, *Jane Eyre*
3. Every property of matter is a school for the understanding—its solidity or resistance, its **inertia**, its extension, its figure, its divisibility. —R. W. Emerson, *Nature*
4. What other dungeon* is so dark as one's own heart! What jailer so **inexorable** as one's self! —Nathaniel Hawthorne, *The House of the Seven Gables*
5. In England the police system, if not the most **infallible** in the world, is certainly the most incorruptible. —E. Phillips Oppenheim, *The Yellow Crayon*
6. No sooner did the hook touch the sea, than a hundred **infatuates** contended for the honor of capture. —Herman Melville, *The Encantadas*

****

1. **inebriating**; intoxicating, besotting, befuddling. —inebriation, —inebriate.
2. **ineffable**; unutterable, inexpressible, indefinable. ※ ineffaceable; unerasable, memorable, indelible: *ineffaceable scars.*
3. **inertia**; 1. inactivity, lethargy, torpor, stupor, stagnancy. 2. unwillingness to change. —inert *adj.*
4. **inexorable**; pitiless, ruthless, merciless. * dungeon; underground prison.
5. **infallible**; unfailing, unerring, flawless, perfect, impeccable.
6. **infatuate**; 1. *n.* the obsessed, the captivated. 2. *v.* enchant, intoxicate, bewitch, enamor. —infatuation.

♣ How luscious lies the pea within
The pod that Duty locks!

—Emily Dickinson, "Forbidden fruit a flavor has"

1. In point of fact the three actions of perceiving, determining, and responding were sequential; but so **infinitesimal** were the intervals of time between them that they appeared simultaneous. —Jack London, *The Call of the Wild*

2. A friend should bear his friend's **infirmities**. —Shakespeare, *Julius Caesar*

3. All **infractions** of love and equity* in our social relations are speedily punished. They are punished by fear. —R. W. Emerson, *Compensation*

4. Among these men there was a stringent* code of honour, any **infringement** of which was punished by death. —Arthur Conan Doyle, *A Study in Scarlet*

5. When attacked sometimes, Becky had a knack* of adopting a demure,* ***ingénue*** air, under which she was most dangerous. —W. M. Thackeray, *Vanity Fair*

6. He was very gentle, with **ingratiating** eyes and soft lips. —Joseph Conrad, *Under Western Eyes*

****

1. **infinitesimal**; infinitely minute or tiny, microscopic, atomic. —infinitesimalness, —infinitesimally. ※ minuscule; very small, minute, tiny: *The reward for the information was too minuscule.*
2. **infirmity**; 1. weakness, feebleness, frailty, defect. 2. disease, malady, ailment. —infirmary; clinic, health center, hospital.
3. **infraction**; violation, breach, infringement, transgression, contravention. —infract. * equity; 1. fairness, justice. 2. stock, value of property.
4. **infringement**; violation, breach, infraction, encroachment. * stringent; 1. strict, rigorous. 2. urgent, *see p. 301, no. 2.*
5. **ingénue**; innocent girl, an actress playing such a part. ※ ingenuous; innocent, naïve, artless. —ingenuousness. ※ ingenious; 1. creative, smart. 2. subtle. —ingenuity. * knack; talent, aptitude. * demure; shy and reserved, modest.
6. **ingratiating**; fawning, flattering, courtly. —ingratiation, —ingratiate.

1. When any creature is by its make **inimical** to other creatures, nature in effect labels that creature, much as an apothecary* does a poison. —Herman Melville, *The Confidence-Man*

2. When he had been enlightened, he turned to Newman with an **inimitable** elderly grace. —Henry James, *The American*

3. Lead us not into temptation. Forgive us our sins. Wash away our **iniquities**. —Oscar Wilde, *The Picture of Dorian Gray*

4. The ill-assorted* and **injudicious** attire of the individual only served to render his awkwardness more conspicuous. —James Fenimore Cooper, *The Last of the Mohicans*

5. Whatever crushes individuality is despotism, by whatever name it may be called, and whether it professes to be enforcing the will of God or the **injunctions** of men. —John Stuart Mill, *On Liberty*

6. Industry is a means and not an end; and mankind work only to get something which they want. What that something is depends partly on their **innate**, and partly on their acquired, desires. —Thomas Henry Huxley, *Science and Culture*

****

1. **inimical**; 1. hostile, antagonistic, rancorous. 2. harmful, injurious, adverse. —inimicalness. * apothecary; 1. pharmacist. 2. pharmacy, dispensary.
2. **inimitable**; supreme, peerless, unsurpassable, nonpareil, consummate.
3. **iniquity**; sin, injustice, wickedness, evil. —iniquitous.
4. **injudicious**; unwise, indiscreet, imprudent. * ill-assorted; mismatched.
5. **injunction**; order, dictate, command, mandate, ordinance. —injunctive.
6. **innate**; inherent, connate, intrinsic, immanent. —innateness, —innately.

♣ God is alone,—but the devil, he is far from being alone; he sees a great deal of company; he is legion. —Henry David Thoreau, *Walden*

1. Her mind was a store-house of **innocuous** anecdote and any question about her acquaintances brought forth a volume of detail. —Edith Wharton, *Ethan Frome*
2. What is the universal sense of want and ignorance, but the fine **innuendo** by which the soul makes its enormous claim? —R. W. Emerson, *The Over-Soul*
3. **Inordinate** desires, of whatever kind, ought to be repressed upon yet a higher consideration; they must be considered as enemies not only to HAPPINESS but to VIRTUE. —Samuel Johnson, *The Adventurer*
4. He would have let the house, but could find no tenant, in consequence of its ineligible* and **insalubrious** site. —Charlotte Brontë, *Jane Eyre*
5. To suppose that the maze is **inscrutable** to diligence, or the heights inaccessible to perseverance, is to submit tamely* to the tyranny of fancy. —Samuel Johnson, *The Rambler*
6. Treacherous drafts* came down chimneys and **insidious** currents of deadly cold found their way through key-holes. —Kate Chopin, *The Awakening*

****

1. **innocuous**; 1. harmless, inoffensive, innoxious. 2. dull. —innocuousness.
2. **innuendo**; indirect implication or intimation, allusive remark, insinuation.
3. **inordinate**; intemperate, immoderate, extravagant. —inordinacy.
4. **insalubrious**; unhealthy, unwholesome. —insalubrity. * ineligible; 1. unfit, unsuitable. 2. disqualified. ※ inedible; uneatable. ※ illegible; unreadable, indecipherable. ※ inept; 1. inapt, absurd. 2. clumsy, maladroit. —ineptitude: *the surgeon's ineptitude*. ※ ineluctable; inevitable, ineludible: *The hero is facing his ineluctable fate.*
5. **inscrutable**; inexplicable, enigmatic, arcane. * tamely; mildly, docilely.
6. **insidious**; sly, treacherous, crafty, cunning, wily. * draft; air current.

1. He **insinuated** that his aloofness was due to distaste for all that was common and low. —W. Somerset Maugham, *Of Human Bondage*
2. The mind, which has feasted* on the luxurious wonders of fiction, has no taste of the **insipidity** of truth. —Samuel Johnson, *Preface to Shakespeare*
3. Youth is **insolent**; it is its right—its necessity; it has got to assert itself, and all assertion in this world of doubts is a defiance, is an insolence. —Joseph Conrad, *Lord Jim*
4. The ladies of Watteau [French painter, 1684–1721], gay and **insouciant**, seemed to wander with their cavaliers* among the great trees, whispering to one another careless, charming things, and yet somehow oppressed by a nameless fear. —W. Somerset Maugham, *Of Human Bondage*
5. The iniquity* of the **instigation** proved its antidote.* —Charlotte Brontë, *The Professor*
6. How **insular** and pathetically solitary are all the people we know! —R. W. Emerson, *Society and Solitude*

****

1. **insinuate**; imply, intimate, suggest indirectly, allude. —insinuation.
2. **insipidity**; dullness, vapidity. —insipid; lackluster, jejune. * feast; indulge.
3. **insolent**; arrogant, haughty, impudent, smug. —insolence; presumption. ※ hubris; insolence: *Doctor Faustus committed a sin of hubris in* Doctor Faustus.
4. **insouciant**; carefree, indifferent, apathetic, listless. —insouciance. * cavalier; knight. ※ cavalry; horse-soldier: *the valiant cavalry.*
5. **instigation**; incitement, provocation, agitation, goading. —instigate. * iniquity; wickedness, *see p. 163, no. 3.* * antidote; antitoxin, antivenom.
6. **insular**; isolated, detached. —insularity, —insulate; maroon, sequester.

♣ Silence is the only Voice of our God. —Herman Melville, *Pierre*

1. The attention of the **insurgents** had been drawn away from murder to plunder* . . .—Arthur Conan Doyle, *The White Company*

2. And never yet did **insurrection** want
   Such water-colors to impaint his cause.
   —Shakespeare, *King Henry IV, Part I*

3. Self-respect, self-help, application,* industry, **integrity**—all are of the nature of habits, not beliefs. —Samuel Smiles, *Self Help*

4. . . . I conjured* him to **intercede** for me with the natives, and endeavour to procure their consent to my leaving them. —Herman Melville, *Typee*

5. Yes, the paper was booming right along, for the **Interdict** made no impression, got no grip, while the war lasted. —Mark Twain, *A Connecticut Yankee*

6. The East Wind, an **interloper** in the dominions of Westerly weather, is an impassive-faced tyrant with a sharp poniard* held behind his back for a treacherous stab. —Joseph Conrad, *The Mirror of the Sea*

****

1. **insurgent**; 1. *n.* rebel, mutineer, revolter, insurrectionary. 2. *adj.* revolting, rebellious, mutinous. —insurgence. * plunder; pillage, marauding, rapine.
2. **insurrection**; revolt, rebellion, insurgence, mutiny. —insurrectionary.
3. **integrity**; 1. honesty, rectitude, probity. 2. wholeness. ※ integration; synthesis, ※ holism; a theory that a part cannot be present without relation to the whole. —holistic: *holistic medicine*. * application; 1. attention. 2. utilization.
4. **intercede**; mediate, arbitrate. —intercession, —intercessor. ※ intercept; interrupt. —interception, —interceptor. * conjure; 1. appeal strongly. 2. evoke.
5. **interdict**; 1. ban, prohibition, restraint. 2. *v.* forbid, debar. ※ outlaw; bandit.
6. **interloper**; intruder, interferer, meddler. ※ interlocutor; dialogist. ※ interpolate; insert. ※ extrapolate; infer, estimate: *extrapolating an incredible result from the research*. ※ redact; edit. —redactor. * poniard; dagger.

1. The forest seemed **interminable**; nowhere did he discover a break in it, not even a woodman's road. —Ambrose Bierce, *An Occurrence at Owl Creek Bridge*

2. It was the only battle which I have ever witnessed, the only battle-field I ever trod while the battle was raging; **internecine** war; the red republicans [the red ants] on the one hand, and the black imperialists [the black ants] on the other. —Henry David Thoreau, *Walden*

3. The **interregnum** has been long, both as to time and distance. —Mark Twain, *The Innocents Abroad*

4. The narrow-leaved willow lay along the surface of the water in masses of light green foliage, **interspersed** with the large white balls of the button-bush.* —Henry David Thoreau, *A Week on the Concord and Merrimack Rivers*

5. The light in the room found its way outward through the **interstices** of closed wooden shutters. —Wilkie Collins, *The Two Destinies*

6. My courage always rises with every attempt to **intimidate** me. —Jane Austen, *Pride and Prejudice*

****

1. **interminable**; endless, everlasting, infinite. —interminableness. ※ eon *or* aeon; everlastingness, eternity: *Now he wants to sleep for eons.*
2. **internecine**; mutually fatal, destructive to both sides.
3. **interregnum**; 1. pause, interval, hiatus. 2. temporary suspension of a government's function between two regimes. ※ interim; 1. temporary. 2. *n.* interval.
4. **intersperse**; scatter, diffuse, distribute, sprinkle, bestrew, disperse. —interspersion. * button-bush; North American shrub with ball-shaped flower heads.
5. **interstice**; crevice, cleft. —interstitial.
6. **intimidate**; threaten, menace, browbeat, bulldoze. —intimidatory; minatory.

1. He has a sullen, rebellious spirit; a violent temper; and an untoward,* **intractable** disposition. —Charles Dickens, *David Copperfield*

2. Assurance and **intrepidity**, under the white banner of seeming modesty, clear the way for merit, that would otherwise be discouraged by difficulties in its journey. —4th Earl of Chesterfield, *Letters to His Son*

3. Some men classify objects by color and size and other accidents of appearance; others by **intrinsic** likeness, or by the relation of cause and effect. —R. W. Emerson, *History*

4. . . . and so the heart of man might be bathed by an **inundation** of eternal love . . . —R. W. Emerson, *Compensation*

5. Thy Fates open their hands; let thy blood and spirit embrace them; and, to **inure** thyself to what thou art like to be, cast thy humble slough* and appear fresh. —Shakespeare, *Twelfth Night*

6. MANY have made witty **invectives** against Usury.* —Francis Bacon, *Essays*

****

1. **intractable**; obstinate, stubborn, headstrong, bullheaded, obdurate. * untoward; 1. unmanageable, unruly, perverse, refractory. 2. unlucky.
2. **intrepidity**; bravery, dauntlessness, valour, pluck. —intrepid; gallant, valiant.
3. **intrinsic**; inborn, inbred, inherent. ***ant.*** extrinsic. —intrinsically.
4. **inundation**; flood, overflow, deluge. —inundate *v.*
5. **inure**; adapt, adjust, accommodate, habituate, accustom, naturalize, acclimatize. —inurement. * slough; swamp, bog.
6. **invective**; abuse, vituperation, venom, revilement, obloquy. —invectiveness. * usury; excessive rate of interest, *see p. 327, no. 1.*

♣ A beauty not explicable is dearer than a beauty which we can see to the end of. —R. W. Emerson, *The Poet*

1. A hundred _______ contended for the honor of capture.
2. The properties of the root are both _______ and medicinal.
3. She sighed a sigh of _______ satisfaction.
4. The solidity, resistance, or _______ of matter is a school fo the understanding.
5. What other jailer is so _______ as one's self!
6. The police system, if not the _______ in the world, is the most incorruptible.

[**inexorable, infallible, infatuates, inebriating, inertia, ineffable**]

****

1. Any _______ of the code was punished by death.
2. When attacked sometimes, she had a knack of adopting a demure, _______ air.
3. He was very gentle, with _______ eyes and soft lips.
4. So _______ were the intervals of time between perceiving and responding.
5. A friend should bear his friend's _______.
6. All _______ of love and equity in our social relations are speedily punished.

[**infringement, infirmities, infractions, ingénue, ingratiating, infinitesimal**]

****

1. Her attire is ill-assorted and _______.
2. Despotism professes to be enforcing the will of God or the _______ of men.
3. It depends partly on their _______, and partly on their acquired, desires.
4. He turned to Newman with an _______ elderly grace.
5. Lead us not into temptation. Forgive us our sins. Wash away our _______.
6. The creature is by its make _______ to other creatures.

[**inimitable, iniquities, injudicious, inimical, injunctions, innate**]

****

1. _______ desires ought to be repressed upon yet a higher consideration.
2. _______ currents of deadly cold found their way through key-holes.
3. Her mind was a store-house of _______ anecdote.
4. The soul makes its enormous claim by the fine _______.
5. The maze is not _______ to diligence.
6. The site of the house was ineligible and _______.

[**insalubrious, inordinate, innuendo, insidious, inscrutable, innocuous**]

Review Exercise: Sentence Completions (pp. 165–68)

1. The iniquity of the _______ proved its antidote.
2. How _______ and pathetically solitary are all the people we know!
3. He _______ that his aloofness was due to distaste for all that was common.
4. The mind has no taste of the _______ of truth.
5. The ladies of Watteau were gay and _______.
6. Youth is _______; it is its right—its necessity; it has got to assert itself.

[**insular, instigation, insouciant, insolent, insinuated, insipidity**]

****

1. And never yet did _______ want such water-colors to impaint his cause.
2. I conjured him to _______ for me with the natives.
3. The _______ made no impression, got no grip, while the war lasted.
4. The East Wind is an _______ in the dominions of Westerly weather.
5. The attention of the _______ had been drawn away from murder to plunder.
6. Self-respect, application, _______—all are of the nature of habits, not beliefs.

[**integrity, insurgents, interloper, intercede, interdict, insurrection**]

****

1. The _______ has been long, both as to time and distance.
2. It was a raging, _______ war.
3. My courage always rises with every attempt to _______ me.
4. The surface of the water was _______ with the large balls of the button-bush.
5. The forest seemed _______; nowhere did he discover a break in it.
6. The light found its way outward through the _______ of closed shutters.

[**interregnum, interminable, internecine, interstices, intimidate, interspersed**]

****

1. He has a sullen, rebellious spirit; and an untoward, _______ disposition.
2. Some men classify objects by color and size; others by _______ likeness.
3. Many have made witty _______ against usury.
4. _______, under the white banner of modesty, clears the way for merit.
5. To _______ thyself to what thou art like to be, cast thy humble slough.
6. And so the heart of men might be bathed by an _______ of eternal love.

[**intractable, intrinsic, inundation, inure, intrepidity, invectives**]

1. We not uncommonly hear the doctrine of utility **inveighed** against as a godless doctrine. —John Stuart Mill, *Utilitarianism*
2. She will be sacrificed. She will be **inveigled** and married to that connection of yours. —Charles Dickens, *Our Mutual Friend*
3. An **inveterate** selfishness will imagine all advantages diminished in proportion as they are communicated.* —Samuel Johnson, *The Rambler*
4. Either the change in the quality of air from heavy to light, or the sense of being amid new scenes where there were no **invidious** eyes upon her, sent up her spirits wonderfully. —Thomas Hardy, *Tess*
5. Alfred in his funeral ode on the victor of Waterloo ventures not to call him the greatest soldier of all time, though in the same ode he **invokes** Nelson as 'the greatest sailor since our world began.' —Herman Melville, *Billy Budd*
6. Being of an **irascible** temper, he [Benvenuto Cellini] was constantly getting into scrapes,* and was frequently under the necessity of flying for his life. —Samuel Smiles, *Self Help*

****

1. **inveigh**; upbraid, rail, chastise, vituperate, castigate. —inveigher.
2. **inveigle**; entice, seduce, allure. —inveiglement.
3. **inveterate**; ingrained, incorrigible. —inveteracy. * communicate; share. ※ invertebrate; 1. spineless. 2. spineless animal. ***ant.*** vertebrate.
4. **invidious**; disagreeable, unpleasant, offensive. —invidiousness.
5. **invoke**; 1. call forth, summon, conjure. 2. beg, implore. —invocation.
6. **irascible**; irritable, peevish, choleric, fretful, waspish, splenetic, spleenful. * scrape: predicament, quandary.

♣ Almost all the processes employed in the arts and manufactures fall within the range either of physics or of chemistry. —Thomas Henry Huxley, *Science and Culture*

1. Then the sun rose, a ray of yellow gold stole across the sky, and the sky was **iridescent**.—W. Somerset Maugham, *Of Human Bondage*

2. My first quarter at Lowood seemed an age; and not the golden age either: it comprised* an **irksome** struggle with difficulties in habituating myself to new rules and unwonted* tasks. —Charlotte Brontë, *Jane Eyre*

3. The summer came, breathless and sultry,* and even at night there was no coolness to rest one's **jaded** nerves. —W. Somerset Maugham, *The Moon and Sixpence*

4. At last, though long, our **jarring** notes agree:
   And time it is, when raging war is done.
   —Shakespeare, *The Taming of the Shrew*

5. All seems infected that th' infected spy,
   As all looks yellow to the **jaundiced** eye.
   —Alexander Pope, *An Essay on Criticism*

6. He continued to wear his spruce* black coat and his bowler hat, always a little too small for him, in a dapper,* **jaunty** manner. —W. Somerset Maugham, *The Moon and Sixpence*

****

1. **iridescent**; showing rainbow colours, colourful, prismatic. —iridescence
2. **irksome**; boring, tedious, wearisome, prosaic. —irksomeness, —irk *v.* * comprise; include, consist of. * unwonted; unconventional, atypical.
3. **jaded**; tired, wearied, exhausted. —jade *v.*; 1. wear out. 2. green stone of jadeite or nephrite. * sultry; sweltering, torrid. —sultriness, —sultrily.
4. **jarring**; 1. discordant, dissonant, cacophonous. 2. harsh, raspy. —jarringly.
5. **jaundiced**; 1. affected with jaundice. 2. biased. —jaundice; 1. the yellows, a disease of the liver. 2. yellowing of the skin or tissues by diseases.
6. **jaunty**; sprightly, buoyant, debonair. —jauntiness; buoyancy. ※ jaunt; excursion, outing. ※ expedition; exploration. * spruce; neat, snug. * dapper; trim.

1. We pass in the world for sects and schools, for erudition* and piety,* and we are all the time **jejune** babes. —R. W. Emerson, *Spiritual Laws*

2. He is a pleasant fellow, and would **jilt** you creditably. —Jane Austen, *Pride and Prejudice*.

3. I was afraid he would ask me to give him the berth* in some ghastly **jocular** hint that I could not refuse to take. —Joseph Conrad, *The Mirror of the Sea*

4. Prayer is the contemplation of the facts of life from the highest point of view. It is the soliloquy of a beholding and **jubilant** soul. —R. W. Emerson, *Self-Reliance*

5. It sounds nothing to hear, but it was hellish to see. It wasn't like a man; it was like some damned **Juggernaut**. —Robert L. Stevenson, *Dr. Jekyll and Mr. Hyde*

6. Just at this **juncture**, however, down came the rain with a violence that put all thoughts of slumber to flight. —Herman Melville, *Typee*

****

1. **jejune**; 1. immature, juvenile, puerile. 2. dull, banal, prosaic, insipid. 3. barren. * erudition; knowledge, learning, *see p. 106, no. 3.* * piety; devoutness.
2. **jilt**; 1. cast off, desert, betray. 2. woman who forsakes a lover.
3. **jocular**; humorous, jocose, facetious. —jocularity. * berth; 1. bunk on a ship. 2. accommodations. 3. dock, wharf, anchorage, quay.
4. **jubilant**; cheerful, rejoicing, exultant, gleeful. —jubilance, —jubilation; bliss, glee, rapture. ※ euphoria; jubilation: *Euphoria induces euphoria.*
5. **Juggernaut**; 1. overpowering force, overwhelming object. 2. idol of Krishna, Hindu deity.
6. **juncture**; 1. turning point, landmark. 2. junction, connection, nexus. —junctural.

♣ To the idea of life victory or strife is necessary; as virtue consists not simply in the absence of vices, but in the overcoming of them. —S. T. Coleridge, *On Poesy or Art*

1. Preserve the right of thy place; but stir not questions of **jurisdiction**: and rather assume thy right in silence and *de facto** [as an accepted fact], than voice it with claims and challenges. —Francis Bacon, *Essays*

2. The feelings excited by improper art are **kinetic**, desire or loathing . . . The arts which excite them, pornographical or didactic, are therefore improper arts. —James Joyce, *A Portrait of the Artist as a Young Man*

3. When a youthful nobleman steals jewellery we call the act **kleptomania**. —George Eliot, *Middlemarch*

4. No, no, I am a rascal; a scurvy* railing* **knave**, a very filthy rogue. —Shakespeare, *Troilus and Cressida*

5. . . . McDougal's cave was but a vast **labyrinth** of crooked aisles that ran into each other and out again and led nowhere. —Mark Twain, *The Adventures of Tom Sawyer*

6. He dreaded to expose his **lacerated** feeling to her neutrality* and misconception. —George Eliot, *Middlemarch*

****

1. **jurisdiction**; legal authority, the right to practice laws, the power to supervise justice. —jurisdictional. ※ jurisprudence; science of law: *medical jurisprudence*; forensic medicine. * de facto; 1. actual. 2. in fact.
2. **kinetic**; of motion, energizing, dynamic. ***ant.*** static. —kinetics, —kineticist. ※ kinesthetic; of the sensation of bodily movement: *kinaesthetic learning*.
3. **kleptomania** *also* **cleptomania**; obsessive and irresistible habit to steal without economic motivation. —kleptomaniac; habitual stealer. ※ recidivism; customary relapse into crime. —recidivate, —recidivous.
4. **knave**; villain, rogue, scoundrel. —knavish. * scurvy; mean. * rail; abuse, revile.
5. **labyrinth**; 1. maze, jungle. 2. tangle. —labyrinthic; intricate, complicated.
6. **lacerated**; torn, hurt. * neutrality; noninterference. ※ neuter; asexual.

1. He was by turns devout* and obscene, merry and **lachrymose**. —W. Somerset Maugham, *Of Human Bondage*

2. There is no doubt whatever that I was a **lackadaisical** young spooney.* —Charles Dickens, *David Copperfield*

3. Like most men of action, he is **laconic** in speech . . . —Arthur Conan Doyle, *The Lost World*

4. It is a close night, though the damp cold is searching too, and there is a **laggard** mist a little way up in the air. —Charles Dickens, *Bleak House*

5. My counsel is, that you use the point of your pen, not the feather; let your first attempt be a *coup d'éclat** in the way of libel, **lampoon**, or satire. —Jonathan Swift, *A Letter of Advice to a Young Poet*

6. Mrs. Highcamp hung with **languid** but unaffected interest upon the warm and impetuous* volubility* of her left-hand neighbor, Victor Lebrun. —Kate Chopin, *The Awakening*

****

1. **lachrymose**; weepy, mournful, woeful, dolorous, lugubrious. —lachrymation, —lachrymatory: *lachrymatory shell; tear shell.* * devout; reverent.
2. **lackadaisical**; languid, listless, lethargic, inert. —lackadaisy. * spooney *also* spoony; 1. fool. 2. *adj.* silly, excessively sentimental, gushy.
3. **laconic**; concise, terse, succinct, compendious. —laconism, —laconically.
4. **laggard**; 1. slow, dilatory, sluggard. 2. lounger, straggler, dawdler. —laggardly.
5. **lampoon**; 1. satire, parody. 2. *v.* ridicule, satirize. —lampoonery, —lampoonist. * *coup d'éclat* ; brilliant stroke.
6. **languid**; 1. uninterested, indifferent, listless. 2. inert, languorous, torpid, lethargic, enervated, feckless. —languor. * impetuous; ardent. * volubility; fluency.

♣ Prosperity doth best discover vice, but Adversity doth best discover virtue. —Francis Bacon, *Essays*

1. I had Miss Sophia's bird in my hand, and thinking the poor creature **languished** for liberty, I own I could not forbear giving it what it desired. —Henry Fielding, *Tom Jones*

2. He is a public offender. What has he been guilty of? Murder, manslaughter . . . **larceny**, conspiracy, fraud? —Charles Dickens, *Little Dorrit*

3. He capers* nimbly* in a lady's chamber.
   To the **lascivious** pleasing of a lute.

   —Shakespeare, *King Richard III*

4. A terrible **lassitude** settled upon Philip. —W. Somerset Maugham, *Of Human Bondage*

5. I see very plainly* ABRAHAM LINCOLN's dark brown face, with the deep-cut lines, the eyes, always to me with a deep **latent** sadness in the expression. —Walt Whitman, *Abraham Lincoln*

6. Having supposed that there was sense where there is no sense, and a **laudable** ambition where there is not a laudable ambition, I am well out of my mistake. —Charles Dickens, *A Tale of Two Cities*

****

1. **languish**; flag, droop, weaken, wither. —languished; feeble, wasted.
2. **larceny**; thievery, theft, pilferage. —larcenous, —larcener; thief.
3. **lascivious**; lewd, libidinous, bawdy, lecherous, salacious. —lasciviousness. * caper; frisk, gambol, frolic. * nimbly; agilely, lightly.
4. **lassitude**; 1. languor, lethargy, enervation, inertia, ennui. 2. fatigue, exhaustion.
5. **latent**; potential, lurking, dormant, quiescent, immanent. —latency. * plainly; obviously, unmistakably, apparently.
6. **laudable**; commendable, praiseworthy, meritorious. —laud. ※ meritocracy; a society where promotion depends on one's ability: *They say America is a meritocracy.* —meritocratic.

1. So vainly is wit **lavished** upon fugitive* topics, so little can architecture secure duration when the ground is false. —Samuel Johnson, *The Idler*

2. It is common to find young men ardent and diligent in the pursuit of knowledge, but the progress of life very often produces **laxity** and indifference. —Samuel Johnson, *The Idler*

3. Much drink may be said to be an equivocator* with **lechery**: it makes him, and it mars him . . . and disheartens* him. —Shakespeare, *Macbeth*

4. He never was **leery** of anything on two feet . . . —Jack London, *The Valley of the Moon*

5. . . . , and the frightful forms of odious* and oppressive poll-taxes, have been played off with all the ingenious dexterity of political **legerdemain**. —Alexander Hamilton, *The Federalist Papers*

6. Abate thy rage, great duke!
   Good bawcock,* bate* thy rage! Use **lenity**, sweet chuck!*
   —Shakespeare, *King Henry V*

****

1. **lavish**; 1. waste, shower, squander. 2. bounteous, munificent, unstinting. 3. abundant, exuberant. —lavishness. * fugitive; 1. passing. 2. runaway.
2. **laxity**; looseness, slackness, negligence, remissness. —lax, —laxly, —laxative; purgative, cathartic. ※ loll; hang laxly, droop, flag, sag.
3. **lechery**; lust, lewdness, salaciousness, prurience. * equivocator; hedger, prevaricator. —equivocation; ambiguity, evasion, shuffling. * dishearten; dispirit.
4. **leery**; 1. dubious, skeptical, suspicious. 2. wary, cautious, chary. —leeriness.
5. **legerdemain**; trickery, deception, juggling, chicanery. * odious; detestable.
6. **lenity**; mercy, clemency, benevolence, grace. —lenience, —lenient. * bawcock; fine fellow. * bate; lessen, moderate. * chuck; darling, dear.

1. . . . he said this complete restoration, though only temporary, was a hopeful sign, proving that there was no permanent **lesion** to prevent ultimate recovey. —George Eliot, *The Mill on the Floss*

2. Competition allowed, stimulus would be given. There would be no **lethargy** of monopoly. —Herman Melville, *The Confidence-Man*

3. Love, which is the essence of God, is not for **levity**, but for the total worth of man. —R. W. Emerson, *Friendship*

4. In nature, as in law, it may be **libelous** to speak some truths. —Herman Melville, *The Encantadas*

5. A great **licentiousness** treads on the heels of a reformation.* —R. W. Emerson, *History*

6. Particularly loathsome to the **Lilliputians** are crimes of false accusation, treason, and fraud—all of which are associated with ambition, the primary vice against order. —Jonathan Swift, *Gulliver's Travels*

****

1. **lesion**; 1. injury, sore, bruise, trauma. 2. *v.* hurt.
2. **lethargy**; stupor, torpor, lassitude, languor, inertia. —lethargize, —lethargic.
3. **levity**; fickleness, frivolity, flippancy.
4. **libelous**; defamatory, slanderous, calumnious *or* calumniatory. —libel *n.*, *v.*
5. **licentiousness**; immorality, wantonness, dissipation, profligation. —licentiously. * reformation; improvement, amelioration. ***ant.*** deformation.
6. **Lilliputian**; 1. tiny person in Lilliput [a country in the novel]. 2. dwarf. 3. petty.

♣ In many respects man is the most ruthlessly ferocious of beasts. —William James, *The Principles of Psychology*

Review Exercise: Sentence Completions (pp. 171–74)

1. She will be _______ and married to that connection of yours.
2. There were no _______ eyes upon her.
3. An ______ selfishness will imagine all advantages diminished.
4. In the ode he _______ Nelson as 'the greatest sailor since our world began.'
5. Being of an _______ temper, he was constantly getting into scrapes.
6. We often hear the doctrine of utility _______ against as a godless doctrine.

[**invidious, inveterate, inveighed, irascible, invokes, inveigled**]

****

1. At last, our _______ notes agree.
2. All looks yellow to the _______ eye.
3. Then the sun rose . . . and the sky was _______.
4. My first quarter at Lowood comprised an _______ struggle with difficulties.
5. He wore his spruce black coat and his bowler hat in a dapper, _______ manner.
6. Even at night there was no coolness to rest one's _______ nerves.

[**iridescent, jarring, jaundiced, irksome, jaunty, jaded**]

****

1. It wasn't like a man; it was like some damned _______.
2. Just at this _______, however, down came the rain with a violence.
3. Prayer is the soliloquy of a beholding and _______ soul.
4. We are all the time _______ babes.
5. He asked me to give him the berth in some ghastly _______ hint.
6. He is a pleasant fellow, and would _______ you creditably.

[**juggernaut, jubilant, juncture, jilt, jocular, jejune**]

****

1. No, no, I am a rascal; a scurvy railing _______, a very filthy rogue.
2. The feelings excited by improper art are _______, desire or loathing.
3. McDougal's cave was but a vast _______ of crooked aisles.
4. Preserve the right of thy place; but stir not questions of _______.
5. When a youthful nobleman steals jewellery we call the act _______.
6. He dreaded to expose his _______ feeling to her neutrality.

[**jurisdiction, labyrinth, knave, kinetic, lacerated, kleptomania**]

Review Exercise: Sentence Completions (pp. 175–78)

1. Let your first attempt be a *coup d'éclat* in the way of libel, _______, or satire.
2. Mrs. Highcamp hung with _______ but unaffected interest upon the gentleman.
3. Like most men of action, he is _______ in speech.
4. There is a _______ mist a little way up in the air.
5. He was by turns devout and obscene, merry and _______.
6. There is no doubt whatever that I was a _______ young spooney.

[**lackadaisical, lachrymose, lampoon, languid, laggard, laconic**]

****

1. I saw a deep _______ sadness in the expression.
2. What has he been guilty of? Murder, arson, forgery, swindling, _______?
3. I thought the poor creature (Miss Sophia's bird) _______ for liberty.
4. A terrible _______ settled upon him.
5. There was a _______ ambition where there is not a laudable ambition.
6. He capers nimbly in a lady's chamber to the _______ pleasing of a lute.

[**larceny, latent, lassitude, languished, laudable, lascivious**]

****

1. The poll-taxes have been played off with all the dexterity of political _______.
2. The progress of life very often produces _______ and indifference.
3. He never was _______ of anything on two feet.
4. Good bawcock, bate thy rage! Use _______, sweet chuck!
5. So vainly is wit _______ upon fugitive topics.
6. Much drink may be said to be an equivocator with _______.

[**lavished, lechery, legerdemain, laxity, lenity, leery**]

****

1. There was no permanent _______ to prevent ultimate recovery.
2. Particularly loathsome to the _______ are crimes of treason and fraud.
3. Competition allowed, there would be no _______ of monopoly.
4. A great _______ treads on the heels of a reformation.
5. Love is not for _______, but for the total worth of man.
6. In nature, as in law, it may be _______ to speak some truths.

[**Lilliputians, libelous, levity, lethargy, lesion, licentiousness**]

1. Now this was written at a time when the black **limber** bone of the Greenland or Right whale was largely used in ladies' bodices. —Herman Melville, *Moby Dick*

2. The water is of great depth, **limpid**, and supplied from a thousand springs. —James Fenimore Cooper, *The Pioneers*

3. My father was a bronco.* Nothing as to **lineage**—that is, nothing as to recent lineage—but plenty good enough when you go a good way back. —Mark Twain, *A Horse's Tale*

4. She spoke of me as her dearest friend. I had only met her once before, but she took it into her head to **lionize** me. —Oscar Wilde, *The Picture of Dorian Gray*

5. Dorian Gray watched with **listless** eyes the sordid shame of the great city. —Oscar Wilde, *The Picture of Dorian Gray*

6. He was cat-footed, and **lithe**, and strong, always strong. I likened him to some great tiger, a beast of prowess* and prey. —Jack London, *The Sea Wolf*

****

1. **limber**; 1. flexible, pliable, plastic, elastic, lithe, lissome. 2. agile, nimble. —limberly, —limberness.
2. **limpid**; 1. clear, transparent, translucent, pellucid. 2. serene. —limpidity.
3. **lineage**; bloodline, ancestry, genealogy, pedigree. * bronco; mustang, wild pony of North America.
4. **lionize**; ennoble, respect as a celebrity. —lionization.
5. **listless**; languid, sluggish, lethargic, torpid, enervated, lymphatic, supine.
6. **lithe**; flexible, lissome, supple, pliable, pliant, willowy. —litheness, —lithely, —lithesome; willowy. ※ svelte; 1. slim, slender. 2. lithe: *a very svelte fashion model.* * prowess; 1. valor, intrepidity, *see p. 244, no. 2.* 2. adroitness.

♣ Eloquence, when at its highest pitch, leaves little room for reason or reflection. —David Hume, *An Enquiry Concerning Human Understanding*

1. He whose fortune is endangered by **litigation**, will not refuse to augment the wealth of the lawyer. —Samuel Johnson, *The Rambler*

2. In few seconds she stretched herself out stiff, and turned up her eyes, while her cheeks, at once blanched* and **livid**, assumed the aspect of death. —Emily Brontë, *Wuthering Heights*

3. Talkers may sow, but the silent reap. "Let us be *doing* something," was his [David Wilkie's] oblique* mode of rebuking the **loquacious** and admonishing the idle. —Samuel Smiles, *Self Help*

4. He was a London boy, with a **loutish** air, a heavy fellow with the beginnings of a moustache on his lip . . . —W. Somerset Maugham, *Of Human Bondage*

5. One of our most **lucrative** means of laying out money is in the shape of loans, where the security is unimpeachable.* —Arthur Conan Doyle, *The Adventures of Sherlock Holmes*

6. Some things are so completely **ludicrous** that a man *must* laugh, or die. —Edgar Allan Poe, *The Assignation*

****

1. **litigation**; legal proceeding, lawsuit, prosecution. —litigate, —litigious.
2. **livid**; 1. pallid, ashen. 2. mad, furious. —lividity. * blanch; whiten, bleach, blench.
3. **loquacious**; verbose, wordy, garrulous. —loquacity. * oblique; aslant, diagonal.
4. **loutish**; boorish, churlish, uncouth, clumsy. ***ant.*** urbane. —lout *n.*; rustic, boor.
5. **lucrative**; profitable, beneficial, remunerative. —lucrativeness. * unimpeachable; irreproachable, blameless, impeccable.
6. **ludicrous**; comic, farcical, funny, humorous. —ludicrousness.

♣ The way of paradoxes is the way of truth. —Oscar Wilde, *The Picture of Dorian Gray*

1. In some houses the thrumming* of **lugubrious** guitars added to the depression of the *triste** night. —O. Henry, *Shoes*

2. A quibble* is to *Shakespeare*, what **luminous** vapours are to the traveller; he follows it at all adventures; it is sure to lead him out of his way, and sure to engulf him in the mire. —Samuel Johnson, *The Preface to Shakespeare*

3. They had a **lurid** altercation,* in which they damned each other's souls with frequence. —Stephen Crane, *Maggie: A Girl of the Streets*

4. The cook, placed upon her mettle,* served a delicious repast*—a **luscious** tenderloin broiled *á point.** —Kate Chopin, *The Awakening*

5. The whale rushed round in a sudden **maelstrom**; seized the swimmer between his jaws; and rearing high up with him, plunged headlong* again, and went down. —Herman Melville, *Moby Dick*

6. 'I'll give you another opportunity of showing your Christian **magnanimity**,' sneered he. —Anne Brontë, *The Tenant of Wildfell Hall*

****

1. **lugubrious**; sad, mournful, woeful, doleful. —lugubriousness. * thrum; play monotonously. ※ strum; play unskillfully: *to strum a guitar.* * triste; sad.
2. **luminous**; 1. bright, shining, lustrous, radiant, resplendent. 2. clear, lucid, perspicuous. —luminosity. * quibble; petty criticism, carping, caviling.
3. **lurid**; 1. glowing, flaring, fiery. 2. horrid, frightful, gruesome, ghastly, grisly, macabre *or* macaber. —luridness, —luridly. * altercation; argument, wrangle.
4. **luscious**; 1. savory, flavorful, palatable. 2. sensual. * upon one's mettle; urged to do one's best. * repast; meal. * *á point* ; relevantly, apropos, appositely.
5. **maelstrom**; 1. whirlpool, swirl, vortex. 2. disturbance, turbulence, pandemonium, bedlam. * headlong; headfirst.
6. **magnanimity**; generosity, largess, munificence, lenience. —magnanimous.

1. An aunt of my father's, and consequently a great-aunt of mine, of whom I shall have more to relate by and by, was the principal **magnate** of our family. —Charles Dickens, *David Copperfield*

2. Neither party expected for the war, the **magnitude**, or the duration, which it has already attained. —Abraham Lincoln, *The Second Inaugural Address*

3. Mr. Babcock's moral ***malaise***, I am afraid, lay deeper than where any definition of mine can reach it. —Henry James, *The American*

4. The man Dante Alighieri received unforgivable affronts* and insults from the world; and the poet Dante Alighieri bequeathed his immortal curse to it, in the sublime **malediction** of the *Inferno*. —Herman Melville, *Pierre*

5. A general amnesty* is proclaimed; all **malefactors** may return to their town. —Henry David Thoreau, *Walden*

6. What **malevolence** you must have to wish to convince me that there is no happiness in the world! —Emily Brontë, *Wuthering Heights*

****

1. **magnate**; very rich and influential leader, mogul, tycoon.
2. **magnitude**; 1. size, extent. 2. immensity, vastness. 3. importance, significance.
3. **malaise**; 1. vague unease, nonspecific depression. 2. physical discomfort before any ailment.
4. **malediction**; curse, damnation, imprecation, execration. ***ant.*** benediction. —maledict *v.*, —maledictive. * affront; insult, offense.
5. **malefactor**; 1. lawbreaker, criminal, outlaw, sinner. 2. evildoer. —malefaction. * amnesty; general pardon or acquittal.
6. **malevolence**; hatred, ill will, malice, rancor, malignity, spite, grudge, venom. ***ant.*** benevolence. —malevolent; hostile, malicious, vicious.

♣ The bondage of art is very exacting. —Joseph Conrad, *The Mirror of the Sea*

1. Deep **malice** makes too deep incision.
—Shakespeare, *King Richard II*

2. The **malignity** of soldiers and sailors against each other has been often experienced at the cost of their country. —Samuel Johnson, *The Rambler*

3. Pike, the **malingerer**, who, in his lifetime of deceit, had often successfully feigned a hurt leg, was now limping in earnest. —Jack London, *The Call of the Wild*

4. When the substance is in a proper state for the next process, it betrays evidences of incipient decomposition*; the fibres are relaxed and softened, and rendered perfectly **malleable**. —Herman Melville, *Typee*

5. "Send me the provost marshal,*" said he [the Duke of Wellington], "and put him under my orders; till some of the **marauders** are hung, it is impossible to expect order or safety." —Samuel Smiles, *Self Help*

6. . . . and here were we **marooned** upon this desert island of a world, without companions, hopes, or aspirations. —Arthur Conan Doyle, *The Poison Belt*

****

1. **malice**; malevolence, malignity, spite, enmity, rancor, venom. —malicious.
2. **malignity**; hatred, malice, malevolence, rancor, grudge. —malignant.
3. **malingerer**; a person pretending illness, someone feigning sickness.
4. **malleable**; tractable, pliable, ductile. * decomposition; corruption, disintegration. —decompose. ※ discompose; disconcert, discomfit. —discomposure.
5. **marauder**; plunderer, pillager, ravager, raider, depredator. —maraud. * provost marshal; supervising officer of military police.
6. **maroon**; 1. abandon, desert, forsake. 2. brownish-red. 3. *n.* a person marooned.

♣ Those who do not love Beauty more than Truth never know the inmost shrine of Art. —Oscar Wilde, *The Decay of Lying*

1. He was a **martinet**. —Robert L. Stevenson, *The Misadventures of John Nicholson*
2. He writhed and wriggled under the infliction but, fully convinced of my skill, endured the pain like a **martyr**. —Herman Melville, *Typee*
3. The fat boy rose, opened his eyes, swallowed the huge piece of pie he had been in the act of **masticating** when he last fell asleep . . . —Charles Dickens, *The Pickwick Papers*
4. He knew, of course, that whatever man dared (within Fifth Avenue's limits) that old Mrs. Manson Mingott, the **Matriarch** of the line, would dare. —Edith Wharton, *The Age of Innocence*
5. . . . it is beautiful to see how the exact adaptation of the current of water to the specific gravity of the gold, so easily separates the powdered **matrix** from the metal. —Charles Darwin, *The Voyage of the Beagle*
6. . . . he sang ancient **maudlin** vaudeville songs and pelted* his screaming parrot with banana peels . . . —O. Henry, *A Double-Dyed Deceiver*

****

1. **martinet**; strict disciplinarian, rigid moralist. —martinetish.
2. **martyr**; one who willingly suffers death, refusing to abandon his religion. —martyrdom.
3. **masticate**; chew, gnaw, nibble, munch, crunch. —mastication, —masticatory.
4. **Matriarch**; female leader of a family or tribe. ***ant.*** patriarch. —matriarchy.
5. **matrix**; 1. principal metal, solid matter. 2. womb. 3. mould.
6. **maudlin**; tearful, sentimental, mawkish, lachrymose. * pelt; batter, pummel, pommel.

♣ Adversity is the first path to truth.

—Lord Byron, *Don Juan*

1. 'Tis sport to **maul** a runner.

—Shakespeare, *Antony and Cleopatra*

2. At Heidelberg I met a fat veterinary surgeon whose voice broke with sobs as he repeated some **mawkish** poetry. —E. M. Forster, *Howards End*

3. Indeed, we all speak different dialects; one shall be copious* and exact, another loose and **meager**; but the speech of the ideal talker shall correspond and fit upon the truth of fact. —Robert L. Stevenson, *Truth of Intercourse*

4. In the deepest snows, the path which I used from the highway to my house, about half a mile long, might have been represented by a **meandering** dotted line. —Henry David Thoreau, *Walden*

5. They won't **meddle** with persons who touch nothing. —Emily Brontë, *Wuthering Heights*

6. I was no boy of fourteen, living the **mediocre** ways of the sleepy town called Oakland. —Jack London, *John Barleycorn*

****

1. **maul**; beat, batter, ill-treat, thrash, bruise, manhandle, lacerate. —mauler.
2. **mawkish**; tearful, sentimental, maudlin, lachrymose.
3. **meager**; scanty, paltry, scarce. * copious; abundant, plentiful, ample.
4. **meandering**; winding, twisting, curving. —meanders; winding of stream.
5. **meddle**; interfere, interlope, intervene, tamper. —meddler, —meddlesome.
6. **mediocre**; ordinary, average, run-of-the-mill. —mediocrity, —mediocritize.

♣ We hold these truths to be self-evident, that all men are created equal, that they are endowed by their Creator with certain unalienable Rights, that among these are Life, Liberty, and the pursuit of Happiness. —Thomas Jefferson, *The Declaration of Independence*

1. He was humble and **meek**, filled with self-disparagement and abasement. —Jack London, *Martin Eden*

2. The victors pushed their success to the opposite shore, and gained the solid ground in the ***mêlée*** of the fight. —James Fenimore Cooper, *The Prairie*

3. Put upon* his good faith, and finding it in collision with his inclinations, Sloppy threw back his head and uttered a **mellifluous** howl, rounded off* with a sniff.* —Charles Dickens, *Our Mutual Friend*

4. She had been his wife's friend, and, as such, he had given her that silver vinaigrette* as a **memento**. —E. M. Forster, *Howards End*

5. The Enemy of Mankind is represented holding subtly **mendacious** dialogues with some tempted soul. —Joseph Conrad, *Under Western Eyes*

6. The persons are such as we; the Europe, an old faded garment of dead persons; the books their ghost. Let us drop this idolatry. Let us give over this **mendicancy**. —R. W. Emerson, *Friendship*

****

1. **meek**; 1. spiritless, submissive. 2. mild, gentle. —meekness, —meekly.
2. **mêlée** *also* **melee**; fray, fracas, brawl, tussle.
3. **mellifluous**; sweet, honeyed, mellow, dulcet, euphonious. —mellifluence. * put upon; impose on. * round off; complete *v.* * sniff; sniffle, snuff.
4. **memento**; memorial, remembrance, souvenir, keepsake. * vinaigrette; small bottle containing a fragrant restorative, with a pierced top.
5. **mendacious**; false, deceptive, prevaricating, fraudulent. —mendacity.
6. **mendicancy**; begging, beggary. —mendicant; 1. *adj.* begging. 2. beggar.

♣ There is no odor so bad as that which arises from goodness tainted. —Henry David Thoreau, *Walden*

Review Exercise: Sentence Completions (pp. 181–84)

1. The water is of great depth, _______, and supplied from a thousand springs.
2. My father was a bronco, but nothing as to recent _______.
3. The black _______ bone of the Right whale was largely used in ladies' bodices.
4. He was cat-footed, and _______, and strong, always strong.
5. Dorian Gray watched with _______ eyes the sordid shame of the great city.
6. I had only met her once before, but she took it into her head to _______ me.

[**lionize, limpid, listless, lineage, lithe, limber**]

****

1. One of our most _______ means of laying out money is in the shape of loans.
2. Some things are so completely _______ that a man must laugh, or die.
3. His fortune was endangered by _______.
4. Her cheeks, at once blanched and _______, assumed the aspect of death.
5. He was a London boy, with a _______ air.
6. He rebuked the _______ and admonished the idle.

[**loquacious, loutish, lucrative, ludicrous, litigation, livid**]

****

1. A quibble is to *Shakespeare*, what _______ vapours are to the traveller.
2. The thrumming of _______ guitars added to the depression of the triste night.
3. I'll give you another opportunity of showing your Christian _______.
4. They had a _______ altercation, in which they damned each other's souls.
5. The cook served a delicious repast—a _______ tenderloin broiled *á point.*
6. The whale rushed round in a sudden _______.

[**lugubrious, maelstrom, luscious, luminous, magnanimity, lurid**]

****

1. A great-aunt of mine was the principal _______ of our family.
2. Neither party expected for the war, the _______, or the duration.
3. A general amnesty is proclaimed; all _______ may return to their town.
4. What _______ you must have to wish to convince me that he is an evil!
5. The poet left his curse to the world, in the sublime _______ of the *Inferno*.
6. His moral _______ lay deeper than where any definition of mine can reach it.

[**malevolence, magnate, magnitude, malefactors, malediction, malaise**]

Review Exercise: Sentence Completions (pp. 185–88)

(pp. 185–88)

1. Deep _______ makes too deep incision.
2. Pike, the _______, was now limping in earnest.
3. The _______ of soldiers against each other has been often experienced.
4. The fibres are relaxed and softened, and rendered perfectly _______.
5. Here were we _______ upon this desert island of a world, without hopes.
6. Till some of the _______ are hung, it is impossible to expect order or safety.

[**malignity, malleable, malice, marooned, marauders, malingerer**]

****

1. He endured the pain like a _______.
2. The _______ of the line would dare whatever man dared in the avenue.
3. The powdered _______ was so easily separated from the metal.
4. He had been in the act of _______ the huge piece of pie when he fell asleep.
5. He was a _______.
6. He sang ancient _______ vaudeville songs.

[**matriarch, matrix, masticating, martinet, martyr, maudlin**]

****

1. They won't _______ with persons who touch nothing.
2. I lived the _______ ways of the sleepy town called Oakland.
3. 'Tis sport to _______ a runner.
4. His voice broke with sobs as he repeated some _______ poetry.
5. One dialect shall be copious and exact, another loose and _______.
6. The path might have been represented by a _______ dotted line.

[**meddle, mediocre, mawkish, maul, meandering, meager**]

****

1. He had given her that silver vinaigrette as a _______.
2. He was humble and _______, filled with self-disparagement and abasement.
3. Let us drop this idolatry. Let us give over this _______.
4. The victors gained the solid ground in the _______ of the fight.
5. Sloppy uttered a _______ howl, rounded off with a sniff.
6. He is holding subtly _______ dialogues with some tempted soul.

[**meek, mêlée, mellifluous, mendicancy, mendacious, memento**]

1. She was not proposing to go out again, so he got her slippers and took off her boots. It delighted him to perform **menial** offices. —W. Somerset Maugham, *Of Human Bondage*

2. "I'm afraid you are **mercenary**, Tom."
"Mercenary," repeated Tom. "Who is not mercenary?" —Charles Dickens, *Hard Times*

3. They [Laws in the country] are expressed in the most plain and simple terms, wherein those people are not **mercurial** enough to discover above one interpretation. —Jonathan Swift, *Gulliver's Travels*

4. He hankered* after the **meretricious** glory of a showy performance. —Joseph Conrad, *The Mirror of the Sea*

5. Natures that have much heat and great and violent desires and perturbations,* are not ripe for action till they have passed the **meridian** of their years. —Francis Bacon, *Essays*

6. . . . she **mesmerized** me by the grace and alertness of her action— . . . —Charlotte Brontë, *The Professor*

****

1. **menial**; lowly, base, humble, ignoble, mean, demeaning, vile. —menially.
2. **mercenary**; money-motivated, venal. —mercenariness, —mercenarily.
3. **mercurial**; 1. ready-witted, shrewd. 2. volatile, fickle. —mercurialness.
4. **meretricious**; vulgar, gaudy, tawdry, garish. * hanker: long, yearn, crave, yen. —hankering; strong desire, yearning.
5. **meridian**; peak, pinnacle, acme, culmination. * perturbation; agitation, upset.
6. **mesmerize**; hypnotize, spellbind, grip, entrance, enthrall. —mesmeric.

♣ Prudence operates on life in the same manner as rules on composition. —Samuel Johnson, *The Idler*

1. It does not seem probable that the most ancient beds have been quite worn away by denudation,* or that their fossils have been wholly obliterated* by **metamorphic** action. —Charles Darwin, *The Origin of Species*

2. Law is intended to **mete** out justice. Sometimes it fails. —Mark Twain, *A Connecticut Yankee*

3. It is not to be supposed that species in a state of nature ever change so quickly as domestic animals under the guidance of **methodical** selection. —Charles Darwin, *The Origin of Species*

4. And now their pride and **mettle** is asleep.
—Shakespeare, *King Henry IV, Part I*

5. The attacks of illness which arise from **miasma** never fail to appear most mysterious. —Charles Darwin, *The Voyage of the Beagle*

6. . . . his friend Mr. Darcy soon drew the attention of the room by his fine, tall person, handsome features, noble **mien** . . . —Jane Austen, *Pride and Prejudice*

****

1. **metamorphic**; transformational. —metamorphosis. ※ metastasis; 1. spread. 2. transformation. 3. metabolism. —metastasize, —metastatic. ※ anabolism; molecular synthesis as a phase of metabolism. ***ant.*** catabolism. * denudation; 1. erosion. 2. stripping. —denude; divest, disarray. * obliterate; destroy.
2. **mete**; 1. allot, distribute. 2. measure. 3. *n.* limit, boundary.
3. **methodical**; orderly, systematic, structured. —methodicalness, —methodize; systematize, orchestrate, choreograph: *to methodize the asymmetric findings*.
4. **mettle**; spirit, courage, valor, fortitude, gallantry, pluck. —mettlesome; intrepid.
5. **miasma**; poisonous atmosphere. —miasmatic, —miasmic.
6. **mien**; manner, bearing, demeanor, carriage.

1. I don't know that the arts have a ***milieu*** here, any of them; they're more like a very thinly settled outskirt. —Edith Wharton, *The Age of Innocence*

2. His features had lost their delicately benevolent aspect; his words were **minatory**. —E. Phillips Oppenheim, *The Vanished Messenger*

3. With the **mincing** step of a demirep*
   Some sidled up the stairs.
   —Oscar Wilde, *The Ballad of Reading Gaol*

4. . . . his abstraction* was evidently so deep, and his whole aspect so **misanthropical**, that I shrank from disturbing him again. —Emily Brontë, *Wuthering Heights*

5. The most undersigned word, the most accidental look, the least familiarity, or most innocent freedom, will be **misconstrued**, and magnified into I know not what, by some people. —Henry Fielding, *Tom Jones*

6. Thou art a traitor and a **miscreant**.
   —Shakespeare, *King Richard II*

****

1. **milieu**; environment, surrounding, setting.
2. **minatory**; menacing, threatening, minacious. ※ minacity; threat, menace.
3. **mincing**; affectedly genteel, pretentiously refined. * demirep; whore, harlot.
4. **misanthropical**; antisocial, hating humans. —misanthropy, —misanthrope. ※ misogyny; hatred of women. * abstraction; absent-mindedness.
5. **misconstrue**; misunderstand, misinterpret, misapprehend. —misconstruction.
6. **miscreant**; 1. villain, rogue, rascal, knave, scoundrel. 2. heretic, infidel. 3. vicious. —miscreancy. ※ recreant; 1. cowardly. 2. disloyal, renegade.

♣ The speaking in a perpetual hyperbole is comely in nothing but in love. —Francis Bacon, *Essays*

1. In the meantime, Don Munio sent forth **missives** in every direction, and had viands* and dainties* of all kinds collected from the country round. —Washington Irving, *Legend of Don Munio Sancho de Hinojosa*

2. A faint light from no particular source **mitigated** the shadows of the halls. —O. Henry, *The Furnished Room*

3. She had been steering seven hours! . . . Her **modicum** of strength had been exhausted. —Jack London, *The Sea Wolf*

4. . . . she treated me like the great **Mogul**; so I became the great Mogul as far as she was concerned. —Charlotte Brontë, *The Professor*

5. A lady may traverse* our streets all day, going and coming as she chooses, and she will never be **molested** by any man. —Mark Twain, *A Tramp Abroad*

6. Mr. Chillip was fluttered* again, by the extreme severity of my aunt's manner; so he made her a little bow and gave her a little smile, to **mollify** her. —Charles Dickens, *David Copperfield*

****

1. **missive**; letter, written message. * viands; gourmet food, haute cuisine, *see p. 333, no. 4.* * dainties; choice food, delicacies.
2. **mitigate**; moderate, alleviate, appease, relieve, allay, placate. —mitigative.
3. **modicum**; very small amount, bit, jot, iota.
4. **mogul**; big businessman, very powerful man, tycoon, magnate.
5. **molest**; abuse, harass, harry. —molestation. * traverse; go or pass through, *see p. 28, no. 5.* ※ ford; cross, wade: *The refugees forded the bloody river.*
6. **mollify**; soothe, pacify, mitigate, allay, placate. * fluttered; agitated.

♣ All that glisters is not gold.

—Shakespeare, *The Merchant of Venice*

1. . . . groups of excursionists, arrayed in unattractive traveling costumes, were moping* about in a drizzling rain and looking as droopy* and woe-begone* as so many **molting** chickens. —Mark Twain, *The Innocents Abroad*

2. God help those who wander into the great mire now, for even the firm uplands are becoming a **morass**. —Arthur Conan Doyle, *The Hound of the Baskervilles*

3. I now discovered that he also kept a particularly mellow Scotch whiskey, an excellent cigar, and a fund of anecdote of which a **mordant** wit was the worthy bursar.* —E. W. Hornung, *A Thief in the Night*

4. In a far corner upon a few mats the **moribund** woman, already speechless and unable to lift her arm, rolled her head over, and with a feeble movement of her hand seemed to command—'No! No!' —Joseph Conrad, *Lord Jim*

5. Pluto grew more and more haggard* and **morose**, and looked more like an imp of darkness than a human being. —Washington Irving, *Guests From Gibbet Island*

6. He was horribly **mortified**. —W. Somerset Maugham, *Of Human Bondage*

****

1. **molt** *also* **moult**; cast off covering, shed coat. * mope; 1. loiter, dawdle. 2. be dejected. * droopy; sagging, dejected, disheartened. * woe-begone; woeful.
2. **morass**; swamp, marsh, bog, quagmire, slough. ※ mores; customs, convention.
3. **mordant**; cutting, biting, sarcastic, acerbic, caustic. —mordancy, —mordantly. ※ mordacious; mordant. —mordacity. * bursar; treasurer, especially of a university.
4. **moribund**; 1. dying, waning, fading, declining. 2. stagnant.
5. **morose**; gloomy, depressed, sullen, sour, pessimistic, morbid. —moroseness. * haggard; gaunt, emaciated, *see p. 138, no. 1.* —haggardness.
6. **mortify**; 1. shame, humiliate, abase, disgrace. 2. discipline. —mortification.

♣ To be a great autocrat you must be a great barbarian. —Joseph Conrad, *The Mirror of the Sea*

1. I did not realize how **motley** are the qualities that go to make up a human being. —W. Somerset Maugham, *The Moon and Sixpence*

2. Surely, as there are **mountebanks** for the natural body, so are there mountebanks for the politic body. —Francis Bacon, *Essays*

3. "My mind's in a **muddle**," said Geoffrey. "I'll try a bath." —Wilkie Collins, *Man and Wife*

4. And heaved and heaved, still unrestingly heaved the black sea, as if its vast tides were a conscience; and the great **mundane** soul were in anguish and remorse for the long sin and suffering it had bred. —Herman Melville, *Moby Dick*

5. Whilst a merchant, he [David Barclay] was as much distinguished for his talents, knowledge, integrity, and power, as he afterwards was for his patriotism and **munificent** philanthropy.* —Samuel Smiles, *Self Help*

6. Overhead the stars were **mustering**, and in the west the sky was still a pale, bright, almost greenish blue. —H. G. Wells, *The War of the Worlds*

****

1. **motley**; 1. variegated, diversified, heterogenous. 2. mottled, dappled.
2. **mountebank**; 1. quack, charlatan. 2. fraud, swindler. —mountebankery.
3. **muddle**; 1. confusion, chaos, disarray, jumble. 2. *v.* confound, befuddle.
4. **mundane**; worldly, earthly, terrestrial, secular. —mundaneness.
5. **munificent**; lavish, magnanimous, unstinted. * philanthropy; charity.
6. **muster**; rally, aggregate, convene. ※ convoke; convene: *The council was convoked immediately to discuss the issue.* —convocation.

♣ Truth, after all, wears a different face to everybody. —James Russell Lowell, *Democracy*

1. Nature is a **mutable** cloud which is always and never the same. —R. W. Emerson, *History*
2. **Mutiny** was effectually laid to rest for the moment. —Mark Twain, *The Adventures of Tom Sawyer*
3. Humanity is immense, and reality has a **myriad** forms. —Henry James, *The Art of Fiction*
4. In certain fishes the swim-bladder seems to be rudimentary for its proper function of giving buoyancy,* but has become converted into a **nascent** breathing organ or lung. —Charles Darwin, *The Origin of Species*
5. . . . the floor was dry and level and had a sort of small loose gravel* upon it, so that there was no **nauseous** or venomous* creature to be seen. —Daniel Defoe, *Robinson Crusoe*
6. The remoter stars seem a **nebula** of united light, yet there is no group which a telescope will not resolve. —R. W. Emerson, *Society and Solitude*

****

1. **mutable**; changeable, transformable, alterable. —mutation, —mutate.
2. **mutiny**; revolt, uprising, rebellion, insurrection. —mutineer, —mutinous.
3. **myriad**; 1. innumerable, incalculable. 2. *n.* multitude, indefinite quantity.
4. **nascent**; beginning, immature, rudimentary, incipient. —nascence. * buoyancy; 1. floatability, weightlessness. 2. cheerfulness, liveliness.
5. **nauseous**; sickening, nauseating, queasy. —nausea; vomiting, qualm. —nauseate *v.* ※ queasy; nauseating: *The rat made me feel queasy.* ※ nautical; naval, marine. ※ emetic; 1. agent causing vomiting: *The worm was an emetic to me.* 2. vomitive *adj.* * gravel; pebble. * venomous; noxious.
6. **nebula** (*pl.* –lae *or* -las); mass of gas and dust among the stars. —nebulous; murky, hazy, misty, vague, obscure, ambiguous. —nebulocity, —nebulize.

1. By his skill in **necromancy** he has a power of calling whom he pleases from the dead, and commanding their service for twenty-four hours, but no longer. —Jonathan Swift, *Gulliver's Travels*

2. Less figuratively speaking, he came up into the printing-office to expose from the book the **nefarious** plagiarism* of an editor in a neighboring city . . . —W. D. Howell, *My Literary Passions*

3. The person who is **negligent** of time and its employment is usually found to be a general disturber of others' peace and serenity. —Samuel Smiles, *Self Help*

4. . . . and in their haste, and encumbered* with the debris* of their smashed companion, they no doubt overlooked many such a stray* and **negligible** victim as myself. —H. G. Wells, *The War of the Worlds*

5. There is the terrible **Nemesis** following on some errors. —George Eliot, *Middlemarch*

6. You have no right to preach to me, you **neophyte**, that have not passed the porch of life . . . —Charlotte Brontë, *Jane Eyre*

****

1. **necromancy**; magic, witchcraft, conjuration, sorcery. —necromancer.
2. **nefarious**; vicious, wicked, villainous, odious, heinous, iniquitous, execrable. —nefariousness. * plagiarism; copying, infringement, piracy. —plagiaristic.
3. **negligent**; careless, casual, lax, slack, remiss, inadvertent. —negligence.
4. **negligible**; trivial, trifling, petty, insignificant. * encumber; burden, hamper, hinder. * debris; 1. remains. 2. wreckage. * stray; roaming, vagrant.
5. **nemesis**; retributive justice, vengeance, karma. —nemeses *pl.* ※ kismet; destiny, karma: ※ kitsch; vulgar art, tawdriness in such an art.
6. **neophyte**; novice, novitiate, rookie, tyro. ※ neonate; newborn child.

♣ False Action is the fruit of false Speculation. —Thomas Carlyle, *Characteristics*

Review Exercise: Sentence Completions (pp. 191–94)

1. “Mercenary,” repeated Tom. “Who is not _______?”
2. They are not _______ enough to discover above one interpretation in the law.
3. He took off her boots. It delighted him to perform _______ offices.
4. He hankered after the _______ glory of a showy performance.
5. Natures are not ripe for action till they have passed the _______ of their years.
6. She _______ me by the grace and alertness of her action.

[**mercurial, mercenary, menial, meretricious, mesmerized, meridian**]

****

1. The attacks of illness which arise from _______ appear most mysterious.
2. And now their pride and _______ is asleep.
3. Mr. Darcy soon drew the attention of the room by his noble _______.
4. Law is intended to _______ out justice. Sometimes it fails.
5. They never change as animals under the guidance of _______ selection.
6. The fossils have been wholly obliterated by _______ action.

[**methodical, mien, mete, metamorphic, miasma, mettle**]

****

1. With the _______ step of a demirep some sidled up the stairs.
2. His whole aspect was so _______ that I shrank from disturbing him again.
3. Thou art a traitor and a _______.
4. I don’t know that the arts have a _______ here, any of them.
5. His features had lost their benevolent aspect; his words were _______.
6. The most innocent freedom will be _______ by some people.

[**misconstrued, mincing, misanthropical, miscreant, minatory, milieu**]

****

1. A faint light from no particular source _______ the shadows of the halls.
2. He made her a little bow and gave her a little smile, to _______ her.
3. She will never be _______ by any man.
4. In the meantime, Don Munio sent forth _______ in every direction.
5. She treated me like the great _______.
6. Her _______ of strength had been exhausted.

[**mollify, molested, missives, Mogul, modicum, mitigated**]

Review Exercise: Sentence Completions (pp. 195–98)

1. He also kept a fund of anecdote of which a _______ wit was the worthy bursar.
2. The ______ woman rolled her head over, and seemed to command—'No! No!'
3. He was horribly _______.
4. Pluto grew more and more haggard and _______.
5. Even the firm uplands are becoming a _______.
6. They looked as droopy and woe-begone as so many _______ chickens.

[**molting, morass, morose, mortified, mordant, moribund**]

****

1. The sea heaved and heaved as if the great _______ soul were in anguish.
2. He was very distinguished for his patriotism and _______ philanthropy.
3. Overhead the stars were _______.
4. "My mind's in a _______," said Geoffrey. "I'll try a bath."
5. I realized how _______ are the qualities that go to make up a human being.
6. There are _______ not just for the natural body, but for the politic body.

[**mundane, munificent, motley, mountebanks, muddle, mustering**]

****

1. The swim-bladder has become converted into a _______ breathing organ.
2. On the floor, there was no _______ or venomous creature to be seen.
3. Nature is a _______ cloud which is always and never the same.
4. The remoter stars seem a _______ of united light.
5. Humanity is immense, and reality has a _______ forms.
6. _______ was effectually laid to rest for the moment.

[**nauseous, nascent, myriad, nebula, mutable, mutiny**]

****

1. There is the terrible _______ following on some errors.
2. You, _______, have not passed the porch of life.
3. By his skill in _______ he can call whom he pleases from the dead.
4. They no doubt overlooked many such a stray and _______ victim as myself.
5. He exposed from the book the _______ plagiarism of an editor.
6. The person was _______ of time and its employment.

[**negligent, neophyte, nefarious, Nemesis, necromancy, negligible**]

1. By experience a man soon learns that obstacles are to be overcome by grappling* with them; that the **nettle** feels as soft as silk when it is boldly grasped. —Samuel Smiles, *Self Help*

2. There was no time to wait for any **nicety** of service. —Kate Chopin, *The Awakening*

3. "Don't ye be nervous, my dear good soul," expostulated,* between his coughs, a young man with a wet face, and his straw hat so far back upon his head that the brim encircled it like the **nimbus** of a saint. —Thomas Hardy, *Tess*

4. I do not know to what inscrutable **Nirvana** you aim. Do you know yourself? —W. Somerset Maugham, *The Moon and Sixpence*

5. Within that **noisome** den* from which I had emerged, I had thought with a narrow intensity only of our immediate security. I had not realized what had been happening to the world. —H. G. Wells, *The War of the Worlds*

6. The geography of Asia and of Africa necessitated a **nomadic** life. —R. W. Emerson, *History*

****

1. **nettle**; 1. prickly plant. 2. predicament. * grapple; struggle.
2. **nicety**; 1. detail, fine point. 2. accuracy, precision. —nice; fastidious.
3. **nimbus**; halo, aura, corona. * expostulate; counsel, exhort, remonstrate.
4. **nirvana**; 1. absolute freedom. 2. beatitude, perfect bliss.
5. **noisome**; 1. harmful, detrimental, noxious. 2. foul, stinking, malodorous. —noisomeness. * den; 1. cave for shelter. 2. lair for wild animals.
6. **nomadic**; 1. migrant, roving, vagrant, itinerant. 2. pastoral. —nomadism, —nomad *n.*; migrant, rover.

♣ Loose libels ought to be passed by in silence and contempt. —Edmund Burke, *A Letter to a Noble Lord*

1. She wore a gown as beautiful and immaterial* as the mist from an unseen cataract* in a mountain gorge.*The **nomenclature** of this gown is beyond the guess of the scribe.* —O. Henry, *Transients in Arcadia*

2. The quiet **nonchalance** of death
No daybreak can bestir.*
—Emily Dickinson, "On this long storm the rainbow rose"

3. It was a stormy, windy night, such as raises whole squadrons* of **nondescript** noises in rickety* old houses. —H. B. Stowe, *Uncle Tom's Cabin*

4. A purely disembodied human emotion is a **nonentity**. —William James, *The Principles of Psychology*

5. Yes, that's right, lad—make much of me—I'm a **nonpareil**; there's nothing like me in the common herd. —Charlotte Brontë, *The Professor*

6. Rose was one of the children who observe and meditate much, and now and then **nonplus** their friends by a wise or curious remark. —Louisa May Alcott, *Eight Cousins*

****

1. **nomenclature**; terminology, a system of names. —nomenclatural. * immaterial; airy. * cataract; cascade. * gorge; 1. ravine. 2. glut. ***ant.*** regorge. * scribe; writer.
2. **nonchalance**; indifference, listlessness, insouciance. * bestir; rouse.
3. **nondescript**; 1. undistinguished, unremarkable, indeterminate. 2. *n.* indescribable thing or person. * squadron; a cavalry unit. * rickety; shaky, decrepit.
4. **nonentity**; nonexistence, nonbeing, nullity, nothingness. ***ant.*** entity.
5. **nonpareil**; 1. nonesuch, ideal, apotheosis, paragon. 2. *adj.* supreme, unrivaled, matchless, peerless. ※ optimum; 1. the best condition. 2. supreme, ideal. —optimization, —optimal. ※ non sequitur; unreasonable inference.
6. **nonplus**; bewilder, perplex, puzzle, baffle, abash, befuddle, bemuse.

1. I disapprove of arsenic as a means of destroying **noxious** insects infesting flowers and plants. —Wilkie Collins, *The Law and the Lady*

2. However, he had **nullified** the force of the enchantment by prayer . . . —Mark Twain, *A Connecticut Yankee*

3. **Nuptial** love maketh mankind; friendly love perfecteth it; but wanton* love corrupteth and embaseth it. —Francis Bacon, *Essays*

4. But, sirs, be sudden in the execution,
   Withal* **obdurate**, do not hear him plead.
   —Shakespeare, *King Richard III*

5. The most attractive class of people are those who are powerful **obliquely** and not by the direct stroke; men of genius, but not yet accredited. —R. W. Emerson, *Experience*

6. There was a carpet: a good one, but the pattern was **obliterated** by dust. —Emily Brontë, *Wuthering Heights*

****

1. **noxious**; harmful, poisonous, pernicious, noisome, baneful.
2. **nullify**; annul, void, invalidate, rescind, abrogate.
3. **nuptial**; marital, matrimonial, connubial, conjugal, bridal. * wanton; immoral.
4. **obdurate**; dogged, forward, tenacious. —obduracy. * withal; therewith.
5. **obliquely**; 1. indirectly, circuitously. 2. aslant, diagonally. —oblique.
6. **obliterate**; delete, efface, expunge, destroy. —obliteration, —obliterative.

♣ In general, if any branch of trade, or any division of labour, be advantageous to the public, the freer and more general the competition, it will always be the more so. —Adam Smith, *The Wealth of Nations*

1. Come hither! bury thyself in a life which, to your now equally abhorred and abhorring, landed world, is more **oblivious** than death. —Herman Melville, *Moby Dick*

2. . . . he would divulge* the secret and so remove somewhat of the **obloquy** that attached to his niece's fame. —Mark Twain, *The Innocents Abroad*

3. In private, men are more bold in their own humours; and in consort,* men are more **obnoxious** to others' humours. —Francis Bacon, *Essays*

4. Those men are most apt to be **obsequious** and conciliating abroad, who are under the discipline of shrews* at home. —Washington Irving, *Rip Van Winkle*

5. The cabin floor was thickly strewn with strange, iron-clasped folios,* and mouldering* instruments of science, and **obsolete** long-forgotten charts. —Edgar Allan Poe, *Ms. Found in a Bottle*

6. Billy's name seemed to have a quieting effect on **obstreperous** males. —Jack London, *The Valley of the Moon*

****

1. **oblivious**; forgetful, unaware, unconscious, incognizant, disregardful. —oblivion.
2. **obloquy**; defamation, disgrace, vilification, opprobrium, calumny, slander. * divulge; leak, disclose, *see p. 88, no. 1.*
3. **obnoxious**; nasty, odious, loathsome, disgusting, repellent, abhorrent, detestable, execrable, vile. * consort; 1. company. 2. agreement, accord.
4. **obsequious**; fawning, flattering, sycophantic. * shrew; termagant.
5. **obsolete**; dated, outmoded, passé, antiquated, anachronistic. * folio; 1. leaf of paper. 2. book of the largest size. * moulder *also* molder; rot, decompose.
6. **obstreperous**; unruly, rampageous, rambunctious. —obstreperousness.

♣ The lewd inflame the lewd, the audacious harden the audacious. —Samuel Johnson, *The Idler*

1. Mr. Tulliver felt very much as if the air had been cleared of **obtrusive** flies now the women were out of the room. —George Eliot, *The Mill on the Floss*

2. He remembered with what a callous selfishness his uncle had treated her, how **obtuse** he had been to her humble, devoted love. —W. Somerset Maugham, *Of Human Bondage*

3. Rules may **obviate** faults, but can never confer beauties; and Prudence keeps life safe, but does not often make it happy. —Samuel Johnson, *The Idler*

4. From the man's distorted body and twisted mind, in **occult** ways, like mists rising from malarial* marshes, came emanations* of the unhealth within. —Jack London, *White Fang*

5. No picture of life can have any veracity* that does not admit the **odious** facts. —R. W. Emerson, *Fate*

6. Extinguished brands* were lying around a spring, the **offals** of a deer were scattered about the place, and the trees bore evident marks of having been browsed by the horses. —James Fenimore Cooper, *The Last of the Mohicans*

****

1. **obtrusive**; 1. protrusive, blatant. 2. meddlesome. —obtrusion, —obtrude.
2. **obtuse**; 1. dull, insensitive. 2. blunt, not pointed. —obtusity, —obtusely.
3. **obviate**; 1. prevent, forefend, deflect. 2. remove, preclude. —obviation.
4. **occult**; mysterious, arcane, rarefied, abstruse. ※ recondite; abstruse: *recondite philosophy*. * malarial; poisonous, miasmatic. * emanation; emission, efflux.
5. **odious**; hateful, detestable, loathsome, abhorrent, repugnant, abominable, execrable. —odium. * veracity; integrity, probity, rectitude. —veracious.
6. **offal**; 1. viscera, entrails, intestinal parts. 2. remains of a butchered animal. 3. rubbish, waste, refuse. * brand; a piece of firewood.

♣ Little strokes fell great oaks. —Benjamin Franklin, *Poor Richard's Almanac*

1. I have seen a duchess fairly knocked down, by the precipitancy* of an **officious** coxcomb* running to save her the trouble of opening a door. —Jonathan Swift, *A Treatise on Good Manners and Good Breeding*
2. She was outrageously painted and **ogled** the students impudently with large black eyes; her smiles were grossly alluring. —W. Somerset Maugham, *Of Human Bondage*
3. . . . nothing had so chilled their blood as that voice of an **ogre**, sounding suddenly out of a silent and empty inn. —G. K. Chesterton, *The Wisdom of Father Brown*
4. Monsieur Defarge's **olfactory** sense was by no means delicate. —Charles Dickens, *A Tale of Two Cities*
5. Millions of people were starving, while the **oligarchs** and their supporters were surfeiting* on the surplus. —Jack London, *The Iron Heel*
6. . . . *my* task was not the least **onerous** . . . —Charlotte Brontë, *Villette*

****

1. **officious**; interfering, meddlesome, obtrusive. * precipitancy; hastiness, rashness. —precipitant. * coxcomb; dandy, fop, beau. —coxcombry.
2. **ogle**; wink, leer, gaze at lecherously, take a look at amorously. —ogler.
3. **ogre**; monster, fiend, demon, devil. —ogrish, ※ wraith; spirit, apparition.
4. **olfactory**; of the sense of smell. —olfaction; the sense of smell.
5. **oligarch**; member of oligarchy. —oligarchy; business or political system by a small clique. ***ant.*** polyarchy; regime by many rulers. ※ junta; temporary regime. * surfeit; 1. *v.* sate, satiate, gorge, *see p. 306, no. 6.* 2. *n.* satiety, glut.
6. **onerous**; burdensome, taxing, cumbersome. —onerousness, —onerously.

♣ Simplify, simplify. —Henry David Thoreau, *Walden*

1. . . . she would plunder* the preserves, drink the sweet wine, break jars and bottles, and so contrive as to throw the **onus** of suspicion on the cook and kitchen-maid. —Charlotte Brontë, *Villette*

2. The sky had grown brighter, the setting moon was becoming pale and **opaque** in the luminous blue of the day. —H. G. Wells, *The Island of Doctor Moreau*

3. It was unspeakably comfortable to stretch our weary limbs between the cool, damp sheets. And how we did sleep!—for there is no **opiate** like Alpine pedestrianism. —Mark Twain, *A Tramp Abroad*

4. She was **oppressed** by ennui* . . . —George Eliot, *Middlemarch*

5. . . . and because I had turned against him to avert farther irrational violence, I was loaded with general **opprobrium**. —Charlotte Brontë, *Jane Eyre*

6. Take but degree away, untune that string,
   And, hark, what discord follows. Each thing meets
   In mere **oppugnancy**.

   —Shakespeare, *Troilus and Cressida*

****

1. **onus**; 1. stigma, infamy. 2. burden, duty, obligation. * plunder; rob, pillage.
2. **opaque**; nontransparent, murky, hazy, turbid. ***ant.*** lucid. —opaqueness.
3. **opiate**; 1. sleeping pill, soporific. 2. narcotic. 3. sedative, pacifier. —opium.
4. **oppress**; 1. trouble, burden, depress, dishearten. 2. overpower, subdue, subjugate, suppress. * ennui; tedium, listlessness, lassitude, *see p. 103, no. 5.*
5. **opprobrium**; 1. disgrace, disrepute, infamy, ignominy, obloquy. 2. reproach.
6. **oppugnancy**; opposition, antagonism. —oppugn *v.*, —oppugnant *adj.*

♣ The weak in courage is strong in cunning.

—William Blake, *The Marriage of Heaven and Hell*

1. In **opulent** states and regular governments, the temptations to wealth and rank, and to the distinctions* that follow them, are such as no force of understanding finds it easy to resist. —Samuel Johnson, *The Adventurer*

2. Certainly the great multiplication of virtues upon human nature resteth upon societies well **ordained** and disciplined. —Francis Bacon, *Essays*

3. It was a genuine relief to the whole congregation when the **ordeal** was over and the benediction* pronounced. —*The Adventures of Tom Sawyer*

4. Behold the **ordnance** on their carriages,
   With fatal mouths gaping on girded Harfleur.*
   —Shakespeare, *King Henry V*

5. . . . as he passed under the shadow of one handsome villa with verandas and wide **ornate** gardens, he heard a noise that made him almost involuntarily stop. —G. K. Chesterton, *The Wisdom of Father Brown*

6. I was so ignorant, and so kind of low-down and **ornery**. —Mark Twain, *The Adventures of Huckleberry Finn*

****

1. **opulent**; well-off, prosperous, affluent. —opulence. * distinction; honor.
2. **ordain**; 1. order, dictate, decree. 2. appoint to holy orders. —ordination.
3. **ordeal**; suffering, trial, tribulation. * benediction; blessing, grace.
4. **ordnance**; 1. cannon, artillery, heavy weapon. 2. munitions, ammunition. ※ ordinance; canon, decree * Harfleur; a commune in northern France.
5. **ornate**; 1. elaborately ornamented, overelaborate, rococo, baroque. 2. flowery in writing style. —ornateness, —ornately.
6. **ornery**; ill-natured, disagreeable, cantankerous, grumpy. —orneriness.

♣ The truth is rarely pure and never simple. —Oscar Wilde, *The Importance of Being Earnest*

1. The geography of Asia and of Africa necessitated a _______ life.
2. The _______ feels as soft as silk when it is boldly grasped.
3. There was no time to wait for any _______ of service.
4. The brim of his straw hat encircled his head like the _______ of a saint.
5. I do not know to what inscrutable _______ you aim.
6. Within that _______ den, I had thought only of our immediate security.

[**Nirvana, noisome, nomadic, nicety, nettle, nimbus**]

****

1. The _______ of the gown is beyond the guess of the scribe.
2. It was a stormy night, such as raises whole squadrons of _______ noises.
3. The children now and then _______ their friends by a wise remark.
4. I'm a _______; there's nothing like me in the common herd.
5. No daybreak can bestir the quiet _______ of death.
6. A purely disembodied human emotion is a _______.

[**nondescript, nonplus, nonpareil, nomenclature, nonentity, nonchalance**]

****

1. But, sirs, be sudden in the execution, withal _______, do not hear him plead.
2. There was a carpet: a good one, but the pattern was _______ by dust.
3. _______ love maketh mankind; friendly love perfecteth it.
4. I disapprove of arsenic as a means of destroying _______ insects.
5. The most attractive class of people are those who are powerful _______.
6. He had _______ the force of the enchantment by prayer.

[**nullified, noxious, obliquely, nuptial, obliterated, obdurate**]

****

1. In consort, men are more _______ to others' humours.
2. Come hither! Bury thyself in a life which is more _______ than death.
3. He removed somewhat of the _______ that attached to his niece's fame.
4. Billy's name seemed to have a quieting effect on _______ males.
5. The cabin floor was strewn with iron-clasped folios and _______ charts.
6. They are most apt to be _______ and conciliating abroad.

[**obsequious, obnoxious, obsolete, oblivious, obloquy, obstreperous**]

Review Exercise: Sentence Completions (pp. 205–8)

1. He remembered how _______ he had been to her humble, devoted love.
2. No picture of life can have any veracity that does not admit the _______ facts.
3. Rules may _______ faults, but can never confer beauties.
4. The _______ of a deer were scattered about the place.
5. In _______ ways, mists rose from the malarial marshes.
6. Mr. Tulliver felt very much as if the air had been cleared of _______ flies.

[**obtrusive, obtuse, occult, offals, obviate, odious**]

****

1. An _______ coxcomb ran to save her the trouble of opening a door.
2. Monsieur Defarge's _______ sense was by no means delicate.
3. My task was not the least _______.
4. The _______ and their supporters were surfeiting on the surplus.
5. She _______ the student impudently with large black eyes.
6. Nothing had so chilled their blood as that voice of an _______.

[**olfactory, onerous, officious, oligarchs, ogled, ogre**]

****

1. There is no _______ like Alpine pedestrianism.
2. She was _______ by ennui.
3. She broke jars and so contrived as to throw the _______ of suspicion on him.
4. I was loaded with general _______.
5. The setting moon was becoming pale and _______.
6. . . . and, hark, what discord follows. Each thing meets in mere _______.

[**oppressed, opiate, opprobrium, opaque, oppugnancy, onus**]

****

1. The _______ was over and the benediction pronounced.
2. Behold the _______ on their carriages, with fatal mouths.
3. The society was well _______ and disciplined.
4. I was so ignorant, and so kind of low-down and _______.
5. The state was so _______ and dominant.
6. There was one handsome villa with verandas and wide _______ gardens.

[**ornery, ornate, ordnance, opulent, ordeal, ordained**]

1. All geological facts tell us plainly that each area has undergone numerous slow **oscillations** of level, and apparently these oscillations have affected wide spaces. —Charles Darwin, *The Origin of Species*

2. He's politically and **ostensibly** dead. —O. Henry, *The Moment of Victory*

3. Let faith **oust** fact; let fancy oust memory; I look deep down and do believe. —Herman Melville, *Moby Dick*

4. We wish to learn all the curious, **outlandish** ways of all the different countries, so that we can "show off" and astonish people when we get home. —Mark Twain, *The Innocents abroad*

5. Do not smile at me, that I boast her off,
   For thou shalt find she will **outstrip** all praise,
   And make it halt behind her.

   —Shakespeare, *Tempest*

6. Julius, on being stopped at the door, mentioned his name—and received an **ovation**. —Wilkie Collins, *Man and Wife*

****

1. **oscillation**; swing, fluctuation, vacillation. —oscillate, —oscillatory.
2. **ostensibly**; seemingly, apparently, outwardly, superficially, speciously.
3. **oust**; cast out, expel, banish, depose, dislodge. —ouster; forcing out, ousting, ejection, expulsion, supplanting.
4. **outlandish**; strange, foreign, alien, exotic. —outlander, —outlandishness.
5. **outstrip**; exceed, outrun, surpass. ※ outwit; outsmart; *outwitting the enemy.*
6. **ovation**; acclamation, applause, laudation, plaudits. ※ ovate; oval.

♣ Intemperance not only wastes the earnings, but the health and the minds of men. —W. Ellery Channing, *On the Elevation of the Laboring Classes*

1. He's a widower, thirty-six years old, without any children, and is proud of his money and **overbearing** . . . —Mark Twain, *Tom Sawyer, Detective*
2. Her head was large and **overshadowed** her body. —Sherwood Anderson, *Winesburg, Ohio*
3. Without one **overt** act of hostility, one upbraiding word, he contrived to impress me momently with the conviction that I was put beyond the pale* of his favour. —Charlotte Brontë, *Jane Eyre*
4. I grant I was not looking well, but on the contrary, thin, haggard, and hollow-eyed; like a sitter-up at night, like an **overwrought** servant, or a placeless person in debt. —Charlotte Brontë, *Villette*
5. Loud **paeans** chanted through the valley announced the approach of the victors. —Herman Melville, *Typee*
6. Alas, their love may be call'd appetite,
   No motion of the liver, but the **palate**,
   That suffer surfeit, cloyment* and revolt.

   —Shakespeare, *Twelfth Night*

****

1. **overbearing**; 1, haughty, arrogant, imperious. 2. predominant, overwhelming.
2. **overshadow**; overshade, outshine, overcast, obscure, adumbrate.
3. **overt**; apparent, obvious, manifest, plain. —overtness. * pale; boundary.
4. **overwrought**; 1. *pp.* of overwork, overdone. 2. strained. 3. agitated.
5. **paean**; 1. song of triumph. 2. song of praise.
6. **palate**; liking, taste, appetite. —palatable. ※ palatial; magnificent: *a palatial residence*. * cloyment; fullness, satiation, repletion.

♣ The thankful receiver bears a plentiful harvest.

—William Blake, *The Marriage of Heaven and Hell*

1. A great chocolate-coloured **pall** lowered over heaven, but the wind was continually charging and routing* these embattled vapours. —R. L. Stevenson, *Dr. Jekyll and Mr. Hyde*

2. Friends are often chosen for similitude of manners, and therefore each **palliates** the other's failings, because they are his own. —Samuel Johnson, *The Rambler*

3. Along the entire east the invisible sun sent **pallid** intimations of his coming. —Herman Melville, *The Encantadas*

4. They [the colours] were sombre blues, opaque like a delicately carved bowl in lapis lazuli,* and yet with a quivering lustre that suggested the **palpitation** of mysterious life. —W. Somerset Maugham, *The Moon and Sixpence*

5. When he stood before the murdered man, he shook as with a **palsy**, and he put his face in his hands and burst into tears. —Mark Twain, *The Adventures of Tom Sawyer*

6. Now, when any vicious simpleton* excites my disgust by his **paltry** ribaldry,* I cannot flatter myself that I am better than he. —Charlotte Brontë, *Jane Eyre*

****

1. **pall**; 1. covering, veil, shroud, mantle. 2. cloth over a coffin. 3. *v.* cover with a pall. * rout; drive off, scatter, stampede, *see p. 276, no. 1.*
2. **palliate**; 1. mitigate, extenuate. 2. soothe, relieve. —palliation, —palliative.
3. **pallid**; 1. dim, dull, wan. 2. pale, ashen, sallow, cadaverous. —pallidness.
4. **palpitation**; pulsation, throbbing. * lapis lazuli; azure semiprecious gemstone. ※ laissez-faire; noninterference, nonintervention: *a policy of laissez-faire.*
5. **palsy**; 1. paralysis, immobility. 2. inactivity, stagnation. 3. *v.* paralyze.
6. **paltry**; petty, trivial. —paltriness. * simpleton; fool. * ribaldry; vulgarity.

♣ Infancy conforms to nobody; all conform to it. —R. W. Emerson, *Self-Reliance*

1. Mr. Snagsby has to lay upon the table half-a-crown, his usual **panacea** for an immense variety of afflictions.* —Charles Dickens, *Bleak House*
2. Knowledge of itself, unless wisely directed, might merely make bad men more dangerous, and the society in which it was regarded as the highest good, little better than a **pandemonium**. —Samuel Smiles, *Self Help*
3. He then launched forth into a **panegyric** on Allworthy's goodness; into the highest encomiums on his friendship. —Henry Fielding, *Tom Jones*
4. My young lady was no philosopher, and no **paragon** of patience. —Emily Brontë, *Wuthering Heights*
5. Wild was the wrestle which should be **paramount**. —Charlotte Brontë, *Jane Eyre*
6. The desire of all of them was to have a mistress. It was part of the **paraphernalia** of the art-student in Paris. It gave consideration in the eyes of one's fellows. —W. Somerset Maugham, *Of Human Bondage*

****

1. **panacea**; cure-all, elixir, nostrum. —panacean *adj.* * affliction; suffering, hardship, misfortune, misery.
2. **pandemonium**; commotion, turmoil, uproar, bedlam. —pandemoniac.
3. **panegyric**; eulogy, encomium, paean, extolment. —panegyrist, —panegyrize.
4. **paragon**; archetype, paradigm, criterion, apotheosis, quintessence.
5. **paramount**; 1. prime, superior, predominant, capital. 2. *n.* supreme ruler, overlord. —paramountcy. —paramountly.
6. **paraphernalia**; 1. accessory, personal effects. 2. apparatus, gadget.

♣ Trifles light as air
Are to the jealous confirmations strong
As proofs of holy writ.

—Shakespeare, *Othello*

1. There passed a weary time. Each throat
   Was **parched**, and glazed each eye.
   —S. T. Coleridge, *The Rime of the Ancient Mariner*

2. Tom came upon the juvenile **pariah** of the village, Huckleberry Finn, son of the town drunkard. —Mark Twain, *The Adventures of Tom Sawyer*

3. He did indeed consider a **parity** of fortune and circumstances to be physically as necessary an ingredient in marriage as difference of sexes, or any other essential. —Henry Fielding, *Tom Jones*

4. The town sounds a **parley**. —Shakespeare, *King Henry V*

5. Unable to turn his back on the fanged danger and go on, the bull would be driven into **paroxysms** of rage. —Jack London, *The Call of the Wild*

6. Will you say, the disasters which threaten mankind are exceptional, and one need not lay his account* for cataclysms* every day? Aye, but what happens once may happen again, and so long as these strokes are not to be **parried** by us they must be feared. —R. W. Emerson, *Fate*

****

1. **parch**; 1. burn, roast, scorch. 2. dry out, desiccate.
2. **pariah**; 1. outcast, castaway, outlaw. 2. wanderer, vagabond.
3. **parity**; equality, equivalence, parallelism.
4. **parley**; talk, meeting, conference, colloquy. ⋇ tonsorial parlor: barber's shop. ⋇ beauty parlor; beauty salon or shop.
5. **paroxysm**; fit, spasm, convulsion. —paroxysmal, —paroxysmic.
6. **parry**; dodge, evade, shun, fend off, stave off. * lay one's account for; be ready, be prepared for. * cataclysm; deluge, catastrophe, *see p. 43, no. 6.*

♣ All beauty comes from beautiful blood and a beautiful brain. —Walt Whitman, *Preface to Leaves of Grass*

1. He built himself, as usual, a vast house, out of ostentation*; but left the greater part of it unfinished and unfurnished, out of **parsimony**. —Washington Irving, *The Devil and Tom Walker*

2. . . . and each of these three [the Knower, the Doer and the Sayer] has the power of the others latent* in him and his own, **patent**. —R. W. Emerson, *The Poet*

3. What arrested him now as of value in life was less its beauty than its **pathos**. —Thomas Hardy, *Tess*

4. Even the word *lord* is the luckiest style that is used in any language to designate a **patrician**. —R. W. Emerson, *English Traits*

5. A young man who ran through his **patrimony**, spending it in profligacy,* was at length reduced to utter want and despair. —Samuel Smiles, *Self Help*

6. There are a thousand and one odd little youthful **peccadilloes**, that we think we may as well not divulge* to them [our young children], Pierre. —Herman Melville, *Pierre*

****

1. **parsimony**; miserliness, meanness, stinginess, niggardliness. —parsimonious. * ostentation; showing off, guise, veneer. —ostentatious; flaunting.
2. **patent**; 1. evident, manifest, palpable. 2. official privilege for an inventor to make and sell an invention. * latent; potential, immanent, *see p. 176, no. 5.*
3. **pathos**; pity, sympathy, commiseration. ⋇ ethos; character of a group or an era: *the ethos of the royal family.* ⋇ zeitgeist; spirit or general trend of a period: *His poetry reflects the zeitgeist of the 18th century.*
4. **patrician**; aristocrat, nobleman, blue blood. ***ant.*** plebeian.
5. **patrimony**; inheritance, legacy, heritage, bequest. —patrimonial. * profligacy; dissipation, prodigality, dissoluteness, —profligate.
6. **peccadillo**; slight sin or fault, misdemeanor. * divulge; confide, confess, reveal.

1. The greatest things which have been done for the world have not been accomplished by rich men, nor by subscription* lists, but by men generally of small **pecuniary** means. —Samuel Smiles, *Self Help*

2. He must be a miserable prig who would act the **pedagogue** here. —George Eliot, *Adam Bede*

3. What a wretched and **peevish** fellow is this King of England, to mope* with his fat-brained* followers so far out of his knowledge! —Shakespeare, *King Henry V*

4. Our strong arms be our conscience, swords our law.
   March on, join bravely, let us to 't **pell-mell**.
   —Shakespeare, *King Richard III*

5. Successive nations perchance have drank at, admired, and fathomed it [White Pond], and passed away, and still its water is green and **pellucid** as ever. —Henry David Thoreau, *Walden*

6. If I have a **penchant**, it is for a philosopher. —Edgar Allan Poe, *Bon-Bon*

****

1. **pecuniary**; monetary, financial. —pecuniarily. * subscription; 1. donation, contribution. 2. agreement, consent by signing.
2. **pedagogue**; 1. pedant, prig. 2. teacher, educator, instructor. —pedagogy, —pedagogical; pedantic, priggish. ※ didactic; moralistic, —didactics.
3. **peevish**; touchy, irritable, choleric, irascible, fretful, liverish, petulant, splenetic, waspish. —peevishness. * mope; loiter, dawdle. * fat-brained; foolish.
4. **pell-mell**; 1. disorder, melee. 2. *adj.* confused, disorderly, chaotic, tumultuous.
5. **pellucid**; clear, transparent, lucid, limpid. —pellucidity, —pellucidly.
6. **penchant**; tendency, bent, inclination, propensity, disposition, proclivity.

♣ Energy is Eternal Delight.

—William Blake, *The Marriage of Heaven and Hell*

penitential

1. The first fever of his intoxication had cooled, with time, into a mild, **penitential** glow. —Wilkie Collins, *No Name*
2. She rested there, **pensive** and still. —O. Henry, *By Courier*
3. Then crushing **penury**
   Persuades me I was better when a king.
   — Shakespeare, *King Richard II*
4. Ah! how cheerfully we consign ourselves to **perdition!** —Herman Melville, *Moby Dick*
5. Holding an honored place in the best society, he [Thomas Carlyle] has stood for the people, for the Chartist, for the pauper, intrepidly* and scornfully, teaching the nobles their **peremptory** duties. —R. W. Emerson, *Carlyle*
6. There is no vice that doth so cover a man with shame as to be found false and **perfidious**. —Francis Bacon, *Essays*

****

1. **penitential**; repentant, remorseful, compunctious. —penitence.
2. **pensive**; pondering, brooding, contemplative, meditative. —pensiveness.
3. **penury**; poverty, impoverishment, destitution, indigence. —penurious.
4. **perdition**; 1. downfall, destruction, ruin, damnation. 2. hell.
5. **peremptory**; obligatory, imperative, compelling. * intrepidly; valiantly.
6. **perfidious**; unfaithful, treacherous, treasonous, recreant. —perfidy; recreance.

♣ In every profession, the exertion of the greater part of those who exercise it, is always in proportion to the necessity they are under of making that exertion. — Adam Smith, *The Wealth of Nations*

Review Exercise: Sentence Completions (pp. 211–14)

1. Julius mentioned his name at the door—and received an _______.
2. Let faith oust fact; let fancy _______ memory.
3. We wish to learn all the curious, _______ ways of all the different countries.
4. Thou shalt find she will _______ all praise, and make it halt behind her.
5. Each area has undergone numerous slow _______ of level.
6. He's politically and _______ dead.

[**outstrip, ovation, oscillations, outlandish, ostensibly, oust**]

****

1. Without one _______ act of hostility, he convinced me that I was outrageous.
2. I was thin, haggard, and hollow-eyed, like an _______ servant.
3. Her head was large and _______ her body.
4. The _______ suffers surfeit, cloyment and revolt.
5. Loud _______ chanted through the glen announced the approach of the victors.
6. He is proud of his money and _______.

[**paeans, overbearing, overt, overwrought, palate, overshadowed**]

****

1. The vicious simpleton excited my disgust by his _______ ribaldry.
2. When he stood before the murdered man, he shook as with a _______.
3. A great chocolate-coloured _______ lowered over heaven.
4. Each of friends _______ the other's failings, because they are his own.
5. The quivering lustre suggested the _______ of mysterious life.
6. Along the entire east the invisible sun sent _______ intimations of his coming.

[**paltry, pallid, palsy, palpitation, pall, palliates**]

****

1. Knowledge of itself might make a society little better than a _______.
2. He then launched forth into a _______ on Allworthy's goodness.
3. A mistress was part of the _______ of the art-student in Paris.
4. He laid upon the table half-a-crown, his usual _______ for a variety of afflictions.
5. Wild was the wrestle which should be _______.
6. My young lady was no philosopher, and no _______ of patience.

[**paragon, panegyric, paraphernalia, panacea, pandemonium, paramount**]

Review Exercise: Sentence Completions (pp. 215–18)

1. So long as the strokes are not to be _______ by us they must be feared.
2. There passed a weary time. Each throat was _______, and glazed each eye.
3. The town sounds a _______.
4. He considered a _______ of fortune to be a necessary ingredient in marriage.
5. The bull was driven into _______ of rage.
6. Tome came upon the juvenile _______ of the village, Huckleberry Finn.

[**parched, parley, pariah, parity, parried, paroxysms**]

****

1. There are a thousand and one odd little youthful _______.
2. He built a house; but left the greater part of it unfinished, out of _______.
3. Each of three has the power of the others latent in him and his own, _______.
4. The young man ran through his _______, spending it in profligacy.
5. Even the word *lord* is used in any language to designate a _______.
6. What arrested him now as of value in life was less its beauty than its _______.

[**patrimony, patrician, peccadilloes, parsimony, pathos, patent**]

****

1. He must be a miserable prig who would act the _______ here.
2. Still the water of White Pond is green and _______ as ever.
3. If I have a _______, it is for a philosopher.
4. They have been accomplished by men generally of small _______ means.
5. March on, join bravely, let us to 't _______.
6. What a wretched and _______ fellow is this King of England!

[**pedagogue, pellucid, penchant, peevish, pell-mell, pecuniary**]

****

1. Ah! how cheerfully we consign ourselves to _______.
2. Thomas Carlyle taught the nobles their _______ duties.
3. The first fever of his intoxication had cooled, with time, into a _______ glow.
4. Then crushing _______ persuades me I was better when a king.
5. There is no vice that doth so cover a man with shame as to be found _______.
6. She rested there, _______ and still.

[**perfidious, penury, penitential, peremptory, perdition, pensive**]

1. The **perforated** pipe gurgled, choked, spat, and splashed in odious ridicule of a swimmer fighting for his life. —Joseph Conrad, *Lord Jim*
2. The furnished room received its latest guest with a first glow of pseudo-hospitality, a hectic,* haggard,* **perfunctory** welcome like the specious* smile of a demirep. —O. Henry, *The Furnished Room*
3. Like a **peripatetic** philosopher, Mr. Verloc, strolling along the streets of London, had modified Stevie's view of the police by conversations full of subtle reasonings. —Joseph Conrad, *The Secret Agent*
4. A *Greek* writer of sentences has laid down as a standing maxim, that *he who believes not another on his oath, knows himself to be* ***perjured****.* —Samuel Johnson, *The Rambler*
5. Life is ghost land, where appearances change, transfuse, **permeate** each the other and all the others . . . —Jack London, *John Barleycorn*
6. But all extremes are **pernicious** in various ways. —Alexander Hamilton, *The Federalist Papers*

****

1. **perforate**; hole, pierce, puncture. —perforation.
2. **perfunctory**; careless, routine, superficial. —perfunctoriness. * hectic; feverish. * haggard; wasted. * specious; spurious, plausible, *see p. 294, no. 5.*
3. **peripatetic**; 1. of Aristotelian method of teaching philosophy while pacing, Aristotelian. 2. itinerant, ambulant, wayfaring. ※ ambulatory; able to walk, ambulant: *Few of the patients were ambulatory.* ※ promenade; ramble.
4. **perjure**; lie under oath, give false testimony. —perjury, —perjurious.
5. **permeate**; pervade, penetrate, infiltration. —permeable; pervasive.
6. **pernicious**; 1. ruinous, lethal. 2. noisome, baneful. —perniciousness.

♣ Every calamity is a spur and valuable hint. —R. W. Emerson, *Fate*

1. When plunder* bears the name of impost,* and murder is **perpetrated** by a judicial sentence, fortitude is intimidated and wisdom confounded. —Samuel Johnson, *The Rambler*

2. With **perseverance**, the very odds and ends* of time may be worked up into results of the greatest value. —Samuel Smiles, *Self Help*

3. I was tall and **personable**, but a little too smooth-faced for a man. —Daniel Defoe, *Moll Flanders*

4. There is not much **perspicacity** in the world. —Joseph Conrad, *Under Western Eyes*

5. The first thing necessary in writing letters of business, is extreme clearness and **perspicuity**. —4th Earl of Chesterfield, *Letters to His Son*

6. There was nothing **pert** or flippant* in her manner now, as when she walked with Mr. Hatfield. —Anne Brontë, *Agnes Grey*

****

1. **perpetrate**; commit, execute. —perpetrator, —perpetration. * plunder *n.*; seizure, maraud, *see p. 227, no. 5.* * impost; tax, customs, tariff.
2. **perseverance**; endurance, persistence, tenacity. —persevere. ※ gritty; 1. perseverant, tenacious. 2. courageous, audacious, plucky. —grit; spirit. * odds and ends; pieces, remnants, leftovers, miscellaneous items, scraps.
3. **personable**; agreeable, pleasing, sociable, gregarious, amiable, affable.
4. **perspicacity**; insight, discernment, acumen, sagacity. —perspicacious; judicious, shrewd, canny. ※ savvy; well-informed: *savvy about high-tech.*
5. **perspicuity**; clearness, intelligibility, lucidity. —perspicuous.
6. **pert**; bold, saucy, cheeky, impudent, forward. —pertness, —pertly. * flippant; lighthearted, frivolous, *see p. 124, no. 5.*

♣ Occasionally, the brave and gentle character may be found under the humblest garb. —Samuel Smiles, *Self Help*

1. They [two races of ants] fought with more **pertinacity** than bulldogs. —Henry David Thoreau, *Walden*

2. Rest, rest, **perturbed** spirit!

   —Shakespeare, *Hamlet*

3. Mr. Pickwick **perused** the lineaments* of his face with an expression of great interest. —Charles Dickens, *The Pickwick Papers*

4. Yet I am not more sure that my soul lives, than I am that **perverseness** is one of the primitive impulses of the human heart. —Edgar Allan Poe, *The Black Cat*

5. The trees, burdened with the last infinitesimal* pennyweight of snow their branches could hold, stood in absolute **petrifaction**. —Jack London, *Burning Daylight*

6. She ceased to be a woman, complex, kind and **petulant**, considerate and thoughtless; she was a Mænad.* She was desire. —W. Somerset Maugham, *The Moon and Sixpence*

****

1. **pertinacity**; doggedness, persistence, obduracy, tenacity. —pertinacious.
2. **perturbed;** disturbed, distracted, troubled. —perturbation. ***ant.*** imperturbation; composure. —perturbable. ⨳ sangfroid; composure: *feigning sangfroid.*
3. **peruse**; examine, scrutinize. —perusal. * lineament; features, contour.
4. **perverseness**; 1. contrariness, orneriness. 2. obduracy. —perversity.
5. **petrifaction** *also* **petrification**; 1. consternation, astonishment, stupefaction. 2. ossification. —petrify, —petrifactive. ⨳ ossify; harden, stiffen: *the ossified system of the agency.* ⨳ osteoporosis; fragility of the bones by loss of calcium. * infinitesimal; microscopic, *see p. 162, no. 1.*
6. **petulant**; fretful, irritable, cross, peevish, waspish, choleric. —petulance. * Mænad; 1. frenzied woman. 2. bacchante.

1. Do you think I'm going to let you hustle* for wages while I **philander** in the regions of high art? —O. Henry, *A Service of Love*

2. A **philanthropist** is necessarily an enthusiast. —Herman Melville, *The Confidence-Man*

3. The youth turned, with sudden, livid* rage, toward the battlefield. He shook his fist. He seemed about to deliver a **philippic**. —Stephen Crane, *The Red Badge of Courage*

4. "You know, he's not at all literary," she said. "He's a perfect **philistine**." —W. Somerset Maugham, *The Moon and Sixpence*

5. I am by nature **phlegmatic**, slow to wrath, and prone to lechery. —Christopher Marlowe, *Doctor Faustus*

6. The sweets of **Pillage** can be known
   To no one but the Thief.
   —Emily Dickinson, "The sweets of Pillage can be known"

****

1. **philander**; chase woman, flirt. * hustle; 1. work energetically. 2. hurry.
2. **philanthropist** *also* **philanthrope**; humanitarian, benefactor, altruist, almsgiver. ***ant.*** misanthrope; hater of mankind. —philanthropy; charity, mercy.
3. **philippic**; 1. denunciation, revilement. 2. tirade. * livid; mad, *see p.182, no. 2.*
4. **philistine**; snob, vulgarian. —philistinism. ※ lowbrow. ***ant.*** highbrow; intellectual: *a highbrow magazine.* ※ dilettante: amateur: *a dilettante in literature.*
5. **phlegmatic**; calm, impassive, composed, tranquil, placid. —phlegm.
6. **pillage**; robbery, plunder, ravage, maraud, despoilment. —pillager.

♣ Kings, in one sense, are undoubtedly the servants of the people, because their power has no other rational end than that of the general advantage. —Edmund Burke, *On the Revolution in France*

1. When the formidable* Huron was completely **pinioned**, the scout* released his hold. —James Fenimore Cooper, *The Last of the Mohicans*

2. I was a civil,* **pious** boy, and could rattle off* my catechism that fast, as you couldn't tell one word from another. —Robert L. Stevenson, *Treasure Island*

3. "Revenge!"
   There was no name signed, and no date. It was an inscription* well calculated to **pique** curiosity. —Mark Twain, *A Tramp Abroad*

4. Then, his preaching was ingenious* and **pithy**, like the preaching of the English Church in its robust age, and his sermons were delivered without book. —George Eliot, *Middlemarch*

5. In a moment the visible world seemed to wheel slowly round, himself the **pivotal** point, and he saw the bridge, the fort, . . . the two privates, his executioners. —Ambrose Bierce, *An Occurrence at Owl Creek Bridge*

6. Nearly all of us have, at some point in our lives—either to excuse our own stupidity or **placate** our consciences—promulgated* some theory of fatalism. —O. Henry, *The Enchanted Kiss*

****

1. **pinion**; 1. shackle, fasten, manacle. 2. feather. * formidable; 1. overwhelming, indomitable. 2. awesome. *see p. 126, no. 5.* * scout; 1. reconnoiterer. 2. reconnoiter. 3. scoff.
2. **pious**; religious, devout, pietistic. * civil; polite. * rattle off; recite rapidly.
3. **pique**; arouse, excite, stir, irritate, provoke, goad. * inscription; words engraved on stone or metal.
4. **pithy**; 1. forceful, cogent, trenchant. 2. concise, terse, laconic, succinct. —pith; core, crux, marrow, —pithiness, —pithily. * ingenious; creative, —ingenuity.
5. **pivotal**; 1. central, polar. 2. decisive, vital, crucial. —pivot.
6. **placate**; appease, soothe, pacify, mollify, assuage. —placation, —placatory. * promulgate; enunciate, propound. *see p. 241, no. 5.*

1. Strickland remained **placid**. —W. Somerset Maugham, *The Moon and Sixpence*
2. A **plagiary** is a man who steals other people's thoughts, and puts them off for his own. —4th Earl of Chesterfield, *Letters to His Son*
3. Every night at midnight, the **plaintive** tones floated out over the silent land. —Mark Twain, *A Tramp Abroad*
4. The Dean believes that single species of each genus were created in an originally highly **plastic** condition. —Charles Darwin, *The Origin of Species*
5. The secret of their [the Dullards'] power is their insensibility to blows; tickle them with a bludgeon* and they laugh with a **platitude**. —Ambrose Bierce, *The Devil's Dictionary*
6. This performance was sure to be hailed with loud **plaudits** . . . —Herman Melville, *Typee*

****

1. **placid**; calm, serene, tranquil, collected, self-possessed. —placidity.
2. **plagiary**; 1. one who steals another's ideas, pirate, plagiarist. 2. piracy, plagiarism, copyright infringement. —plagiarize.
3. **plaintive**; sorrowful, melancholy, mournful, grievous, doleful, woeful, rueful, pathetic. —plaintiveness, —plaintively.
4. **plastic**; 1. pliable, flexible, malleable, elastic, tensile, ductile, supple. 2. molding. —plasticity. ※ plastic surgery; operation to remodel a body part.
5. **platitude**; commonplace, triteness, cliché, banality, bromide, truism, insipidity. —platitudinarian, —platitudinize. * bludgeon; *see p. 33, no. 4.*
6. **plaudits**; usu. in *pl.* applause, acclaim, commendation.

♣ Ofttimes it is very wonderful to trace the rarest and profoundest things, and find their probable origin in something extremely trite or trivial. —Herman Melville, *Pierre*

1. He was always a villain, smooth-spoken and **plausible**, but a dangerous, subtle villain all the same. —Arthur Conan Doyle, *Beyond the City*

2. . . . then, the **plebeian** herds crouch abased before the tremendous centralization. —Herman Melville, *Moby Dick*

3. There are younger nations—living nations! Nations that do not snore and gurgle helplessly in paroxysms of **plethora** upon beds of formality and red tape!* —H. G. Wells, *The War in the Air*

4. The future is **pliant** and ductile,* and will be easily moulded by a strong fancy into any form. —Samuel Johnson, *The Rambler*

5. I must store my **plunder** at this inn, since the hostess is an honest woman. —Arthur Conan Doyle, *The White Company*

6. In the heart of a **plutocracy** tradesmen become cunning enough to be more fastidious than their customers. —G. K. Chesterton, *The Innocence of Father Brown*

****

1. **plausible**; likely, credible, verisimilar, feasible. ***ant***. implausible.
2. **plebeian**; 1. low, humble, vulgar. ***ant.*** patrician. 2. *n*. commoner. —plebeianism.
3. **plethora**; 1. excess of blood, overabundance of red corpuscles. 2. surfeit, oversupply, glut, superfluity. * red tape; bureaucracy, officialdom.
4. **pliant**; pliable, supple, tensile, elastic. ***ant.*** unruly. —pliancy. * ductile; lissome.
5. **plunder**; 1. *n*. pillage, booty, loot. 2. *v.* rob, maraud, foray. —plunderage.
6. **plutocracy**; government by the wealthy. —plutocrat, —plutocratic.

♣ Virtue is harder to be got than a knowledge of the world. —John Locke, *Some Thoughts Concerning Education*

1. . . . if any one of us makes an ass of himself he is **poaching** on their preserves. —Oscar Wilde, *The Picture of Dorian Gray*

2. To be "run ashore*" has the littleness,* **poignancy**, and bitterness of human error. —Joseph Conrad, *The Mirror of the Sea*

3. Avoid as much as you can, in mixed companies, argumentative, **polemical** conversations. —4th Earl of Chesterfield, *Letters to His Son*

4. The war is, perhaps, severest between the males of **polygamous** animals . . .—Charles Darwin, *The Origin of Species*

5. My dear Jane, Mr. Collins is a conceited,* **pompous**, narrow-minded, silly man. —Jane Austen, *Pride and Prejudice*

6. At an angle of the **ponderous** wall frowned a more ponderous gate. It was riveted* and studded* with iron bolts, and surmounted* with jagged* iron spikes. —Edgar Allan Poe, *William Wilson*

****

1. **poach**; 1. encroach, trespass. 2. steal, plunder. —poacher.
2. **poignancy**; 1. sharpness, pungency, piquancy. 2. sorrowfulness, pathos. —poignant. * run ashore; grounded. * littleness; 1. stinginess. 2. pettiness.
3. **polemical**; controversial, argumentative, contentious. —polemist.
4. **polygamous**; having more than one mate. —polygamy, ***ant.*** monogamy. ※ polyglot; person fluent in several languages. ※ polygyny; mating and living with more than one wife. ***ant.*** polyandry. ※ endogamy; intermarriage. ***ant.*** exogamy.
5. **pompous**; 1. grandiose, vainglorious, ostentatious. 2. arrogant, presuming, forward. —pomposity, —pomp; grandeur, parade, panoply. ※ pageantry; panoply: *the pageantry of Independence Day.* * conceited; presumptuous.
6. **ponderous**; heavy, weighty. —ponderosity. * rivet; fix. * stud; set. * surmount; 1. cap, crown. 2. conquer, vanquish. * jagged; zigzag, indented.

1. The furnished room received its latest guest with a _______ welcome.
2. He who believes not another on his oath, knows himself to be _______.
3. The _______ pipe gurgled, choked, spat, and splashed.
4. All extremes are _______ in various ways.
5. Like a _______ philosopher, Mr. Verloc strolled along the streets of London.
6. Appearances change, transfuse, _______ each the other and all the others.

[**pernicious, perforated, peripatetic, perfunctory, perjured, permeate**]

****

1. I am tall and _______, but a little too smooth-faced for a man.
2. There is not much _______ in the world.
3. The first thing necessary in writing letters of business, is extreme _______.
4. There was nothing _______ in her manner now, as when she walked with him.
5. Murder was _______ by a judicial sentence.
6. With _______ , the pieces of time may be worked up into the greatest value.

[**perpetrated, pert, perspicuity, personable, perspicacity, perseverance**]

****

1. Rest, rest, _______ spirit.
2. _______ is one of the primitive impulses of the human heart.
3. She ceased to be a woman, complex, kind and _______; she was Maenad.
4. Mr. Pickwick _______ the lineaments of his face.
5. The trees, burdened with snow, stood in absolute _______.
6. They [two races of ants] fought with more _______ than bulldogs.

[**pertinacity, perturbed, perverseness, petulant, perused, petrifaction**]

****

1. The sweets of _______ can be known to no one but the thief.
2. I am by nature _______, slow to wrath, and prone to lechery.
3. A _______ is necessarily an enthusiast.
4. He shook his fist. He seemed about to deliver a _______.
5. I won't let you hustle for wages while I _______ in the regions of high art.
6. "You know, he's not at all literary," she said. "He is a perfect _______."

[**phlegmatic, philanthropist, pillage, philistine, philippic, philander**]

Review Exercise: Sentence Completions (pp. 225–28)

(pp. 225–28)

1. Then, his preaching was ingenious and _______.
2. "Revenge!" It was an inscription well calculated to _______ curiosity.
3. The visible world seemed to wheel slowly round, himself the _______ point.
4. When the savage was completely _______, the scout released his hold.
5. We have promulgated some theory of fatalism to _______ our consciences.
6. I was a civil, _______ boy, and could rattle off my catechism so fast.

[**pithy, pique, pinioned, pious, placate, pivotal**]

****

1. A _______ is a man who steals other people's thoughts.
2. Strickland remained _______.
3. Single species of each genus were created in an originally _______ condition.
4. This performance was sure to be hailed with loud _______.
5. Tickle them with a bludgeon and they laugh with a _______.
6. Every night at midnight, the _______ tones floated out over the silent land.

[**plaudits, placid, plagiary, plaintive, platitude, plastic**]

****

1. In the heart of a _______ tradesmen become cunning and cunning.
2. He was always a villain, smooth-spoken and _______.
3. The _______ herds crouch abased before the tremendous centralization.
4. The nations snore and gurgle in paroxysms of _______ upon beds of red tape!
5. The future is _______ and ductile.
6. I must store my _______ at this inn, since the hostess is an honest woman.

[**plausible, plutocracy, plunder, pliant, plebeian, plethora**]

****

1. Avoid as much as you can, in mixed companies, _______ conversations.
2. To be run ashore has the littleness, _______, and bitterness of human error.
3. If any one of us makes an ass of himself he is _______ on their preserves.
4. Mr. Collins is a conceited, _______, narrow-minded, silly man.
5. The war is, perhaps, severest between the males of _______ animals.
6. At an angle of the _______ wall frowned a more ponderous gate.

[**ponderous, polemical, poignancy, poaching, pompous, polygamous**]

1. After several **portentous** yawns, he pronounced his book to be "cursed trash," and threw it on the table. —Anne Brontë, *The Tenant of Wildfell*

2. Sometimes the beam of her view gilded my foot, sometimes my **portly** belly. —Shakespeare, *The Merry Wives of Windsor*

3. Sir William Blackstone was the **posthumous** son of a silk-mercer. —Samuel Smiles, *Self Help*

4. Between the **postulated** Matter and the postulated Thinker, the sheet of phenomena would then swing, some of them (the 'realities') pertaining more to the matter, others (the fictions, opinions, and errors) pertaining more to the Thinker. —William James, *The Principles of Psychology*

5. The poet is not any permissive **potentate**, but is emperor in his own right. —R. W. Emerson, *The Poet*

6. Occasionally, fairies played **pranks** with new-born children by exchanging them. —Shakespeare, *The Winter's Tale*

****

1. **portentous**; ominous, foreboding, bodeful, sinister. —portent *n.*; omen, augury. —portend *v.*; foreshadow, augur, presage.
2. **portly**; fat, fleshy, obese, plump, rotund, corpulent. —portliness.
3. **posthumous**; 1. born after the death of one's father. 2. happening after one's death. —posthumousness, —posthumously.
4. **postulate**; 1. assume, presume, hypothesize. 2. *n.* premise. ※ posit; 1. assume. 2. place. 3. submit, suggest: *He posited that she was guilty.*
5. **potentate**; ruler, monarch, sovereign. —potent, —potency.
6. **prank**; joke, mischievous trick, escapade. —prankish, —prankishly.

♣ The liberty of the individual must be thus far limited; he must not make himself a nuisance to other people. —John Stuart Mill, *On Liberty*

1. Mere **prattle**, without practice,
   Is all his soldiership.
   —Shakespeare, *Othello*
2. I'll plunge into the matter without further **preamble**. —Arthur Conan Doyle, *Memoirs of Sherlock Holmes*
3. Impenetrable and heartless, the sea has given nothing of itself to the suitors* for its **precarious** favors. —Joseph Conrad, *The Mirror of the Sea*
4. The place of justice is an hallowed place; and therefore not only the bench, but the foot-pace* and **precincts** and purprise* thereof, ought to be preserved without scandal and corruption. —Francis Bacon, *Essays*
5. Precious as thought is, the love of truth is still more precious; for without it, thought wanders and wastes itself, and **precipitates** men into guilt and misery. —W. Ellery Channing, *On the Elevation of the Laboring Classes*
6. I know she goes in for* giving a rapid **précis** of all her guests. —Oscar Wilde, *The Picture of Dorian Gray*

****

1. **prattle**; chatter, twitter, babble, prate. —prattler, —prattlingly.
2. **preamble**; introduction, preface, prelude, foreword. —preambulary *adj.*
3. **precarious**; uncertain, insecure, unsteady, unreliable, unstable, risky, dubious. —precariousness. * suitor; 1. wooer, beau. 2. suer, plaintiff, petitioner.
4. **precinct**; boundary, purlieus. * foot-pace; 1. lobby. 2. dais. * purprise; enclosure.
5. **precipitate**; hasten, expedite, accelerate. ***ant.*** decelerate. —precipitation, —precipitous. ※ precipitant; sudden, abrupt. —precipitancy. ※ precipice; cliff.
6. **précis**; summary, abstract, synopsis, epitome. * go in for; like, enjoy.

♣ Reputation is an idle and most false imposition; oft got without merit, and lost without deserving. —Shakespeare, *Othello*

1. Miss Temple had always something of serenity in her air, of state in her mien, of refined propriety in her language, which **precluded** deviation into the ardent, the excited, the eager. —Charlotte Brontë, *Jane Eyre*

2. Many artists have been **precocious**, but without diligence their precocity would have come to nothing. —Samuel Smiles, *Self Help*

3. An intense anticipation itself transforms possibility into reality; our desires being often but the **precursors** of the things which we are capable of performing. — Samuel Smiles, *Self Help*

4. They [men of the aggressive turn] are of their nature warlike, **predatory**, eager for fight, plunder, dominion. —W. M. Thackeray, *Jonathan Swift*

5. It is difficult for a seaman to believe that his stranded ship does not feel as unhappy at the unnatural **predicament** of having no water under her keel* as he is himself at feeling her stranded. —Joseph Conrad, *The Mirror of the Sea*

6. Your I is both subject and object; it **predicates** things of itself and is the things predicated. —Jack London, *John Barleycorn*

****

1. **preclude**; exclude, rule out, obviate, debar. —preclusion, —preclusive.
2. **precocious**; premature, forward. —precocity. ※ *preterm infant.*
3. **precursor**; forerunner, herald, harbinger. —precursory.
4. **predatory**; 1. rapacious, voracious, vulturine, ravening. 2. plundering, ravaging, marauding. 3. predacious, raptorial, carnivorous. ***ant.*** herbivorous. —predator; 1. carnivorous animal. 2. marauder.
5. **predicament**; difficulty, dilemma, quandary, plight, scrape, deadlock. * keel; main structure along the central bottom of a ship.
6. **predicate**; 1. affirm, assert, maintain. 2. imply, connote. 3. the other main part of a sentence or clause, describing the subject. —predication, —predicative.

1. The aristocracy are marked by their **predilection** for country-life. They are called the county-families. —R. W. Emerson, *English Traits*
2. It was impossible for a girl of the fond* age of eighteen, highly **predisposed** for love and matrimony,* not to be pleased with so gallant* a cavalier. —Washington Irving, *The Spectre Bridegroom*
3. The parrot sat, **preening** her plumage, on Long John's shoulder. —Robert L. Stevenson, *Treasure Island*
4. We shall, also, presently see that the tail is a highly useful **prehensile** organ to some of the species; and its use would be much influenced by its length. —Charles Darwin, *The Origin of Species*
5. Sensible objects conform to the **premonitions** of Reason and reflect the conscience. —R. W. Emerson, *Nature*
6. In balancing his faults with his perfections, the latter seemed rather to **preponderate**. —Henry Fielding, *Tom Jones*

****

1. **predilection**; fondness, partiality, preference.
2. **predisposed**; inclined, given, minded. —predisposition. * fond; tender. * matrimony; marriage. * gallant; 1. polite to women. 2. valiant.
3. **preen**; trim, primp, plume, array, dress up.
4. **prehensile**; 1. capable of grasping. 2. perceptible, insightful. —prehensility.
5. **premonition**; forewarning, foreboding, portent, presage, presentiment. —premonish, —premonitory.
6. **preponderate**; predominate, prevail, outweigh, outbalance. —preponderance, —preponderation, —preponderant; prevalent, prepotent.

♣ Be not afraid of greatness: some are born great, some achieve greatness, and some have greatness thrust upon them. —Shakespeare, *Twelfth Night*

1. Your honour is **prepossessed** against me, and resolved not to believe anything I say. —Henry Fielding, *Tom Jones*

2. This whole world is a **preposterous** one, with many preposterous people in it. —Herman Melville, *Pierre*

3. The *Imagination* is one of the highest **prerogatives** of man. —Charles Darwin, *The Descent of Man*

4. If I may trust the flattering truth of sleep,
   My dreams **presage** some joyful news at hand.
   —Shakespeare, *Romeo and Juliet*

5. The most exact calculator has no **prescience** that somewhat incalculable may not balk* the very next moment. —R. W. Emerson, *The Over-Soul*

6. Of the **presentiments** which some people are always having, *some* surely must come right. —W. M. Thackeray, *Vanity Fair*

****

1. **prepossessed**; prejudiced, biased, predetermined. —prepossessing; engaging, winning, enchanting, bewitching. ※ myopic; nearsighted, prejudiced: *The myopic critics blamed the party for its myopic policy.* —myopia. ***ant.*** presbyopia.
2. **preposterous**; absurd, irrational, inept. —preposterousness; ineptitude.
3. **prerogative**; privilege, exclusive right, perquisite. ※ prerequisite; precondition: *What is a prerequisite for the prerogative?*
4. **presage**; foretell, portend, foreshadow.
5. **prescience**; foreknowledge, foresight, precognition, clairvoyance. —prescient.
   * balk; 1. hinder, thwart, *see p. 25, no.* 2. 2. recoil, flinch, evade.
6. **presentiment**; foreboding, premonition, portent, presage. —presentient *adj.*

♣ Things sequent in time, ditto.* —William James, *The Principles of Psychology*

* ditto; repeat.

1. He had had nothing out of them [immense sums]—nothing of the **prestigious** or the desirable things of the earth, craved for by predatory natures. —Joseph Conrad, *Chance*

2. James Crawley, when his aunt had last beheld him, was a gawky* lad, at that uncomfortable age when the voice varies between an unearthly treble* and a **preternatural** bass. —W. M. Thackeray, *Vanity Fair*

3. I felt that you were the last man in the world whom I could ever be **prevailed** on to marry. —Jane Austen, *Pride and Prejudice*

4. He does not shuffle* or **prevaricate**, dodge or skulk*; but is honest, upright, and straightforward. —Samuel Smiles, *Self Help*

5. He was rough, absent-minded, careless, and awkward, rather **priggish**, and not at all agreeable to a dainty,* beauty-loving girl like Rose. —Louisa May Alcott, *Eight Cousins*

6. He had been suddenly jerked from the heart of civilization and flung into the heart of things **primordial**. —Jack London, *The Call of the Wild*

****

1. **prestigious**; 1. eminent, distinguished, renowned. 2. esteemed. —prestige.
2. **preternatural**; extraordinary, superhuman, supernatural. * gawky; awkward, ungainly, *see p. 134, no. 3.* * treble; the highest voice.
3. **prevail**; predominate, preponderate, triumph. —prevalence, —prevalent.
4. **prevaricate**; evade, hedge, palter, equivocate, waffle. —prevarication. * shuffle; deceive. * skulk; 1. hide, lurk. 2. evade, shirk.
5. **priggish**; pedantic, pedagogic, scholastic. * dainty; 1. delicate. 2. *n.* delicacies.
6. **primordial**; primitive, primeval, prehistoric, pristine. —primordially.

♣ Labour is not only a necessity and a duty, but a blessing—only the idler feels it to be a curse. —Samuel Smiles, *Self Help*

1. Mythology is the crop which the Old World bore before its soil was exhausted, before the fancy and imagination were affected with blight*; and which it still bears, wherever its **pristine** vigor is unabated.* —Henry David Thoreau, *Walking*

2. Many artists have had to encounter **privations** which have tried their courage and endurance to the utmost before they succeeded. —Samuel Smiles, *Self Help*

3. New York was inexorable* in its condemnation of business irregularities. So far there had been no exception to its tacit* rule that those who broke the law of **probity** must pay. —Edith Wharton, *The Age of Innocence*

4. Clancy was an American with an Irish diathesis* and cosmopolitan **proclivities**. —O. Henry, *The Shamrock and the Palm*

5. Never **procrastinate**, never put off till tomorrow what you can do today. —4th Earl of Chesterfield, *Letters to His Son*

6. I felt a **prod** at the back of my neck, and turned dizzy with the shock. —Arthur Conan Doyle, *The Lost World*

****

1. **pristine**; 1. original, primitive. 2. clean, pure, undefiled, immaculate, unsullied. * blight; 1. distress. 2. calamity. 3. v. wither. * unabated; undiminished.
2. **privation**; poverty, neediness, destitution, indigence, penury.
3. **probity**; honesty, integrity. * inexorable; cruel, merciless, relentless, ruthless, implacable. * tacit; reticent, taciturn, *see p. 311, no. 2.*
4. **proclivity**; tendency, inclination, penchant, propensity. * diathesis; constitutional predisposition.
5. **procrastinate**; delay, postpone, defer, adjourn. —procrastination.
6. **prod**; 1. *n.* urge, stir, poke, goad, nudge. 2. *v.* prick, incite. —prodder.

1. Tahiti is smiling and friendly; it is like a lovely woman graciously **prodigal** of her charm and beauty. —W. Somerset Maugham, *The Moon and Sixpence*

2. Nature, when she grants but one child, always compensates by making it a **prodigy**; and so it was with the daughter of the baron. —Washington Irving, *The Spectre Bridegroom*

3. We both know that he has been **profligate** in every sense of the word. —Jane Austen, *Pride and Prejudice*

4. Her hair, thick and dark like her mother's, fell over her shoulders in fine **profusion**, and she had the same kindly expression and sedate,* untroubled eyes. —W. Somerset Maugham, *The Moon and Sixpence*

5. The unknown **progenitor** of the Vertebrata* probably possessed many vertebræ.* —Charles Darwin, *The Origin of Species*

6. There were local tales of his having exerted his powers of **prognosis**, . . . and it was said that in every instance the person whose friends he had warned had died suddenly at the appointed time, and from no assignable cause. —Ambrose Bierce, *Can Such Things Be?*

****

1. **prodigal**; 1. abundant, profuse, lavish. 2. spendthrift, squandering, extravagant. 3. bountiful, unstinted. —prodigality, —prodigalize.
2. **prodigy**; 1. young genius. 2. wonder. —prodigious; 1. vast. 2. marvelous.
3. **profligate**; libertine, dissolute, dissipated, debauched. —profligacy.
4. **profusion**; 1. abundance, plenitude, exuberance, luxuriance. 2. bounty, prodigality. 3. extravagance, lavishness. —profuse *adj.* * sedate; calm, serene.
5. **progenitor**; ancestor, ascendant, forefathers. ***ant.*** descendant; offspring, progeny. —progenitorial. * the Vertebrata; a division of vertebrate (animal with a backbone). * vertebræ *also* vertebras; *pl.* of vertebra (spine).
6. **prognosis**; forecast, prognostication. —prognostic, —prognosticate.

1. So was the Matter as the Thinker was _______.
2. After several _______ yawns, he pronounced his book to be "cursed trash."
3. Sir William Blackstone was the _______ son of a silk-mercer.
4. Sometimes the beam of her view gilded my foot, sometimes my _______ belly.
5. The poet is not any permissive _______, but is emperor in his own right.
6. The fairies played _______ with new-born children by exchanging them.

[**pranks, potentate, portentous, postulated, portly, posthumous**]

****

1. The bench, the foot-pace and _______ ought to be preserved without scandal.
2. The sea has given nothing of itself to the suitors for its _______ favors.
3. I will plunge into the matter without further _______.
4. Mere _______, without practice, is all his soldiership.
5. I know she goes in for giving a rapid _______ of all her guests.
6. Without the love of truth, thought _______ men into guilt and misery.

[**precarious, precincts, prattle, preamble, precipitates, précis**]

****

1. Our desires are often but the _______ of the things.
2. Many artists have been _______.
3. The seaman believes that his stranded ship feels unhappy at the _______.
4. Your I _______ things of itself and is the things predicated.
5. They are of their nature warlike, _______, eager for fight, plunder, dominion.
6. She had something of state in her air, which _______ deviation into the eager.

[**predicates, predicament, precursors, precocious, precluded, predatory**]

****

1. She was a girl of the fond age of eighteen, highly _______ for love.
2. The parrot sat, _______ her plumage, on Long John's shoulder.
3. The tail is a highly useful _______ organ to some of the species.
4. In balancing his faults with his perfections, the latter seemed to _______.
5. Sensible objects conform to the _______ of Reason.
6. The aristocracy are marked by their _______ for country-life.

[**predilection, premonitions, preponderate, predisposed, preening, prehensile**]

Review Exercise: Sentence Completions (pp. 235–38)

1. This whole world is a _______ one.
2. The imagination is one of the highest _______ of man.
3. Your honour is _______ against me.
4. The exact calculator has no _______ that somewhat incalculable may not balk.
5. Some people are always having some trustworthy _______.
6. My dreams _______ some joyful news at hand.

[**prerogatives, preposterous, prepossessed, presentiments, presage, prescience**]

****

1. You were the last man in the world whom I could ever be _______ on to marry.
2. He does not shuffle or _______, dodge or skulk; but is honest and upright.
3. He was rough, careless, awkward, and rather _______.
4. He had been suddenly flung into the heart of things _______.
5. He had nothing of the _______ things, craved for by predatory natures.
6. The voice varies between an unearthly treble and a _______ bass.

[**prevailed, preternatural, prevaricate, priggish, prestigious, primordial**]

****

1. Those who broke the law of _______ must pay.
2. Clancy was an American with an Irish diathesis and cosmopolitan _______.
3. I felt a _______ at the back of my neck, and turned dizzy with the shock.
4. Many artists have had to encounter _______ which have tried their courage.
5. The _______ vigor of the Old World is unabated in the city.
6. Never _______, never put off till tomorrow what you can do today.

[**probity, procrastinate, proclivities, prod, pristine, privations**]

****

1. There were local tales of his having exerted his powers of _______.
2. The _______ of the Vertebrata probably possessed many vertebrae.
3. Her hair, thick and dark, fell over her shoulders in fine _______.
4. Tahiti is like a lovely woman graciously _______ of her charm and beauty.
5. Nature, when she grants but one child, compensates by making it a _______.
6. We both know that he has been _______ in every sense of the word.

[**prognosis, profusion, progenitor, profligate, prodigal, prodigy**]

1. Captain the Honorable Edward Fairfax Vere, to give his full title, was a bachelor of forty or thereabouts, a sailor of distinction even in a time **prolific** of renowned seamen. —Herman Melville, *Billy Budd*

2. He secured silence, at the outset, by a humorous allusion to the **prolix** speaker who had preceded him. —Wilkie Collins, *I Say No*

3. She's never been **promiscuous** like some of these girls . . . she's never been touched by a native. —W. Somerset Maugham, *The Moon and Sixpence*

4. Their house was in Wickham Place, and fairly quiet, for a lofty **promontory** of buildings separated it from the main thoroughfare. —E. M. Forster, *Howards End*

5. Music is the sound of the universal laws **promulgated**. —Henry David Thoreau, *A Week on the Concord and Merrimack Rivers*

6. A large number of individuals of an animal or plant can be reared only where the conditions for its **propagation** are favorable. —Charles Darwin, *The Origin of Species*

****

1. **prolific**; fertile, fecund, productive. ***ant.*** barren; sterile. —proliferate *v.*; grow or increase rapidly, mushroom, multiply. —prolificacy.
2. **prolix**; 1. wordy, lengthy, verbose. 2. tedious. —prolixity, —prolixly.
3. **promiscuous**; loose, sluttish, unchaste. —promiscuity.
4. **promontory**; 1. projecting part. 2. headland, foreland. —promontoried *adj.*
5. **promulgate**; announce, declare, proclaim, enunciate. —promulgation.
6. **propagation**; dissemination, proliferation. —propagate, —propagative.

♣ There are a vast number of absurd and mischievous fallacies, which pass readily in the world for sense and virtue while in truth they tend only to fortify error and encourage crime. —Sydney Smith, *Fallacies of Anti-Reformers*

1. The Government sometimes participates in the national **propensity**, and adopts through passion what reason would reject. —George Washington, *Farewell Address*

2. Here I disclaim all my paternal care,
   Propinquity and property of blood.

   —Shakespeare, *King Lear*

3. He carried his head on one side, partly in modest depreciation* of himself, partly in modest **propitiation** of everybody else. —Charles Dickens, *David Copperfield*

4. The dew fell, but with **propitious** softness; no breeze whispered. —Charlotte Brontë, *Jane Eyre*

5. From a circular lately issued it appears that Dr. Freke, in 1851 ('Dublin Medical Press,' p. 322), **propounded** the doctrine that all organic beings have descended from one primordial form. —Charles Darwin, *The Origin of Species*

6. To the whale, his tail is the sole means of **propulsion**. —Herman Melville, *Moby Dick*

****

1. **propensity**; bent, tendency, inclination, proclivity, penchant.
2. **propinquity**; nearness, closeness, kinship, similarity, proximity.
3. **propitiation**; 1. appeasement, mollification, placation, soothing. 2. atonement, expiation. —propitiatory. * depreciation; devaluation. ***ant.*** appreciation.
4. **propitious**; favorable, auspicious. —propitiousness, —propitiously.
5. **propound**; 1. offer, propose, proffer. 2. present, submit.
6. **propulsion**; driving force, momentum, impulse, impetus. —propulsive.

♣ No man was ever yet a great poet, without being at the same time a profound philosopher. —S. T. Coleridge, *Biographia Literaria*

1. Every language has likewise its improprieties and absurdities, which it is the duty of the lexicographer to correct or **proscribe**. —Samuel Johnson, *Preface to the English Dictionary*

2. In politics, as in religion, it is equally absurd to aim at making **proselytes** by fire and sword. Heresies in either can rarely be cured by persecution. —Alexander Hamilton, *The Federalist Papers*

3. She is **prostrate** with fear. —E. Phillips Oppenheim, *The Yellow Crayon*

4. . . . it must not be forgotten that John Barleycorn is **protean**. . . . He can tuck in his arm the arm of any man in any mood. He can throw the net of his lure over all men. —Jack London, *John Barleycorn*

5. Life **protracted** is protracted woe.
   —Samuel Johnson, *The Vanity of Human Wishes*

6. The old gentleman lifted his shaggy* eyebrows, **protruded** his thick nether* lip, and tapped the arms of his chair with his cushioned fingertips. —Kate Chopin, *The Awakening*

****

1. **proscribe**; banish, outlaw, expel. —proscription, —proscriptive.
2. **proselyte**; convert. —proselytism, —proselytize.
3. **prostrate**; 1. exhausted, worn out, drained. 2. beaten, overcome, defeated. 3. lying flat, prone. ***ant.*** supine. —prostration.
4. **protean**; 1. versatile, polymorphous, like Proteus. 2. variable, mutable, volatile.
5. **protract**; 1. prolong, lengthen. 2. extend, protrude. —protraction, —protractile.
6. **protrude**; project, jut. —protrusion, —protrudent; protrusive, protuberant. * shaggy; hairy, bushy, hirsute. * nether; 1. lower. 2. of hell, infernal.

♣ Jealousy is never satisfied with anything short of an omniscience that would detect the subtlest fold of the heart. —George Eliot, *The Mill on the Floss*

1. And now she began to think of her husband's will, which had been made at the time of their marriage, leaving the bulk of his property to her, with **proviso** in case of her having children. —George Eliot, *Middlemarch*

2. Nor should thy **prowess** want praise and esteem,
   But that 'tis shown ignobly,* and in treason.
   —Shakespeare, *King Henry VI, Part II*

3. The Princess was married by **proxy**, at her father's residence, by the Count de Schlüsselback. —W. M. Thackeray, *Vanity Fair*

4. What is her character? Is she solemn? Is she queer? Is she **prudish**? —Jane Austen, *Mansfield Park*

5. There is no folly so besotted* that the idiotic rivalries of society, the **prurience**, the rashness, the blindness of youth, will not hurry a man to its commission. —Charlotte Brontë, *Jane Eyre*

6. . . . I chose his name for my first **pseudonym** when I began to write for the newspapers . . . —William Dean Howells, *My Literary Passions*

****

1. **proviso**; condition, term, stipulation. —provisory; conditional. ※ provisional; temporary, interim, pro tempore.
2. **prowess**; bravery, valor, gallantry. —prow; 1. valiant, undaunted, plucky, intrepid, gritty. 2. *n.* forecastle, bow. * ignobly; basely, meanly.
3. **proxy**; deputy, substitute, surrogate.
4. **prudish**; overmodest, prim, demure. —prude, —prudishness, —prudishly. ※ poser *or* poseur; one who acts affectedly.
5. **prurience**; lechery, carnality, lubricity. —prurient. * besotted; foolish, doting.
6. **pseudonym**; pen name. ※ epithet; *see p. 105, no. 2.* ※ sobriquet; nickname.

1. There was always, in her conversation, the same odd mixture of audacity and **puerility**. —Henry James, *Daisy Miller*
2. Isaac Barrow, when at the Charterhouse School, was notorious for his **pugilistic** encounters. —Samuel Smiles, *Self Help*
3. The latter was a small, alert, dark-eyed man about thirty years of age, very sturdily built, with thick black eyebrows and a strong, **pugnacious** face. —Arthur Conan Doyle, *The Hound of the Baskervilles*
4. I cried in a loud voice, "Long live the most **puissant** king of Lilliput!*" —Jonathan Swift, *Gulliver's Travels*
5. They writhed* in their chairs to gaze around and over the impending* form of Tildy, that Aileen's **pulchritude** might season and make ambrosia* of their bacon and eggs. —O. Henry, *The Brief Debut of Tildy*
6. . . . there were no absolutely alarming symptoms, nothing touching the **pulmonary** complaint . . . —Jane Austen, *Emma*

****

1. **puerility**; childhood, immaturity. —puerility, —puerile; young, juvenile, jejune. ※ puberty; adolescence, teenage. ※ juvenile; young: *juvenile delinquency.*
2. **pugilistic**; of boxing, like boxing. —pugilist, —pugilism.
3. **pugnacious**; combative, hostile, bellicose, belligerent. —pugnacity.
4. **puissant**; powerful, mighty, potent. —puissance. * Lilliput; *see p. 178, no. 6.* ※ behemoth; huge creature, something enormous, colossus, leviathan, titan: *a new economic behemoth.*
5. **pulchritude**; fairness, comeliness. —pulchritudinous. * writhe; wriggle.* impending; imminent. * ambrosia; food of the gods. ※ nectar; drink of the gods.
6. **pulmonary**; of the lungs, pneumonic. ※ *pulmonary artery.*

♣ Nakedness is uncomely, as well in mind as body. —Francis Bacon, *Essays*

1. The wheels of the dairyman's spring cart, as he sped home from market, licked up the **pulverized** surface of the highway, and were followed by white ribands* of dust . . . —Thomas Hardy, *Tess*

2. What was to be done? To disobey the king's positive commands was monstrous in the eyes of the obsequious* courtiers of a **punctilious** court—but to obey him, and bury him alive, would be downright* regicide!* —Washington Irving, *Legend of the Rose of the Alhambra*

3. The meaner the type by which a law is expressed, the more **pungent** it is, and the more lasting in the memories of men. —R. W. Emerson, *The Poet*

4. It [aerial warfare] had this unique feature, that both sides lay open to **punitive** attack. —H. G. Well, *The War in the Air*

5. My uncle was a thin, **puny** little man, very meek and acquiescent,* and no match for my aunt. —Washington Irving, *The Adventure of My Aunt*

6. What I saw their bravest and their fairest do last night, the lowest multitude that could be scraped up* out of the **purlieus** of Christendom would blush to do, I think. —Mark Twain, *The Innocents Abroad*

****

1. **pulverize**; 1. grind, crumble. 2. demolish. —pulverizable. * riband; ribbon.
2. **punctilious**; 1. rigid, ceremonious. 2. meticulous. —punctilio. * obsequious; toadyish, sycophantic. * downright; plain. * regicide; the killing of a monarch.
3. **pungent**; sharp, piercing, biting, sarcastic, edgy, poignant, caustic. —pungency.
4. **punitive**; retaliative, retaliatory, retributive, vindictive. ※ punitive justice; Nemesis. ※ quid pro quo: 1. retaliation, reprisal, tit for tat. 2. compensation.
5. **puny**; 1. feeble, frail. 2. tiny. —puniness, —punily. * acquiescent; yielding.
6. **purlieus**; neighborhood, environs, outskirts. * scrape up; gather, garner.

♣ Only so much do I know, as I have lived. —R. W. Emerson, *The American Scholar*

1. Accordingly, the forger* was put to Death; the utterer of a bad note was put to Death; . . . the **purloiner** of forty shillings and sixpence was put to Death. —Charles Dickens, *A Tale of Two Cities*

2. Now, by all odds,* the most ancient extant* portrait anyways **purporting** to be the whale's, is to be found in the famous cavern-pagoda of Elephanta, in India. —Herman Melville, *Moby Dick*

3. All sounds are her [silence's] servants and **purveyors**. —Henry David Thoreau, *A Week on the Concord and Merrimack Rivers*

4. It is a **pusillanimous** desertion of our work to gaze after our neighbors. It is peeping. —R. W. Emerson, *Spiritual Laws*

5. I rehearsed **putative** parts in hypothetical conversations. I got up stories. —E. W. Hornung, *The Amateur Cracksman*

6. Sorrow is a kind of rust of the soul, which every new idea contributes in its passage to scour* away. It is the **putrefaction** of stagnant life, and is remedied by exercise and motion. —Samuel Johnson, *The Rambler*

****

1. **purloiner**; stealer, thief, burglar, filcher, pilferer. —purloin. * forger; counterfeiter. —forge; 1. furnace, smithy. 2. counterfeit. 3. form metal.
2. **purport**; 1. mean, intend, signify. 2. meaning, import, intention. * by all odds; unquestionably, definitely. * extant; surviving, subsisting, *see p. 114, no. 6.*
3. **purveyor**; 1. supplier, provider. 2. distributor. —purveyance, —purvey.
4. **pusillanimous**; cowardly, spiritless, timid, timorous. —pusillanimity.
5. **putative**; supposed, alleged, presumed. —putatively.
6. **putrefaction**; rot, decay, moldering, decomposition. —putrefy, —putrescent; decayed, putrid. ※ carrion; dead decomposing flesh. * scour; 1. brighten. 2. cleanse.

♣ The things which hurt, instruct. —Benjamin Franklin, *Poor Richard's Almanac*

1. Why is it that a bucket of water soon becomes **putrid**, but frozen remains sweet forever? It is commonly said that this is the difference between the affections and the intellect. —Henry David Thoreau, *Walden*

2. It [the swamp] was full of pits and **quagmires**, partly covered with weeds and mosses. —Washington Irving, *The Devil and Tom Walker*

3. . . . when it fell in reproof upon those servants, they shrunk and **quailed** as timid people do when the lightning flashes out of a cloud. —Mark Twain, *A Connecticut Yankee*

4. Some sudden **qualm** hath struck me at the heart,
   And dimm'd mine eyes, that I can read no further.
   —Shakespeare, *King Henry VI, Part II*

5. He asked one or two insidious* questions, so innocent in appearance that Hayward, not seeing into what a **quandary** they led him, answered blandly.* —W. Somerset Maugham, *Of Human Bondage*

6. The ship is lying here in the harbor of Naples—**quarantined**. . . . She is a prison, now. —Mark Twain, *The Innocents Abroad*

****

1. **putrid**; 1. rotten, corrupt, decayed, spoiled. 2. reeking, stinking. —putridity.
2. **quagmire**; 1. marsh, bog, slough. 2. predicament.
3. **quail**; shrink, recoil, flinch, cringe, cower.
4. **qualm**; 1. uneasiness, misgivings, scruple. 2. *n.* faint. 3. nausea. —qualmish.
5. **quandary**; predicament, impasse. * insidious; tricky. * blandly; mildly.
6. **quarantine**; isolate, separate, segregate.

♣ There is not a creed which is not shaken, not an accredited dogma which is not shown to be questionable, not a received tradition which does not threaten to dissolve. —Matthew Arnold, *The Study of Poetry*

1. She's a good girl. She's never been _______ like some of these girls.
2. Captain was a sailor of distinction even in a time _______ of renowned seamen.
3. Music is the sound of the universal laws _______.
4. The conditions for the _______ of the plant are favorable.
5. A lofty _______ of buildings separated the house from the main thoroughfare.
6. He secured silence by a humorous allusion to the _______ speaker.

[**promontory, promiscuous, prolific, prolix, propagation, promulgated**]

****

1. Dr. Freke, in 1851, _______ the doctrine.
2. The dew fell, but with _______ softness; no breeze whispered.
3. He carried his head on one side, in modest _______ of everybody else.
4. The Government sometimes participates in the national _______.
5. To the whale, his tail is the sole means of _______.
6. Here I disclaim all my paternal care, _______ and property of blood.

[**propounded, propitious, propinquity, propulsion, propensity, propitiation**]

****

1. It is the duty of the lexicographer to _______ the absurdities of our language.
2. In religion, it is absurd to aim at making _______ by fire and sword.
3. The old gentleman _______ his thick nether lip.
4. Life protracted is _______ woe.
5. It must not be forgotten that John Barleycorn is _______.
6. She is _______ with fear.

[**prostrate, proscribe, protean, protracted, proselytes, protruded**]

****

1. Nor should thy _______ want praise and esteem, but that 'tis shown ignobly.
2. What is her character? Is she solemn? Is she queer? Is she _______?
3. He willed all of his property to her, with _______ in case of her having child.
4. The Princess was married by _______, at her father's residence.
5. I chose his name for my first _______ when I began to write articles.
6. The _______ of youth would hurry a man to the commission of such a folly.

[**prudish, prowess, proxy, proviso, pseudonym, prurience**]

Review Exercise: Sentence Completions (pp. 245–48)

1. There was, in her speech, the same odd mixture of audacity and _______.
2. The latter was a small, alert, dark-eyed man with a strong, _______ face.
3. Isaac Barrow, when at the school, was notorious for his _______ encounters.
4. There were no alarming symptoms, nothing touching the _______ complaint.
5. I cried in a loud voice, "Long live the most _______ king of Lilliput!"
6. Aileen's _______ might season and make ambrosia of their bacon and eggs.

[**pulchritude, puissant, pulmonary, puerility, pugnacious, pugilistic**]

****

1. The meaner the type by which a law is expressed, the more _______ it is.
2. The wheels of the cart licked up the _______ surface of the highway.
3. You did what the _______ of Christendom would blush to do.
4. My uncle was a thin, _______ little man, very meek and acquiescent.
5. Both sides lay open to _______ attack.
6. The defiance was monsterous in the eyes of the courtiers of a _______ court.

[**punitive, puny, pungent, pulverized, purlieus, punctilious**]

****

1. It is a _______ desertion of our work to gaze after our neighbors.
2. The _______ of forty shillings and sixpence was put to death.
3. Sorrow is the _______ of stagnant life.
4. The old portrait _______ to be the whale's was found in the cavern-pagoda.
5. I rehearsed _______ parts in hypothetical conversations.
6. All sounds are her [silence's] servants and _______.

[**purloiner, pusillanimous, purporting, putrefaction, purveyors, putative**]

****

1. Some sudden _______ hath struck me at the heart.
2. When it fell in reproof upon those servants, they shrunk and _______.
3. The swamp was full of pits and _______.
4. Hayward couldn't see into what a _______ they led him.
5. The ship is lying here in the harbor of Naples—_______.
6. A bucket of water soon becomes _______, but frozen remains sweet forever.

[**qualm, quagmires, quailed, quandary, putrid, quarantined**]

1. If you want excitement, the excitement of a dangerous chase after a tremendous **quarry**, take your life in your hands, go in and win. —E. Phillips Oppenheim, *The Yellow Crayon*
2. The mutiny was **quelled**. —Charlotte Brontë, *The Professor*
3. His basilisk* eyes were nearly **quenched** by sleeplessness—and weeping, perhaps, for the lashes were wet then. —Emily Brontë, *Wuthering Heights*
4. Nothing was stirring except a brindled,* grey cat, which crept from the ashes, and saluted me with a **querulous** mew. —Emily Brontë, *Wuthering Heights*
5. Now, no philanthropist* likes to be opposed with **quibbling**. —Herman Melville, *The Confidence-Man*
6. She folded herself in the large chair, and leaned her head against it in fatigued **quiescence**. —George Eliot, *Middlemarch*

****

1. **quarry**; 1. prey, game. 2. target. 3. stone pit. 4. *v.* excavate.
2. **quell**; 1. overpower, subdue, suppress, squelch, subjugate. 2. pacify, soothe, appease, mitigate, alleviate. —queller.
3. **quench**; 1. put out, extinguish, smother. 2. suppress. —quenchable, —quenchless. * basilisk; legendary serpent.
4. **querulous**; complaining, grumbling, whining. * brindled; mottled, spotted.
5. **quibble**; 1. cavil, carp. 2. evade, prevaricate. * philanthropist; benefactor.
6. **quiescence**; 1. inactivity, inertia, dormancy, desuetude, suspension, abeyance. 2. repose. —quiescent. ※ abeyance; pause, quiescence, suspension: *The government held the project in abeyance.*

♣ The deviation of man from the stage in which he was originally placed by nature seems to have proved to him a prolific source of diseases. —Edward Jenner, *Vaccination Against Smallpox*

1. What a piece of work is a man! How noble in reason! How infinite in faculties! . . . The beauty of the world, the paragon* of animals! And yet, to me, what is this **quintessence** of dust? —Shakespeare, *Hamlet*

2. No **quips** now, Pistol!

   —Shakespeare, *The Merry Wives of Windsor*

3. I have felt so many **quirks** of joy and grief,
   That the first face of neither, on the start,
   Can woman me* unto't.

   —Shakespeare, *All's Well that Ends Well*

4. She is ready prey to any man who knows how to play adroitly either on her affectionate ardor or her **Quixotic** enthusiasm. —George Eliot, *Middlemarch*

5. The senators are to be chosen for the period of six years; . . . and no state is to be entitled to more than two senators; a **quorum** of the body is to consist of sixteen members. —Alexander Hamilton, *The Federalist Papers*

6. If I could meet that fancy-monger,* I would give him some good counsel, for he seems to have the **quotidian** of love upon him. —Shakespeare, *As You Like It*

****

1. **quintessence**; essence, core, kernel, marrow, pith. —quintessential. * paragon; perfection, beau ideal, nonpareil, apotheosis, *see p. 214, no. 4.*
2. **quip**; 1. jest, wisecrack, gibe, sally. 2. repartee, retort.
3. **quirk**; 1. freak, caprice. 2. trait. * woman me; make me feminine (i.e., cry).
4. **quixotic**; fanciful, unrealistic, unpractical, romantic, chimerical. —quixotism, —quixotry, —quixotically. ※ chimera; fancy, illusion, delusion, hallucination.
5. **quorum**; the least number of members to be present for a valid meeting.
6. **quotidian**; 1. daily fever. 2. daily, diurnal. 3. trivial, commonplace. * fancy-monger; 1. capricious lover. 2. love-monger, love dealer.

1. The **rabble** call him lord.

—Shakespeare, *Hamlet*

2. Mugridge seemed to be in **rabid** fear of the water, and he exhibited a nimbleness and speed we did not dream he possessed. —Jack London, *The Sea Wolf*

3. He bowed cordially to the lady in charge of Miss de Barral's education, whom he saw in the hall engaged in conversation with a very good-looking but somewhat **raffish** young gentleman. —Joseph Conrad, *Chance*

4. It will generally be found that the men who are thus habitually behind time are as habitually behind success; and the world generally casts them aside to swell the ranks* of the grumblers and the **railers** against fortune. —Samuel Smiles, *Self Help*

5. God gave the righteous man a certificate entitling him to food and **raiment** . . . —Henry David Thoreau, *Life without Principle*

6. There was a **rakish**, vagabond smartness, and a kind of boastful rascality,* about the whole man that was worth a mine of gold. —Charles Dickens, *The Pickwick Papers*

****

1. **rabble**; mob, swarm, throng, horde, the lower crowd.
2. **rabid**; 1. raging, fanatical, maniacal. 2. of rabies (hydrophobia *or* lyssa) : *rabid dogs*. —rabidity, —rabidness, —rabidly. ※ acrophobia; morbid dread of heights. ※ xenophobia; abnormal fear of aliens. ※ claustrophobia; pathological fear of narrow place. ※ hydrophobia; 1. unreasonable dread of water. 2. rabies.
3. **raffish**; disreputable, discreditable, vulgar, rakish. —raffishness.
4. **railer**; scolder, vilifier, reviler. * swell the ranks; multiply the number.
5. **raiment**; garment, apparel, array, garb.
6. **rakish**; 1. sporty, dapper. 2. jaunty, debonair. * rascality; roguery.

1. He knew all the **ramifications** of New York's cousinships. —Edith Wharton, *The Age of Innocence*

2. The weeds had taken advantage of Phoebe's absence, and the long-continued rain, to run **rampant** over the flowers and kitchen-vegetables. —Nathaniel Hawthorne, *The House of the Seven Gables*

3. Directly on the shore of the lake, and nearer to its western than to its eastern margin, lay the extensive* earthen **ramparts** and low buildings of William Henry. —James Fenimore Cooper, *The Last of the Mohicans*

4. Under a tree in this commanding yet neglected spot was an old **ramshackle** wooden seat. —G. K. Chesterton, *The Innocence of Father Brown*

5. The dinner was served in two huge tin-plated vessels, whence rose a strong steam redolent* of **rancid** fat. —Charlotte Brontë, *Jane Eyre*

6. He [the free man] recognizes the laws of the state and he can break them without sense of sin, but if he is punished he accepts the punishment without **rancour**. —W. Somerset Maugham, *Of Human Bondage*

****

1. **ramification**; 1. branch, offshoot, extension. 2. upshot, sequel. —ramify.
2. **rampant**; violent, raging, rampageous, rambunctious. —rampancy.
3. **rampart**; bulwark, bastion, barrier, stronghold. * extensive; immense.
4. **ramshackle**; shaky, rickety, decrepit, unstable.
5. **rancid**; stinking, foul, fetid, rank, putrid. —rancidity. * redolent; fragrant.
6. **rancour**; malevolence, spite, grudge, enmity, animosity. —rancorous.

♣ As much experience is 'prudence,' so is much science 'sapience.' —Thomas Hobbes, *Of Man*

1. The snub* which the waitress had inflicted on him **rankled**. —W. Somerset Maugham, *Of Human Bondage*

2. Whilst Soult **ransacked** and carried away with him from Spain numerous pictures of great value, Wellington did not appropriate to himself a single farthing's worth of property. —Samuel Smiles, *Self Help*

3. To speak the honest truth, without any false **rant** or assumed romance, there actually was a moment, six months ago, when I thought her divine. —Charlotte Brontë, *Villette*

4. I have a recollection of large, unbending women with great noses and **rapacious** eyes, who wore their clothes as though they were armour. —W. Somerset Maugham, *The Moon and Sixpence*

5. . . . I had been in **rapport** with you. —Arthur Conan Doyle, *The Memoirs of Sherlock Holmes*

6. Where lies the final harbour, whence we unmoor* no more? In what **rapt** ether* sails the world, of which the weariest will never weary? —Herman Melville, *Moby Dick*

****

1. **rankle**; inflame, fester, chafe, gall. * snub; 1. slight, affront. 2. chill.
2. **ransack**; 1. pillage, plunder, ravage. 2. rummage, forage.
3. **rant**; bombast, bravado, grandiloquence, magniloquence. —ranter.
4. **rapacious**; greedy, avaricious, voracious, ravenous. —rapacity.
5. **rapport**; 1. harmony, affinity, empathy. 2. fellowship, camaraderie. ※ rapprochement; détente, reconciliation: *Two nations reached a rapprochement*.
6. **rapt**; 1. enchanted, captivated. 2. intent, absorbed, engrossed. —raptness. * unmoor; up the anchor. * ether; 1. air, atmosphere. 2. the upper sky.

♣ A good deal of our politics is physiological. —R. W. Emerson, *Fate*

1. The county gentry* of old time lived in a **rarefied** social air. —George Eliot, *Middlemarch*

2. The gift of **ratiocination** and making syllogisms*—I mean in man—for in superior classes of beings, such as angels and spirits—'tis all done, may it please your worships, as they tell me, by Intuition. —Laurence Sterne, *Tristram Shandy*

3. . . . and [he] spoke in a **raucous** undertone as if he had half-forgotten how to speak. —G. K. Chesterton, *The Innocence of Father Brown*

4. It must be more natural to rob for gain, than to **ravage** only for mischief. —Samuel Johnson, *The Rambler*

5. Left alone, the minister summoned a servant of the house, and requested food, which, being set before him, he ate with **ravenous** appetite. —Nathaniel Hawthorne, *The Scarlet Letter*

6. My house has been destroyed—**razed** to the ground. —Charles Dickens, *A Tale of Two Cities*

****

1. **rarefy**; purify, refine, sublimate, subtilize. —rarefaction. * gentry; nobility.
2. **ratiocination**; reasoning, rational thinking. —ratiocinate, * syllogism; reasoning from two premises to a conclusion. ※ induction; reasoning from the particular to the general. ***ant.*** deduction.
3. **raucous**; 1. hoarse, gruff. 2. discordant, dissonant, cacophonous. —raucity.
4. **ravage**; plunder, pillage, maraud, ransack, despoil. —ravagement.
5. **ravenous**; ravening, edacious, esurient. —raven; 1. big crow. 2. *v.* devour.
6. **raze**; break down, destruct, ruin, demolish. —razer.

♣ That character is power, is true in a much higher sense than that knowledge is power. —Samuel Smiles, *Self Help*

1. Of course he was far from being a moss-grown* **reactionary**. —Joseph Conrad, *Under Western Eyes*

2. Sir Joshua Reynolds, when a boy, forgot his lessons, and took pleasure only in drawing, for which his father was accustomed to **rebuke** him. —Samuel Smiles, *Self Help*

3. I never remember being so wrapt up in any book, as I was in Joyce's *Scientific Dialogues*; and I was rather **recalcitrant** to my father's criticisms of the bad reasoning respecting the first principles of physics, which abounds in the early part of that work. —John Stuart Mill, *Autobiography*

4. Had society then beaten him into submission? Was he a coward? Had he been bulldozed* into **recanting**? —Jack London, *The Iron Heel*

5. The scientific attainments of Professor Summerlee are too well known for me to trouble to **recapitulate** them. —Arthur Conan Doyle, *The Lost World*

6. Affection, when **reciprocated**, gives rights. —E. M. Forster, *Howards End*

****

1. **reactionary**; ultraconservative, right-winger. * moss-grown; antiquated
2. **rebuke**; chide, reproach, reprimand, upbraid, reprove. —rebukingly. ※ rebut; retort, refute, confute, contradict: *The lawyer rebutted the testifier's rebuttal.*
3. **recalcitrant**; objecting to, contrary, defiant, unwilling, refractory, renitent. —recalcitrance, —recalcitration, —recalcitrate.
4. **recant**; 1. withdraw, retract, revoke, renounce, abjure. 2. deny, disavow, repudiate. —recantation. ※ renege on; recant: *He reneged on his promise to witness the suspect's innocence at the court.* * bulldoze; bully, intimidate, coerce.
5. **recapitulate**; 1. reiterate the main points. 2. summarize, epitomize. —recapitulation. ※ replicate; copy, duplicate, *see p. 266, no.5.*
6. **reciprocate**; 1. interchange, exchange. 2. return, requite. —reciprocation.

1. . . . she was a perfect **recluse**; and, apparently, perfectly contented. —Emily Brontë, *Wuthering Heights*

2. I'm just goin' to **reconnoiter**. I won't go close. —Jack London, *The Valley of the Moon*

3. I really cannot allow this matter to go any further without some explanation. Tupman, **recount** the circumstances. —Charles Dickens, *The Pickwick Papers*

4. I had no parish to have **recourse** to for my nourishment in my infancy. —Daniel Defoe, *Moll Flanders*

5. Delinquencies,* from whatever causes, would be productive of complaints, **recriminations**, and quarrels. —Alexander Hamilton, *The Federalist Papers*

6. In the sublimest flights of the soul, **rectitude** is never surmounted,* love is never outgrown. —R. W. Emerson, *Divinity School Address*

****

1. **recluse**; hermit, eremite, anchorite, the secluded. —reclusive.
2. **reconnoiter**; check out, scout. —reconnaissance, —reconnoiterer.
3. **recount**; 1. tell or relate in detail, describe. 2. enumerate. ※ raconteur; good relater or storyteller, narrator, anecdotist.
4. **recourse**; resort, resource, refuge, expedient.
5. **recrimination**; countercharge, counteraccusation, retort. —recriminate. * delinquency; 1. negligence, dereliction. 2. misconduct, crime.
6. **rectitude**; honesty, righteousness, equity, uprightness, integrity, verity, probity. —rectitudinous. * surmount; overcome, vanquish.

♣ How far that little candle throws his beams!
So shines a good deed in a naughty world.

—Shakespeare, *The Merchant of Venice*

1. The mutiny was _______.
2. His basilisk eyes were nearly _______ by sleeplessness.
3. She leaned her head against the large chair in fatigued _______.
4. Now, no philanthropist likes to be opposed with _______.
5. A brindled, grey cat saluted me with a _______ mew.
6. Do you want the excitement of a dangerous chase after a tremendous _______?

[quibbling, quelled, quenched, quarry, querulous, quiescence]

****

1. What a piece of work is a man! . . . What is this _______ of dust?
2. No _______ now, Pistol!
3. A _______ of the body is to consist of sixteen members.
4. He knows how to play adroitly on her _______ enthusiasm.
5. The fancy-monger seems to have the _______ of love upon him.
6. I have felt many _______ of joy and grief.

[quips, quorum, quixotic, quirks, quotidian, quintessence]

****

1. God gave the righteous man a certificate entitling him to food and _______.
2. There was a _______, vagabond smartness about the whole man.
3. The world is swelling the ranks of the _______ against fortune.
4. He was a very good-looking but somewhat _______ young gentleman.
5. The _______ call him lord.
6. Mugridge seemed to be in _______ fear of the water.

[railers, raiment, rakish, raffish, rabid, rabble]

****

1. If the free man is punished he accepts the punishment without _______.
2. From two huge tin-plated vessels rose a strong steam redolent of _______ fat.
3. The weeds had run _______ over the flowers and kitchen-vegetables.
4. Directly on the shore of the lake lay the extensive earthen _______.
5. Under a tree in this neglected spot was an old _______ wooden seat.
6. He knew all the _______ of New York's cousinships.

[rancour, rancid, ramshackle, ramparts, ramifications, rampant]

Review Exercise: Sentence Completions (pp. 255–58)

1. I have a recollection of large, unbending women with _______ eyes.
2. I had been in _______ with you.
3. Without any false _______, there was a moment when I thought her divine.
4. In what _______ ether sails the world, of which the weariest will never weary?
5. The snub which the waitress had inflicted on him _______.
6. Soult _______ and carried away with him from Spain numerous pictures.

[**ransacked, rankled, rapt, rapacious, rapport, rant**]

****

1. The minister ate the food with _______ appetite.
2. My house has been destroyed—_______ to the ground.
3. It must be more natural to rob for gain, than to _______ only for mischief.
4. The county gentry of old time lived in a _______ social air.
5. Man has the gift of _______ and making syllogisms.
6. He spoke in a _______ undertone as if he had half-forgotten how to speak.

[**razed, ravenous, raucous, ratiocination, ravage, rarefied**]

****

1. I was rather _______ to my father's criticisms of the bad reasoning.
2. Affection, when _______, gives rights.
3. Had he been bulldozed into _______?
4. I don't have to trouble to _______ his scientific attainments.
5. Of course he was far from being a moss-grown _______.
6. His father was accustomed to _______ him for taking pleasure in drawing.

[**rebuke, recalcitrant, reactionary, recapitulate, reciprocated, recanting**]

****

1. Delinquencies would be productive of quarrels and _______.
2. She was a perfect _______; and, apparently, perfectly contented.
3. I'm just goin' to _______. I won't go close.
4. In the sublimest flights of the soul, _______ is never surmounted.
5. I had no parish to have _______ to for my nourishment in my infancy.
6. I really cannot understand this matter. Tupman, _______ the circumstances.

[**recourse, recluse, recriminations, recount, reconnoiter, rectitude**]

1. Even after the stars were glimmering above his head, he was able to distinguish the **recumbent** forms of his companions, as they lay stretched on the grass. —James Fenimore Cooper, *The Last of the Mohicans*

2. The week's rest had **recuperated** the dogs and put them in thorough trim. —Jack London, *The Call of the Wild*

3. He delighted to witness Hindley degrading himself past **redemption**. —Emily Brontë, *Wuthering Heights*

4. On every side, Oxford is **redolent** of age and authority. —R. W. Emerson, *English Traits*

5. Bert was **redoubtable**. —Jack London, *The Valley of the Moon*

6. . . . she was quite a child, perhaps seven or eight years old, slightly built, with a pale, small-featured face, and a **redundancy** of hair falling in curls to her waist. —Charlotte Brontë, *Jane Eyre*

****

1. **recumbent**; 1. inactive, reposing. 2. leaning, reclining. —recumbency.
2. **recuperate**; recover, heal, regain, restore. —recuperation.
3. **redemption**; 1. deliverance, rescue, salvation. 2. compensation, reparation. 3. atonement, expiation. —redeem, —redemptive.
4. **redolent**; 1. odorous, fragrant. 2. reminiscent, suggestive. —redolence.
5. **redoubtable**; dreadful, terrific, awful, formidable. ※ redoubt; stronghold.
6. **redundancy**; 1. excess, superfluity, surfeit. 2. repetition. —redundant.

♣ Death is like the insect
Menacing the tree,
Competent to kill it,
But decoyed may be.

—Emily Dickinson, "Death is like the insect"

1. The sunset fires, **refracted** from the cloud-driftage of the autumn sky, bathed the canyon with crimson* . . . —Jack London, *The Valley of the Moon*

2. He knew the game, and could conquer the most **refractory** lion with a broom handle—not outside the cage, but inside and locked in. —Jack London, *Michael, Brother of Jerry*

3. The flashes of her dark **refulgent** eye were like sparks of fire on the withered, yet combustible,* heart of Aben Habuz. —Washington Irving, *Legend of the Arabian Astrologer*

4. The accusation had been eagerly **refuted** at the time. —Jane Austen, *Emma*

5. In heaven's name, I'll ascend* the **regal** throne.

   —Shakespeare, *King Richard II*

6. Who would think, then, that such fine ladies and gentlemen should **regale** themselves with an essence found in the inglorious bowels of a sick whale! —Herman Melville, *Moby Dick*

****

1. **refract**; change the direction of a ray, deflect. —refractile; refractive, refractable, refrangible. * crimson; deep red.
2. **refractory**; wilful, unruly, intractable, recalcitrant. —refractoriness.
3. **refulgent**; radiant, resplendent, effulgent. * combustible; inflammable.
4. **refute**; contradict, retort, rebut, confute, disprove. —refutation, —refutable.
5. **regal**; royal, sovereign. —regality; 1. royalty, sovereignty. 2. kingdom. —regalia; privilege or emblem of royalty. * ascend; climb, go up, gain.
6. **regale**; entertain, feast. —regalement, —regaler.

♣ Error may flourish for a time, but Truth will prevail in the end. —John Henry Newman, *The Idea of University*

1. It is, perhaps, from their meat **regimen** that the Gauchos,* like other carnivorous animals, can abstain long from food. —Charles Darwin, *The Voyage of the Beagle*
2. The worthy gentleman then became once more the life and soul of the society, being again **reinstated** in his old post of lion . . . —Charles Dickens, *Nicholas Nickleby*
3. Her eyes darkened, and he expected an indignant **rejoinder**. —Edith Wharton, *The Age of Innocence*
4. She was fast **relapsing** into stupor*; nor did her mind again rally*: at twelve o'clock that night she died. —Charlotte Brontë, *Jane Eyre*
5. . . . at once I am **relegated** from cabin table to galley* . . . —Jack London, *The Sea Wolf*
6. The words cut Dorothea to the heart, and made her **relent**. —George Eliot, *Middlemarch*

****

1. **regimen**; diet. * Gaucho; cowboy of the South American plains.
2. **reinstate**; restore, reestablish, rehabilitate. —reinstatement. ※ refurbish; remodel, renovate, revamp, repair: *The old man refurbished the old house.*
3. **rejoinder** *n.*; reply, response, retort. —rejoin *v.*; rebut, riposte *also* ripost.
4. **relapse**; revert, regress. * stupor; torpor, inertia. * rally; recuperate.
5. **relegate**; oust, banish, expel, deport, exile. —relegation, —relegable. * galley; 1. kitchen of a ship. 2. an ancient large rowboat.
6. **relent**; soften, become lenient, be merciful. —relentingly. ※ relentless; 1. merciless, ruthless. 2. persistent, unremitting.

♣ The most sublime act is to set another before you.

—William Blake, *The Marriage of Heaven and Hell*

1. **Relinquish** your labours: you must be weary, and let me have the happiness of giving you rest. —Charlotte Brontë, *The Professor*

2. . . . and the cheerfulness of the children added a **relish** to his existence. —Jane Austen, *Sense and Sensibility*

3. He took his hat and went out, with a dragging, **reluctant** step. —Stephen Crane, *Maggie, A Girl of the Streets*

4. In proportion as I addicted myself more and more to loose pleasure, I must grow more and more **remiss** in application to my studies. —Henry Fielding, *Tom Jones*

5. She answered her sister's **remonstrance** with a faint smile. —Wilkie Collins, *No Name*

6. O, let not virtue seek
   Remuneration for the thing it was!

   —Shakespeare, *Troilus and Cressida*

****

1. **relinquish**; surrender, renounce, waive. —relinquishment. ※ jettison; abandon, relinquish: *The company jettisoned the project because the risk was too high.*
2. **relish**; 1. delight, gratification, enjoyment. 2. taste, zest, gusto, palate. 3. seasoning, condiment. 4. *vt., vi.* taste, savor. —relishable.
3. **reluctant**; disinclined, grudging, loath, averse, recalcitrant. —reluctance.
4. **remiss**; negligent, slack, slothful. —remissness. ※ remission; 1. subsidence, abatement: *His pancreatic cancer is now in remission.* 2. pardon, remittal.
5. **remonstrance**; 1. admonition, reproof, reproach, reprimand, expostulation. 2. complaint, protest. —remonstrate, —remonstrant.
6. **remuneration**; 1. compensation, recompense, reimbursement. 2. payment, wages, salary. —remunerative; profitable, gainful, lucrative.

1. . . . seen with arms in his hands and in a questionable attitude, he was shot for a **renegade** seaman. —Herman Melville, *Benito Cereno*
2. The man who **renounces** himself, comes to himself. —R. W. Emerson, *Divinity School Address*
3. After such wrong as he had suffered, there is no **reparation**. —Nathaniel Hawthorne, *The House of the Seven Gables*
4. I intended no pointed **repartee**; it was only a blunder.* —Charlotte Brontë, *Jane Eyre*
5. At length the jackal* had got together a compact **repast** for the lion, and proceeded to offer it to him. —Charles Dickens, *A Tale of Two Cities*
6. They who make laws may, without doubt, amend or **repeal** them; and it will not be disputed that they who make treaties may alter or cancel them. —James Madison, *The Federalist Papers*

****

1. **renegade**; 1. traitorous, treasonous, mutinous. 2. betrayer, apostate.
2. **renounce**; abandon, abdicate, relinquish. —renunciation, —renunciant.
3. **reparation**; 1. compensation, amends, restitution. 2. repair. —reparable.
4. **repartee**; witty retort, riposte. * blunder; error, faux pas. ※ gaffe; blunder: *The ambassador made a big gaffe at the party; he spilled hot soup on the queen's dress.* ※ solecism; 1. ungrammatical usage. 2. gaffe. ※ neologism; 1. new word: *The development of science has caused many neologisms.* 2. coinage.
5. **repast**; meal, table. * jackal; 1. fawner performing servile tasks for another. 2. canine mammal in Asia and Africa.
6. **repeal**; 1. *v.* abolish, nullify, revoke, rescind, abrogate, countermand. 2. *n.* abolition, withdrawal, invalidation, revocation, nullification. —repealable.

♣ Every act rewards itself. —R. W. Emerson, *Compensation*

1. Science has proved that forces, sensible and occult,* physical and metaphysical, simple and complex, surround, traverse, vibrate, rotate, **repel**, attract, without stop. —Henry Adams, *The Education of Henry Adams*

2. The sage precepts* of the first instructors of the world are transmitted from age to age with little variation, and echoed from one author to another, not perhaps without some loss of their original force at every **repercussion**. —Samuel Johnson, *The Rambler*

3. He loved books, never going to sea without a newly **replenished** library, compact but of the best. —Herman Melville, *Billy Budd*

4. Her looks do argue her **replete** with modesty;
   Her words do show her wit incomparable.
   —Shakespeare, *King Henry VI, Part III*

5. When the two are made with equal skill the **replica** is the more valuable, for it is supposed to be more beautiful than it looks. —Ambrose Bierce, *The Devil's Dictionary*

6. His impassive* **repose** (he seldom stirred a limb when once he sat down) was like a display of dignity. —Joseph Conrad, *Lord Jim*

****

1. **repel**; drive back, reject, repulse, rebuff, resist. —repellent; repugnant, rebarbative. —repellence. * occult; mysterious, esoteric.
2. **repercussion**; echo, reverberation. —repercussive. * precept; aphorism, adage.
3. **replenish**; refill, restock, reload, reinforce. —replenishment.
4. **replete**; filled, stuffed, abounding, brimming, teeming. —repletion.
5. **replica**; duplicate of a work of art. —replication, —replicate; duplicate: *replicating Picasso's* Guernica.
6. **repose**; 1. calmness, tranquility, composure, serenity, equanimity, aplomb. 2. rest, relaxation. * impassive; emotionless, aloof, apathetic, *see p. 147, no. 1.*

1. She never **reprehended** him but mildly.
—Shakespeare, *The Comedy of Errors*

2. However brilliant a contest or a victory might be, no sign or sound betrayed that any one was moved. A dignified gravity and **repression** were maintained at all times. —Mark Twain, *A Tramp Abroad*

3. Death, that inexorable* judge, had passed sentence on him, and refused to grant him a **reprieve**. —Henry Fielding, *Tom Jones*

4. Let us affront* and **reprimand** the smooth mediocrity* and squalid* contentment of the times. —R. W. Emerson, *Self-Reliance*

5. Letters of **reprisal** were granted, and a war ensued.* —Alexander Hamilton, *The Federalist Papers*

6. Robert Clive was a dunce,* if not a **reprobate**, when a youth; but always full of energy, even in badness. —Samuel Smiles, *Self Help*

****

1. **reprehend**; reprove, admonish, reprobate, reproach, reprimand, rebuke, blame, criticize. —reprehension, —reprehensible.
2. **repression**; 1. restraint, constraint. 2. suppression, subjugation. —repressive.
3. **reprieve**; 1. parole, respite, stay of execution. 2. pardon, acquittal, remission, remittal. —reprieval. * inexorable; relentless, implacable.
4. **reprimand**; scold, admonish, reproach, rebuke, chide, upbraid, reprove. * affront; offend, outrage. * mediocrity; commonplace. * squalid; filthy.
5. **reprisal**; retaliation, retribution, requital, vengeance. * ensue; follow.
6. **reprobate**; 1. rascal, scoundrel, ruffian. 2. *v.* condemn. ※ the reprobate; the damned. ***ant.*** the elect. * dunce; dullard, dolt, blockhead, simpleton.

♣ There is no such thing as a moral or an immoral book. Books are well written, or badly written. —Oscar Wilde, *The Picture of Dorian Gray*

1. "Your humility, Mr. Bingley," said Elizabeth, "must disarm **reproof**." —Jane Austen, *Pride and Prejudice*

2. Dalton, the chemist, **repudiated** the notion of his being "a genius," attributing everything which he had accomplished to simple industry and accumulation. —Samuel Smiles, *Self Help*

3. Overcoming the **repugnance** natural to one who had never before touched a dead body, I stooped and turned him over to feel for his heart. —H. G. Wells, *The War of the Worlds*

4. Without contraries is no progression. Attraction and **Repulsion**, Reason and Energy, Love and Hate, are necessary to Human existence.
—William Blake, *The Marriage of Heaven and Hell*

5. We skirted around two-thirds of the island, four miles from shore, and all the opera glasses in the ship were called into **requisition** to settle disputes as to whether mossy spots on the uplands were groves of trees or groves of weeds. —Mark Twain, *The Innocents Abroad*

6. To do good to mankind is the chivalrous* plan
   And is always as nobly **requited**.
   —Lord Byron, "When a man hath no freedom to fight for at home"

****

1. **reproof**; blame, rebuke, reproval, objurgation. ※ reprove; reproach.
2. **repudiate**; deny, negate, refuse, disavow. —repudiation, —repudiable.
3. **repugnance**; antipathy, abhorrence, aversion, reluctance. —repugnant.
4. **repulsion**; 1. repelling. 2. abhorrence, repugnance. —repulsive, —repulse.
5. **requisition**; 1. demand, request. 2. summons. —requisite; required.
6. **requite**; 1. recompense, reciprocate, indemnify. 2. avenge, retaliate. —requital.
   * chivalrous; 1. knightly. 2. courteous, gallant.

1. On every side, Oxford is _______ of age and authority.
2. Bert was _______.
3. The week's rest had _______ the dogs and put them in thorough trim.
4. She was quite a child with a _______ of hair falling in curls to her waist.
5. He delighted to witness Hindley degrading himself past _______.
6. He was able to distinguish the _______ forms of his companions.

[**redoubtable, redolent, redundancy, recuperated, redemption, recumbent**]

****

1. The flashes of her dark _______ eye were like sparks of fire on his heart.
2. The accusation had been eagerly _______ at the time.
3. They _______ themselves with an essence found in the bowels of a sick whale.
4. In heaven's name, I'll ascend the _______ throne.
5. The sunset fires were _______ from the cloud-driftage of the autumn sky.
6. He could conquer the most _______ lion with a broom handle.

[**regal, refracted, refulgent, regaled, refuted, refractory**]

****

1. At once I am _______ from cabin table to galley.
2. Her eyes darkened, and he expected an indignant _______.
3. The Gauchos can abstain long from food, perhaps, from their meat _______.
4. The words cut Dorothea to the heart, and made her _______.
5. The worthy gentleman was again _______ in his old post of lion.
6. She was fast _______ into stupor.

[**relapsing, reinstated, relegated, rejoinder, relent, regimen**]

****

1. _______ your labours; you must be weary.
2. O, let not virtue seek _______ for the thing it was!
3. The cheerfulness of the children added a _______ to his existence.
4. He took his hat and went out, with a dragging, _______ step.
5. She answered her sister's _______ with a faint smile.
6. I grew more and more _______ in application to my studies.

[**reluctant, remonstrance, remuneration, relish, remiss, relinquish**]

Review Exercise: Sentence Completions (pp. 265–68)

1. They who make laws may, without doubt, amend or _______ them.
2. At length the jackal had got together a compact _______ for the lion.
3. After such wrong as he had suffered, there is no _______.
4. I intended no pointed _______; it was only a blunder.
5. He was shot for a _______ seaman.
6. The man who _______ himself, comes to himself.

[**repartee, reparation, renounces, repeal, renegade, repast**]

****

1. He never went to sea without a newly _______ library.
2. Forces, physical and metaphysical, vibrate, _______, attract, without stop.
3. The sage precepts have lost somewhat of their original force at every _______.
4. When the two are made with equal skill the _______ is the more valuable.
5. His impassive _______ was like a display of dignity.
6. Her looks do argue her _______ with modesty.

[**replete, repose, replenished, replica, repercussion, repel**]

****

1. Death had passed sentence on him, and refused to grant him a _______.
2. A dignified gravity and _______ were maintained at all times.
3. Robert Clive was a dunce, if not a _______, when a youth.
4. She never _______ him but mildly.
5. Letters of _______ were granted, and a war ensued.
6. Let's _______ the smooth mediocrity and squalid contentment of the times.

[**reprisal, reprimand, reprehended, reprieve, repression, reprobate**]

****

1. Dalton, the chemist, _______ the notion of his being a genius.
2. Your humility must disarm _______.
3. To do good to mankind is the chivalrous plan and is always as nobly _______.
4. Overcoming the _______ to a dead body, I turned him over to feel for his heart.
5. Attraction and _______, love and hate, are necessary to human existence.
6. All the opera glasses in the ship were called into _______.

[**repugnance, reproof, repudiated, requisition, repulsion, requited**]

1. One party to a contract may violate it—break it, so to speak, but does it not require all to lawfully **rescind** it? —Abraham Lincoln, *The First Inaugural Address*

2. The volatile* truth of our words should continually betray the inadequacy of the **residual** statement. —Henry David Thoreau, *Walden*

3. The blaze of tropic suns was in his face, and in his swelling, **resilient** muscles was the primordial vigor of life. —Jack London, *Martin Eden*

4. He had a deep, **resonant** voice, fitted to his massive frame. —W. Somerset Maugham, *The Moon and Sixpence*

5. We deferred our excursion till the afternoon; a golden afternoon of August: every breath from the hills so full of life, that it seemed whoever **respired** it, though dying, might revive. —Emily Brontë, *Wuthering Heights*

6. O injurious love,
   That **respites** me a life, whose very comfort
   Is still a dying horror!
   —Shakespeare, *Measure for Measure*

****

1. **rescind**; repeal, revoke, abrogate. —rescindment; annulment, rescission.
2. **residual**; remaining, leftover, surplus. —residue. * volatile; 1. inconstant, variable. 2. fickle, mercurial.
3. **resilient**; bouncy, elastic, buoyant. —resilience.
4. **resonant**; 1. resounding, reverberating. 2. ringing, sonorous. —resonance.
5. **respire**; breathe, inhale and exhale. —respiration, —respiratory.
6. **respite**; 1. *v.* defer, reprieve. 2. *n.* delay, suspension. 3. interval. ※ moratorium; 1. permission to a debtor to suspend payments. 2. *n.* respite.

♣ The universe is fluid and volatile. —R. W. Emerson, *Circles*

1. Adam and Eve were then created by God and placed in Eden, in the plain of Damascus, that lovely garden **resplendent** with sunlight and colour, teeming with luxuriant* vegetation. —James Joyce, *A Portrait of the Artist as a Young Man*
2. He owed no man, and **restitution** was unthinkable. —Jack London, *Burning Daylight*
3. In fact, precisely as a rash,* **restive** horse is said to feel his oats,* so Turkey felt his coat. —Herman Melville, *Bartleby*
4. Let me but **retaliate** upon him, by degrees, however slow—let me but begin to get the better of* him, let me but turn the scale*—and I can bear it. —Charles Dickens, *Nicholas Nickleby*
5. He was not eloquent, but there was a dignity in this constitutional **reticence**, there was a high seriousness in his stammerings. —Joseph Conrad, *Lord Jim*
6. He was a sober, steady-looking young man of **retiring** manners, with a comic head of hair, and eyes that were rather wide open. —Charles Dickens, *David Copperfield*

****

1. **resplendent**; brilliant, radiant, irradiant, refulgent, effulgent. —resplendence. * luxuriant; abundant, lush, rank.
2. **restitution**; 1. compensation, recompense, reimbursement, reparation, redress, indemnification. 2. restoration, reinstatement. —restitute *v.*
3. **restive**; 1. unruly, recalcitrant, refractory. 2. fretful, fractious. * rash; hasty, impetuous, reckless. * feel one's oats; 1. be frisky. 2. feel self-important.
4. **retaliate**; avenge, revenge, reciprocate, requite. —retaliation. * get the better of; defeat, surmount, outwit. * turn the scale; change the situation.
5. **reticence**; 1. quiet, tacitness, taciturnity. 2. reserve, restraint. —reticent.
6. **retiring**; shy, unsocial, uncommunicative, diffident. —retiringness.

1. All that he [the Journalist] can do is to consider attentively, and determine impartially, to admit no falsehoods by design,* and to **retract** those which he shall have adopted by mistake. —Samuel Johnson, *Miscellaneous Essays*

2. I must **retrench** where I can, and learn to be a better manager. —Jane Austen, *Mansfield Park*

3. What we call **retribution** is the universal necessity by which the whole appears wherever a part appears. —R. W. Emerson, *Compensation*

4. Am I to lose all, without a chance of **retrieval**? —Emily Brontë, *Wuthering Heights*

5. The development has assuredly been **retrograde.** —Charles Darwin, *The Origin of Species*

6. For fifteen days the castle was given up to joy and **revelry**. —Washington Irving, *Legend of Don Munio Sancho de Hinojosa*

****

1. **retract**; 1. cancel, withdraw, revoke, recant. 2. deny, disavow, disown, repudiate. —retractation, —retractable. * by design; on purpose.
2. **retrench**; reduce, economize, husband, curtail. —retrenchment.
3. **retribution**; requital, punitive justice, retaliation, Nemesis, karma. —retributive. ※ comeuppance; retribution: *The devil at last got his comeuppance*.
4. **retrieval**; retaking, recovery, regain, restoration. —retrieve, —retrievable.
5. **retrograde**; 1. reverting, regressive, relapsing, retreating, retrogressive, inverse. ***ant.*** progressive. 2. degenerative. 3. *v.* return, revert. —retrogradation.
6. **revelry**; merrymaking, spree, carousal, orgy, bacchanalia, festivity.

♣ No one, indeed, acknowledges to himself that his standard of judgement is his own liking. —John Stuart Mill, *On Liberty*

1. The effect of the wine upon Victor was to change his accustomed volubility* into silence. He seemed to have abandoned himself to a **reverie**, and to be seeing pleasing visions in the amber* bead. —Kate Chopin, *The Awakening*
2. They all began at once, *una voce,** to rebuke* and **revile** him, repeating often that none but a coward ever struck a woman. —Henry Fielding, *Tom Jones*
3. For Heaven's sake, sir, **revoke** your warrant, and do not send her to a place which must unavoidably prove her destruction. —Henry Fielding, *Tom Jones*
4. He walked up one street, and down another, until exercise had abated the first passion of his grief; and then the **revulsion** of feeling made him thirsty. —Charles Dickens, *Oliver Twist*
5. The **ribaldry** of this miserable man is despicably* disgusting. —Charles Dickens, *The Pickwick Papers*
6. I love to see that Nature is so **rife** with life that myriads* can be afforded to be sacrificed and suffered to prey on one another. —Henry David Thoreau, *Walden*.

****

1. **reverie** *also* **revery**; daydream, fantasy, woolgathering. * volubility; talkativeness, garrulity, loquacity. * amber; 1. semitransparent fossil resin used in making ornaments. 2. yellowish brown.
2. **revile**; abuse, rail, vilify. —revilement, —reviler. * *una voce*; unanimously. * rebuke; reprove, reprimand, admonish, *see p. 257, no. 2.*
3. **revoke**; withdraw, annul, abrogate, rescind, recant. —revocation, —revocable.
4. **revulsion**; 1. abrupt change of feeling, strong reaction in feeling. 2. disgust, abomination, repulsion, odium, detestation. —revulsed; affected with revulsion.
5. **ribaldry**; vulgarity, indecency. —ribald. * despicably; vilely, ignobly.
6. **rife**; abounding, teeming, swarming. —rifeness. * myriad; great number, great number of plants, animals or things.

1. Laws and principles are not for the times when there is no temptation; they are for such moments as this, when body and soul rise in mutiny* against their **rigor**. —Charlotte Brontë, *Jane Eyre*

2. The sisters had stood, **riveted** to one spot, horror-stricken, and nearly helpless. —James Fenimore Cooper, *The Last of Mohicans*

3. . . . she was a woman of **robust** frame, square-shouldered and strong-limbed, not tall, and, though stout, not obese. —Charlotte Brontë, *Jane Eyre*

4. I had forgotten I was a plebeian,* I was remembering I was a man. Cost what it might, I would mount that **rostrum**. —Mark Twain, *A Connecticut Yankee*

5. Our own active effort is the essential thing; and no facilities, no books, no teachers, no amount of lessons learned by **rote** will enable us to dispense with* it. —Samuel Smiles, *Self Help*

6. His appearance, so **rotund** and yet so startled, could never fail to excite a smile. —W. Somerset Maugham, *The Moon and Sixpence*

****

1. **rigor**; strictness, rigidity, severity, grimness, sternness, austerity. —rigorous; harsh, stringent. ⋇ draconian; rigorous: *He was draconian to the others, but not to himself.* * mutiny; insurgence, rebellion, insurrection, *see p. 197, no. 2.*
2. **rivet**; 1. fix firmly, fasten tightly. 2. focus. —riveting; arresting, captivating.
3. **robust**; muscular, sinewy, stout, sturdy, brawny. —robustness.
4. **rostrum**; platform, podium, dais. * plebeian; commoner. ⋇ pulpit; 1. raised platform for the sermon in a church. 2. ministry.
5. **rote**; memorizing by repetition. ⋇ mnemonic; 1. *adj.* of the memory. 2. *n.* device to help the memory. * dispense with; do without.
6. **rotund**; plump, chubby, round, obese, corpulent, portly. —rotundity.

♣ The depths are fathomless and therefore calm. —Walt Whitman, *Preface to Leaves of Grass*

1. Shame and confusion! All is on the **rout**.

   —Shakespeare, *King Henry VI, Part II*

2. . . . we had little to say, but sat absorbed in thought, or in silence listened to the monotonous sound of our oars, a sort of **rudimental** music . . . —Henry David Thoreau, *A Week on the Concord and Merrimack Rivers*

3. After **ruminating** for some minutes with his chin sunk on his breast, he raised his head . . . —Charles Dickens, *Oliver Twist*

4. I am grieved, though I cannot be astonished at your **rupture** with Mr. De Courcy. —Jane Austen, *Lady Susan*

5. He's not a rough diamond—a pearl-containing oyster of a **rustic**; he's a fierce, pitiless, wolfish man. —Emily Brontë, *Wuthering Heights*

6. Most **sacrilegious** murder hath broke ope*
   The Lord's anointed* temple, and stole thence
   The life o' th' building.

   —Shakespeare, *Macbeth*

****

1. **rout**; 1. crushing defeat, chaotic retreat, stampede. 2. *v.* stampede. 3. rabble.
2. **rudimental** *or* **rudimentary**; primary, primordial, primitive. —rudiment.
3. **ruminate**; 1. meditate, brood, excogitate. 2. masticate again. —ruminator.
4. **rupture**; split, breakup, breach, tear, crack, fracture.
5. **rustic**; 1. boor, churl. 2. boorish, churlish. 3. plain, homespun. —rusticity.
6. **sacrilegious**; profane, blasphemous, desecrating. ***ant.*** devout; sacred, pious, hallowed, consecrate. —sacrilege. * ope; open. * anoint; choose.

♣ If I can stop one heart from breaking,
I shall not live in vain.

—Emily Dickinson, "If I can stop one heart from breaking"

1. A slavish nature would find consolation in the fact that the principal robber was an exalted and almost a **sacrosanct** person—a grand duke, in fact. —Joseph Conrad, *Under Western Eyes*

2. Fear is an instructor of great **sagacity** and the herald of all revolutions. —R. W. Emerson, *Compensation*

3. There are people who seem to have no notion of sketching a character, or observing and describing **salient** points, either in persons or things. —Charlotte Brontë, *Jane Eyre*

4. The quadruped is often obliged to lick the earth, in order to obtain the **saline** particles. —James Fenimore Cooper, *The Last of the Mohicans*

5. Nippers, the second on my list, was a whiskered, **sallow**, and, upon the whole, rather piratical-looking young man of about five and twenty. —Herman Melville, *Bartleby*

6. His features were pretty yet, and his eye and complexion brighter than I remembered them, though with merely temporary luster borrowed from the **salubrious** air and genial sun. —Emily Brontë, *Wuthering Heights*

****

1. **sacrosanct**; sacred, inviolable, hallowed, sanctified. —sacrosanctity.
2. **sagacity**; wisdom, sageness, judiciousness. —sagacious; judicious, savvy.
3. **salient**; 1. noticeable, outstanding, prominent, eminent, conspicuous, remarkable. 2. projecting, protruding. ***ant.*** reentrant. —salience.
4. **saline**; salty, brackish, briny. —salinity, —salinize.
5. **sallow**; pale, pallid, ashen, anemic. ***ant.*** ruddy. —sallowness.
6. **salubrious**; 1. pleasant, agreeable. 2. healthy, wholesome, sanitary, hygienic. —salubrity. ※ hygiene; 1. sanitary condition. 2. hygienics. —hygienist.

♣ O, how full of briers is this working-day world! —Shakespeare, *As You Like It*

1. Also, while aware that poverty was anything but delectable,* she had a comfortable middle-class feeling that poverty was **salutary**. —Jack London, *Martin Eden*

2. The directors voted you three hundred guineas as **salvage**, and you refused them. —Arthur Conan Doyle, *Beyond the City*

3. As we found them within gunshot, our leader ordered the two wings to advance swiftly, and give them a **salvo** on each wing with their shot. —Daniel Defoe, *The Further Adventures of Robinson Crusoe*

4. He was donned* in his Sunday garments, with his most **sanctimonious** and sourest face. —Emily Brontë, *Wuthering Heights*

5. . . . I reasonably concluded that the wars of the natives were marked by no very **sanguinary** traits. —Herman Melville, *Typee*

6. Now, as always, Clare's father was **sanguine** as a child. —Thomas Hardy, *Tess*

****

1. **salutary**; 1. healthful, wholesome. 2. beneficial, advantageous. ※ salutation; 1. greeting, salute. 2. opening address. —salutatory, —salute *v.* * delectable; pleasant, *see p. 73, no. 6.*
2. **salvage**; 1. *n.* rescue, salvation, relief. 2. *v.* save, deliver, relieve. 3. crew or property rescued. —salvageable; salvable, redeemable.
3. **salvo**; simultaneous or continuing firing, volley, barrage, fusillade.
4. **sanctimonious**; pretending piety, feigning righteousness. —sanctimony. ※ imprimatur; sanction, approval: *the government's imprimatur.* * don; dress. ***ant.*** doff.
5. **sanguinary**; bloody, slaughterous, gory. —sanguinariness, —sanguinarily.
6. **sanguine**; 1. cheerful, buoyant. 2. confident, assured. 3. hopeful, optimistic: *sanguine expectations.* 4. bloody, ruddy. —sanguinity, —sanguinely.

1. Whoever _______ the breath from the hills, though dying, might revive.
2. Does it not require all to lawfully _______ it?
3. O injurious love, that _______ me a life!
4. He had a deep, _______ voice, fitted to his massive frame.
5. The volatile truth of words betray the inadequacy of the_______ statement.
6. In his swelling, _______ muscles was the primordial vigor of life.

[**respites, resilient, resonant, residual, rescind, respired**]

****

1. He owed no man, and _______ was unthinkable.
2. He was a sober, steady-looking young man of _______ manners.
3. He was not eloquent, but there was a dignity in this constitutional _______.
4. Precisely as a rash, _______ horse is said to feel his oats, so Tom felt his coat.
5. The garden was _______ with sunlight and colour.
6. Let me but _______ upon him, by degrees, however slow.

[**retiring, restitution, restive, resplendent, retaliate, reticence**]

****

1. The journalist has to _______ those which he has adopted by mistake.
2. I must _______ where I can, and learn to be a better manager.
3. What we call _______ is the universal necessity.
4. Am I to lose all, without a chance of _______?
5. For fifteen days the castle was given up to joy and _______.
6. The development has assuredly been _______.

[**retrograde, revelry, retrieval, retract, retrench, retribution**]

****

1. The _______ of feeling made him thirsty.
2. He seemed to have abandoned himself to a _______.
3. They all began at once, *una voce*, to rebuke and _______ him.
4. Nature is so _____ with life that myriads can be sacrificed to prey on one another.
5. The _______ of this miserable man is despicably disgusting.
6. For Heaven's sake, sir, _______ your warrant, and do not send her to prison.

[**rife, revile, revoke, ribaldry, revulsion, reverie**]

Review Exercise: Sentence Completions (pp. 275–78)

1. The sisters had stood, _______ to one spot, horror-stricken, and nearly helpless.
2. Cost what it might, I would mount that _______.
3. His appearance, so _______ and yet so startled, could never fail to excite a smile.
4. No amount of lessons learned by _______ will enable us to dispense with it.
5. She was a woman of _______ frame, square-shouldered and strong-limbed.
6. Laws are for the moments when body and soul rise in mutiny against their _____.

[**rotund, rote, robust, riveted, rigor, rostrum**]

****

1. I am grieved, though I cannot be astonished at your _______ with him.
2. He _______ for some minutes with his chin sunk on his breast.
3. He's not a rough diamond—a pearl-containing oyster of a _______.
4. We listened to the monotonous sound of our oars, a sort of _______ music.
5. Shame and confusion! All is on the _______.
6. Most _______ murder hath broke ope the Lord's anointed temple.

[**ruminated, rupture, sacrilegious, rout, rustic, rudimental**]

****

1. The quadruped often licks the earth in order to obtain the _______ particles.
2. They have no notion of describing _______ points, either in persons or things.
3. The temporary luster was borrowed from the _______ air and genial sun.
4. The principal robber was an exalted and almost a _______ person.
5. Fear is an instructor of great _______ and the herald of all revolutions.
6. Nippers was a whiskered, _______, young man of about five and twenty.

[**salubrious, saline, sallow, sagacity, salient, sacrosanct**]

****

1. He ordered the two wings to give them a _______ on each wing with their shot.
2. He was donned in his Sunday garments, with his most _______ face.
3. Now, as always, Clare's father was _______ as a child.
4. She had a comfortable middle-class feeling that poverty was _______.
5. The wars of the natives were marked by no very _______ traits.
6. The directors voted you three hundred guineas as _______.

[**salvo, sanguine, sanguinary, salvage, salutary, sanctimonious**]

1. Oh, **sapient** servant of the law, condescend to tell us, then, what you *know*. —Mark Twain, *A Connecticut Yankee*
2. Dominic, too, devoted himself to his business, but his taciturnity* was **sardonic**. —Joseph Conrad, *The Arrow of Gold*
3. Sleep is necessary to the happy, to prevent **satiety** and to endear* life by a short absence; and to the miserable, to relieve* them by intervals of quiet. —Samuel Johnson, *The Adventurer*
4. This world only *seems* to be **saturated** and soaking with lies; but in reality it does not so lie soaking and saturate; along with some lies, there is much truth in this world. —Herman Melville, *Pierre*
5. He twisted his heavy mouth into a faint smile—he was one of those **saturnine** people who smile with the corners of the mouth down. —H. G. Wells, *The Island of Doctor Moreau*
6. The **savant** becomes unpoetic. —R. W. Emerson, *Nature*

****

1. **sapient**; *generally used ironically,* wise, clever, sagacious, perspicacious. —sapience, —sapiential. ※ sapiens; of modern humans: *homo sapiens.*
2. **sardonic**; biting, acerbic, sarcastic, satiric, taunting, caustic. —sardornicism. * taciturnity; reticence, tacitness, reserve. —taciturn; reticent.
3. **satiety**; 1. satiation, surfeit. 2. repletion, plethora. —satiate, —satiable. * endear; make beloved. —endearing, —endearment. * relieve; 1. soothe. 2. rescue. —relief.
4. **saturate**; 1. fill, suffuse. 2. wet, soak, drench. —saturation.
5. **saturnine**; gloomy, sullen, glum, morose. —saturnineness, —saturninely.
6. **savant**; scholar, expert, polymath. ※ pundit; savant: *sports pundit.*

♣ We are all in the gutter, but some of us are looking at the stars. —Oscar Wilde, *Lady Windermere's Fan*

1. However, a warm **savoury** steam from the kitchen served to belie the apparently cheerless prospect before us. —Herman Melville, *Moby Dick*
2. The cries of the two parties were now in sound an interchange of **scathing** insults. —Stephen Crane, *The Red Badge of Courage*
3. . . . and **schisms** are the fruit of disputation. —James Fenimore Cooper, *The Pioneers*
4. Excellent, Watson! You are **scintillating** this evening. —Arthur Conan Doyle, *The Return of Sherlock Holmes*
5. I must not forget that these coarsely-clad little peasants are of flesh and blood as good as the **scions** of gentlest genealogy.* —Charlotte Brontë, *Jane Eyre*
6. The next morning Archer **scoured** the town in vain for more yellow roses. —Edith Wharton, *The Age of Innocence*

****

1. **savoury**; tasty, delicious, spicy, palatable, delectable, luscious. —savour.
2. **scathing**; biting, cutting, sarcastic, sulfurous, caustic, mordant, vitriolic, trenchant, excoriating, mordacious. —scathe; 1. harm, injure. 2. criticize.
3. **schism**; split, division, disunion. —schismatic, —schismatize. ※ scheme; tactic, ploy. ※ gambit; 1. scheme, maneuver. 2. opening remark. ※ dichotomy; division, polarity, disjunction: *a dichotomy between his saying and action.*
4. **scintillating**; bright, brilliant, witty. —scintillation, —scintillate; sparkle.
5. **scion** *also* **cion**; 1. offspring, descendant, progeny. ***ant.*** ancestor. 2. heir, inheritor. 3. shoot for grafting. * genealogy; family tree, lineage, pedigree.
6. **scour**; 1. search, scan, rummage, ransack. 2. clean by rubbing.

♣ The science of conduct, like all other sciences, must be "fruitful"; and, like all other sciences, it must be founded upon experience. —Francis Bacon, *Essays*

1. Fondly do we hope—fervently do we pray—that this mighty **scourge** of war may speedily pass away. —Abram Lincoln, *Second Inaugural Address*
2. In the yard, which was kept **scrupulously** neat, were flowers and plants of every description which flourishes in South Louisiana. —Kate Chopin, *The Awakening*
3. He indulges in **scurrilous** jests, and the bride was his affianced* one! —Charlotte Brontë, The *Professor*
4. Get thee glass eyes;
   And, like a **scurvy** politician, seem
   To see the things thou dost not.

   —Shakespeare, *King Lear*
5. And oh, the deceit! I have seen a good deal of the **seamy** side this last week. The deceit of the most promising people. My dear Lucy, the deceit! —E. M. Forster, *A Room With A View*
6. Thy crown does **sear** mine eyeballs.

   —Shakespeare, *Macbeth*

****

1. **scourge**; 1. affliction, misery, misfortune, visitation. 2. whip, lash.
2. **scrupulously**; meticulously, fastidiously, conscientiously. —scrupulosity.
3. **scurrilous**; abusive, foulmouthed, gross, vulgar. —scurrility; gross abuse. ※ scurry; hurry, rush, scuttle, scamper. * affianced; engaged, betrothed.
4. **scurvy**; base, mean, ignoble, despicable, contemptible. —scurviness.
5. **seamy**; 1. sordid, nasty, squalid. 2. having a seam. —seam; 1. joint by sewing. 2. line joining two edges. ※ *the seamy side of life*.
6. **sear**; 1. burn, scorch, parch, char. 2. shrivel, wither. —searingly.

♣ The finite is a manifestation of the infinite. —W. Ellery Channing, *On the Elevation of the Laboring Classes*

1. Plainly, the central idea of **secession** is the essence of anarchy. —Abraham Lincoln, *The First Inaugural Address*

2. In the swamp in **secluded** recesses,*
A shy and hidden bird is warbling* a song.
—Walt Whitman, "When Lilacs Last in the Dooryard Bloom'd"

3. Miss Ladd broke through her rule of attending to **secular** affairs on weekdays only . . . —Wilkie Collins, *I Say No*

4. All progress slow, contemplative, **sedate**. —Ambrose Bierce, *The Devil's Dictionary*

5. Ease is the utmost that can be hoped from a **sedentary** and unactive habit. —Samuel Johnson, *The Rambler*

6. At the bottom of the ocean where no **sediment** is accumulating, seaweed, zoophytes,* fish, and even shells, may multiply for ages and decompose, leaving no vestige of their form or substance behind. —Charles Lyell, *Uniformity of Change*

****

1. **secession**; split, withdrawal, separation. —secessionism, —secede.
2. **secluded**; isolated, remote, reclusive, cloistered, sequestered, solitary. —seclusion. * recess; remote place, nook. * warble; twitter, chirp.
3. **secular**; worldly, earthly, mundane. —secularity.
4. **sedate**; calm, composed, serene, tranquil, collected, placid. —sedation.
5. **sedentary**; 1. stationary, not migratory. 2. sitting. —sedentariness.
6. **sediment**; 1. dregs, grounds, deposit. 2. fragments of rock. —sedimentary. * zoophyte; plantlike animal such as a coral.

♣ A government cannot have too much of the kind of activity which does not impede, but aids and stimulates, individual exertion and development. —John Stuart Mill, *On Liberty*

1. To the community **sedition** is a fever, corruption is a gangrene,* and idleness an atrophy.* —Samuel Johnson, *The Idler*
2. The son of a Scotch minister, he [David Wilkie] gave early indications of an artistic turn; and though he was a negligent* and inapt scholar, he was a **sedulous** drawer of faces and figures. —Samuel Smiles, *Self Help*
3. There was a **seedy** old chest, and an old hair trunk with the hinges broke. —Mark Twain, *The Adventures of Huckleberry Finn*
4. We could not **segregate** the sick, nor could we care for them. We were packed like sardines. —Jack London, *South Sea Tales*
5. Since I have undertaken to manhandle this Leviathan [the whale], it behoves* me to approve* myself omnisciently exhaustive* in the enterprise; not overlooking the minutest **seminal** germs of his blood, and spinning him out to the uttermost coil of his bowels. —Herman Melville, *Moby Dick*
6. I was growing old, or wise, or both, or **senile** as an alternative. —Jack London, *John Barleycorn*

****

1. **sedition**; riot, revolt, rebellion, insurrection. —seditionary, —seditious. gangrene; death of tissue. * atrophy; degeneration. ***ant.*** hypertrophy.
2. **sedulous**; diligent, assiduous, industrious. —sedulity. * negligent; slack, remiss.
3. **seedy**; 1. worn, run-down, dilapidated. 2. with many seeds. —seediness.
4. **segregate**; 1. isolate, seclude, sequester. ***ant.*** desegregate. 2. separate, discriminate, demarcate. —segregative. ※ tabulate; classify, categorize.
5. **seminal**; 1. embryonic, germinal. 2. original. —seminality. * behove; be necessary for. * approve; prove. * exhaustive; thoroughgoing, comprehensive.
6. **senile**; old, senescent, decrepit. —senility; aging, decrepitude. ※ senescence; senility. —senesce *v.*, —senescent.

1. Your reasons at dinner have been sharp and **sententious**; pleasant without scurrility,* witty without affection, audacious without impudency,* . . . and strange without heresy.* —Shakespeare, *Love's Labour's Lost*

2. The doll, duly* night-capped and night-gowned, lay in its cradle; she was rocking it to sleep, with an air of the most perfect faith in its possession of **sentient** and somnolent* faculties. —Charlotte Brontë, *Villette*

3. She knew the **sequestered** spots where the hens laid their eggs. —W. M. Thackeray, *Vanity Fair*

4. The knife-edge backbone was deeply **serrated**, and into one of the notches both men disappeared. —Jack London, *The Valley of the Moon*

5. He took off his hat with an air of gorgeous **servility**. —Oscar Wilde, *The Picture of Dorian Gray*

6. One moment Alleyne saw the galley's* poop* crowded with rushing figures, waving arms, exultant faces; the next it was a blood-smeared **shambles**, with bodies piled three deep upon each other . . . —Arthur Conan Doyle, *The White Company*

****

1. **sententious**; 1. concise, terse, pithy. 2. aphoristic, moralizing, axiomatic. —sententiousness. * scurrility; indecent abuse. * impudency; insolence. * heresy; heterodoxy, unorthodoxy. ***ant.*** orthodoxy; 1. canon. 2. standard.
2. **sentient**; sensate, perceptible, sensible. ***ant.*** insensate. —sentience. * duly; appropriately. * somnolent; sleepy, drowsy. —somnolence.
3. **sequester**; isolate, seclude, segregate, cloister. —sequestered; retired.
4. **serrate**; make saw-toothed, jag, notch. —serration, —serrated.
5. **servility**; slavery, thralldom. —servile; slavish. —servitor; slave, thrall.
6. **shambles**; usu. in *pl.* but regarded as *sing.* 1. butchery, slaughterhouse, a place of carnage or havoc. 2. mess, bedlam, maelstrom, muddle. * galley; *see p. 263, no. 5.* * poop; stern. ***ant.*** forecastle; bow.

1. When the young tendrils [the common small white bush bean's] make their appearance, they [woodchucks*] have notice of it, and will **shear** them off with both buds and young pods* . . . —Henry David Thoreau, *Walden*

2. He was more alive, there was an excitement in **sheer** being, an eager vehemence* of soul, which made life now a trifle dull. —W. Somerset Maugham, *Of Human Bondage*

3. Life is easy to chronicle, but bewildering to practice, and we welcome "nerves"* or any other **shibboleth** that will cloak* our personal desire. —E. M. Forster, *A Room with a View*

4. She was not amusing or clever, her mind was common; she had a vulgar* **shrewdness** . . . —W. Somerset Maugham, *Of Human Bondage*

5. We are afraid of truth, afraid of fortune, afraid of death, . . . We **shun** the rugged battle of fate, where strength is born. —R. W. Emerson, *Self-Reliance*

6. The sparkling points of light flashed past me in an interminable* stream, as though the whole **sidereal** system were dropping into the void. —Jack London, *The Sea Wolf*

****

1. **shear**; cut, trim, prune, clip. —shearer, —shears; a pair of scissors. * woodchuck; a marmot in North America. * pod; seed vessel of the bean.
2. **sheer**; 1. perfect, absolute, unmitigated, consummate. 2. pure. 3. transparent, thin, gossamer, diaphanous. —sheerness. * vehemence; passion, ardor, verve.
3. **shibboleth**; saying, catchword, slogan. * nerve; courage. * cloak; hide.
4. **shrewdness**; smartness, keenness, acuteness. —shrewd. * vulgar; indecent.
5. **shun**; avoid, escape, evade, elude, eschew, circumvent. —shunless.
6. **sidereal**; stellar, of the stars. ※ asteroid; minor planet, planetoid. ※ meteor; shooting star. * interminable; endless.

1. In Mary Ann there was a certain affected **simper**, and a craving for notice, that I was sorry to observe. —Anne Brontë, *Agnes Grey*

2. Some laughed; some said by way of complete excuse, that the post was virtually a **sinecure**, and any fool who could spell his name was good enough for it. —Charles Dickens, *Little Dorrit*

3. With every daybreak the rising sun had to wade* through a crimson stream, luminous* and **sinister**, like the spilt blood of celestial bodies murdered during the night. —Joseph Conrad, *The Mirror of the Sea*

4. The hills are wooded, the course of the ravine* is **sinuous**. —Ambrose Bierce, *Can Such Things Be*?

5. The **skirmish** fire increased to a long chattering sound. With it was mingled faraway cheering. A battery* spoke. —Stephen Crane, *The Red Badge of Courage*

6. No, if I digged up thy forefathers' graves,
   And hung their rotten coffins up in chains,
   It could not **slake** mine ire,* nor ease my heart.
   —Shakespeare, *King Henry VI, Part III*

****

1. **simper**; silly smile, affected smile, smirk, coy smile. —simperingly.
2. **sinecure**; job that needs little work but gives a salary and benefits. —sinecurist, —sinecurism.
3. **sinister**; ominous, inauspicious, foreboding, bodeful. —sinisterness. * wade; walk through water. * luminous; radiant, resplendent, *see. p. 183, no. 2.*
4. **sinuous**; winding, curvy, coiling, serpentine, tortuous, meandering, sinuate. —sinuosity. * ravine; deep narrow valley, canyon, gorge.
5. **skirmish**; minor battle, conflict, argument. * battery; a set of cannonry.
6. **slake**; 1. calm, assuage, allay. 2. satisfy, gratify. * ire; rage. —ireful; wrathful.

1. Sleep is necessary to the happy, to prevent _______by a short absence.
2. This world only seems to be _______ and soaking with lies.
3. He was a _______ man who smiles with the corners of the mouth down.
4. The _______ becomes unpoetic.
5. Dominic, too, devoted himself to his business, but his taciturnity was _______.
6. Oh, _______ servant of the law, condescend to tell us, then, what you know.

[**saturated, savant, sapient, sardonic, saturnine, satiety**]

****

1. Their cries were now in sound an interchange of _______ insults.
2. _______ are the fruit of disputation.
3. A _______ steam from the kitchen served to belie the cheerless prospect.
4. The next morning Archer _______ the town in vain for more yellow roses.
5. Excellent, Watson! You are _______ this evening.
6. They are of flesh and blood as good as the _______ of gentlest genealogy.

[**scathing, schisms, scions, scintillating, savoury, scoured**]

****

1. Thy crown does _______ mine eyeballs.
2. He indulges in _______ jests, and the bride was his affianced one!
3. Fondly do we hope that his mighty _______ of war may speedily pass away.
4. In the yard, which was kept _______ neat, were plants of every description.
5. Like a _______ politician, seem to see the things thou dost not.
6. And oh, the deceit! I have seen a good deal of the _______ side this last week.

[**scrupulously, sear, scurrilous, scurvy, seamy, scourge**]

****

1. All progress slow, contemplative, _______.
2. No _______ is accumulating at the bottom of the ocean.
3. Ease is the utmost that can be hoped from a _______ and unactive habit.
4. She broke through her rule of attending to _______ affairs on weekdays only.
5. Plainly, the central idea of _______ is the essence of anarchy.
6. In the swamp in _______ recesses, a shy and hidden bird is warbling a song.

[**secluded, secession, secular, sedentary, sedate, sediment**]

Review Exercise: Sentence Completions (pp. 285–88)

1. To the community _______ is a fever, and corruption is a gangrene.
2. We could not _______ the sick, nor could we care for them.
3. There was a _______ old chest, and an old hair trunk with the hinges broke.
4. I did not overlook the minutest _______ germs of the whale's blood.
5. I was growing old, or wise, or both, or _______ as an alternative.
6. David Wilkie was a _______ drawer of faces and figures.

[**seminal, seedy, sedulous, senile, segregate, sedition**]

****

1. The knife-edge backbone was deeply _______.
2. Your reasons at dinner have been sharp and _______.
3. She knew the _______ spots where the hens laid their eggs.
4. He took off his hat with an air of gorgeous _______.
5. She believed in the doll's possession of _______ and somnolent faculties.
6. The next moment it [the galley's poop] was a blood-smeared _______.

[**shambles, sentient, serrated, sequestered, servility, sententious**]

****

1. They flashed as though the whole _______ system were dropping into the void.
2. There was an excitement in _______ being.
3. Her mind was common; she had a vulgar _______.
4. We _______ the rugged battle of fate, where strength is born.
5. We welcome any _______ that will cloak our personal desire.
6. Woodchucks _______ off the young tendrils with both buds and young pods.

[**shrewdness, sheared, shun, sidereal, sheer, shibboleth**]

****

1. Some said by way of complete excuse, that the post was virtually a _______.
2. The _______ fire increased to a long chattering sound.
3. Digging up thy father's grave could not _______ mine ire, nor ease my heart.
4. In Mary Ann there was a certain affected _______, and a craving for notice.
5. The rising sun had to wade through a crimson stream, luminous and _______.
6. The hills are wooded, the course of the ravine is _______.

[**slake, sinuous, simper, sinecure, sinister, skirmish**]

1. **Slander** lives upon succession.

—Shakespeare, *The Comedy of Errors*

2. By a dexterous **sleight**, pitching his cap up into the mizzen-top* for a shelf, he goes down rollicking. —Herman Melville, *Moby Dick*

3. Not only in the slumber of **sloth**, but in the dissipation of ill directed industry, is the shortness of life generally forgotten. —Samuel Johnson, *The Rambler*

4. In the woods, too, a man casts off his years, as the snake his **slough**, and at what period soever* of life is always a child. —R. W. Emerson, *Nature*

5. He was clad in a professional but rather **slovenly** fashion, for his frock-coat was dingy* and his trousers frayed.* —Arthur Conan Doyle, *The Hound of the Baskervilles*

6. They climbed out of the **smelting** town, where eyrie* houses perched insecurely on a precipitous landscape. —Jack London, *The Valley of the Moon*

****

1. **slander**; defamation, libel, vilification, calumny, denigration. —slanderous.
2. **sleight**; adeptness, adroitness, dexterity. ※ *sleight of hand* ; jugglery, legerdemain, prestidigitation. * mizzen-top; top of the fore-and-aft sail.
3. **sloth**; indolence, sluggishness, faineance. —slothful; slack, laggard, faineant.
4. **slough**; 1. the covering of a snake's skin. 2. *v.* molt, cast off. 3. bog, swamp. * soever; 1. in any way. 2. whatever.
5. **slovenly**; untidy, sloppy, slipshod, slatternly, unkempt. —sloven; untidy person. * dingy; 1. grimy, squalid. 2. murky, dreary. * fray; wear out, tatter.
6. **smelt**; extract metal by melting or fusing ores. —smelter, —smeltery. * eyrie *also* eyry; an aerie, a lofty nest of a big bird.

♣ A true man belongs to no other time or place, but is the centre of things. —R. W. Emerson, *Self-Reliance*

1. Now let us do what we can to rekindle the **smouldering,** nigh* quenched* fire on the altar. —R. W. Emerson, *Divinity School Address*

2. His [Jim's] manner was very **sober** and set; his bearing was that of a naturally taciturn man possessed by an idea. —Joseph Conrad, *Lord Jim*

3. . . . among his intimate friends he was better known by the ***sobriquet*** of "The artful Dodger," . . . —Charles Dickens, *Oliver Twist*

4. Nothing can be more hurtful to a youth than to have his soul **sodden** with pleasure. —Samuel Smiles, *Self Help*

5. At present I am a **sojourner** in civilized life again. —Henry David Thoreau, *Walden*

6. Your air was often diffident, and altogether that of one refined by nature, but absolutely unused to society, and a good deal afraid of making herself disadvantageously conspicuous by some **solecism** or blunder. —Charlotte Brontë, *Jane Eyre*

****

1. **smoulder** *also* **smolder**; 1. smoke, fume, burn without a flame. 2. rage, boil, simmer, seethe, * nigh; near. * quench; put out, extinguish, *see p. 251, no. 3.*
2. **sober**; 1. grave, severe, solemn, staid. 2. temperate, abstemious, abstinent. 3. composed, sedate. —sobriety.
3. **sobriquet**; nickname, assumed name, alias. ※ eponym; one after whom something is named. —eponymous: *The eponymous heroine of the novel,* Moll Flanders *is of course Moll Flanders.*
4. **sodden**; soaked, drenched, saturated, soggy.
5. **sojourner**; temporary stayer, temporary resident or occupier.
6. **solecism**; 1. bad manner, error, gaffe. 2. misusage. —solecist, —solecistic.

♣ We can never have enough of Nature. —Henry David Thoreau, *Walden*

1. I was still by nature **solicitous** to be neat. —Charlotte Brontë, *Jane Eyre*

2. I prefer to be owned as sound and **solvent**, and my word as good as my bond, and to be what cannot be skipped, or dissipated, or undermined, to all the éclat* in the universe. —R. W. Emerson, *Illusions*

3. The West Wind is too great a king to be a dissembler*: he is no calculator plotting deep schemes in a **somber** heart; he is too strong for small artifices. —Joseph Conrad, *The Mirror of the Sea*

4. We wonder superfluously* when we hear of a **somnambulist** walking a plank securely,—we have walked a plank all our lives . . . —Henry David Thoreau, *A Week on the Concord and Merrimack Rivers*

5. He had a **sonorous** bass voice, and an air of defiant self-confidence inclining to brazenness. —George Eliot, *The Mill on the Floss*

6. The night programme in Coralio never varied. The recreations of the people were **soporific** and flat. They wandered about, barefoot and aimless, speaking lowly and smoking cigar or cigarette. —O. Henry, *Shoes*

****

1. **solicitous**; 1. longing, eager, anxious. 2. concerned. —solicitude.
2. **solvent**; 1. solid, reliable. ***ant.*** insolvent. 2. financially sound. 3. dissolvent, resolvent. —solvency. * éclat; 1. reputation. 2. great success, acclamation.
3. **somber**; 1. gloomy, dismal. 2. dark, drab. —somberness. * dissembler; hypocrite, dissimulator.
4. **somnambulist**; sleepwalker, noctambulist. —somnambulate, —somnambulistic. * superfluously; excessively.
5. **sonorous**; resounding, resonant, orotund, deep and rich in sound. —sonority.
6. **soporific** *or* **soporiferous**; 1. drowsy, somnific, somniferous. 2. hypnotic.

♣ The world is emblematic. —R. W. Emerson, *Nature*

1. Men in great place are thrice servants: servants of the **sovereign** or state; servants of fame; and servants of business. —Francis Bacon, *Essays*
2. . . . apparently a **spasm** caught his breath. —Charlotte Brontë, *Jane Eyre*
3. In this steady rain the springs of the mountain were broken up; every glen* gushed water like a cistern*; every stream was in high **spate**. —Robert L. Stevenson, *Kidnapped*
4. . . . shoals* of golden and silver minnows* rose to the surface to behold the heavens, and then sheered* off into more sombre aisles; they swept by as if moved by one mind, continually gliding past each other, and yet preserving the form of their battalion unchanged, as if they were still embraced by the transparent membrane* which held the **spawn**. —Henry David Thoreau, *A Week on the Concord and Merrimack Rivers*
5. I am not sure, my dear girl, but that it may be wise and **specious** to preserve that outward indifference. —Charles Dickens, *Bleak House*
6. Fie,* What a **spendthrift** is he of his tongue!

   —Shakespeare, *The Tempest*

****

1. **sovereign**; ruler, monarch, potentate. —sovereignty. ※ suzerain; a country dominating another. —suzerainty; the authority of suzerain.
2. **spasm**; convulsion, paroxysm, cramp. —spasmodic.
3. **spate**; flood, deluge, inundation. * glen; narrow valley, gorge, ravine. * cistern; water tank, receptacle for water.
4. **spawn**; 1. eggs of amphibians or aquatic animals. 2. *v.* produce eggs. * shoal; crowd, throng. * minnow; small freshwater fish. * sheer; 1. swerve. 2. diaphanous. 3. perpendicular. * membrane; thin film of tissue.
5. **specious**; plausible, spurious, misleading. —speciocity, —speciously.
6. **spendthrift***;* *n.* prodigal, profligate, wastrel. * fie; exclamation of dismay.

1. . . . it [the Battle of Niagara] passed gradually into a **sporadic** conflict over half a continent. —H. G. Wells, *The War in the Air*

2. . . . the animal was as **spry** as a squirrel? —James Fenimore Cooper, *The Pioneers*

3. I don't want any second-hand, **spurious** sensations; I want the knowledge that leaves a trace—that leaves strange scars and stains and reveries behind it. —Henry James, *A Bundle of Letters*

4. Yet you, my creator, detest and **spurn** me, thy creature, to whom thou art bound by ties only dissoluble* by the annihilation of one of us. —Mary Shelley, *Frankenstein*

5. He's not at a smart hotel. He's living in one tiny room in the most **squalid** way. —W. Somerset Maugham, *The Moon and Sixpence*

6. What was the use of **squandering** the days of his youth in an office when the world was beautiful? —W. Somerset Maugham, *Of Human Bondage*

****

1. **sporadic**; occasional, intermittent, periodic, scattering. —sporadically.
2. **spry**; 1. lively, energetic, vigorous, vivacious, brisk, sprightly. 2. quick, nimble, agile, alert. —spryness, —spryly.
3. **spurious**; false, sham, fake, bogus, forged, inauthentic, counterfeit, fraudulent, adulterate. ※ adulterate *v.*; degrade, debase. ※ ersatz; 1. bogus, counterfeit. 2. artificial, spurious: *The lady has never drunk ersatz coffee.*
4. **spurn**; rebuff, repel, repulse. * dissoluble; capable of being melted, soluble. —dissolve; 1. melt, disintegrate, decompose. 2. solve. —dissolution.
5. **squalid**; dirty, foul, sordid, filthy, soiled, blemished, sullied. —squalidity.
6. **squander**; waste, lavish, dissipate, frivol away. —squanderingly.

♣ To arrogate is to dishonor. —Thomas Hobbes, *Of Man*

1. Philip was **squeamish**, and the way in which Miss Price ate took his appetite away. She ate noisily, greedily, a little like a wild beast in a menagerie. —W. Somerset Maugham, *Of Human Bondage*

2. Her appearance always acted as a damper* to the curiosity raised by her oral oddities: hard-featured and **staid**, she had no point to which interest could attach. —Charlotte Brontë, *Jane Eyre*

3. In the meantime the state of affairs was not that of a truce but of a **stalemate**. —Jack London, *Jerry of the Islands*

4. The apartment and furniture would have been nothing extraordinary as belonging to a homely,* northern farmer, with a stubborn countenance, and **stalwart** limbs set out to advantage in knee-breeches and gaiters. —Emily Brontë, *Wuthering Heights*

5. Little Jimmie was striving to **stanch** the flow of blood from his cut lips. —Stephen Crane, *Maggie: A Girl of the Streets*

6. I think you are all mated or **stark** mad.

—Shakespeare, *The Comedy of Errors*

****

1. **squeamish**; 1. sensitive, delicate. 2. scrupulous. 3. easily nauseated.
2. **staid**; 1. steady, sober. 2. calm, sedate. —staidness. * damper; depressor.
3. **stalemate**; deadlock, dead end. ※ impasse; stalemate: *The dialogue to end the war reached an impasse.* ※ stale; 1. decayed. 2. fetid.
4. **stalwart**; stout, robust, sturdy, muscular, hefty. —stalwartness. * homely; plain.
5. **stanch**; 1. stop, staunch, stem, arrest bleeding. 2. *adj.* staunch, steadfast. ※ hemostasis; stopping of haemorrhage. —hemostatic.
6. **stark**; 1. completely, utterly, absolutely. 2. *adj.* sheer. —starkness, —starkly.

♣ A man often pays dear for a small frugality. —R. W. Emerson, *Compensation*

1. In a **stealthy** and sneaking* manner they [the jays*] flit* from tree to tree, nearer and nearer, and pick up the kernels which the squirrels have dropped. —Henry David Thoreau, *Walden*

2. Jemmy recognized the **stentorian** voice of one of his brothers at a prodigious* distance. —Charles Darwin, *The Voyage of the Beagle*

3. It cannot be maintained that species when intercrossed are invariably **sterile**, and varieties invariably fertile. —Charles Darwin, *The Origin of Species*

4. As is the case with men of talent, his gifts adorn his **sterling** soundness. —Joseph Conrad, *The Mirror of the Sea*

5. Her belief in comradeship was **stifled**, and . . . —E. M. Forster, *Howards End*

6. Do not return to your families with the **stigma** of disgrace marked on your brows. —Mary Shelley, *Frankenstein*

****

1. **stealthy**; covert, furtive, clandestine, surreptitious. —stealthiness, —stealthily. * sneaking; secret, skulking, sneaky, *see p. 156, no. 1,* ※ *sneak.* * jay; 1. a gregarious bird of the crow family. 2. fool. 3. chatterer. * flit; flick, flutter.
2. **stentorian**; blaring, ringing, sonorous, powerful in voice. —stentorianly. * prodigious; 1. tremendous, phenomenal. 2. marvelous, fabulous, superb.
3. **sterile**; barren, infecund, infertile. ***ant.*** prolific; fertile. — sterility, —sterilize.
4. **sterling**; 1. genuine, trustworthy. 2. superlative. 3. British currency.
5. **stifle**; choke, strangle, suffocate, smother.
6. **stigma**; shame, disgrace, dishonor, smirch. —stigmatic, —stigmatize.

♣ Never do two things at a time: pursue your object, be it what it will, steadily and indefatigably. —4th Earl of Chesterfield, *Letters to His Son*

1. The letters were formal and a little **stilted**. —W. Somerset Maugham, *Of Human Bondage*

2. We must not **stint**
   Our necessary actions, in the fear
   To cope malicious censurers.
   —Shakespeare, *King Henry VIII*

3. The **stipend** arising hence would hardly have indulged* the schoolmaster in the luxuries of life, had he not added to this office those of clerk and barber. —Henry Fielding, *Tom Jones*

4. Was it possible that this **stolidly** respectable person was of the same blood as one of the most notorious criminals in the country? —Arthur Conan Doyle, *The Hound of the Baskervilles*

5. They [the ruddy cliffs] were curiously **striated**, in a manner which is, I believe, characteristic of basaltic* upheavals. —Arthur Conan Doyle, *The Lost World*

6. The insipidity* and yet the noise; the nothingness and yet the self-importance of all these people! What would I give to hear your **strictures** on them! —Jane Austen, *Pride and Prejudice*

****

1. **stilted**; pompous, bombastic, grandiloquent. —stilt *n.* ; column, pillar.
2. **stint**; control, withhold, restrict, curb. —stintless; unstinted, unstinting, overgenerous, unsparing, lavish, prodigal, bountiful. —stintingly.
3. **stipend**; pay, salary, wage, allowance. —stipendiary. * indulge; gratify.
4. **stolidly**; insensitively, impassively, apathetically. —stolidity, —stolid.
5. **striated**; striped, streaked. —stria *n.* (*pl.* striae); stripe. —striate *v.* * basaltic; of volcanic rocks. —basalt. ※ seismic; of earthquake.
6. **stricture**; 1. severe criticism, censorious remark, censure. 2. restriction, limitation, demarcation. * insipidity; boringness, *see p. 165, no. 2.* —insipid.

1. In the slumber of _______, is the shortness of life generally forgotten.
2. _______ lives upon succession.
3. In the woods, too, a man casts off his years, as the snake his _______.
4. He was clad in a professional but rather _______ fashion.
5. They climbed out of the _______ town.
6. By a dexterous _______, he pitched his cap up into the mizzen-top for a shelf.

[**sleight, smelting, slovenly, sloth, slander, slough**]

****

1. At present I am a _______ in civilized life again.
2. Jim's manner was very _______ and set.
3. The most hurtful to a youth is to have his soul _______ with pleasure.
4. She made herself disadvantageously conspicuous by some _______.
5. He was better known by the _______ of "The artful Dodger."
6. Now let us rekindle the _______, nigh quenched fire on the altar.

[**sober, sodden, sobriquet, smouldering, solecism, sojourner**]

****

1. The recreations of the people were _______ and flat.
2. He had a _______ bass voice.
3. We wonder superfluously when we hear of a _______ walking a plank.
4. The West Wind is no calculator plotting deep schemes in a _______ heart.
5. I prefer to be owned as sound and _______.
6. I was still by nature _______ to be neat.

[**sonorous, soporific, solicitous, somnambulist, somber, solvent**]

****

1. Every glen gushed water like a cistern; every stream was in high _______.
2. The transparent membrane is still holding the _______.
3. Apparently a _______ caught his breath.
4. Fie, what a _______ is he of his tongue!
5. Men in great place are servants of the _______ or state.
6. It may be wise and _______ to preserve that outward indifference.

[**spate, spendthrift, sovereign, specious, spawn, spasm**]

Review Exercise: Sentence Completions (pp. 295–98)

1. Yet you, my creator, detest and _______ me, thy creature.
2. He's living in one tiny room in the most _______ way.
3. What was the use of _______ the days of his youth in an office.
4. The Battle of Niagara passed gradually into a _______ conflict.
5. I don't want any second-hand, _______ sensations.
6. The animal was as _______ as a squirrel?

[**squandering, spry, spurious, sporadic, spurn, squalid**]

****

1. I think you are all mated or _______ mad.
2. Philip was _______, and the way in which she ate took his appetite away.
3. He is a homely farmer with a stubborn countenance and _______ limbs.
4. Hard-featured and _______, she had no point to which interest could attach.
5. Little Jimmie was striving to _______ the flow of blood from his cut lips.
6. In the meantime the state of affairs was not that of a truce but of a _______.

[**staid, stanch, stalwart, stark, squeamish, stalemate**]

****

1. As is the case with men of talent, his gifts adorn his _______ soundness.
2. It cannot be maintained that species when intercrossed are invariably _______.
3. Don't return to your home with the _______ of disgrace marked on your brows.
4. In a _______ and sneaking manner they [the jays] flit from tree to tree.
5. Her belief in comradeship was _______.
6. Jemmy recognized the _______ voice of one of his brothers.

[**stifled, stentorian, sterling, sterile, stealthy, stigma**]

****

1. The _______ arising hence hasn't indulged the schoolmaster.
2. What would I give to hear your _______ on all these people!
3. The _______ respectable person was of the same blood as the criminal.
4. The ruddy cliffs were curiously _______.
5. The letters were formal and a little _______.
6. We must not _______ our necessary actions, in the fear to cope censurers.

[**strictures, stipend, stint, stilted, stolidly, striated**]

1. The hissing of a kettle upon the stove rose sharp and **strident** to the ear. —Arthur Conan Doyle, *The Valley of Fear*

2. No laws, however **stringent**, can make the idle industrious, the thriftless provident, or the drunken sober. —Samuel Smiles, *Self Help*

3. Life's but a walking shadow; a poor player
   That **struts** and frets his hour upon the stage
   And then is heard no more.
   —Shakespeare, *Macbeth*

4. The ripest fruit of reason the **stultification** of reason. From the topmost peak of reason James teaches to cease reasoning and to have faith that all is well and will be well . . . —Jack London, *John Barleycorn*

5. Such is our desire of abstraction* from ourselves, that very few are satisfied with the quantity of **stupefaction** which the needs of the body force upon the mind. —Samuel Johnson, *The Idler*

6. Principles and opinions may be maintained with perfect **suavity**, without coming to blows or uttering hard words. —Samuel Smiles, *Self Help*

****

1. **strident**; harsh, jarring, grating, raspy, raucous. —stridence. ※ raspy; grating.
2. **stringent**; 1. rigid, stern, rigorous, severe. 2. tight, urgent. —stringency.
3. **strut**; 1. show off, display, parade. 2. swagger, prance, peacock. —strutter.
4. **stultification**; making useless, nullification, annulling, crippling. —stultify.
5. **stupefaction**; 1. unconsciousness, stupor, torpor. 2. amazement, astonishment, consternation. —stupefy; daze, astound, stun, bewilder, bemuse. —stupefactive. * abstraction; 1. withdrawing, remotion. 2. absent-mindedness, oblivion.
6. **suavity**; 1. affableness, amiableness, unctuousness, debonairness. 2. civility, urbanity. —suave, —suavely.

1. Unlike the earth, it [the sea] cannot be **subjugated** at any cost of patience and toil. —Joseph Conrad, *The Mirror of the Sea*

2. Now I find I had **suborn'd** the witness,
   And he's indicted* falsely.

   —Shakespeare, *Othello*

3. No one ever had so complete an alibi; I could **subpoena** half Westminster. —G. K. Chesterton, *The Wisdom of Father Brown*

4. It was a street of small shops **subservient** to the needs of poor people. —W. Somerset Maugham, *The Moon and Sixpence*

5. It is a common thing for the countenances of the dead, even in that fixed and rigid state, to **subside** into the long-forgotten expression of sleeping infancy, and settle into the very look of early life. —Charles Dickens, *Oliver Twist*

6. In the general course of human nature, *a power over a man's* ***subsistence*** *amounts to a power over his will.* —Alexander Hamilton, *The Federalist Papers*

****

1. **subjugate**; conquer, vanquish, subdue, quell. —subjugation, —subjugate.
2. **suborn**; instigate somebody to commit perjury or a wrong act. —subornative. * indict; accuse, incriminate, prosecute, *see p. 157, no. 5.*
3. **subpoena**; 1. summon, serve with a writ. 2. writ to send for a witness.
4. **subservient**; 1. contributory, conducive. 2. obsequious, subordinate. —subservience, —subserve.
5. **subside**; 1. go down, sink. 2. abate. —subsidence; alleviation, remission. ※ subsidize; fund, finance: *Many people live in subsidized houses.* —subsidy.
6. **subsistence**; 1. existence, survival. 2. living, livelihood. —subsist.

♣ More helpful than all wisdom is one draught of simple human pity that will not forsake us. —George Eliot, *The Mill on the Floss*

1. . . . as many thoughts in succession **substantiate** themselves, we shall by and by stand in a new world of our own creation . . . —R. W. Emerson, *Friendship*

2. . . . they were impressed because he was not deceived by their little **subterfuges**. —W. Somerset Maugham, *Of Human Bondage*

3. From beneath their feet rose always the **subterranean** rumbles* of revolt. —Jack London, *The Iron Heel*

4. So impossible is it for arbitrary* human ordinations* permanently to degrade human nature, or **subvert** the principles of justice and freedom. —W. Ellery Channing, *On the Elevation of the Laboring Classes*

5. It is as **succinct** as an invoice. —Mark Twain, *A Tramp Abroad*

6. He would have called aloud for **succor**; but the slow eyes opened upon him; and slowly he felt the girl's supineness* leaving her; and now she recovers herself a little. —Herman Melville, *Pierre*

****

1. **substantiate**; confirm, demonstrate, verify, attest, corroborate, authenticate. —substantiation, —substantial. ※ substantive; 1. real. 2. considerable. 3. acting as a noun: *substantive clause*.
2. **subterfuge**; trick, device, artifice, manoeuvre *also* maneuver.
3. **subterranean** *or* **subterraneous**; underground, covert. * rumble; thunder.
4. **subvert**; upset, overthrow. —subversion. * arbitrary; 1. despotic, dogmatic. 2. random. * ordination; 1. ordering. 2. ordainment; conferring holy office.
5. **succinct**; precise, concise, terse, laconic. —succinctly.
6. **succor** *or* **succour**; assistance, relief. * supineness; inertia, *see p. 306, no. 2.*

♣ From exertion come wisdom and purity; from sloth ignorance and sensuality. —Henry David Thoreau, *Walden*

1. I love to see the herd of men feeding heartily on coarse* and **succulent** pleasures, as cattle on the husks* and stalks of vegetables. —Henry David Thoreau, *A Week on the Concord and Merrimack Rivers*

2. In short, the poor candle-maker's scrupulous* morality **succumbed** to his unscrupulous necessity, as is now and then apt to be the case. —Herman Melville, *The Confidence-Man*

3. Absolve you to yourself, and you shall have the **suffrage** of the world. —R. W. Emerson, *Self-Reliance*

4. The hall was not dark, nor yet was it lit, only by the high-hung bronze lamp; a warm glow **suffused** both it and the lower steps of the oak staircase. —Charlotte Brontë, *Jane Eyre*

5. Ahab's soul, shut up in the caved trunk of his body, there fed upon the **sullen** paws of its gloom! —Herman Melville, *Moby Dick*

6. I did wrong: I would have **sullied** my innocent flower—breathed guilt on its purity. —Charlotte Brontë, *Jane Eyre*

****

1. **succulent**; 1. delightful, delectable. 2. juicy. —succulence. * coarse; harsh. * husk; covering of a fruit or seed.
2. **succumb**; yield, submit, surrender. * scrupulous; 1. ethical. 2. meticulous.
3. **suffrage**; 1. consent, approval. 2. vote, right to vote, franchise. —suffragist; advocate, esp. of women's suffrage. ※ egalitarian; equalitarian: *The suffragist was an egalitarian, not an egoist.* ※ referendum; public vote, plebiscite. ※ franchise; 1. *v.* give the right to vote. ***ant.*** disfranchise. 2. *n.* dealership.
4. **suffuse**; cover, flood, spread over. —suffusion.
5. **sullen**; gloomy, dismal, morose, surly. —sullenness.
6. **sully**; 1. defile, besmirch, taint, denigrate. 2. spoil, mar, impair, vitiate.

1. . . . the air is **sultry** and stifling; an intolerable thirst is provoked, for which no running stream offers its kind relief. —Herman Melville, *The Encantadas*

2. The dark panelling, the massive, tarnished* gold of the cornice,* the mahogany tables, gave the room an air of **sumptuous** comfort, and the leather-covered seats along the wall were soft and easy. —W. Somerset Maugham, *Of Human Bondage*

3. Above the chimney were **sundry** villainous old guns and a couple of horse-pistols, and, by way of ornament, three gaudily painted canisters* disposed along its ledge.* —Emily Brontë, *Wuthering Heights*

4. I cannot agree with the painters who claim **superciliously** that the layman can understand nothing of painting. —W. Somerset Maugham, *The Moon and Sixpence*

5. **Superfluous** wealth can buy superfluities only. —Henry David Thoreau, *Walden*

6. Intellectual tasting of life will not **supersede** muscular activity. —R. W. Emerson, *Experience*

****

1. **sultry**; humid and hot, sweltering, muggy, torrid. —sultriness, —sultrily.
2. **sumptuous**; luxurious, extravagant, deluxe, lavish. —sumptuousness. * tarnished; discolored, rusted. * cornice; see *p. 12, no. 6.*
3. **sundry**; multifarious, miscellaneous, motley. —sundries; various items. * canister; metal bin, tin. * ledge; 1. shelf. 2. projection from a rock wall.
4. **superciliously**; 1. haughtily, overbearingly. 2. sneeringly, disdainfully.
5. **superfluous**; excessive, surplus, redundant. —superfluity, —superfluously.
6. **supersede** *also* **supercede**; replace, substitute, supplant. —supersedure *n.*

♣ The light of human minds is perspicuous words. —Thomas Hobbes, *Of Man*

1. No crisis, apparently, had **supervened**. —Thomas Hardy, *Tess*
2. The wind was light; the waves languid*; the stars twinkled with a faint effulgence*; all nature seemed **supine** with the long night watch. —Herman Melville, *The Encantadas*
3. I knew a boy who, from his peculiar energy, was called "Buster"* by his playmates, and this rightly **supplanted** his Christian name. —Henry David Thoreau, *Walking*
4. So we see, in languages the tongue is more pliant* to all expressions and sounds, the joints are more **supple** to all feats* of activity and motions, in youth than afterwards. —Francis Bacon, *Essays*
5. A man can scarce allege* his own merits with modesty, much less extol* them; a man cannot sometimes brook to **supplicate** or beg. —Francis Bacon, *Essays*
6. I am off—**surfeited** with endearment—to live my own life, and do my own work. —George Bernard Shaw, *An Unsocial Socialist*

****

1. **supervene**; follow immediately, ensue. —supervention.
2. **supine**; 1. inactive, inert, lethargic, torpid. 2. lying on the back. ***ant.*** prone; 1. prostrate. 2. liable, inclined, disposed. —supineness; inactivity, inertia, lethargy, torpor. * languid; feeble, anemic. * effulgence; radiance, refulgence.
3. **supplant**; substitute, supersede. * buster; 1. robust child. 2. blockbuster.
4. **supple**; flexible, tractable, pliable. ***ant.*** stiff. —suppleness. * pliant; compliant, *see p. 227, no. 4.* * feat; 1. stunt, tour de force. 2. exploit, accomplishment.
5. **supplicate**; entreat, beseech, petition. —supplication; prayer, petition, litany. —supplicatory. * allege; profess. * extol; laud, applaud, acclaim.
6. **surfeit**; 1. overindulge, satiate, glut, cloy. 2. *n.* satiety, plethora. —surfeiter.

♣ Nothing is at last sacred but the integrity of your own mind. —R. W. Emerson, *Self-Reliance*

1. We must see that the world is rough and **surly**, and will not mind drowning a man or a woman, but swallows your ship like a grain of dust. —R. W. Emerson, *Fate*

2. You shall have my facts for your **surmises**. —E. Phillips Oppenheim, *The Yellow Crayon*

3. The State leaders may even make a merit of their **surreptitious** invasions of it [the Constitution] on the ground of some temporary convenience, exemption,* or advantage. —Alexander Hamilton, *The Federalist Papers*

4. Every spy was under **surveillance** himself. —Mark Twain, *The Innocents Abroad*

5. . . . and I never saw a child so **susceptible** of flattery as she was. —Anne Brontë, *Agnes Grey*

6. Never had such a set of noisy, roistering,* **swaggering** varlets* landed in peaceful Communipaw. —Washington Irving, *Guests from Gibbet Island*

****

1. **surly**; unfriendly, sullen, brusquely, gruff. —surliness, —surlily.
2. **surmise**; 1. guess, conjecture, speculation. 2. *v.* speculate, presume, fancy.
3. **surreptitious**; covert, stealthy, clandestine, furtive, privy. —surreptitiousness. * exemption; immunity, absolution, impunity, exoneration.
4. **surveillance**; watch, vigilance, superintendence. —surveillant.
5. **susceptible**; 1. sensitive, receptive, vulnerable. 2. allowing, permitting.
6. **swaggering**; prideful, boastful. * roistering; blustering. * varlet; attendant.

♣ Art is long, and time is fleeting,
And our hearts, though stout and brave,
Still, like muffled drums, are beating
Funeral marches to the grave.

—H. W. Longfellow, "A Psalm of Life"

1. He was a big, **swarthy** Netherlander, with black moustaches and a bold glance. —Joseph Conrad, *The Mirror of the Sea*
2. I was **swathed** in cant* . . . —E. M. Forster, *Howards End*
3. The heat was **sweltering**, and the men grumbled fiercely over their work. —Robert L. Stevenson, *Treasure Island*
4. They **swindle**, right and left, but they always make the other person *seem* to swindle himself. —Mark Twain, *Tom Sawyer Abroad*
5. Not to speak it harshly or scornfully, it seemed Clifford's nature to be a **Sybarite**. —Nathaniel Hawthorne, *The House of Seven Gables*
6. . . . and the wonder is that they so seldom err as they do, beset, as they continually are, by the wiles* of parasites* and **sycophants** . . . —Alexander Hamilton, *The Federalist Papers*.

****

1. **swarthy**; darkish, dusky, brunette. —swarthiness, —swarthily.
2. **swathe**; wrap, bind, enfold, envelop. * cant; hypocrisy, pretence, humbug.
3. **sweltering**; sultry, torrid, broiling, oppressively hot. —swelteringly.
4. **swindle**; cheat, defraud, bamboozle. —swindler.
5. **sybarite**; 1. sensualist, voluptuary, hedonist, one devoted to indulgence and luxury. ***ant.*** ascetic. 2. *adj.* sybaritic. ※ Stoicism; asceticism, *see p. 17, no. 6.*
6. **sycophant**; yes-man, flatterer, fawner, toady. —sycophancy, —sycophantic. * wiles (usu. in *pl.*) ; crafts, chicaneries. * parasite; fellow guest, sponger.

♣ The inbred politeness which springs from right-heartedness and kindly feelings is of no exclusive rank or station. The mechanic who works at the bench may possess it, as well as the clergyman, or the peer. —Samuel Smiles, *Self Help*

1. No laws, however _______, can make the idle industrious.
2. Life is a poor player that _______ and frets his hour upon the stage.
3. Principles may be maintained with perfect _______, without coming to blows.
4. The hissing of a kettle upon the stove rose sharp and _______ to the ear.
5. Very few are satisfied with the quantity of _______.
6. The ripest fruit of reason the _______ of reason.

[**stultification, stupefaction, stringent, struts, strident, suavity**]

****

1. It was a street of small shops _______ to the needs of poor people.
2. The sea cannot be _______ at any cost of patience and toil.
3. A power over a man's _______ amounts to a power over his will.
4. Now I find I had _______ the witness, and he's indicted falsely.
5. No one ever had so complete an alibi; I could _______ half Westminster.
6. The countenances of the dead _______ into the expression of sleeping infancy.

[**subsistence, subpoena, suborn'd, subsided, subjugated, subservient**]

****

1. It is as _______ as an invoice.
2. He would have called aloud for _______.
3. Many thoughts in succession _______ themselves.
4. They were impressed because he was not deceived by their little _______.
5. It is impossible for human ordinations to _______ the principles of justice.
6. From beneath their feet rose always the _______ rumbles of revolt.

[**succor, succinct, subterranean, subvert, subterfuges, substantiate**]

****

1. His scrupulous morality _______ to his unscrupulous necessity.
2. I did wrong: I would have _______ my innocent flower.
3. Absolve you to yourself, and you shall have the _______ of the world.
4. Ahab's soul, there fed upon the _______ paws of the gloom!
5. They were feeding heartily on coarse and _______ pleasures.
6. A warm glow _______ both the hall and the lower steps of the oak staircase.

[**suffused, succulent, sullen, sullied, succumbed, suffrage**]

Review Exercise: Sentence Completions (pp. 305–8)

1. The air is _______ and stifling; an intolerable thirst is provoked.
2. Above the chimney were _______ villainous old guns.
3. Intellectual tasting of life will not _______ muscular activity.
4. The mahogany tables gave the room an air of _______ comfort.
5. He claimed _______ that the layman can understand nothing of painting.
6. _______ wealth can buy superfluities only.

[**superfluous, sundry, sultry, supersede, sumptuous, superciliously**]

****

1. I am off—_______ with endearment—to live my own life.
2. The joints are more _______ to all feats of activity, in youth than afterwards.
3. A man cannot sometimes brook to _______ or beg.
4. The wind was light . . . all nature seemed _______ with the long night watch.
5. This [Buster] rightly _______ his Christian name.
6. No crisis, apparently, had _______.

[**supple, supervened, supplanted, surfeited, supplicate, supine**]

****

1. Never had such a set of _______ varlets landed in peaceful Communipaw.
2. The State leaders made a merit of their _______ invasions of the Constitution.
3. Every spy was under _______ himself.
4. I never saw a child so _______ of flattery as she was.
5. You shall have my facts for your _______.
6. We must see that the world is rough and _______.

[**surly, swaggering, surveillance, surmises, susceptible, surreptitious**]

****

1. The heat was _______, and the men grumbled fiercely over their work.
2. They are beset by the wiles of parasites and _______.
3. Not to speak it harshly, it seemed Clifford's nature to be a _______.
4. He was a big, _______ Netherlander, with black moustaches and a bold glance.
5. The swindlers always make the other person seem to _______ himself.
6. I was _______ in cant.

[**Sybarite, sycophants, swarthy, sweltering, swindled, swathed**]

1. . . . had he been a single hair's breadth taller, the matchless **symmetry** of his form would have been destroyed. —Herman Melville, *Typee*

2. Mr. Pontellier had been a rather courteous husband so long as he met a certain **tacit** submissiveness in his wife. —Kate Chopin, *The Awakening*

3. The greater part of the structure was the brain, sending enormous nerves to the eyes, ear, and **tactile** tentacles.* —H. G. Wells, *The War of the Worlds*

4. Here is a **talisman** will remove all difficulties. —Charlotte Brontë, *Jane Eyre*

5. So cowards fight, when they can fly no further;
   So doves do peck the falcon's* piercing **talons**.
   —Shakespeare, *King Henry VI, Part III*

6. The dead man's papers had not been **tampered** with. —Arthur Conan Doyle, *The Return of Sherlock Holmes*

****

1. **symmetry**; balance, proportion, harmony, equivalence, correspondence, congruity. —symmetric, —symmetrize.
2. **tacit**; silent, reticent, taciturn. —tacitness, —tacitly.
3. **tactile**; 1. perceptible, tangible. 2. tactual. —tactility. * tentacle; feeler.
4. **talisman**; charm, amulet. ※ fetish *or* fetiche; totem, cult object.
5. **talon**; claw of a bird of prey. * falcon; hawk, any bird of prey.
6. **tamper**; interfere, meddle, intervene, interpose. —tamperer.

♣ Love is anterior to life,
Posterior to death,
Initial of creation, and
The exponent of breath.

—Emily Dickinson, "Love is anterior to life"

1. He pierced* the emblematic* or spiritual character of the visible, audible, **tangible** world. —R. W. Emerson, *The American Scholar*

2. Oh, devilish **tantalization** of the gods! —Herman Melville, *Moby Dick*

3. I cannot make your consciousness **tantamount** to mine. —R. W. Emerson, *Friendship*

4. His greatest fear in the world was that his large, stout wife, at table, should crown him with a plate of hot soup. Twice, in a **tantrum**, she had done this during their earlier married life. —Jack London, *Michael, Brother of Jerry*

5. I thought you a broken toy that had lasted its time; a worthless spangle that was **tarnished**, and thrown away. —Charles Dickens, *David Copperfield*

6. Away ass, you'll lose the tide,* if you **tarry** any longer. —Shakespeare, *The Two Gentlemen of Verona*

****

1. **tangible**; perceptible, palpable. ※ haptic; of the sense of touch, tactile, tactual. * pierce; penetrate. * emblematic; symbolic. —emblem.
2. **tantalization**; teasing, molestation, irritation, vexation, annoyance. —tantalize.
3. **tantamount**; equal, equivalent.
4. **tantrum**; fit, explosion, outburst, hot temper.
5. **tarnish**; 1. stain, discolor, spoil, taint, sully. 2. corrode, rust. —tarnishable.
6. **tarry**; 1. delay, be late, be tardy. 2. stay, sojourn, remain. * tide; 1. a favorable opportunity. 2. variation.

♣ Nor is the people's judgement always true:
The most may err as grossly as the few.

—John Dryden, *Absalom and Achitophel*

1. The cruel **taunt** was more than hunger, and cold, and nakedness. —Harriet Beecher Stowe, *Uncle Tom's Cabin*

2. . . . in English, when we have used a word a couple of times in a paragraph, we imagine we are growing **tautological**, . . . Repetition may be bad, but surely inexactness is worse. —Mark Twain, *A Tramp Abroad*

3. The last scene of her dismal Vanity Fair comedy was fast approaching; the **tawdry** lamps were going out one by one; and the dark curtain was almost ready to descend. —W. M. Thackeray, *Vanity Fair*

4. Here and there a **tawny** brook prattled* out from among the underwood and lost itself again in the ferns and brambles* upon the further side. —Arthur Conan Doyle, *The White Company*

5. Terror seized me, a horror of my **temerity**. —H. G. Wells, *The War of the Worlds*

6. I ask you now, is such a theory **tenable**? —Arthur Conan Doyle, *The Adventures of Sherlock Holmes*

****

1. **taunt**; 1. *n.* ridicule, sneer, scoff, jeer, gibe. 2. *v.* despise, deride. —tauntingly.
2. **tautological**; redundant, pleonastic. —tautology, —tautologize.
3. **tawdry**; gaudy, garish. ※ counterfeit; shoddy.
4. **tawny**; yellowish brown. —tawniness, —tawnily. * prattle; babble, chatter, *see p. 232, no. 1.* * bramble; prickly shrub.
5. **temerity**; rashness, recklessness, foolhardiness. —temerarious.
6. **tenable**; maintainable, defensible, justifiable, viable, rational. ***ant.*** untenable. —tenableness, —tenably.

♣ The reality *exists* as a *plenum*.* —William James, *The Principles of Psychology*

* plenum; fullness. ***ant.*** vacuum.

1. There are certain animals to which **tenacity** of position is a law of life. —George Eliot, *The Mill on the Floss*

2. He felt himself losing his footing in the depths of this **tenebrous** affair. —Joseph Conrad, *The Secret Agent*

3. This gentleman and Mr Thwackum scarce ever met without a disputation*; for their **tenets** were, indeed, diametrically opposite to each other. —Henry Fielding, *Tom Jones*

4. The sound of tools to a clever workman who loves his work is like the **tentative** sounds of the orchestra to the violinist who has to bear his part in the overture. —George Eliot, *Adam Bede*

5. There was a **tenuous** mist in the distance, and it softened exquisitely the noble lines of the buildings. —W. Somerset Maugham, *Of Human Bondage*

6. It is worth notice that a decoction* of cabbage leaves is far more exciting and probably nutritious to Drosera* than an infusion* made with **tepid** water. —Charles Darwin, *Insectivorous Plants*

****

1. **tenacity**; obstinacy, persistence, pertinacity, obduracy. —tenacious.
2. **tenebrous**; dark, shadowy, gloomy, dour. —tenebrosity, —tenebrific.
3. **tenet**; principle, doctrine, creed, credo, belief. * disputation; 1. argument, debate. 2. contradiction, gainsay. —dispute.
4. **tentative**; 1. experimental, provisional. 2. hesitant. —tentativeness.
5. **tenuous**; thin, gossamer, flimsy, airy, dilute. —tenuity, —tenuously.
6. **tepid**; 1. warmish, lukewarm. 2. halfhearted. —tepidity. * decoction; boiling down. * Drosera; a species of sundew. * infusion; extraction.

♣ The regal and parental tyrant differ only in the extent of their dominions, and the number of their slaves. —Samuel Johnson, *The Rambler*

1. Bald and **terse** as the statement was, I now found it infinitely alluring. —Ambrose Bierce, *Can Such Things Be?*
2. . . . Margaret fell asleep, **tethered** by affection, and lulled by the murmurs of the river that descended all the night from Wales. —E. M. Forster, *Howards End*
3. He had thin silver bracelets upon his arms, and on his neck a collar of the same metal, bearing the inscription, "Wamba, the son of Witless, is the **thrall** of Cedric Rotherwood." —Walter Scott, *Ivanhoe*
4. He could hear nothing, but the drip, drip on the **threadbare** carpet. —Oscar Wilde, *The Picture of Dorian Gray*
5. He had borne himself to the lawyer with a sort of murderous mixture of **timidity** and boldness, and he spoke with a husky, whispering and somewhat broken voice. —Robert L. Stevenson, *Dr. Jekyll and Mr. Hyde*
6. She stopped, out of breath but seething with the **tirade** yet to come.—Jack London, *The Valley of the Moon*

****

1. **terse**; concise, compact, succinct, curt, laconic. —terseness, —tersely.
2. **tether**; 1. *v.* chain, tie, rein, halter, fetter. 2. restraint, limit of one's capacity.
3. **thrall**; 1. slave, servitor, bondsman. 2. slavery. 3. enslave.
4. **threadbare**; worn, frayed, shabby, ragged, tattered, scruffy. —threadbareness.
5. **timidity**; cowardice, diffidence, timorousness, recreancy. —timid.
6. **tirade**; 1. harangue, long and violent speech. 2. denunciation, philippic.

♣ Neither a borrower nor a lender be;
For loan oft loses both itself and friend,
And borrowing dulls the edge of husbandry.

—Shakespeare, *Hamlet*

1. . . . the landlady, assisted by a chamber-maid, proceeded to vinegar the forehead, beat the hands, **titillate** the nose, and unlace the stays of the spinster aunt . . . —Charles Dickens, *The Pickwick Papers*

2. A man is to carry himself in the presence of all opposition as if every thing were **titular** and ephemeral* but he. —R. W. Emerson, *Self-Reliance*

3. I leave my **toady**, Miss Briggs, at home. My brothers are my toadies here, my dear, and a pretty pair they are! —W. M. Thackeray, *Vanity Fair*

4. When hibernation was observed, it was found that whilst some animals became **torpid** in winter, others were torpid in summer: hibernation then was a false name. —R. W. Emerson, *Fate*

5. They [the rat and mouse] live under the cold climate of Faroe in the north and of the Falklands in the south, and on many an island in the **torrid** zones. —Charles Darwin, *The Origin of Species*

6. Even when he could not follow the reasoning, it gave him a curious pleasure to follow the **tortuosities** of thoughts that threaded their nimble way on the edge of the incomprehensible. —W. Somerset Maugham, *Of Human Bondage*

****

1. **titillate**; tickle, stimulate, excite, arouse, provoke. —titillation, —titillative.
2. **titular**; nominal, theoretical. —titularly. * ephemeral; passing, transitory.
3. **toady**; 1. fawner, flatterer, sycophant. 2. *v.* flatter. —toadism, —toadish.
4. **torpid**; 1. inactive, inert, dormant, lethargic. 2. dull, sluggish, indolent, languorous. —torpor; stupor, stagnancy. —torpidity, —torpify.
5. **torrid**; 1. sultry, sweltering, broiling. 2. tropical. 3. ardent, fervent. —torridity.
6. **tortuosity**; distortion, contortion, crookedness, warpage. —tortuous.

♣ It is a happy thing that time quells the longings of vengeance, and hushes the promptings of rage and aversion. —Charlotte Brontë, *Jane Eyre*

1. His **tousled** hair streamed wildly, and his face was dark with vexation and wrath. —Stephen Crane, *The Red Badge of Courage*

2. . . . what with **touting** for parcels at the station and selling the Bun Hill *Weekly Express*, he was making three shillings a week, or more . . . —H. G. Wells, *The War in the Air*

3. My lady is too high in position, too handsome, too accomplished,* too superior in most respects to the best of those by whom she is surrounded, not to have her enemies and **traducers**, I dare say. —Charles Dickens, *Bleak House*

4. She might have been in a **trance**, her eyes open, yet unseeing. —Thomas Hardy, *Tess*

5. He stood **transfixed** to the spot, gazing on vacancy. —Charles Dickens, *The Pickwick Papers*

6. It would have been a much better **transgression,** had I broken the bond of secrecy and told you everything. —Jane Austen, *Emma*

****

1. **tousle**; disarrange, dishevel, rumple, ruffle. —tousy; tangled, tousled.
2. **tout**; recommend, solicit, importune, canvass. —touter.
3. **traducer**; slanderer, libeler, vilifier, detractor, decrier. —traducement. * accomplished; educated, cultivated, civilized.
4. **trance**; 1. daze, reverie, abstraction. 2. rapture, ecstasy. 3. *v.* fascinate, captivate, enamor, entrance. —trancelike.
5. **transfix**; 1. pin, fix, impale. 2. bewitch, hypnotize, paralyze.
6. **transgression**; sin, crime, misdemeanor, felony, offence, iniquity, contravention. —transgressive. ⋇ trespassing; intrusion, encroach. ⋇ malfeasance; wrongdoing by an official. ⋇ misfeasance; unlawful act by lawful authority. ⋇ nonfeasance; dereliction, failure to do one's legal duty.

1. It is very easy to be entirely kind and pleasant to servants, without the least touch of any shade of **transient** good-fellowship with them. —Herman Melville, *Pierre*

2. He knew that all things human are **transitory**. —W. Somerset Maugham, *Of Human Bondage*

3. Above him was the light, **translucent**, billowing globe of shining brown oiled silk and the blazing sunlight and the great deep blue dome of the sky. —H. G. Wells, *The War in the Air*

4. . . . the twopence-halfpenny was **transmuted** into gold in the heart of the grateful waiting-maid . . . —W. M. Thackeray, *Vanity Fair*

5. Some damning circumstance always **transpires**. —R. W. Emerson, *Compensation*

6. For Johnson and Leach the **travail** of existence had ceased. —Jack London, *The Sea Wolf*

****

1. **transient**; fleeting, ephemeral, transitory, evanescent. —transience.
2. **transitory**; passing, temporary, fleeting, fugacious. —transitoriness.
3. **translucent**; clear, lucid, pellucid, semitransparent.
4. **transmute**; transform, transfigure, metamorphose. —transmutation.
5. **transpire**; 1. take place, arise, occur. 2. vapor, emit. —transpiration.
6. **travail**; 1. pang, labor, suffering. 2. toil, effort.

♣ Superstition is the religion of feeble minds. —Edmund Burke, *Reflections on the Revolution in France*

1. The brain sent enormous nerves to the eyes, ear, and _______ tentacles.
2. The _______ of his form has been matchless in the community.
3. The dead man's papers had not been _______ with.
4. He met a certain _______ submissiveness in his wife.
5. Here is a _______ will remove all difficulties.
6. So doves do peck the falcon's piercing _______.

[**talons, symmetry, tampered, talisman, tacit, tactile**]

****

1. I cannot make your consciousness _______ to mine.
2. Twice, in a _______, she, at table, had crowned him with a plate of hot soup.
3. He pierced the spiritual character of the visible, audible, _______ world.
4. Oh, devilish _______ of the gods!
5. Away ass, you'll lose the tide, if you _______ any longer.
6. I thought you a worthless spangle that was _______, and thrown away.

[**tantrum, tantalizaion, tantamount, tangible, tarnished, tarry**]

****

1. Terror seized me, a horror of my _______.
2. I ask you now, is such a theory _______?
3. The _______ lamps were going out one by one.
4. Here and there a _______ brook prattled out from among the underwood.
5. Having used a word several times in a paragraph, I am growing _______.
6. The cruel _______ was more than hunger, and cold, and nakedness.

[**tawny, taunt, tautological, temerity, tenable, tawdry**]

****

1. He felt himself losing his footing in the depths of this _______ affair.
2. There are certain animals to which _______ of position is a law of life.
3. The infusion was made with _______ water.
4. The sound of tools is like the _______ sounds of the orchestra.
5. There was a _______ mist in the distance.
6. Their _______ were, indeed, diametrically opposite to each other.

[**tenacity, tepid, tenebrous, tenets, tentative, tenuous**]

Review Exercise: Sentence Completions (pp. 315–18)

1. She stopped, out of breath but seething with the _______ yet to come.
2. Wamba, the son of Witless, is the _______ of Cedric Rotherwood.
3. Margaret fell asleep, _______ by affection.
4. He had borne himself to the lawyer with a mixture of _______ and boldness.
5. He could hear nothing, but the drip, drip on the _______ carpet.
6. Bald and _______ as the statement was, I now found it infinitely alluring.

[**tethered, terse, threadbare, tirade, thrall, timidity**]

****

1. She proceeded to vinegar the forehead, beat the hands, and _______ the nose.
2. Whilst some animals became _______ in winter, others were torpid in summer.
3. It gave him a curious pleasure to follow the _______ of thoughts.
4. The rat and mouse live on many an island in the _______ zones.
5. I leave my _______, Miss Brigs, at home. My brothers are my toadies here.
6. Everything was _______ and ephemeral but he.

[**titular, tortuosities, titillate, torpid, toady, torrid**]

****

1. He _______ for parcels at the station and sold the Bun Hill *Weekly Express*.
2. My lady doesn't have her enemies and _______, I dare say.
3. It would have been a much better _______, had I told you everything.
4. His _______ hair streamed wildly, and his face was dark with vexation.
5. She might have been in a _______, her eyes open, yet unseeing.
6. He stood _______ to the spot, gazing on vacancy.

[**trance, transfixed, touted, transgression, traducers, tousled**]

****

1. Some damning circumstance always _______.
2. The twopence-halfpenny was _______ into gold in the heart of the maid.
3. I have never had any shade of _______ good-fellowship with the servants.
4. For Johnson and Leach the _______ of existence had ceased.
5. He knew that all things human are _______.
6. Above him was the light, _______, billowing globe of shining brown silk.

[**transient, transmuted, translucent, transitory, travail, transpires**]

1. If we look wider, things are all alike; laws and letters and creeds and modes of living seem a **travesty** of truth. —R. W. Emerson, *Spiritual Laws*

2. I am justly kill'd with mine own **treachery**.

   —Shakespeare, *Hamlet*

3. She exhibited her hospitality in bread and **treacle** . . . —George Eliot, *The Mill on the Floss*

4. His [Henry D. Thoreau's] **trenchant** sense was never stopped by his rules of daily prudence,* but was always up to the new occasion. —R. W. Emerson, *Thoreau*

5. I stood still, in **trepidation**. —Jack London, *The Sea Wolf*

6. She used never to make any return to my affection before, but now **tribulation** has opened her heart. —George Eliot, *Adam Bede*

****

1. **travesty**; 1. farcical imitation, parody, mockery, burlesque, vaudeville. 2. *v.* mock. ※ burlesque; 1. mockery, a variety show. 2. *v.* make a travesty: *The lawyer burlesqued justice at the court, together with the perjurer.*
2. **treachery**; disloyalty, betrayal, treason, perfidy. —treacherous.
3. **treacle**; 1. syrup *or* sirup, molasses. 2. inordinately sentimental writing. 3. something cloying. —treacly *adj.*
4. **trenchant**; sarcastic, acerbic, acidulous, caustic, pungent, scathing, astringent, vitriolic, mordant. —trenchancy. * prudence; cautiousness.
5. **trepidation**; 1. dread, panic, apprehension. 2. trembling, quivering, tremor.
6. **tribulation**; 1. suffering, affliction, distress. 2. trial, hardship, ordeal. —tribulate *v.*

♣ No face which we can give to a matter will stead us so well at last as the truth. —Henry David Thoreau, *Walden*

1. Before that unjust **tribunal** there was little or no order of procedure ensuring to any accused person any reasonable hearing. —Charles Dickens, *A Tale of Two Cities*.

2. Don't cling so tenaciously* to ties of the flesh; save your constancy* and ardour* for an adequate cause; forbear* to waste them on **trite** transient objects. Do you hear, Jane? —Charlotte Brontë, *Jane Eyre*

3. Bitter and **truculent** when excited, I spoke as I felt, without reserve or softening. —Charlotte Brontë, *Jane Eyre*

4. The country rises in successive steps of table-land,* interspersed* with some **truncate** conical hills. —Charles Darwin, *The Voyage of the Beagle*

5. It even occurred to me that some sentimental maidservant had stolen in to keep a **tryst** with her sweetheart. —Henry James, *The Aspern Papers*

6. Nothing was burning on the hillside, though from the common* there still came a red glare and a rolling **tumult** of ruddy smoke beating up against the drenching hail.* —H. G. Wells, *The War of the Worlds*

****

1. **tribunal**; court, a board of adjudication. ※ the bench; judges.
2. **trite**; threadbare, prosaic, pedestrian, banal. —triteness. * tenaciously; persistently. * constancy; loyalty. * ardour; verve. * forbear; abstain from.
3. **truculent**; combative, aggressive, belligerent, pugnacious. —truculence.
4. **truncate**; 1. *adj.* cut short. 2. *v.* shorten by cutting off. —truncation. * table-land; upland, plateau. ※ knoll; small mound, hillock. * intersperse; disperse.
5. **tryst**; 1. clandestine appointment. 2. meeting. 3. keep a tryst. —tryster.
6. **tumult**; turmoil, bedlam, pandemonium, fracas. —tumultuous. * common; public land. * hail; pellets (small solid balls) of snow.

♣ No man lives without jostling and being jostled. —Thomas Carlyle, *Sir Walter Scott*

1. The **turbid** water, swollen by the heavy rain, was rushing rapidly on below. —Charles Dickens, *Oliver Twist*
2. There is indeed nothing more unsuitable to the nature of man in any calamity* than rage and **turbulence**. —Samuel Johnson, *The Rambler*
3. I always used to get up with the lark,* till I came under the petrifying* influence of your **turgid** intellect. —Mark Twain, *A Tramp Abroad*
4. Minds, sway'd by eyes, are full of **turpitude**.
   —Shakespeare, *Troilus and Cressida*
5. I hardly know which is myself and which the butcher, we are always in such a tangle* and **tussle**, knocking about upon the trodden grass. —Charles Dickens, *David Copperfield*
6. Michael's crowning* achievement, under Daughtry's **tutelage**, in the first days in the stateroom,* was to learn to count up to five. —Jack London, *Michael, Brother of Jerry*

****

1. **turbid**; unclear, murky, muddy. —turbidity.
2. **turbulence**; disturbance, commotion, turmoil, pandemonium. —turbulent; tempestuous. * calamity; catastrophe, mischance, mishap, *see p. 38, no. 6.*
3. **turgid**; swollen, inflated, pompous, orotund. —turgidity. * get up with the lark; rise early in the morning. * petrifying; frightening, stunning, paralyzing.
4. **turpitude**; 1. baseness, meanness, vileness, abjectness,. 2. viciousness.
5. **tussle**; 1. *n.* struggle, grapple, scuffle. 2. *v.* wrestle, contend. * tangle; muddle.
6. **tutelage**; 1. tuition, instruction. 2. charge, protection, guardianship. * crowning; highest. * stateroom; private room on a passenger ship or train.

♣ One thought fills immensity.
—William Blake, *The Marriage of Heaven and Hell*

1. I was still a **tyro** so far as concerned knowing how to behave in desperate circumstances. —Jack London, *The Iron Heel*

2. Life is not given us for the mere sake of Living, but always with an **ulterior** external Aim. —Thomas Carlyle, *Characteristics*

3. Tahiti is a lofty green island, with deep folds of a darker green, in which you divine* silent valleys; there is mystery in their sombre* depths, down which murmur and plash* cool streams, and you feel that in those **umbrageous** places life from immemorial* times has been led according to immemorial ways. —W. Somerset Maugham, *The Moon and Sixpence*

4. A human visage, as fiercely wild as savage art and **unbridled** passions could make it, peered* out on the retiring footsteps of the travellers. —James Fenimore Cooper, *The Last of the Mohicans*

5. Indeed, they had all seemed remarkably taciturn, and when they did speak, endowed with very **uncanny** voices. —H. G. Wells, *The Island of Doctor Moreau*

6. His appearance was wild and **uncouth**; there was aloofness in his eyes and sensuality in his mouth. —W. Somerset Maugham, *The Moon and Sixpence*

****

1. **tyro**; apprentice, novice, entrant, probationer, novitiate, neophyte. ※ manqué; 1. frustrated, unsuccessful, unfulfilled: *a novelist manqué*. 2. would-be.
2. **ulterior**; hidden, concealed, covert, surreptitious. —ulteriorly.
3. **umbrageous**; 1. shady, shading. 2. incensed. —umbrageousness. * divine; discover. * sombre; gloomy. * plash; splash. * immemorial; ancient.
4. **unbridled**; uncontrolled, unconstrained, unrestrained. * peer; peep, pry.
5. **uncanny**; 1. weird, eerie, preternatural. 2. incredible. —uncanniness.
6. **uncouth**; unrefined, rough, coarse, gross, crude, clumsy, boorish, rustic, ungainly, loutish. —uncouthness, —uncouthly.

1. The **unction**, the suavity of her behaviour offered, for one who knew her, a sure token that suspicion of some kind was busy in her brain. —Charlotte Brontë, *Villette*

2. The **undulating** common seemed now dark almost to blackness, except where its roadways lay grey and pale under the deep-blue sky of the early night. —H. G. Wells, *The War of the Worlds*

3. On land it [the penguin] stumps*; afloat it sculls*; in the air it flops.* As if ashamed of her failure, Nature keeps this **ungainly** child hidden away at the ends of the earth, in the Straits of Magellan, and on the abased* sea-story of Rodondo. —Herman Melville, *The Encantadas*

4. Oh! his character is **unimpeachable**. —Charlotte Brontë, *Jane Eyre*

5. His aspect was miserably **unkempt** and wildly sorrowful. —Joseph Conrad, *The Mirror of the Sea*

6. The black mounted the steps of the poop,* and, like a brave prisoner, brought up to receive sentence, stood in **unquailing** muteness before Don Benito, now recovered from his attack. —Herman Melville, *Benito Cereno*

****

1. **unction**; 1. soothing words, flattery, compliment. 2. anointing, ointment. 3. balm, balsam, salve. —unctuous.
2. **undulating**; waving, wavy, rippling, ruffling, surging. —undulation, —undulately, —undulatory *also* undulant. ※ unwavering; steadfast, resolute, unswerving.
3. **ungainly**; 1. ungraceful, clumsy, awkward. 2. unmanageable, unwieldy, unruly. —ungainliness. * stump; walk heavily. * scull; oar, paddle. * flop; fall flat. * abased; degraded.
4. **unimpeachable**; irreproachable, impeccable, inculpable, unblemished.
5. **unkempt**; untidy, sloppy, slovenly, slipshod, slatternly.
6. **unquailing**; dauntless, unshrinking, intrepid, unflinching. ***ant.*** cowering. * poop; stern, *see p. 286, no. 6.*

1. History is a tangled skein* that one may take up at any point, and break when one has **unraveled** enough; but complexity precedes evolution. —Henry Adams, *The Education of Henry Adams*

2. Every skilled touch of the artist's brush or chisel, though guided by genius, is the product of **unremitting** study. —Samuel Smiles, *Self Help*

3. I have observed, Mrs. Elton, in the course of my life, that if things are going **untowardly** one month, they are sure to mend the next. —Jane Austen, *Emma*

4. Any sportiveness in cattle is unexpected. I saw one day a herd of a dozen bullocks* and cows running about and frisking* in **unwieldy** sport, like huge rats, even like kittens. —Henry David Thoreau, *Walking*

5. Though the world scouts* at us whale hunters, yet does it **unwittingly** pay us the profoundest homage*; yea, an all-abounding adoration! for almost all the tapers,* lamps, and candles that burn round the globe, burn, as before so many shrines, to our glory! —Herman Melville, *Moby Dick*

6. The clock **upbraids** me with the waste of time.

—Shakespeare, *Twelfth Night*

****

1. **unravel**; solve, untangle, unsnarl. * skein; coil of yarn.
2. **unremitting**; incessant, persistent, incessant, constant. —unremittingly.
3. **untowardly**; 1. unluckily, unfortunately, unpropitiously. 2. refractorily.
4. **unwieldy**; burdensome, cumbersome, unmanageable, ungainly. —unwieldiness, —unwieldily. * bullock; castrated bull. * frisk; rollick, gambol.
5. **unwittingly**; unintentionally, unawarely, inadvertently. ※ subliminal; subconscious, unaware: *her subliminal advertisement of her lofty birth.* * scout; deride, jeer, taunt. * homage; respect, honor. * taper; slender candle.
6. **upbraid**; reproach, chide, chastise, reprimand, berate. —upbraidingly.

1. Banish your dotage!* Banish **usury**,
   That makes the Senate ugly!
   —Shakespeare, *Timon of Athens*

2. He honestly mistook his sensuality for romantic emotion, his **vacillation** for the artistic temperament, and his idleness for philosophic calm. —W. Somerset Maugham, *Of Human Bondage*

3. We did not think it hypocritical to draw over our **vagaries** the curtain of a decent silence. —W. Somerset Maugham, *The Moon and Sixpence*

4. Don't be **vainglorious**. Your lace-mender is too good for you, but not good enough for me; neither physically nor morally does she come up to my ideal of a woman. —Charlotte Brontë, *The Professor*

5. Cowards die many times before their deaths;
   The **valiant** never taste of death but once.
   —Shakespeare, *Julius Caesar*

6. Though held in a sort a barbarian, the backwoodsman* would seem to America what Alexander was to Asia—captain in the **vanguard** of conquering civilization. —Herman Melville, *The Confidence-Man*

****

1. **usury**; inordinate rate of interest. —usurer; loan shark, shylock. —usurious. * dotage; senility, decrepitude.
2. **vacillation**; sway, fluctuation, oscillation, waver, dither. —vacillatory, —vacillate; hesitate. ※ dither; vacillate: *The gourmand was dithering over what to eat.*
3. **vagary**; whim, caprice, crotchet, fancy. —vagarious.
4. **vainglorious**; boastful, conceited, bragging. —vainglory; bravado.
5. **valiant** *or* **valorous**; gallant, plucky, intrepid, doughty. —valor *or* valiance.
6. **vanguard**; 1. foremost position, forefront, van, spearhead. 2. leader, forerunner. * backwoodsman; frontiersman, pioneer.

1. The imagination creating the enemy is already **vanquished**; the combat's result is the combat's cause. —Ambrose Bierce, *Can Such things Be?*
2. She teased me with a thousand **vapid** complaints about school-quarrels and household economy. —Charlotte Brontë, *Villette*
3. Upon her head was a fanciful turban of purple velvet, figured with silver sprigs,* and surmounted* by a tuft* of **variegated** feathers. —Herman Melville, *Typee*
4. Glorious men are the scorn of wise men, the admiration of fools, the idols of parasites, and the slaves of their own **vaunts**. —Francis Bacon, *Essays*
5. It is very natural for young men to be **vehement**, acrimonious,* and severe. —Samuel Johnson, *The Rambler*
6. Houses, gates, churches, haystacks, objects of every kind they shot by, with a **velocity** and noise like roaring waters suddenly let loose. —Charles Dickens, *The Pickwick Papers*

****

1. **vanquish**; overpower, overwhelm, conquer, subdue, quell, subjugate, overcome. —vanquishment, —vanquisher, —vanquishable.
2. **vapid**; lifeless, dull, flat, insipid, jejune. —vapidity, —vapidly.
3. **variegated**; varicolored, polychromatic, multifarious, harlequin, motley. —variegation. ※ monolithic; uniform, monochromatic: *monolithic safety system.* * sprig; small branch, shoot. * surmount; conquer. * tuft; knot, bunch, cluster.
4. **vaunt**; *n.* brag, swagger, bravado, flaunt, grandiloquence. —vaunty *adj.*
5. **vehement**; intense, violent, fervid, ardent. —vehemence, —vehemently. * acrimonious; bitter, sarcastic.
6. **velocity**; 1. speed, pace. 2. rapidity, swiftness, celerity.

♣ To the feeble, the sluggish and purposeless, the happiest accidents avail nothing—they pass them by, seeing no meaning in them. —Samuel Smiles, *Self Help*

1. His _______ sense was never stopped by his rules of daily prudence.
2. I stood still, in _______.
3. She exhibited her hospitality in bread and _______.
4. Now _______ has opened her heart.
5. I am justly kill'd with mine own _______.
6. Laws and letters and creeds and modes of living seem a _______ of truth.

[**tribulation, treachery, trenchant, travesty, treacle, trepidation**]

****

1. Bitter and _______ when excited, I spoke as I felt, without reserve.
2. The country was interspersed with some _______ conical hills.
3. Some maidservant had stolen in to keep a _______ with her sweetheart.
4. From the common there still came a rolling _______ of ruddy smoke.
5. Before that unjust _______ there was no any reasonable hearing.
6. Forbear to waste your constancy and ardour on _______ transient objects.

[**trite, truculent, tribunal, truncate, tryst, tumult**]

****

1. We are always in such a tangle and _______.
2. Minds, sway'd by eyes, are full of _______.
3. I came under the petrifying influence of your _______ intellect.
4. His crowning achievement, under her _______, was to learn to count up to five.
5. The _______ water, swollen by the heavy rain, was rushing rapidly on below.
6. There is nothing more unsuitable to the nature of man in calamity than _______.

[**turgid, turpitude, turbulence, tutelage, tussle, turbid**]

****

1. The human visage was as fiercely wild as _______ passions could make it.
2. I was still a _______ so far as concerned knowing how to behave in calamity.
3. They did speak, endowed with very _______ voices.
4. Life is given us, always with an _______ external aim.
5. His appearance was wild and _______.
6. In those _______ places life has been led according to immemorial ways.

[**tyro, unbridled, umbrageous, uncanny, uncouth, ulterior**]

Review Exercise: Sentence Completions (pp. 325–28)

(pp. 325–28)

1. The _______ common seemed now dark almost to blackness.
2. Nature keeps this _______ child hidden away at the ends of the earth.
3. Oh! His character is _______.
4. The ______ offered a sure token that some suspicion was busy in her brain.
5. Like a brave prisoner, he stood in _______ muteness before Don Benito.
6. His aspect was miserably _______ and wildly sorrowful.

[**ungainly, unimpeachable, undulating, unkempt, unquailing, unction**]

****

1. Every skilled touch of the artist's brush is the product of _______ study.
2. The world _______ pays us [whale hunters] the profoundest homage.
3. The clock _______ me with the waste of time.
4. History is a tangled skein that one may break when one has _______ enough.
5. If things are going _______ one month, they are sure to mend the next.
6. A herd of a dozen bullocks and cows ran about and frisked in _______ sport.

[**unremitting, upbraids, unraveled, unwieldly, untowardly, unwittingly**]

****

1. The backwoodsman was a captain in the _______ of conquering civilization.
2. Banish your dotage! Banish _______, that makes the Senate ugly!
3. He honestly mistook his _______ for the artistic temperament.
4. We think it hypocritical to draw over our _______ the curtain of a decent silence.
5. Don't be _______. Your lace-mender is not good enough for me.
6. The _______ never taste of death but once.

[**vainglorious, vacillation, vanguard, valiant, vagaries, usury**]

****

1. It is very natural for young men to be _______, acrimonious, and severe.
2. They shot by houses, with a _______ and noise like roaring waters.
3. She teased me with a thousand _______ complaints about school-quarrels.
4. Glorious men are the slaves of their own _______.
5. Her fanciful turban was surmounted by a tuft of _______ feathers.
6. The imagination creating the enemy is already _______.

[**variegated, vanquished, vehement, velocity, vaunts, vapid**]

1. Two vacant chairs at it [the little table] extended their arms with **venal** hospitality to the influx* of patrons. —O. Henry, *A Cosmopolite In A Café*
2. As to "going into the bush," this only means that a man has done his duty successfully in the pursuit of a hereditary* **vendetta**. —Joseph Conrad, *The Mirror of the Sea*
3. There was an air of grandeur in it that struck you with awe, and rivalled the beauties of the best Grecian architecture; and it was as commodious* within as **venerable** without. —Henry Fielding, *Tom Jones*
4. To invent might not be precisely a virtue, but it was the most **venial** of faults. —Charlotte Brontë, *Villette*
5. Sweet are the uses of adversity;
   Which, like the toad,* ugly and **venomous**,
   Wears yet a precious jewel in his head.
   —Shakespeare, *As You Like It*
6. Certainty of knowledge not only excludes mistake but fortifies **veracity**. —Samuel Johnson, *The Idler*

****

1. **venal**; buyable, mercenary. —venality. * influx; 1. arrival. 2. inflow. ***ant.*** efflux.
2. **vendetta**; 1. prolonged bloody feud or conflict between two families. 2. violent vengeance. * hereditary; inherited.
3. **venerable**; 1. august, historic and hallowed. 2. honorable, respectable. —veneration. ※ reverend; venerable. * commodious; spacious, capacious.
4. **venial**; minor, slight, pardonable. ***ant.*** mortal: *mortal sin*. —veniality.
5. **venomous**; 1. poisonous, toxic, noxious, virulent. 2. spiteful, rancorous. —venom. * like the toad; indicating the belief that the toad is venomous but with a jewel as an antitoxin.
6. **veracity**; honesty, integrity, rectitude, probity, ingenuousness. —veracious.

1. The skeleton dimensions* I shall now proceed to set down are copied **verbatim** from my right arm, where I had them tattooed. —Herman Melville, *Moby Dick*

2. My way of putting things! My dear fellow, I have merely stripped the rags of business **verbiage** and financial jargon* off my statements. —Joseph Conrad, *Chance*

3. Yet I rarely failed to find, even in midwinter, some warm and springy* swamp* where the grass and the skunk-cabbage still put forth with perennial* **verdure**. —Henry David Thoreau, *Walden*

4. "For the sake of improving the aspect of **verisimilitude**," said Razumov, curtly,* in a desire to affirm his independence. "I must be trusted in what I do." —Joseph Conrad, *Under Western Eyes*

5. . . . every brisk young man who says in succession fine things to each reluctant generation—Boethius, . . . Coleridge—is some reader of Plato, translating into the **vernacular**, wittily, his good things. —R. W. Emerson, *Plato; or, the Philosopher*

6. He would say that she was wonderfully well informed and **versatile**—which was certainly true. —Thomas Hardy, *Tess*

****

1. **verbatim**; word for word, to the letter, literally. * dimension; measure.
2. **verbiage**; wordiness, verbosity. —verbose; talkative, wordy. ※ verboten; forbidden, taboo, prohibited: *Verbal abuse is strictly verboten in this classroom.* * jargon; 1. specialized terminology. 2. dialect, cant.
3. **verdure**; 1. greenness, verdancy. 2. freshness. —verdurous; grassy, verdant. * springy; lively. * swamp; slough. * perennial; active through years.
4. **verisimilitude**; truthfulness, likelihood, reality. —verisimilar. * curtly; tersely.
5. **vernacular**; 1. native language. 2. dialect, jargon, lingo. —vernacularize, —vernacularly.
6. **versatile**; all-around *or* all-round, all-purpose, protean. —versatility.

1. Our courses were converging* like the sides of an angle, the **vertex** of which was at the edge of the fog-bank. —Jack London, *The Sea Wolf*

2. . . . he began to sway from side to side, as from **vertigo** . . . —Ambrose Bierce, *Can Such Things Be?*

3. A baker's cart had already rattled through the street, chasing away the latest **vestige** of night's sanctity with the jingle-jangle of its dissonant* bells. —Nathaniel Hawthorne, *The House of Seven Gables*

4. No matter, since
   They have left their **viands** behind; for we have stomachs.
   —Shakespeare, *The Tempest*

5. But deep below our freckles and hay-coloured hair the unhandsomest of us dream of a prince or a princess, not **vicarious**, but coming to us alone. —O. Henry, *The Brief Debut of Tildy*

6. The greatest **vicissitude** of things amongst men, is the vicissitude of sects and religions. —Francis Bacon, *Essays*

****

1. **vertex**; summit, pinnacle, apex, zenith, acme, consummation. —vertical. * converge; merge, mingle. ***ant.*** diverge. —divergent; digressive, tangential.
2. **vertigo**; dizziness, giddiness, wooziness. —vertiginous.
3. **vestige**; trace, remnant, track. —vestigial. * dissonant; incongruous.
4. **viands**; 1. choice dish, very delicious food. 2. provisions, victuals.
5. **vicarious**; acting, substitute, delegated. —vicariousness, —vicariously. ※ surrogate; 1. *adj.* substitute, vicarious. 2. *n.* mother substitute. —surrogation.
6. **vicissitude**; fluctuation, variation, ups and downs. —vicissitudinous.

♣ Integrity without knowledge is weak and useless, and knowledge without integrity is dangerous and dreadful. —Samuel Johnson, *Rasselas*

1. The dogs do right to be **vigilant**. —Emily Brontë, *Wuthering Heights*

2. . . . if the bill is good, it must have in one corner, mixed in with the **vignette**, the figure of a goose, very small, indeed, all but microscopic.* —Herman Melville, *The Confidence-Man*

3. His decent reticence is branded as hypocrisy, his circumlocutions* are roundly called lies, and his silence is **vilified** as treachery. —W. Somerset Maugham, *The Moon and Sixpence*

4. It is scarcely the province of an author to refute* the arguments of his censors and **vindicate** his own productions. —Anne Brontë, *The Tenant of Wildfell Hall*

5. . . . suffering, for the most part, makes men petty* and **vindictive**. —W. Somerset Maugham, *The Moon and Sixpence*

6. She showed **virile** force in the contest—more than once she almost throttled* him, athletic as he was. —Charlotte Brontë, *Jane Eyre*

****

1. **vigilant**; attentive, alert, wary. —vigilance, —vigil *n.* ; watch, surveillance.
2. **vignette**; 1. small drawing or photograph. 2. short sketch in a book. * microscopic; tiny, infinitesimal.
3. **vilify**; slander, calumniate, malign, traduce, decry. ※ denigrate; vilify, defame: *They deliberately denigrated the scientist's achievement.* —vilification. * circumlocution; indirect expression, *see p. 47, no. 2.*
4. **vindicate**; prove, justify, corroborate. —vindicative. * refute; confute, disprove.
5. **vindictive**; revengeful, punitive, retaliative. * petty; mean, paltry.
6. **virile**; manly, masculine, robust. —virility. ※ macho; 1. masculine. 2. virile man. *see p. 94, no. 6* . ※ machismo; manliness, virility. * throttle; choke, strangle.

♣ Example is always more efficacious than precept. —Samuel Johnson, *Rasselas*

1. It [the room] was adorned with a great number of knickknacks* and curiosities which might have engaged the attention of a **virtuoso**. —Henry Fielding, *Tom Jones*

2. . . . she sincerely looked on me as a compound of **virulent** passions, mean spirit, and dangerous duplicity.* —Charlotte Brontë, *Jane Eyre*

3. . . . we ourselves know how the barometer of our self-esteem and confidence rises and falls from one day to another through causes that seem to be **visceral** and organic* rather than rational . . . —William James, *The Principles of Psychology*

4. . . . under the sinister splendour of that sky the sea, blue and profound, remained still, without a stir, without a ripple, without a wrinkle—**viscous**, stagnant, dead. —Joseph Conrad, *Lord Jim*

5. . . . amusement in excess **vitiates** the whole nature, and is a thing to be carefully guarded* against. —Samuel Smiles, *Self Help*

6. "If you are not good, none is good"—those little words may give a terrific meaning to responsibility, may hold a **vitriolic** intensity for remorse. —George Eliot, *Middle-march*

****

1. **virtuoso**; expert, master, maestro, maven. —virtuosity, —virtuosic. * knick-knack; trinket, gewgaw, ornamental bagatelle.
2. **virulent**; malignant, malevolent, rancorous. —virulence. * duplicity; fraud.
3. **visceral**; instinctive, emotional, illogical, intestinal. * organic; constitutional.
4. **viscous**; sticky, viscid, glutinous. —viscousness.
5. **vitiate**; undermine, impair, devalue, depreciate. —vitiation. * guard; supervise.
6. **vitriolic**; 1. edgy, sarcastic, caustic. 2. of sulfuric acid. —vitriol *n.*, —vitriolize.

♣ Ignorance, when it is voluntary, is criminal. —Samuel Johnson, *Rasselas*

1. The yeomen* separated the incensed priests, who continued to raise their voices, **vituperating** each other in bad Latin. —Walter Scott, *Ivanhoe*

2. Indeed Master Blifil himself now seconded* her with all the **vociferation** in his power. —Henry Fielding, *Tom Jones*

3. Wanting in perseverance,* such **volatile** natures are outstripped* in the race of life by the diligent and even the dull. —Samuel Smiles, *Self Help*

4. The good, by affinity, seek the good; the vile,* by affinity, the vile. Thus of their own **volition**, souls proceed into heaven, into hell. —R. W. Emerson, *Divinity School Address*

5. He greeted Philip with enthusiasm, and with his usual **volubility** told him that he had come to live in London, Ruth Chalice was a hussy,* he had taken a studio . . . —W. Somerset Maugham, *Of Human Bondage*

6. "The **voracious** caterpillar when transformed into a butterfly . . . and the gluttonous maggot* when become a fly" content themselves with a drop or two of honey or some other sweet liquid. —Henry David Thoreau, *Walden*

****

1. **vituperate**; censure, rebuke, reproach. —vituperative. * yeoman; farmer.
2. **vociferation**; shout, roar, yell, bawl. —vociferous. * second; approve.
3. **volatile**; 1. temperamental, fitful, spasmodic. 2. inconstant. —volatility. * perseverance; endurance, persistence, grit. * outstrip; surpass, *see p. 211, no. 5.*
4. **volition**; will, resolution, determination. —volitional. * vile; mean.
5. **volubility**; fluency, loquacity, garrulity. —voluble. * hussy; slut, trollop.
6. **voracious**; greedy, devouring, rapacious, ravenous, ravening, gluttonous, edacious, esurient. * maggot; larva.

♣ No cause more frequently produces bashfulness than too high an opinion of our own importance. —Samuel Johnson, *The Rambler*

1. The legislative department is everywhere extending the sphere of its activity, and drawing all power into its impetuous* **vortex**. —James Madison, *Federalist Papers*

2. . . . yes, the heart of a politician, of a soldier, of a **votary** of glory, a lover of renown, a luster after power, beat under my curate's surplice.* —Charlotte Brontë, *Jane Eyre*

3. Whether Bartleby's eyes improved or not, I could not say. To all appearance, I thought they did. But when I asked him if they did, he **vouchsafed** no answer. —Herman Melville, *Bartleby*

4. Drive away the **vulgar** from the streets.
—Shakespeare, *Julius Caesar*

5. If he was **vulnerable** he was mortal, and if we could wound him we could kill him. —Arthur Conan Doyle, *The Hound of the Baskervilles*

6. A breath of the countryside seemed to be **wafted** into that panelled room in the middle of London. —W. Somerset Maugham, *Of Human Bondage*

****

1. **vortex**; whirlpool, eddy, swirl. * impetuous; hasty, impulsive, *see p. 148, no. 3.*
2. **votary**; devotee, admirer, adherent, disciple. * surplice; white ecclesiastical gown.
3. **vouchsafe**; grant, permit, accord. —vouchsafement. ※ vouch; guarantee.
4. **vulgar**; low, common, indecent, plebeian. —vulgarity, —vulgarize.
5. **vulnerable**; sensitive, susceptible. —vulnerability.
6. **waft**; float, flow, drift, whiff. —waftage, —wafter.

♣ Of all the faculties of the human mind, it will, I presume, be admitted that *Reason* stands at the summit. —Charles Darwin, *The Descent of Man*

1. On gala* days the town fires its great guns, which echo like popguns* to these woods, and some **waifs** of martial music occasionally penetrate thus far. —Henry David Thoreau, *Walden*

2. So shaken as we are, so **wan** with care,
   Find we a time for frighted peace to pant.
   —Shakespeare, *Henry IV, Part I*

3. I have sat before the dense coal fire and watched it all aglow, full of its tormented flaming life; and I have seen it **wane** at last, down, down, to dumbest dust. —Herman Melville, *Moby Dick*

4. If I be **waspish**, best beware my sting.
   —Shakespeare, *The Taming of the Shrew*

5. . . . advice often seems the most **wantonly** wasted of all human breath; . . . we must find the true gem for ourselves. —Herman Melville, *Pierre*

6. The hard-working man would come to the top, the **wastrel** sink to the bottom. —E. M. Forster, *Howards End*

****

1. **waif**; 1. stray item, object abandoned. 2. vagabond. 3. foundling. * gala; 1. festive, celebratory. 2. festival, feast. * popgun; toy gun.
2. **wan**; 1. worn, exhausted. 2. ashen, pale, pallid, livid, sallow, cadaverous. —wanly. ※ throb; pulsate, palpitate, pant.
3. **wane**; lessen, diminish, shrink, decline, dwindle. —waney *also* wany *adj.*
4. **waspish**; ill-tempered, testy, fretful, peevish, fractious, irascible, petulant. —waspishness, —waspishly. ※ WASP; White Anglo-Saxon Protestant.
5. **wantonly**; 1. wilfully, arbitrarily, randomly. 2. playfully, frolicsomely. 3. unchastely, promiscuously, licentiously. —wantonness, —wanton; 1. lewd, lubricious, immoral, libertine. 2. cruel, vicious. 3. capricious, unrestrained.
6. **wastrel**; 1. idler, loafer, shirker. 2. *n.* profligate, prodigal, spendthrift.

1. Certainty of knowledge not only excludes mistake but fortifies _______.
2. The chairs extended their arms with _______ hospitality to the patrons.
3. It was as commodious within as _______ without.
4. To invent might not be precisely a virtue, but it was the _______ of faults.
5. He has done his duty successfully in the pursuit of the hereditary _______.
6. The toad, ugly and _______, wears yet a precious jewel in his head.

[**venomous, venial, venerable, vendetta, veracity, venal**]

****

1. I have merely stripped the rags of business _______ off my statements.
2. The skeleton dimensions were copied _______ from my right arm.
3. They translated into the _______, wittily, his good things.
4. To improve the aspect of _______, I must be trusted in what I do.
5. She was wonderfully well informed and _______.
6. In the warm swamp, the grass still put forth with perennial _______.

[**verbatim, verbiage, verisimilitude, vernacular, verdure, versatile**]

****

1. The greatest _______ of things amongst men, is the vicissitude of sects.
2. A baker's cart had already chased away the latest _______ of night's sanctity.
3. We dream of a prince or a princess, not _______, but coming to us alone.
4. He began to sway from side to side, as from _______.
5. The _______ of our courses was at the edge of the fog-bank.
6. They have left their _______ behind; for we have stomachs.

[**vertex, viands, vicarious, vertigo, vicissitude, vestige**]

****

1. The bill has in one corner, mixed in with the _______, the figure of a goose.
2. The dogs do right to be _______.
3. Suffering, for the most part, makes men petty and _______.
4. His silence is _______ as treachery.
5. She showed _______ force in the contest.
6. It is scarcely the province of an author to _______ his own productions.

[**vignette, vindictive, virile, vindicate, vigilant, vilified**]

Review Exercise: Sentence Completions (pp. 335–38)

1. The causes seem to be _______ and organic rather than rational.
2. Amusement in excess _______ the whole nature.
3. The sea, blue and profound, remained still—_______, stagnant, dead.
4. The curiosities might have engaged the attention of a _______.
5. She looked on me as a compound of _______ passions and mean spirit.
6. Those little words may hold a _______ intensity for remorse.

[**vitiates, vitriolic, visceral, viscous, virtuoso, virulent**]

****

1. With his usual _______ he told Philip that he had taken a studio . . .
2. The _______ caterpillar transformed into a butterfly.
3. Such _______ natures are outstripped in the race of life by the diligent.
4. Master Blifil himself now seconded her with all the _______ in his power.
5. Thus of their own _______, souls proceed into heaven, into hell.
6. The priests continued to raise their voices, _______ each other in bad Latin.

[**volubility, voracious, volatile, volition, vituperating, vociferation**]

****

1. A breath of the countryside seemed to be _______ into that panelled room.
2. When I asked him if his eyes improved, he _______ no answer.
3. Drive away the _______ from the streets.
4. The legislative department is drawing all power into its impetuous _______.
5. The heart of a _______ of glory beat under my curate's surplice.
6. If he was _______ he was mortal.

[**wafted, votary, vulgar, vouchsafed, vulnerable, vortex**]

****

1. If I be _______, best beware my sting.
2. Advice often seems the most _______ wasted of all human breath.
3. Some _______ of martial music occasionally penetrate thus far.
4. So _______ with care, we find a time for frighted peace to pant.
5. The hard-working man would come to the top, the _______ sink to the bottom.
6. I have seen the dense coal fire _______ at last, down, down, to dumbest dust.

[**wane, wan, wastrel, waspish, waifs, wantonly**]

1. Grey Beaver had crossed the great **watershed** between Mackenzie and the Yukon in the late winter, and spent the spring in hunting among the western outlying* spurs* of the Rockies. —Jack London, *White Fang*

2. It is when we try to grapple with another man's intimate need that we perceive how incomprehensible, **wavering**, and misty are the beings that share with us the sight of the stars and the warmth of the sun. —Joseph Conrad, *Lord Jim*

3. Some poor villagers had been **waylaid** and robbed while on their way to Doramin's house with a few pieces of gum or beeswax which they wished to exchange for rice. —Joseph Conrad, *Lord Jim*

4. I knew I was catching at straws; but in the wide and **weltering** deep where I found myself, I would have caught at cobwebs. —Charlotte Brontë, *Villette*

5. Let no world-syren come to sing to me this day, and **wheedle** from me my undauntedness. —Herman Melville, *Pierre*

6. Always the dulness of the fool is the **whetstone** of the wits. —Shakespeare, *As You Like It*

****

1. **watershed**; 1. water parting, divide. 2. turning point, juncture, landmark, milestone. * outlying; remote, secluded. * spur; 1. ridge. 2. projection. 3. stimulus.
2. **wavering**; fluctuating, irresolute, undulating, vacillating. ***ant.*** unwavering; unswerving: *unwavering fidelity, see p. 325, no. 2.*
3. **waylay**; ambush, ambuscade. ※ wayward; 1. wilful, unruly, headstrong. 2. capricious, fickle, flighty: *the wayward hero in the movie.*
4. **weltering**; 1. surging, billowing. 2. wallowing, writhing, floundering.
5. **wheedle**; coax, cajole, inveigle. —wheedler, wheedlingly.
6. **whetstone**; 1. lesson. 2. stone for whetting tools. —whet *v.*; sharpen, hone.

♣ The effect is deep and secular as the cause. —R. W. Emerson, *Fate*

1. Science is a search after identity, and the scientific **whim** is lurking in all corners. —R. W. Emerson, *Illusions*

2. Eve yielded to the **wiles** of the arch* tempter. —James Joyce, *A Portrait of the Artist as Young Man*

3. And nearly always he grinned, and only once or twice did he **wince**, which was when certain coins, tossed by more playful almoners,* came inconveniently nigh to his teeth . . . —Herman Melville, *The Confidence-Man*

4. I swear, if you **winnowed** her out between the stars, like Tomlinson, there would be found in her not one original thought. —Jack London, *Martin Eden*

5. The Sunday newspaper's headliner's work is cut for him.
"**Winsome** Waitress Wins Wealthy Wisconsin Woodsman." —O. Henry, *An Adjustment of Nature*

6. Our little canoe, so neat and strong, drew a favorable criticism from all the **wiseacres** among the tavern* loungers* along the road. —Henry David Thoreau, *The Allegash and East Branch*

****

1. **whim**; 1. sudden idea, fancy. 2. caprice. —whimsy *n.*, —whimsical.
2. **wiles** (usu. in *pl.*); tricks, stratagems, chicaneries. —wily *adj.*, —wilily. * arch; 1. artful, sly, cunning, crafty. 2. mischievous.
3. **wince**; cower, flinch, quail. * almoner; distributer of alms, social worker.
4. **winnow**; 1. screen, sift, sieve. 2. choose, select. —winnower.
5. **winsome**; winning, engaging, fascinating, fetching. —winsomeness.
6. **wiseacre**; 1. person who pretends to be wise, a wisenheimer. 2. upstart. ※ wisecrack; witticism. * tavern; pub. * lounger; idler, loafer.

♣ Of the universal mind each individual man is one more incarnation. —R. W. Emerson, *History*

1. Yes, there would be a day when his face would be wrinkled and **wizen**, his eyes dim and colorless, the grace of his figure broken and deformed. —Oscar Wilde, *The Picture of Dorian Gray*

2. In open courtroom, before all men, Jim Hall had proclaimed* that the day would come when he would **wreak** vengeance on the judge that sentenced him.—Jack London, *White Fang*

3. The smoke came crookedly out of Mr. Flintwinch's mouth, as if it circulated through the whole of his **wry** figure and came back by his wry throat . . .—Charles Dickens, *Little Dorrit*

4. We'll **yoke** together, like a double shadow
To Henry's body, and supply his place.
—Shakespeare, *King Henry VI, Part III*

5. The **zany** was progenitor* to the specialist in humor. —Ambrose Bierce, *The Devil's Dictionary*

6. Again the genial spring burst forth with song and blossom and balmy* **zephyr**. —Washington Irving, *Legend of the Rose of the Alhambra*

****

1. **wizen** *or* **weazen**; 1. *adj.* shriveled, wizened. 2. *v.* wither.
2. **wreak**; inflict, execute. —wreaker, —wreakful. * proclaim; declare.
3. **wry**; 1. twisted, contorted, distorted, crooked, warped, askew. 2. ironic, cynical, sardonic, caustic. —wryness, —wryly.
4. **yoke**; 1. *v.* unite, connect, couple, harness. 2. *n.* bondage, clasp.
5. **zany**; buffoon, clown. * progenitor; 1. predecessor. ***ant.*** successor. 2. forebear.
6. **zephyr**; the west wind, a breeze. * balmy; 1. mild. 2. fragrant.

♣ There is a great responsible Thinker and Actor working wherever a man works. —R. W. Emerson, *Self-Reliance*

Review Exercise: Sentence Completions (pp. 341–43)

1. How _______ are the beings that share with us the sight of the stars!
2. Grey Beaver had crossed the great ______ between Mackenzie and the Yukon.
3. I found myself in the wide and _______ deep.
4. Let no world-syren _______ from me my undauntedness.
5. Always the dulness of the fool is the _______ of the wits.
6. They had been _______ and robbed while on their way to his house.

[**whetstone, weltering, wavering, waylaid, wheedle, watershed**]

****

1. The scientific _______ is lurking in all corners.
2. _______ Waitress Wins Wealthy Wisconsin Woodsman.
3. Eve yielded to the _______ of the arch tempter.
4. Our little canoe drew a favorable criticism from all the _______.
5. And nearly always he grinned, and only once or twice did he _______.
6. You _______ her out between the stars.

[**wiles, wiseacres, winnowed, whim, winsome, wince**]

****

1. He would _______ vengeance on the judge that sentenced him.
2. Again the genial spring burst forth with song and blossom and balmy _______.
3. The smoke circulated through the whole of his _______ figure.
4. We'll _______ together, like a double shadow to Henry's body.
5. Yes, there would be a day when his face would be wrinkled and _______.
6. The _______ was progenitor to the specialist in humor.

[**yoke, zany, wreak, wizen, zephyr, wry**]

Appendix

120 ESSENTIAL SCIENCE TERMS

To take the verbal section of any standardized test

1. **Absolute zero** is an impossibility in reality, but a theoretical possibility.

2. **Acid rain** can damage organisms and infrastructures.

3. The police have already used an **algorithm** to predict the venue* of crime.

4. **Allele** frequency is the proportion of a specific allele in a certain population.

5. The vascular plants with flowers and ovules* are **angiosperms**.

6. So many **anaerobes** live within the human intestines.

7. **Antigens** comprise toxins, viruses, and other immunogens.*

8. **Antithrombin** is a protein released by the liver.

9. **Apoptosis**, cell suicide, is a crucial process for organic growth.

****

1. **absolute zero**; the hypothetically lowest temperature (–273.15°C, or –459.67°F) without any molecular activity.
2. **acid rain**; acidic rain containing chemicals from fossil fuels.
3. **algorithm**; a set of mathematical rules or procedure for solving a problem by a computer. —algorithmic. * venue; scene. ※ encryption algorithm.
4. **allele**; one of alternative types of a gene holding the same locus* on a chromosome. * locus; position, place.
5. **angiosperm**; plant with the seeds in an ovary.* * ovule; unimpregnated seed. * ovary; part of flower bearing ovules.
6. **anaerobe**; organism able to exist without oxygen. —anaerobic.
7. **antigen**; material leading to the production of antibodies. —antigenic. * immunogen; substance that brings about an immunity.
8. **antithrombin**; material that inactivates thrombins* to prevent the coagulation of blood. * thrombin; enzyme in blood that expedites blood clotting.
9. **apoptosis**; cell death, decomposition of cells.

1. Rheumatoid arthritis is one of the major **autoimmune** diseases.
2. Algae are good examples of **autotrophs**; humans of heterotrophs.
3. **Base**, nucleobase, comes about connected to the sugar of DNA* or RNA.
4. **Benthos** comprises two categories: zoobenthos* and phytobenthos.*
5. **Big Bang Theory** states that the universe is continuously expanding.
6. Every organism has a **biome**.
7. A **black hole** can grow by absorbing the neighboring mass.
8. A **caldera** is different from a volcanic crater but occasionally confused with it.

****

1. **autoimmune**; brought about by antibodies acting against the body's own parts such as cells and tissues.
2. **autotroph**; self-nourishing organism such as green plants and some bacteria. ***ant***; heterotroph. —autotrophic.
3. **base**; one of the basic nitrogenous components of DNA or RNA.* * the sugar of DNA; deoxyribose, the sugar of RNA; ribose. * RNA; *see p. 350, no. 3.*
4. **benthos**; 1. group of organisms living at the waters floor. 2. the deepest bottom of a sea or lake. * zoobenthos; animal benthos. * phytobenthos; plant benthos.
5. **Big Bang Theory**; cosmological theory that the universe originated from a massive explosion of highly dense matter about 14 billion years ago.
6. **biome**; main biotic community such as a desert, forest, or everglade. ※ biomass; total organisms in a given habitat.
7. **black hole**, a.k.a., collapsar; region of space-time with strong gravitational attraction that anything (including light) cannot escape.
8. **caldera**; large hole made by the breakdown of the center of a volcano after eruption.

1. Water moves from the roots of a tree towards its leaves by **capillary action**.
2. **Cellulose** is one of the most important substances in manufacturing paper and textiles.
3. The X **chromosome** determines femaleness; the Y chromosome maleness.
4. **Cilia** can cleanse mucus from the lungs, treating a patient for asthma.
5. Dolly, the sheep was the first mammal to be **cloned** in the world.
6. Copper is an exemplary conductor that allows electrical **conduction**.
7. Mikhail Lomonosov, the Russian scientist, first drafted the **conservation of mass,** also called *conservation of matter*, in 1748.
8. **Convection** takes place only in fluids, not in solids.

****

1. **capillary action** *or* **capillarity**; motion of a liquid in contact with a solid, caused by the surface tension on the walls of a very thin tube.
2. **cellulose**; carbohydrate that is the major part of plant cell walls.
3. **chromosome**; any of the thread-like cellular structures including DNA and proteins that carry the genes. —chromosomal.
4. **cilia**, *pl.* of cilium; 1. microscopic organelles* projected from cells. 2. eyelashes.
   * organelle; differentiated cellular part.
5. **clone**; make a copy of an organism from the cells. —clonal, —clonally.
6. **conduction**; transfer of heat or electricity via a material. —conductor.
7. **conservation of mass**; the principle that the total mass of an isolated material system is invariable despite any other change within the system.
8. **convection**; the process of heat transfer by the currents flow in which heated air rises up and cooler air sinks to be heated and rise up again. —convect, —convective.

1. A cyberneticist who studies **cybernetics**, without heart, could be a Frankenstein, creating a cyborg* that would be able to destroy its creator.
2. The patterns of X-ray **diffraction** are very helpful in understanding the structure of an object through which the X-ray waves pass.
3. RNA is called "messenger RNA*" because it sends genetic information from **DNA** to the cytoplasm (the cell substance excepting the nucleus).
4. Bedbugs, the **ectoparasites**, emerge in our bedroom every night.
5. **El Niño** decreases the upwelling of cold, nutrient-rich water, bringing about the decline of plankton and fish, and giving rise to drought and heavy rains.
6. Making use of an **electrode**, they can diagnose and treat some serious cases.

****

1. **cybernetics**; science concerned especially with comparative study of systems in artificial and biological brains. ※ cyborg; cybernetic organism.
2. **diffraction**; modification of water, light, or sound waves encountering an obstacle or aperture. ※ deflection; deviation, veering, fending off, *see p. 73, no. 2.*
3. **DNA**: deoxyribonucleic acid (the main constituent of chromosomes) that carries genetic information and determines hereditary characteristics. * RNA; ribonucleic acid deciding protein synthesis. ※ DNA mutation, DNA replication.
4. **ectoparasite**; parasite living outside its host, such as a flea. ※ endoparasite; parasite living within its host, such as a hookworm or tapeworm.
5. **El Niño**; warming of the ocean surface near the Pacific coast of South America, happening every few years and leading to unusual weather patterns.
6. **electrode**; conductor through which electricity contacts a medium.

♣ All science has one aim, namely, to find a theory of nature. —R. W. Emerson, *Nature*

1. Milk is a good example of an **emulsion** (i.e., fat dispersed in water).
2. **Endocrine** disruptors* can bring about cancers or congenital deformities.
3. In an **endothermic** process, a system absorbs heat from its environment; in an exothermic process, a system releases heat to the environment.
4. Dermis is the vascular tissue layer below the **epidermis**.
5. All organisms except prokaryotes* are **eukaryotes**.
6. **Fermions**, particles such as electrons, protons, and neutrons, have half-integral spins while bosons such as pions, mesons, and photons, have zero or integral spins.
7. The human **genome** consists of approximately 30,000 genes, including more than three billion chemical base pairs.

****

1. **emulsion**; suspension of a liquid in another, a combination of two liquids that do not usually mix. —emulsifier, —emulsification, —emulsify.
2. **endocrine**; 1. secretion, hormone, ductless gland. 2. of endocrine glands. * endocrine disruptor; endocrine-disrupting chemical.
3. **endothermic**; typified by absorption of heat. ***ant***. exothermic; evolving heat.
4. **epidermis**; the external layer of the skin. ※ subcutaneous; subdermal, beneath the epidermis: *subcutaneous injection*.
5. **eukaryote**; organism with cells including a membrane-bound nucleus. * prokaryote; unicellular organism such as a bacterium or alga, lacking a nucleus.
6. **fermion**; subatomic particle with half-integral spin.* * spin; momentum.
7. **genome**; a single set of chromosomes with total genetic information in an organism.

♣ The sacrosanct fetish of today is science. —Joseph Conrad, *The Secret Agent*

1. A **geomagnetic storm** is precipitated by the charged particles released from solar flares.

2. **Global warming** leads to correlative changes in the climate worldwide.

3. **GMO** brings about genetically modified foods.

4. The temperature **gradient** between day and night in deserts is usually steep.

5. The **herpetologis**t also was attacked by a big alligator at his home.

6. **Heuristics** is definitely a gateway to natural science.

7. **Histocompatibility** decides the tolerance of transplanted cell or transfused blood.

****

1. **geomagnetic storm** *or* **magnetic storm**; a passing disturbance in the earth's magnetic field, brought about by sunspots.
2. **global warming**; increase of average temperature over the earth, resulting from the greenhouse effect brought about by the increase of gases, especially carbon dioxide and methane emitted from burning fossil fuels.
3. **GMO**; *abbr.* genetically modified organism (a.k.a., transgenic organism), such as GloFish (genetically modified fluorescent fish).
4. **gradient**; 1. change rate of a quantity such as temperature. 2. slope rate.
5. **herpetologist**; one who studies reptiles and amphibians such as toads and crocodiles.
6. **heuristics**; science of learning by self-education or trial-and-error.
7. **histocompatibility**; tissue compatibility, the condition in which one tissue can be grafted to the other without immunological interference.

♣ But lo! Men have become the tools of their tools. —Henry David Thoreau, *Walden*

1. So many _______ live within the human intestines.
2. The police have already used an _______ to predict the venue of crime.
3. The vascular plants with flowers and ovules are _______.
4. _______ is an impossibility in reality, but a theoretical possibility.
5. _______ can damage organisms and infrastructures.
6. _______ frequency is the proportion of a specific allele in a certain population.

[**allele, algorithm, angiosperms, anaerobes, absolute zero, acid rain**]

****

1. _______, cell suicide, is a crucial process for organic growth.
2. _______ is a protein released by the liver.
3. _______ comprise toxins, viruses, and other immunogens.
4. Rheumatoid arthritis is one of the major _______ diseases.
5. _______, nucleobase, comes about connected to the sugar of DNA or RNA.
6. Algae are good examples of _______; humans of heterotrophs.

[**base, apoptosis, antithrombin, autotrophs, autoimmune, antigens**]

****

1. Water moves from the roots of a tree towards its leaves by _______.
2. A _______ can grow by absorbing the neighboring mass.
3. _______ states that the universe is continuously expanding.
4. Every organism has a _______.
5. _______ comprises two categories: zoobenthos and phytobenthos.
6. A _______ is different from a volcanic crater but occasionally confused with it.

[**biome, caldera, capillary action, benthos, Big Bang Theory, black hole**]

****

1. _______ can cleanse mucus from the lungs, treating a patient for asthma.
2. The _______ is also called *conservation of matter*.
3. Dolly, the sheep was the first mammal to be _______ in the world.
4. The X _______ determines femaleness; the Y chromosome maleness.
5. _______, a carbohydrate, is a very important substance in manufacturing paper.
6. Copper is an exemplary conductor that allows electrical _______.

[**conduction, conservation of mass, cilia, cloned, cellulose, chromosome**]

Review Exercise: Sentence Completions (pp. 349–52)

1. Bedbugs, the _______, emerge in our bedroom every night.
2. A cyberneticist who studies _______, without heart, could be a Frankenstein.
3. _______ gives rise to drought and heavy rains.
4. The patterns of X-ray _______ are very helpful in understanding the structure of an object through which the X-ray waves pass.
5. RNA sends genetic information from _______ to the cytoplasm.
6. _______ takes place only in fluids, not in solids.

[**cybernetics, El Niño, ectoparasites, convection, DNA, diffraction**]

****

1. In an _________ process, a system absorbs heat from its environment; in an exothermic process, a system releases heat to the environment.
2. Making use of an_______, they can diagnose and treat some serious cases.
3. Milk is a good example of an _______.
4. _______ disruptors can bring about cancers or congenital deformities.
5. Dermis is the vascular tissue layer below the _______.

[**electrode, epidermis, endothermic, endocrine, emulsion**]

****

1. The human _____ consists of approximately 30,000 genes, including more than three billion chemical base pairs.
2. _______ have half-integral spin while bosons have zero or integral spin.
3. A _______ is precipitated by the charged particles released from solar flares.
4. All organisms except prokaryotes are _______.
5. _______ leads to correlative changes in the climate worldwide.

[**geomagnetic storm, genome, global warming, fermions, eukaryotes**]

****

1. _______ is definitely a gateway to natural science.
2. The temperature _______ between day and night in deserts is usually steep.
3. _______ brings about genetically modified foods.
4. The _______ also was attacked by a big alligator at his home.
5. _______ decides the tolerance of transplanted cell.

[**histocompatibility, GMO, heuristics, herpetologist, gradient**]

1. It is the growth of civilization that distinguishes the **Holocene**.

2. In 1947, Dennis Gabor invented **holography**, a branch of optics.

3. **Homogenized** milk with the fat globules broken up is uniform in consistency.*

4. The scientist should study the human body to build a **humanoid** robot.

5. You have to add hydrogen to vegetable oils in order to **hydrogenate** them and produce solid fats.

6. Surface tension exists at the surface of a homogenous liquid; interfacial tension at the **interface** between two unmixable liquids.

7. Thanks to the **Internet of Things**, machines have already become wizards.

****

1. **Holocene**; the time from about 12,000 years ago (the end of the Pleistocene*) to the present. * the Pleistocene; the epoch from about 2.6 million to 12,000 years ago, characterized by glaciations and the appearance of Homo sapiens.
2. **holography**; the technique or science of holograms.* * hologram; three-dimensional image made by beams.
3. **homogenize**; make homogenous by mixing. —homogenization, —homogeneity. ※ homologous; analogous in structure but not in operation. ※ homologue; something similar. * consistency; density.
4. **humanoid**; 1. like or corresponding to a human being. 2. human-like creature or machine.
5. **hydrogenate**; unite with hydrogen. —hydrogenous.
6. **interface**; 1. surface boundary between neighboring phases or materials. 2. interacting point between a computer and other electronic device.
7. **Internet of Things (IoT)**; data communication of digital machines through internet. ※ Internet of Everything (IoE); smart networking of data, devices and people: *Many people are afraid that in the near future, robots with artificial intelligence might utilize big data via the Internet of Everything, dominating human beings globally.*

1. A cation is a positively charged **ion**; an anion a negatively charged one.
2. Normal saline is an **isotonic** solution.
3. Stable i**sotopes** have long lives because they don't disintegrate, but radioactive isotopes have short lives because they invariably disintegrate.
4. The **jet stream** has a crucial impact on aviation and weather fronts.
5. Without oxygen, the **Krebs cycle** cannot occur.
6. **Krypton** is one of the unreactive gaseous elements such as a helium or argon.
7. **Light pollution** can have bad effects on human health and nocturnal wildlife.

****

1. **ion**; an atom or a molecule that bears a positive or negative electrical charge by having lost or gained electrons. —ionize.
2. **isotonic**; 1. of the same tension. 2. keeping the same osmotic pressure.
3. **isotope**; any of two or more atoms with an equal number of protons but a variant number of neutrons.
4. **jet stream**; strong winds meandering near the troposphere,* moving from west to east. * troposphere; the lowest layer of atmosphere, 4–11 miles above the earth.
5. **Krebs cycle,** a.k.a., citric acid cycle; sequence of metabolic reactions that generate carbon dioxide and energy.
6. **krypton**; odorless, colorless, inert gaseous element, used mainly in fluorescent lights.
7. **light pollution**; too much artificial light hindering astronomical observation.

♣ The devil can cite scripture for his purpose.

—Shakespeare, *The Merchant of Venice*

1. **Metabolism** consists of two categories: anabolism (the combining of simple substances into complex compounds), and catabolism (the decomposition of organic compounds).
2. **Mitochondrion** is a rod-like organelle that supplies cellular energy.
3. **Mitosis** is the process of cell division that produces new cells in organisms.
4. Glucose molecules are good examples of natural **monomers**.
5. Carbon **monoxide** is more dangerous because it is colorless and odorless.
6. A **mucous** membrane produces mucus* to protect itself against viruses or bacteria.

****

1. **metabolism**; chemical process inside the cells of an organism to produce energy for its growth and maintenance. —metabolite; 1. product of metabolism. 2. material necessary for metabolism. —metabolize.
2. **mitochondrion**, *pl.* -dria; organelle in the cytoplasm* of most eukaryotes, including enzymes significant for cell metabolism through cellular respiration. * cytoplasm; a cell's contents except the nucleus.
3. **mitosis**; cell division causing two nuclei, each of which includes a full copy of parental chromosomes. ※ amitosis; cell division without the generation of chromosomes. ※ meiosis; cell division reproducing four daughter cells with half of the parental chromosomes.
4. **monomer**; key unit of polymer,* molecule uniting with others to make a polymer. * polymer; natural compound consisting of molecules.
5. **monoxide**; oxide* with a single oxygen atom. * oxide; compound of oxygen. ※ carbon dioxide, carbon monoxide.
6. **mucous**; relating to mucus,* secreting mucus. * mucus; slippery and sticky material released by some parts of the body.

1. **Mutualism** and commensalism* are the examples of symbiotic association.
2. According to the theory of 'intelligent design,' organisms are not created and reproduced by **natural selection**, but by an intelligent being, a supreme creator.
3. Fatigue and weight loss are the main symptoms of **neoplasia**.
4. **Newton's laws of motion**, expounding the motion of a body, laid the basis for mechanics, applying to human action.
5. **Niche** is a habitat in which an organism can survive as a member of a species.
6. In **nitrogen cycle**, nitrogen passes from the atmosphere to organisms by nitrification, and back to the atmosphere by denitrification (i.e., decomposition).

****

1. **mutualism**; mutually beneficial union between two variant species. * commensalism; relationship in which an organism benefits from another without harming it. ※ parasitism; relationship between a parasite and the host.
2. **natural selection**; process by which only organisms best adjusted to their ecological environment can survive and reproduce.
3. **neoplasia**; 1. development of neoplasm (tumor). 2. abnormal growth of cells.
4. **Newton's laws of motion;** First Law: An object tends to stay unmoving or in constant motion unless affected by an outside force. Second Law: The momentum of an object is equivalent to the force affecting it. Third Law: A force affecting an object brings about the same and contrary reaction.
5. **niche**; 1. ecological position of an organism. 2. environmental condition.
6. **nitrogen cycle**; circulation of nitrogen between organisms and their environment. —nitrogenous.

♣ A golden mind stoops not to shows of dross.

—Shakespeare, *The Merchant of Venice*

1. **Nucleotide**, an organic molecule, consists of a sugar, a phosphate group, and a nitrogenous base.
2. Osmotic pressure propels **osmosis**, a vital process for an organism.
3. The **outcrop** protruding above the land turned out to be an important mineral vein.
4. Chemicals such as CFC* are believed to be destroying the **ozone shield**.
5. **Peristalsis** drives digestion in an organism.
6. The scientist sampled the **pH** level of the soil in the vineyard.
7. **Phagocytes** shield our bodies from infection by malignant microorganisms.
8. The **phenotypes** of twins are different while their genotypes* are uniform.

****

1. **nucleotide**; a monomer of nucleic acid (DNA or RNA).
2. **osmosis**; the passage of a solvent through a membrane from a lower concentrated to a higher concentrated solution until both solutions have equal concentration. —osmotic, —osmose *v.*
3. **outcrop**; part of a stratum, vein, or bedrock at the surface of the ground.
4. **ozone shield** *or* **ozonosphere**; ozone layer in the stratosphere that blocks solar ultraviolet radiation. * CFC (chlorofluorocarbon); a compound with carbon, chlorine, and etc.; the main cause of ozone destruction. ※ ozone hole.
5. **peristalsis**; wavelike contractions and relaxations of the alimentary tract.
6. **pH**; measure of the acidity or alkalinity in a solution or material.
7. **phagocyte**; cell that absorbs foreign substances. —phagocytosis; the ingestion of foreign materials by phagocytes.
8. **phenotype**; 1. set of properties of an organism influenced by its genes and environment. 2. group of organisms showing a particular phenotype. * genotype; 1. genetic formation of an organism. 2. organisms with the same genotype.

1. Some animals, especially insects, attract the opposite sex by **pheromones**.
2. **Phloem** transports the nutrients made by photosynthesis, from the leaves to the other parts of a plant while xylem* transports water from the roots to the other parts.
3. **Phosphorus** is used in producing matches and pesticides.
4. **Photoelectric** effect is the production of electrons by a material exposed to light.
5. A **photon** has no mass, acting and reacting as a wave or particle.
6. In most cases of **photosynthesis**, oxygen is created as a by-product.
7. Octopus, an invertebrate, is an example of **phylum**, a taxonomic* division.
8. Milk **plasma**, whey, is the watery part staying after milk has been coagulated to obtain curds.*

****

1. **pheromone**; chemical released from an animal, serving as a means of communication with other members of the same species.
2. **phloem**; food-carrying tissue in vascular plants. * xylem; water-conducting tissue.
3. **phosphorus**; phosphorescent* material (white, red, and black element glowing in the dark). —phosphorous; luminescent, fluorescent, phosphorescent.
4. **photoelectric**; relating to or utilizing an electric current caused by radiation.
5. **photon**; part of electromagnetic energy, a particle of light.
6. **photosynthesis**; process in which green plants and some bacteria produce carbohydrates from water and carbon dioxide, using sunlight. —photosynthesize.
7. **phylum**; one of the eight taxonomic ranks (domain, kingdom, phylum, class, order, family, genus, and species). * taxonomic; relating to classification of organisms.
8. **plasma**; the fluid portion of milk or blood. —plasmatic. * curd; solidified milk.

1. Bees **pollinate** plants for honey, enabling their fertilization.
2. The **projectile** force projected the missile into the sky, which drew its trajectory.
3. A toe **prosthesis** was found on the ancient Egyptian mummy.
4. Contracting or expanding, a **pseudopodium** functions as an organ of feeding, grasping, or locomotion.
5. There are four stages in metamorphic insects: embryo, larva, **pupa**, and imago.
6. The **pyroclastic** flows from Mount Vesuvius buried almost everything of the ancient Roman city of Pompeii in AD 79.
7. A hadron, a composite particle, consists of **quarks**, and interworks solidly with other particles.
8. **Quasars** with high redshifts* are intensely luminous.

****

1. **pollinate**; carry pollen from anthers* to the stigmas. * anther: pollen-containing part of a stamen.* * stamen; male organ of a flower, producing pollen.
2. **projectile**; 1. driving forward. 2. capable of being fired. 3. *n.* bullet, missile.
3. **prosthesis**; man-made replacement for a lost part of the body. —prosthetic.
4. **pseudopodium**, *pl.* -podia; temporary protrusion from a phagocyte* or the cells of an organism such as an amoeba. * phagocyte; *see p. 359, no. 7.*
5. **pupa**; dormant stage of metamorphic insects within cocoons or shells, between larva and imago.* * imago; adult insect.
6. **pyroclastic**; formed by rock fragments (ash and pumice) from volcanic eruption.
7. **quark**; any component of elementary particles with electric charges.
8. **quasar**; tremendously distant, celestial object with enormous energy. * redshift; increase in the wavelength of light from a celestial body, caused by the Doppler effect.* * Doppler effect; change in the waves when the source and observer are moving.

1. High **radioactivity** has been detected in the lake near the nuclear power plant.

2. It takes about 365 days for the earth to make one **revolution** around the sun.

3. The **seedling*** grew into a sapling.*

4. **Sirtuin** regulates cellular processes such as apoptosis or transcription.*

5. Plants without seeds, such as algae, fungi and ferns, reproduce by **spores**.

6. The treatment of a disease by using **stem cells** is called "stem cell therapy."

7. Without proof, **string theory** is still hypothetical.

8. Algae can serve as **substrates** for other animals.

9. The sudden breakdown of a star's core causes most **supernovas.**

****

1. **radioactivity**; 1. emission of radiation from nuclear reaction or the breakup of atomic nuclei. 2. radiation from such a source.
2. **revolution**; 1. rotation, orbital motion. 2. cycle of revolution.
3. **seedling**; very young plant less than three years old and not yet about three feet high. * sapling; young tree 3 to 15 years old and 2 to 10 feet high.
4. **sirtuin**; protein controlling a cell's growth. * transcription; *see p. 364, no. 3.*
5. **spore**; unicellular, asexual, reproductive body.
6. **stem cell**; fundamental cell that can develop into many types of specialized cells. ※ two kinds of stem cells: embryonic stem cells, and adult stem cells.
7. **string theory**; theory that the basic units of matter or energy are string-like rather than point-like in a space-time with more than three dimensions.
8. **substrate**; 1. surface on which an organism lives. 2. substance affected by an enzyme. 3. substratum, *pl.* -strata.
9. **supernova**; 1. star that explodes and becomes millions of times brighter than the sun, emitting enormous energy. 2. star explosion.

1. Sugar water is a solution; muddy water a **suspension.**

2. **Synapsis** happens during the beginning of meiosis.*

3. **Synesthesia** occurs when the hearing of a scream causes an image of a red color.

4. **Taiga** is a biome typified by conifers such as firs or spruces.

5. Plate **tectonics** is a theory that explains the motion of the earth's lithosphere,* such as volcanism, seismicity, continental drift, or seafloor spreading.

6. Mars is said to be the most appropriate planet for **terraforming**.

7. **Thigmotropism** occurs more noticeably in twiners or tendrils.

8. Today, scientists can fabricate a prosthesis* by means of a **3-D printer.**

****

1. **suspension**; mixture in which particles are dispersed but not dissolved in a liquid. * solution; mixture in which a solute dissolves in a solvent.
2. **synapsis**; the combination of homologous chromosomes. * meiosis; *see p. 357, no. 3.*
3. **synesthesia**; concurrent sensation in one part of body, caused by tactile stimulation of another. —synesthetic.
4. **taiga**; subarctic forest area covering northern Eurasia and North America, south of the tundra.
5. **tectonics**; geological study of the earth's structural features. * lithosphere; the earth's upper mantle made up of several plates continually moving.
6. **terraform**; transform a planet's environment into one similar to the earth's.
7. **thigmotropism**; directional growth or movement of a plant upon contact with a firm object. ※ heliotropism; plant's orienting response to the sunlight.
8. **3-D printer**; apparatus to synthesize three-dimensional objects from a digital file, making use of additive processes. * prosthesis; *see p. 361, no.3.*

topography

1. The alpinist was very familiar with the **topography** of the Alps.

2. An automatic transmission in a vehicle, of course, uses a **torque** converter in place of a clutch on a manual transmission.

3. **Transcription** of an organism occurs by RNA polymerase.*

4. A **transgenic** organism will naturally transmit a new trait to its offspring.

5. **Translation** happens in the protoplasm* of a cell.

6. Drought usually brings about the decrease of **turgor** pressure in many plants.

7. The **water cycle** is indispensable to the preservation of the earth's ecosystem.

8. **Zymosis** causes an infectious disease.

****

1. **topography**; 1. configuration of an area. 2. study of the contour of a land.
2. **torque**; force that causes rotation, moment of a force.
3. **transcription**; organic process by which RNA is synthesized from DNA, causing a transfer of genetic information. * RNA polymerase; the enzyme catalyzing transcription.
4. **transgenic**; of an organism with a genome changed by the transfer of genes.
5. **translation**; process of protein synthesis directed by the information of messenger RNA. * protoplasm; the jelly-like substance constituting a cell's nucleus.
6. **turgor**; the standard tension or turgidity* of organic cells. * turgidity; swelling.
7. **water cycle** *or* **hydrologic cycle**; cycle of water from the earth to the atmosphere by evaporation and from the atmosphere back to the earth by precipitation.
8. **zymosis**; 1. fermentation. 2. infection. 3. contagious disease. —zymosthenic.

♣ Ah, I have no data. I cannot tell. —Arthur Conan Doyle, *The Adventures of Sherlock Holmes*.

1. The scientist should study the human body to build a _______ robot.
2. In 1947, Dennis Gabor invented _______, a branch of optics.
3. Interfacial tension exists at the _______ between two unmixable liquids.
4. You have to add hydrogen to vegetable oils in order to _______ them.
5. It is the growth of civilization that distinguishes the _______.
6. _______ milk with the fat globules broken up is uniform in consistency.

[**interface, homogenized, humanoid, holography, hydrogenate, Holocene**]

****

1. Stable _______ have long lives because they don't disintegrate.
2. A cation is a positively charged _______; an anion a negatively charged one.
3. _______ is one of the unreactive gaseous elements such as helium and argon.
4. Thanks to the _______, machines have already become wizards.
5. Normal saline is an _______ solution.
6. The _______ has a crucial impact on aviation and weather fronts.
7. Without oxygen, the _______ cannot occur.

[**jet stream, isotonic, Krebs cycle, ion, isotopes, krypton, Internet of Things**]

****

1. _______ consists of two categories: anabolism and catabolism.
2. _______ is a rod-like organelle that supplies cellular energy.
3. _______ can have bad effects on human health and nocturnal wildlife.
4. Carbon _______ is more dangerous because it is colorless and odorless.
5. Glucose molecules are good examples of natural _______.
6. _______ is the process of cell division that produces new cells in organisms.

[**metabolism, monoxide, mitosis, mitochondrion, monomers, light pollution**]

****

1. He believes that organisms can survive by _______, not by a supreme creator.
2. A _______ membrane produces mucus to protect itself against viruses.
3. Fatigue and weight loss are the main symptoms of _______.
4. _______ laid the basis for mechanics, applying to human action.
5. _______ and commensalism are the examples of symbiotic association.

[**neoplasia, mutualism, Newton's laws of motion, natural selection, mucous**]

Review Exercise: Sentence Completions (pp. 358–61)

1. Osmotic pressure propels _______, a vital process for an organism.
2. _______ consists of a sugar, a phosphate group, and a nitrogenous base.
3. The _______ protruding above the land turned out to be a mineral vein.
4. In _______, nitrogen passes from air to organisms and back to air.
5. _______ is a habitat in which an organism can survive.
6. Chemicals such CFF are believed to be destroying the _______.
7. _______ drives digestion in an organism.

[**niche, nucleotide, peristalsis, ozone shield, osmosis, outcrop, nitrogen cycle**]

****

1. _______ shield our bodies from infection by malignant microorganisms.
2. _______ is used in producing matches and pesticides.
3. Some animals, especially insects, attract the opposite sex by _______.
4. _______ transports the nutrients from the leaves to the other parts of a plant.
5. The scientist sampled the _______ level of the soil in the vineyard.
6. The _______ of twins are different while their genotypes are uniform.

[**pheromones, phagocytes, phloem, phosphorus, phenotypes, pH**]

****

1. _______ effect is the production of electrons by a material exposed to light.
2. Milk _______, whey, is the watery part staying after milk has been coagulated.
3. Bees _______ plants for honey, enabling their fertilization.
4. Octopus, an invertebrate, is an example of _______, a taxonomic division.
5. A _______ has no mass, acting and reacting as a wave or particle.
6. In most cases of _______, oxygen is created as a by-product.

[**phylum, plasma, photosynthesis, photon, pollinate, photoelectric**]

****

1. Contracting or expanding, a _______ functions as an organ of locomotion.
2. The _______ flows from Mount Vesuvius buried everything of Pompeii.
3. The _______ force projected the missile into the sky, which drew its trajectory.
4. A toe _______ was found on the ancient Egyptian mummy.
5. Metamorphic insects have four stages: embryo, larva, _______, and imago.

[**pupa, pseudopodium, pyroclastic, prosthesis, projectile**]

1. The _______ grew into a sapling.
2. Plants without seeds, such as algae, fungi and ferns, reproduce by _______.
3. It takes about 365 days for the earth to make one _______ around the sun.
4. High _______ has been detected in the lake near the nuclear power plant.
5. _______ with high redshifts are intensely luminous.
6. A hadron consists of _______ and interworks solidly with other particles.
7. _______ regulates cellular processes such as apoptosis or transcription.

[**sirtuin, seedling, radioactivity, spores, quarks, revolution, quasars**]

****

1. Algae can serve as _______ for other animals.
2. _______ happens during the beginning of meiosis.
3. The sudden breakdown of a star's core causes most _______.
4. Without proof, _______ is still hypothetical.
5. The treatment of a disease by using _______ is called "stem cell therapy."
6. Sugar water is a solution; muddy water a _______.

[**supernovas, substrates, synapsis, suspension, stem cells, string theory**]

****

1. _______ is a biome typified by conifers such as firs or spruces.
2. The alpinist was very familiar with the _______ of the Alps.
3. _______ occurs when the hearing of a scream causes an image of blood.
4. Plate _______ is a theory that explains the motion of the earth's lithosphere.
5. Mars is said to be the most appropriate planet for _______.

[**topography, taiga, synesthesia, tectonics, terraforming**]

****

1. Today, scientists can fabricate a prosthesis by means of a _______.
2. _______ occurs more noticeably in twiners or tendrils.
3. An automatic transmission in a vehicle, of course, uses a _______ converter in place of a clutch on a manual transmission.
4. A _______ organism will naturally transmit a new trait to its offspring.
5. _______ of an organism occurs by RNA polymerase.

[**transcription, 3-D printer, thigmotropism, torque, transgenic**]

Review Exercise: Sentence Completions (p. 364)

1. The _______ is indispensable to the preservation of the earth's ecosystem.
2. Drought usually brings about the decrease of _______ pressure in many plants.
3. _______ causes an infectious disease.
4. _______ happens in the protoplasm of a cell.

[**zymosis, translation, turgor, water cycle**]

Made in the USA
Columbia, SC
21 August 2021